They Laid the Foundation

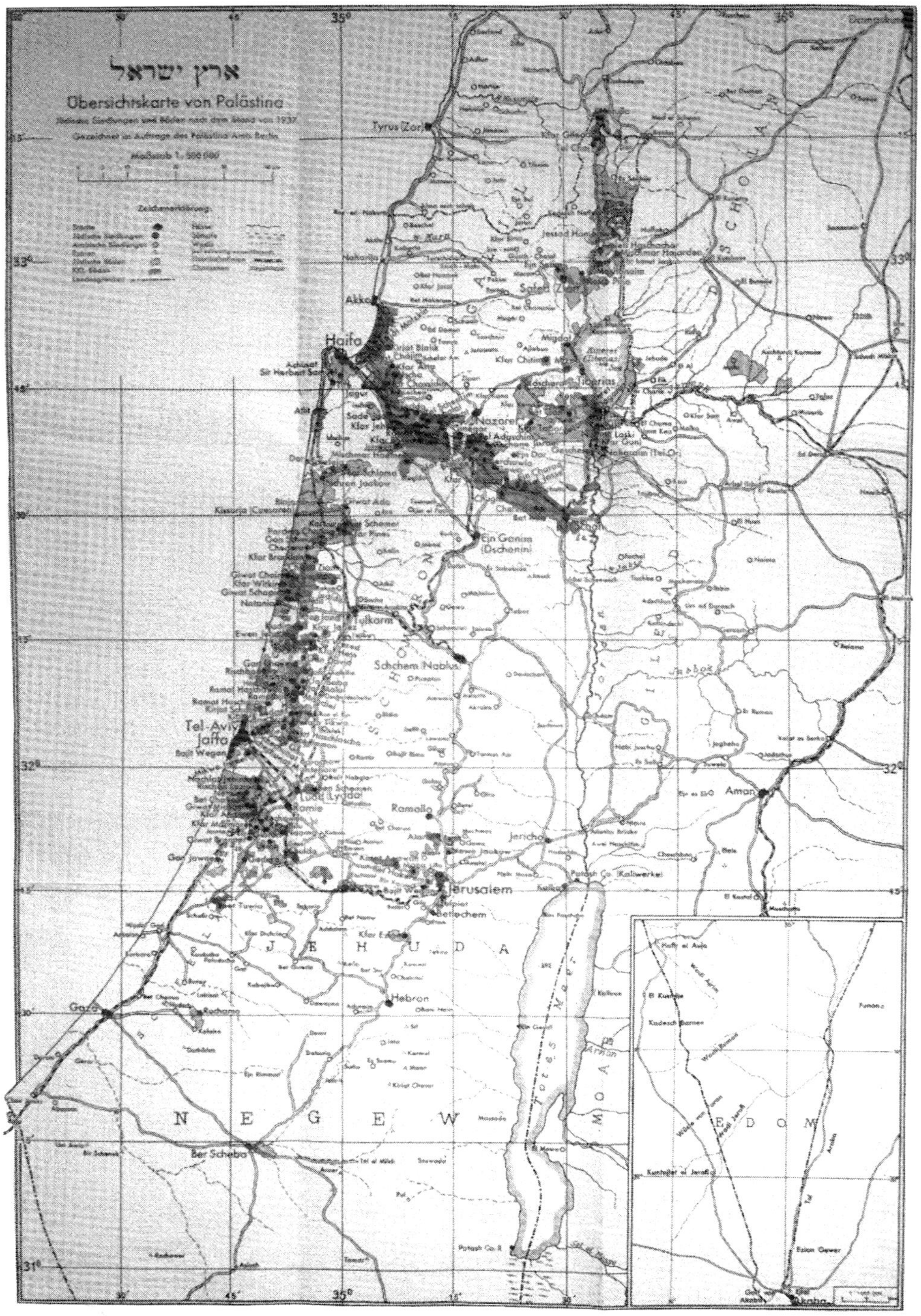

ארץ ישראל
Übersichtskarte von Palästina
Jüdische Siedlungen und Böden nach dem Stand von 1937
Gezeichnet im Auftrage des Palästina-Amts Berlin
Maßstab 1 : 500 000
Zeichenerklärung
Tyrus (Zor)
Akko
Haifa
Safed (Zefat)
Tiberias
Nazareth
Kissarja (Caesarea)
Ejn Ganim (Dschenin)
Natanja
Tulkarm
Schechem Nablus
Tel-Aviv
Jaffa
Lud (Lydda)
Ramle
Ramalla
Jericho
Aman
Jerusalem
Betlechem
Potash Co. (Kaliwerke)
J E H U D A
Gaza
Hebron
N E G E W
Ber Scheba
Potash Co. II
E D O M
Kadesch Barnea
Ezion Gewer
Akaba

Myra Warhaftig

They Laid the Foundation

Lives and Works of German-Speaking Jewish Architects
in Palestine 1918–1948

In memory of my parents Shifra and Noah Warhaftig

This English language edition was sponsored by:
Reuben and Edith Hecht Foundation
Michael Strauss
Michael Federmann
Stef Wertheimer

Photos: Myra Warhaftig (M.W.), Orly Warhaftig (O.W.)

Title of the original German edition:
Sie legten den Grundstein.
Leben und Wirken deutschsprachiger jüdischer Architekten
in Palästina 1918–1948
published by Ernst Wasmuth Verlag Tübingen • Berlin, 1996

Second Edition, Revised and Enlarged

Translated from the German by Andrea Lerner
Copy editing: Geoffrey Steinherz
Printed and bound by AZ Druck und Datentechnik GmbH, Kempten
ISBN-10 3 8030 0676 7
ISBN-13 978 3 8030 0676 9

Available through D.A.P./Distributed Art Publishers
155 Sixth Avenue, 2nd Floor, New York, N.Y. 10013
Tel (212) 627-1999 Fax (212) 627-9484

Printed and bound in Germany

Contents

Preface to the Second Edition

After this book was published in German in 1996, I curated a touring exhibition derived from the contents titled "Architecture in Palestine 1918–1948". The exhibition, with German and Hebrew texts, travelled in subsequent years first to Tel Aviv, Haifa and Jerusalem and then to Berlin, Dessau and Braunschweig. In the fall of 2000, an English version of the exhibition was shown at Columbia University in New York.
In actuality, this chapter on architectural history is not tied to any particular nation, for its protagonists were uprooted and forced to resettle in many different countries. Due to political events, they wandered from continent to continent, under the most difficult conditions, and in the process, the various cultures they encountered shaped their life experiences. That unusual and unprecedented series of events left behind distinct traces in their views on architecture, whose complexity this book conveys in detail.

Ever since it was first published, the wish has been repeatedly expressed in Israel and the USA for the book to be available in at least English or Hebrew. In May 2005 I met Stef Wertheimer in Tefen, Israel and broached this subject to him. Ruthi Ofek, the director and curator of the Open Museums, also was present. Wertheimer immediately agreed and promised to help finance an English edition. But he also stipulated one condition: that it include portraits of the lives and works of some persecuted Jews from Nazi Germany who started out as entrepreneurs when they arrived in Eretz Israel and who, with their descendants, have gone on to represent important branches of Israeli industry. These individuals also laid the foundation of Israel — and several of them lived and worked in buildings designed by the protagonists of this book. We then agreed to focus on four exemplary industrial families: Yekutiel Federmann and his brother Shmuel, who founded the Dan hotel chain in Israel; Dr. Reuben Hecht and his wife Edith, who founded the Dagon silo at the port of Haifa; Dr. Richard Strauss and his wife Hilda, founders of the Strauss Dairies; and Stef Wertheimer himself, founder of the metal cutting tools company ISCAR Ltd. in Tefen.
All these entrepreneurs came from Jewish families that had been established in Germany for at least two or three centuries. As young people, all without exception encountered anti-Semitism. They recognized that it was essential to found a Jewish state. Wherever they lived, they joined Zionist organizations and became active members. Their goal was to immigrate to Eretz Israel. When Hitler came to power in 1933, and anti-Jewish laws were introduced in Germany and later in other European countries, Yekutiel Federmann and Reuben Hecht were involved in illegal actions that secretly brought Jewish persons from Europe to Israel, at that time Palestine. They were forced to cease such operations at the outbreak of World War II. The Federmann, Strauss and Wertheimer families left Germany for Eretz Israel between 1936 and 1940. Yekutiel Federmann, Hilda and Richard Strauss and Stef Wertheimer proved to be very resourceful and courageous as they fought the British mandate government until the state of Israel was founded. For political reasons, the Hecht family was not able to re-enter Israel until 1948. All of the persons mentioned here were possessed by a single vision: to establish a new field of industry for the new state of Israel.

I am extremely grateful to Michael Federmann of the Dan Hotels, to the Reuben and Edith Hecht Foundation, and to Michael Strauss of the Strauss Dairies for helping to make possible the publication of this book, as well as for kindly providing materials about the history of their organizations.
For his sympathy and commitment in helping to secure financing for this new edition, I owe special thanks to Stef Wertheimer. I am also deeply grateful to him for the impetus he provided for the new section. My involvement with the lives and works of the German-Jewish entrepreneurs who helped build Israel from the 1930s to the present led me to the discovery of some very moving life stories. And my deep appreciation to Ruthi Ofek, who brought us together.

Berlin 2006

Myra Warhaftig

Preface to the First Edition

This book presents the lives and works of forty-seven architects. I was personally acquainted with fourteen of them, seven of whom were my teachers at the Technion in Haifa. I was able to meet the relatives – widows, daughters, sons, nieces, nephews – or close friends of the deceased architects, except in the case of Elsa Gidoni-Mandelstamm. I visited them in Israel's major cities of Tel Aviv, Jerusalem and Haifa as well as in the kibbutzim Ein Harod, Ein Gev, Mishmar-Ha'emek and Merchavia. Outside Israel, I visited Judith Stolzer-Segal (who since has died) and Yehuda Bienheim's son in Munich. In London I met Harry Rosenthal's widow. Fortunately, I was able to locate Bruno Kalitzki's wife shortly before she died in Berlin. The architect Werner Wittkower of Tel Aviv, and Robert Friedmann's son, who lives in Italy, visited me here in Berlin. All of these individuals, without exception, did their utmost to help. They gave me information, as far as they could remember, and put materials, photographs, documents and publications at my disposal. Regardless of their circumstances, they took me in or offered me hospitality with indescribable generosity.

I wrote letters to the relatives of architects who had died in America, and to institutions, archives, universities, and registries in every country imaginable. These amounted to 551 inquiries between May 1985 and November 1993.

Without the financial assistance from my mother, and without her constant presence in Haifa in years gone by, this research would have been unthinkable. The book is therefore dedicated to my parents, who did not live to see it published. I would like to say a special word of thanks to Mr. Wolfgang Nagel who, during his time in office as the senator for building in Berlin, gave me the financial support that enabled me to write this manuscript between September 1992 and June 1993.

My heartfelt thanks go to Ms. Jutta Sartory M.A. and to Dr. Hedwig Wingler for their exceptional contributions to this work in its finished form.

For their tireless support over many years, and especially in difficult times, I would like to acknowledge Ms. Annamarie Mommsen, daughter of the architect Ludwig Hoffmann, and Dr. Anna Maria D'Ans. Finally, I would like to thank my daughters Tomari and Orly for their patience.

Berlin 1996

Myra Warhaftig

Introduction

Quand le MODERNE n'était pas un style mais une cause

Anatole Kopp, Paris 1988[1]

In these pages, the lives of 120 architects, including eight women, are profiled. What their biographies have in common is that all studied at German-language universities early in the twentieth century and all emigrated from various countries to Israel, in those days Palestine, between the two world wars.[2] About twenty-five of the architects emigrated during the 1920s. When the National Socialists came to power in 1933, ninety-five more Jewish architects fled persecution in Germany and found a safe home in Eretz Israel.
When researching these individuals' life stories and motivations, and their works, I soon became aware of connections that linked their fates with their biographies and with the buildings that were their creative means of expression. Sifting through all the material gathered from libraries, public and private archives and estates, it became unmistakably clear to what extent world politics had disrupted the lives of these architects, and the strengths they nonetheless were able to mobilize for their creative work.
The majority had gone to battle for their respective homelands, whether Germany, Austria-Hungary or Russia, in World War I. A few, such as Leo Adler or Harry Rosenthal, were so severely injured that they suffered the rest of their lives. The architects had attended a total of eighteen different German-language universities and art academies. Some fifty studied at the Technische Hochschule Charlottenburg, today the Technical University of Berlin; another forty studied at the Technische Hochschule in Vienna. Six were pupils of the Bauhaus in Dessau and five studied in Prague and Brno. Others, such as Josef Neufeld, Carl Rubin, and Eugen Szekey, went to Berlin to launch their careers in the offices of Hans Poelzig, Erich Mendelsohn or Bruno Taut. Alexander Klein, on the other hand, had already built a successful professional practice in Russia before leaving his native country due to the anti-Semitic ferment that followed the 1917 Russian Revolution and World War I. Early in the 1920s Klein moved to Berlin, where he gained renown as both a researcher and a practising architect.
One-third of the architects portrayed here had already seen their designs built before 1933 in cities in Central Europe, primarily in Berlin, and had published articles and books about their own works (and those of other architects). Their buildings characterized twentieth-century German cityscapes, and still do — and not just in Berlin; some of their works have survived in Hamburg and Leipzig as well. Often these architects were members in good standing of professional societies and artists' associations: Oskar Kaufmann was a member of the Deutscher Werkbund (DWB), Ze'ev W. Haller belonged to the Bund Deutscher Architekten (BDA, Federation of German Architects), Robert Friedmann and Alexander Klein to both the BDA and the Architekten-und Ingenieur-Verein (AIV, Association of Architects and Engineers) of Berlin, Erich Mendelsohn was a member of the BDA and the Prussian Academy of the Arts in Berlin, to name only a few. Yet despite their productivity and professional stature, their names – with the exception of Erich Mendelsohn and, lately, Oskar Kaufmann – are rarely mentioned in the architectural literature, their buildings seldom attributed, and their writings are virtually nowhere to be found, not even in national libraries.

Most of the architects included in this book had, from an early age, witnessed or been the target of social exclusion, racist persecution and pogroms in the countries of Eastern and Central Europe. Jochanan Ratner,

Eugen Stolzer, Gideon Kaminka and Werner Wittkower all documented their experiences and dealings with anti-Semitism in Germany and in Austria. They determined early on that they would no longer submit to these oppressive conditions and therefore made the decision to leave their homelands as soon as possible. As they pursued a definition of their Jewish identity, some joined the Jewish youth movement. The future pioneer architects Arieh Sharon and Jacob Pinkerfeld were members of Ha'shomer Ha'tzair (Young Guards), the largest Zionist-Socialist youth federation in the countries of Eastern Europe and Russia. Werner Wittkower and Gideon Kaminka were members of Blau-Weiss (Blue and White), the first Zionist Federation in Germany. Although the established Berlin architects such as Oskar Kaufmann, Erich Mendelsohn, Harry Rosenthal, Arthur Korn and Siegfried Weitzmann were not staunch Zionists, these members of the Jewish bourgeoisie still had to struggle for recognition and renown. They joined the Central-Verein (CV – Central Association of German Citizens of Jewish Faith), which was founded in 1893 in Berlin with the goal of countering discrimination against Jews in public life.

The fact that no Jewish architects were represented in the German Architecture Exhibition of 1931, which took place from May to August in Berlin, prompted the Central-Verein to produce a special issue of its weekly newspaper, the *CV-Zeitung*, titled "Architects and Buildings. From Hitzig to Mendelsohn" on July 3, 1931. In it, art historian Dr. Max Osborn presented a number of successful German-Jewish architects and artists from various disciplines, along with their works, in order to refute the widespread smear campaign that Jews lacked culture.[3] At the same time, the publication also described the affinity existing between Jewish creative activity and German culture.

This account of the biographies and works of architects who found a new homeland in Palestine is therefore also a portrait of Jewish history during the first half of the twentieth century – a period characterized by anti-Semitism, by Theodor Herzl's political Zionism, by the persecution and annihilation of European Jewry and, finally, by the founding of the state of Israel. There, the practice of Modern architecture, which had originated in Germany but was suppressed when Hitler gained power, was resumed and further developed.

The return of Jews to the biblical Land of the Forefathers began late in the nineteenth century under the influence of the Zionist movement – that is, almost two thousand years after the Jews had been driven out. Initially it took place under Ottoman rule. When Great Britain conquered the land from the Turks at the end of World War I, Jewish return continued under the British mandate government. After the state of Israel was established in 1948, an uninterrupted flow of immigration to the new Jewish country ensued. Such immigration, known in Hebrew as aliya (ascent), has been subdivided into historical epochs defined by political events.

The first wave of immigration occurred between 1882 and 1903 as a result of persecution of Jews in Russia and Romania. During that period, about 25,000 Jews came to Palestine, but many soon left the country again because of the extremely harsh living conditions. Those who remained founded the new agricultural settlements such as Rishon-Lezion, Gedera and Rosch-Pina.

The Second Aliya took place between 1903 and 1914, after pogroms in which hundreds of Jews were murdered and hundreds more wounded in the Russian cities of Kishinev (April 1903), Homel (September 1903), Schitomir (April 1904) and other places; many Jewish homes and businesses were destroyed. A further incentive was the failure of the 1905 Russian Revolution, which led to more pogroms. The founding of Degania, the first kibbutz in Eretz-Israel (1910), goes back to the immigrants of this aliya.

Abschrift.

Die
TECHNISCHE HOCHSCHULE
ZU BERLIN
erteilt durch diese Urkunde
Herrn Siegfried Weitzmann
aus Berlin

DIPLOM-INGENIEURS

nachdem er die Diplom-Prüfung der Abteilung für
Architektur
nach der Diplom-Prüfungsordnung vom 18 Januar 1909
abgelegt und in der Haupt-Prüfung das Gesamturteil
„bestanden"
erhalten hat.

Charlottenburg, den 2. Juli 1910.

Der Rektor der Technischen Hochschule zu Berlin
gez. Müller-Breslau.

(Stempel)

Der Vorsteher der Abteilung für Architektur
gez. Koch.

Siegfried Weitzmann's diploma from the Technische Hochschule Berlin, July 2, 1910

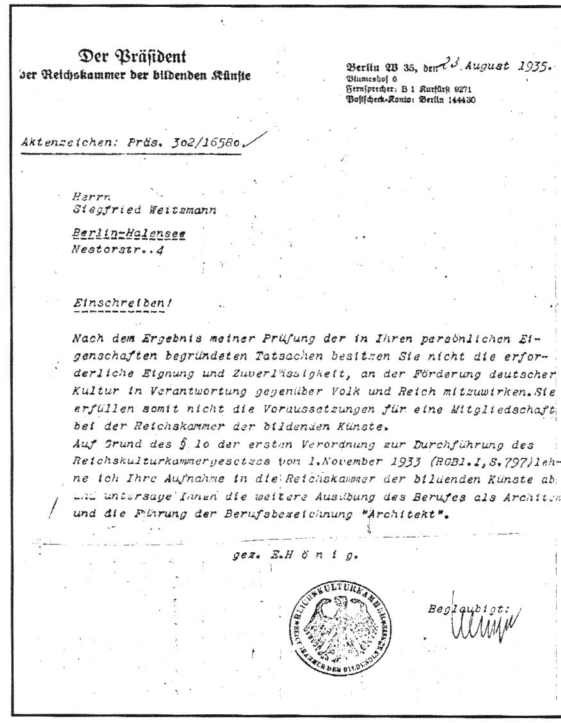

Der Präsident
der Reichskammer der bildenden Künste

Berlin W 35, den 23. August 1935.
Blumeshof 6
Fernsprecher: B 1 Kurfürst 9271
Postscheck-Konto: Berlin 144430

Aktenzeichen: Präs. 302/16580.

Herrn
Siegfried Weitzmann
Berlin-Halensee
Nestorstr. 4

Einschreiben!

Nach dem Ergebnis meiner Prüfung der in Ihren persönlichen Eigenschaften begründeten Tatsachen besitzen Sie nicht die erforderliche Eignung und Zuverlässigkeit, an der Förderung deutscher Kultur in Verantwortung gegenüber Volk und Reich mitzuwirken. Sie erfüllen somit nicht die Voraussetzungen für eine Mitgliedschaft bei der Reichskammer der bildenden Künste.
Auf Grund des § 10 der ersten Verordnung zur Durchführung des Reichskulturkammergesetzes vom 1. November 1933 (RGBl. I, S. 797) lehne ich Ihre Aufnahme in die Reichskammer der bildenden Künste ab und untersage Ihnen die weitere Ausübung des Berufes als Architekt und die Führung der Berufsbezeichnung "Architekt".

gez. E. Hönig.

Beglaubigt:

Letter to Siegfried Weitzmann, Berlin from the president of the Reich Chamber of Fine Arts, August 23, 1935, forbidding him to practise

After the 1917 Russian Revolution and World War I, the Third Aliya took place between 1919 and 1923. Impressed by Zionism's political success, many young people went to Palestine, often without appropriate preparation, to lend their physical efforts to the building of "national homesteads for the Jewish people". They were known in Hebrew as the chalutzim, or pioneers, and they energetically proceeded to settle the country with new kibbutzim. Ein Harod, founded in 1921, was the first large communal settlement that combined agriculture and industry.

The Fourth Aliya occurred between 1924 and 1928, primarily due to the economic collapse in Poland and other Eastern European countries that affected the livelihood of many Jews. Most of the Fourth Aliya immigrants were members of the middle class and many went on to establish themselves as merchants or small factory owners in Tel Aviv.

The horrendous persecution of European Jews under National Socialism in Germany and the outbreak of World War II brought about mass immigration to Palestine from 1933 to 1945, the period of the Fifth Aliya.

Ausschreitungen in Wien und Berlin, Seite 345 ff.

C.V.-Zeitung

Central Verein

Berlin, 3. Juli 1931
X. Jahrgang • Nr. 27
Einzelnummer 20 Pfennig

Blätter für Deutschtum und Judentum.

Organ des Central-Vereins deutscher Staatsbürger jüdischen Glaubens e.V.

Allgemeine Zeitung des Judentums

Vierteljahrsabonnement 2,50 RM. (zuzügl. Bestellgeld)

Verlag und Schriftleitung: Berlin W 15, Emser Str. 42. Fernsprecher: J 2 Oliva 5074. .:. Postscheckkonto: Berlin 304 72. .:. Bankkonto: Dresdner Bank, Depositenkasse H 2, Berlin-Wilmersdorf 1, Hohenzollerndamm 196, und von Goldschmidt - Rothschild & Co., Berlin W 8.
Alleinige Anzeigenannahme: Annoncen-Expedition Rudolf Mosse, Berlin SW 100, und deren Filialen. Anzeigenpreise: 0,90 RM für die 7gespaltene Zeile nach Rudolf Mosses Normalzeilenmesser Nr. 4, Familienanzeigen und Stellengesuche (nicht Stellenangebote) für Mitglieder des Centralvereins 0,45 RM, die 62 mm breite Reklamezeile 3,50 RM.

Baukünstler und Bauten

Die „Deutsche Bau-Ausstellung" in Berlin, die grosse Schau deutschen Bauwesens, gab Anlass zu dieser Sondernummer. Sie will die schöpferische Mitwirkung jüdischer Deutscher in diesem Zweige der Kunst und des Kunsthandwerks zeigen und dadurch doppeltem Zwecke dienen: das judengegnerische Schlagwort von der Unproduktivität jüdischer, angeblich nur „händlerischer" Geisteshaltung widerlegen und zugleich die unlösbare Verbundenheit jüdischen Schaffens, Denkens und Seins mit deutscher Kultur und Heimaterde von neuem erhärten.

Von Hitzig bis Mendelsohn

Von Dr. Max Osborn

Wenn es nach der Theorie ginge, könnte man annehmen, daß im Bereich jüdischer Künstlertätigkeit der Architektur nur ein bescheidener Platz zufiele. Wer in die Geheimnisse jüdischen Wesens und Geistes einzudringen sucht, wird mitunter der Auffassung zuneigen, daß bei allem Reichtum vielfältiger Begabung in der Kunst das Talent zu schöpferischen Leistungen größten Stils und Umfangs sich doch bisher noch nicht in völliger Freiheit entfaltet habe. Wenn es so wäre, und in der Dichtung könnte man auf das Drama verweisen, so wäre das letzten Endes nicht verwunderlich. In dem einen Jahrhundert, das seit der Emanzipation verstrich, konnte unmöglich alles nachgeholt werden, was durch fast zwei Jahrtausende gewaltsam unterdrückt und geknebelt worden war.

Aber die Baukunst, die bei solcher Betrachtung in erster Linie herangezogen werden muß, bietet ein ganz anderes Bild, als erwartet werden konnte. Wer näher zusieht, wird, vielleicht zu seiner eigenen Ueberraschung, erkennen, daß in diesem abgelaufenen Jahrhundert jüdische Kräfte einen erheblichen und bedeutsamen Anteil an der Entwicklung der europäischen, namentlich der deutschen Architektur genommen haben. Hier kommt doch im eigentlichen Sinne alles auf die Fähigkeit machtvoll organisierenden Gestaltens, wuchtigen Zusammenfassens, gegenseitiger Durchdringung phantasievoll erfindenden und derb-handwerklichen Tuns an, also auf Eigenschaften, die manche dem jüdischen Sinn bestreiten möchten — gleichwohl diese erstaunliche, in breiter Front anrückende Schar fruchtbarer Mitstreiter! Ja, das Ergebnis fällt fast noch schwerer ins Gewicht als in den übrigen Künsten (namentlich in der Plastik, wo es bis heute verhältnismäßig bescheiden geblieben ist), da wir es nicht nur mit einer großen Zahl schlechthin tüchtiger Männer, sondern darüber hinaus mit einzelnen Persönlichkeiten zu tun haben, die für ihre ganze Zeit führend geworden sind und auf dem Vormarsch ihrer Kunst zu neuen Zielen weitreichenden Einfluß ausgeübt haben.

Wenn im folgenden der Versuch gemacht wird, einen Ueberblick über diesen Tatbestand zu geben, so sei von vornherein bemerkt, daß keineswegs irgendwelche „Vollständigkeit" angestrebt werden konnte, die im Rahmen eines Zeitschriftenaufsatzes auch niemand erwarten wird, und daß weiterhin dem Verfasser vor allem seine Vertrautheit mit den Berliner Verhältnissen als Ausgangspunkt diente. Doch gerade die Baugeschichte der deutschen Hauptstadt bietet einer derartigen Umschau wesentliche Handhaben. Wenn wir in Schinkel den meisterlichen Erneuerer des Berliner Stadtbildes verehren, so rückt unter seinen Schülern und Fortsetzern sogleich ein Architekt jüdischer Abstammung an den ersten Platz. Friedrich Hitzig

First page of the Central Verein's newspaper, July 3, 1931

Introduction

Although the British mandate government took steps to stem the rising tide of Jewish immigrants (measures documented in the so-called *White Paper* of 1939), twice as many persons arrived in the country during the Fifth Aliya as had entered between the end of World War I and the end of 1932.
By 1941 the number of inhabitants in Palestine had reached 1,616,000, of whom 505,000 (32.2% of the population) were Jews. Between 1933 and 1941, 230,000 persecuted individuals entered the country; one-third of them were Jews from Germany, Austria and Czechoslovakia.[4] Among them were more than one hundred architects.[5]
The Association of Engineers and Architects in (Eretz) Israel had been founded in Haifa in 1922. It soon moved to Tel Aviv, where the organization has maintained its headquarters ever since. From that point onward, it is possible to document the immigration of Jewish architects through its archive.

Those architects who emigrated from Germany and Austria to Palestine during the Third and the Fourth Aliya came with the intention of "building the country and uplifting ourselves" – as the chalutzim anthem

Taking a break at the construction site, Pardess Hanna, ca. 1935

ARCHITEKTEN BAUEN IN PALÄSTINA

Diplom-Ingenieur / Architekt
EDGAR AUERBACH
Tel-Aviv, Trumpeldor St 24

INDUSTRIEBAU
בנין בתי תעשיה

מהנדס מדופלם / אדריכל
אדגר אורבך
תל־אביב, רח׳ טרומפלדור 24

מהנדס מדופלם רוברט פרידמן, אדריכל
בית דרום אפריקה, רחוב אלנבי, חיפה

Dipl. Eng. **ROBERT FRIEDMANN**, Architect
SOUTH AFRICA BUILDING, ALLENBY ST., HAIFA
NEW BUSINESS CENTRE — מרכז חדש

E. GIDONI - L. ZEISLER - ARCH - ENG.
13. FRISHMANN STREET, TEL-AVIV

WOHNHAUS-, SIEDLUNGS-, INDUSTRIE-BAUTEN

HEINRICH GOTTLIEB
INNEN-ARCHITEKT
TEL-AVIV
HAJARDON STREET 17

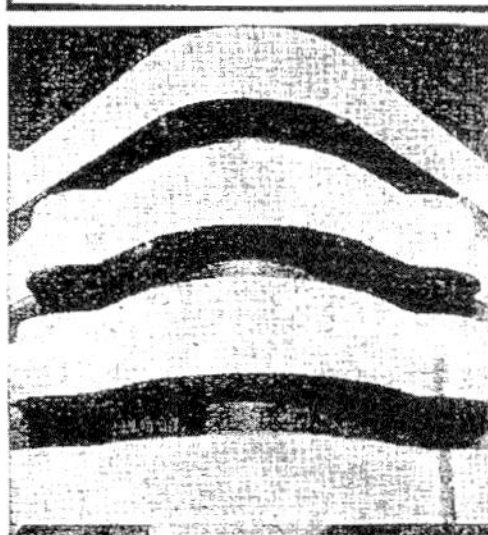

WOHNHAUS
Ecke Jehuda Halevi und Maza Street
Erbaut 1934

Architekt
W. HALLER
TEL-AVIV
60, Jehuda Halevi
(Ecke Maza Street)

Gutachten
Hausverwaltungen
Bebauungspläne
ENTWURF
und
BAULEITUNG
Parzellierungen
Beratung

S. DOSTROVSKY & J. GREEN
ARCHITECTS
BUSINESS CENTRE HAIFA
TELEFON 970

Generalvertretung der „P.N." für
Palästina
HEINZ ZEIMANN
Tel-Aviv, Dizengoffstraße 159

Dr. ing.
Gideon G. Kaminka
Architekt
Haifa P. O. B. 972
Phone: 766

ד״ר אינג׳. גדעון
ג. קאמינקא
אדריכל
היפה ת. ד. 972
טלפ.: 766

Diplom-Architekt
J.-A. Minor — י. מינור

Vorprojekte, Kostenanschläge, Bauleitung, Expertise; Auskunft gratis.

Büro: **Tel-Aviv, Hess Str. 7**

MÜHLBAUER & MITTELMANN
BAU-INGENIEURE
TEL-AVIV · PINSKER 12
מילבואר את מיטלמאן, מהנדסים
תל־אביב, רחוב פינסקר 12

PLÄNE
BAULEITUNG
BAUBERATUNG

תכניות · השגחה · הצאורת לבנין

A. ORDOWER
TEL-AVIV / ALLENBY STREET 43

INNENARCHITEKT

WOHNUNGEN — LADEN
AUSFÜHRUNG IN EIGENER REGIE

ZEHN JAHRE PRAXIS IM LANDE

Architektur-Büro Achad-Haamstr. 42, Tel-Aviv

J. ORNSTEIN — Dipl.-Ing., Wien, 15 Jahre Praxis in Palästina
S. LIASKOWSKI — Architekt, Zürich, Seit 1933 in Tel-Aviv

Geschäfts-, Wohnhaus-, Fabrik-Bau etc.

KALITZKI-ENTIN
ARCHITEKT / HAIFA
NEW BUSINESS CENTRE
HOUSE FREUND, TEL.: 813

קליצקי־אנטין
אדריכלים / היפה
מרכז חדש
בית פרוינד, טלפ.: 813

Architects build in Palestine, page of advertisements (p. 14) in: *Palästina Nachrichten. Zeitschrift für Wirtschaftsentwicklung im Vorderen Orient*, Berlin, October 25, 1935

proclaimed – and were among the creative forces responsible for realizing the first planned housing and settlements in Palestine. Not only did they bring the 'know-how' acquired from building in Europe, they also consciously transplanted an architectural style known in Germany as Neues Bauen (New Building). The lives and works of eleven of these architects are introduced in "The Pioneers" section of this book.[6]
With and because of these architects, Modern architecture achieved its breakthrough in Palestine. The movement soon was strengthened and supported by German, Austrian and Czechoslovakian architects who fled Europe for Palestine after the Nazis came to power on January 30, 1933. The lives and works of twenty-nine of these men and women are documented in the section titled "The Persecuted".
Thus from a historical and socio-political perspective, it was initially possible to distinguish two groups of architects who went to Palestine with differing motivations: the pioneers of the 1920s and those persecuted during the 1930s. But in evaluating the biographical material, I found that there was also a third group whose lives perhaps most vividly illustrate the connection between art and politics: those who graduated from the architecture department of the Bauhaus in Dessau. Four of the six Bauhaus students were avowed chalutzim, having immigrated to Palestine as youths during the Third Aliya. When they learned of the existence of the Bauhaus and its structure and guiding principles, these staunch Zionists set out with intense commitment to study in Dessau.
The Bauhaus director's idea that "artists should consciously enact their social responsibility to the community, and be supported by the community in exchange" corresponded with the consciousness of the young socialists from Palestine.[7] And the working method propagated by the Bauhaus – the use of didactic experiments – also corresponded with the ideals of the chalutzim. With the help of modern teaching methods, they strove to connect their artistic ability with creative thinking in order to construct economical and aesthetic workers' housing that incorporated the latest technological advances, in accordance with Herzl's legacy.[8] A separate section is therefore dedicated to the lives and works of these six Bauhaus disciples.
Within each section, the architects are listed chronologically according to their date of birth.

The three-thousand-year history of the Jewish people as a political continuum is the determining factor behind Israel's architectural development, while starkly different structures from various epochs and cultures bear witness throughout the land to changing historical periods. In Jerusalem one encounters the remains of monumental graves in Hellenistic style from the time of Herod; in Caesarea stand the imposing ruins of a Roman settlement; the churches, cloisters and hospices between Jerusalem in the south and Tiberias in the north recall the Byzantine era. The changeover to Ottoman rule, which lasted four hundred years, left in its aftermath an Eastern culture whose distinguishing features are the domed mosques and slim minarets of Akko and Jaffa, Haifa, Jerusalem and Tiberias.

Alex Baerwald designed the Technion in Haifa using a mixture of stylistic elements derived partly from the Judaic symbolic world and partly from the realm of Islamic architecture.
But Jochanan Ratner, a pupil of Friedrich Ostendorf, eschewed such historic elements in his Jewish administration building, erected 1927 in Jerusalem, instead giving his structure an austere form designed along functional lines.
During the Weimar Republic between 1919 and 1933, Germany had become the centre of an avant-garde architectural concept and style – the aforementioned Neues Bauen – that had a momentous effect on the

architecture of the entire Western world. The fact that the struggle for Modern architecture led to a successful revolution was due mainly to the existence of three outstanding German institutions: the Deutscher Werkbund, the Bauhaus, and Der Ring.

The Deutscher Werkbund was founded in 1907, while the empire was still in existence. It proposed an alternative to historicism, bringing together artists, craftsmen and captains of industry to collaborate in developing better forms for basic objects of everyday use. During the 1920s, the Deutscher Werkbund became an equally energetic advocate for a new architecture. Its journal *Die Form* published pertinent essays on Neues Bauen with photographs of actual examples and models. In 1925 the Werkbund shifted its

German emigrants brought all their worldly possessions into the country in lifts (wooden containers). These were fitted with doors and windows to make them habitable until housing, built according to plans by Alexander Klein, was completed in Kiryat Tivon, 1937

focus from crafts to architecture and decided to mount a major architectural exhibition in Stuttgart on the topic of "contemporary living". The housing ensemble built for the exhibition, the Weissenhofsiedlung, is renowned as a prime example of the avant-garde architecture of the 1920s.[9]

The Bauhaus, founded as a reformist art school in Weimar in 1919, did not have an independent department of architecture until after it moved to Dessau. The department was established in 1927 at the personal behest of Bauhaus founder and architect Walter Gropius, one year before he turned the school's direction over to Hannes Meyer. Meyer encouraged his students to relate their work to sociological and biological research and to view their designs as the result of rational economic and functional factors. His successor Ludwig Mies van der Rohe, who headed the Bauhaus and its architecture department from 1930 until he was forced to close the school in 1933, dismissed Meyer's insistence upon the primacy of social criteria. Instead, Mies emphasized the concept of quality and the use of more elegant architectural materials.

In order to strengthen and spread the modern view of a new architectural culture in a new economic and social era, a group of progressive architects formed an association called "Der Ring" in Berlin in 1925. Its members included Walter Gropius and Ludwig Mies van der Rohe as well as Peter Behrens, Hugo Häring, Ernst May, Hans Poelzig, Bruno Taut and Max Taut. They all propounded the idea of a modern and socially responsible architecture, and were able to point to concrete examples of this approach in the many buildings they had erected. They appealed directly to the public through periodicals, books, lectures and exhibitions. With the help of plans and models, they publicized the new building style among their professional colleagues while also introducing their architectonic political goals. After the traumatic experience of World War I, they repudiated so-called historical architecture. The new style of architecture was intended to give expression to a new era.

Among the general public, Modern architecture thus became associated with terms such as the "new age" or "new Germany".

Historically, Jews have always constituted a tiny minority of no more than 1% of the population of Germany. Only in 1871 did they gain equal rights under the German Reich's constitution — without, however, seeing that equality fully realized during the lifetime of the empire. For decades, Jews were excluded from academic posts, the civil service and high-ranking military positions. As the broader struggle for enlightenment, human rights and social justice progressed, Jews gained admission to nearly all realms of society, politics and culture. By 1909–10 they already accounted for nearly 3% of German university professors.[10]

Soon, however, anti-Semitism of previously unheard of dimensions came to light. And the more the Jews were driven into isolation, the greater became their efforts to assimilate. Their reactions to the changing social conditions were expressed in different ways. There was a strong movement away from religion: artists and scholars, writers and merchants, doctors, lawyers, politicians and others turned away from Judaism. Conflicts arose between Orthodox and liberal, Zionist and assimilated Jews and fissures within Judaism resulted. But the bourgeois notion of the value of education, chosen as the means to overcome isolation within German society, became an ideal all could share.

Following the German defeat in World War I and the difficult beginnings of the Weimar Republic, the right wing political programme began to take on increasingly nationalistic and racist features. Ten years into the Weimar era, political parties of all persuasions avoided the appointment of Jews to any kind of public office, and political discussions about the "Jewish question" took on a tone more threatening than ever before.

Tiberias, the chief Mosque Dahir al-Omar, built ca. 1743. Photo: M.W. 1992

Haifa, the Big Mosque, built ca. 1895. Photo: M.W. 1992

centre:
Jaffa, Chassan Bek Mosque, built ca. 1916. Photo: M.W. 1992
below:
Jerusalem, Russian Cathedral, built ca. 1890. Photo: M.W. 1992

Jews attempted to counter the growing irrationality and longed for a future in which "their dream of fame and recognition could be fulfilled and they would finally assume their long-sought place in society".[11] Jewish avant-garde artists and musicians saw their future in Modernism, perceiving traditional forms of cultural expression as often associated with anti-Semitic ideas. They hoped to further their own integration and equality by means of a new modern language "containing the immanent potential of art as a liberating element in history".[12] Indeed, in literature, theatre, the visual arts, architecture and music, Jews played "a visible and decisive role in upholding Modernism against the forces of tradition".[13]

Among the architects in Berlin who devoted themselves to Neues Bauen and enthusiastically made major contributions to that city's Modern architecture were a surprisingly large number of Jews. Alfons Anker, Fred Forbat, Rudolf Fränkel, Ernst Freud, Erwin Gutkind, the functionalist Alexander Klein, Arthur Korn and Siegfried Weitzmann, Erich Mendelsohn, Richard Neutra, Martin Punitzer, Michael Rachlis, Harry Rosenthal and Paul Zucker, to name only a few of the most prominent, made names for themselves at the time.[14] Josef Neufeld, the pioneer architect who in those days was an active member of CIAM (Congrès Internationaux d'Architecture Moderne) in Berlin, also deserves mention.[15]

With their new language of architecture, these German-Jewish architects also wanted to uphold the vision of a better, more beautiful and more reasonable world without war and hatred, without the negative aspects of the past and, most of all, without discrimination and anti-Semitism.

But these representatives of the new architectural style had barely celebrated their initial successes when they came under vehement attack. Conservative architects raised voices shrill with nationalist and racist arguments; the loudest among them was Paul Schultze-Naumburg in 1928 with his book *Kunst und Rasse* (Art and Race). Opponents of Modernist architecture published papers that tried to convince the public that "art mirrors racial attributes".[16] The basic tenor of these arguments was that the new style of building embodied an "un-German" culture.[17] Der Ring, one of the driving forces behind the reform movement, was denounced as a "Jewish-Bolshevist architects' association" although only three of the twenty-seven men who were members – Arthur Korn, Erich Mendelsohn and the architect and writer Walter Curt Behrendt – were German citizens of Jewish faith.[18]

Early in 1932, National Socialist candidates running for election to the Dessau city council called for the Bauhaus to be disbanded and its building demolished: "With the disappearance of this so-called 'College of Design', one of the most conspicuous sites of the Jewish-Marxist will-to-'art' will disappear from German soil."[19] In fact, however, during the fourteen-year history of the Bauhaus, none of the three directors and none of the twenty-four teachers, except for Marcel Breuer, had been Jews.

The Deutscher Werkbund also became the target of racist vilification: "National Socialist propagandists, who loved to use 'cultural bolshevism' as a catch phrase, often proved to be anti-Semites as well. Not one Jew was a leading member of the Werkbund, but so-called patriots, who imagined that Jews and Marxists had conspired to cordon off nationalistically-minded artists from influence and from the labour market, accused the Werkbund of being a tool of this conspiracy."[20]

Let us look back again to the period around the turn of the twentieth century: it was then that the idea of an independent Jewish state appeared, as if in a vision, to Theodor Herzl. After he visited Palestine in 1899, Herzl decided to write a Zionist utopian novel. In the book *Altneuland* (Old New Land), published in 1902 in

Theodor Herzl, born 1860 in Budapest, died 1904 in Edlach am Semmering
Etching by Hermann Struck

Leipzig, Herzl describes an area in the northern part of the land as it would look in the year 1923: "Thousands of white villas appeared, glowing amidst the green of opulent gardens. From Akko to Carmel, it was as though a great garden had been planted, and the mountain itself also was crowned with gleaming structures."[21] The novel is full of descriptions of cities, artisans' villages, industrial complexes, agricultural settlements, villa colonies and seaside resorts, located side by side and constructed by means of the most modern achievements of technology and the human spirit. Alex Bein, the Herzl scholar, interprets these visions of the future: "Technology, especially electricity (whose significance was just starting to be recognized in Herzl's time), had redesigned the entire world of work. Agriculture, manual labour, lighting, construction, road building — technology put its stamp on them all. Yet not only did it improve the lives of individuals; it made possible, even necessitated, a new, more just, social and economic order, a new, more perfect form of human co-existence."[22]

Theodor Herzl had a decisive influence on settlement politics in Palestine. During the Fifth Zionist Congress in Basel in 1901, Herzl for the first time called for cooperative settlements in Palestine in an attempt to resolve the "Jewish Question". In this context, he set up the Jewish national fund Keren Kayemet Leisrael (KKL) "to be used solely for the purpose of buying land in Palestine and Syria".[23] Zvi Schapira (1840–1898), a mathematics professor at the University of Heidelberg, had conceived the idea for the KKL. Around the same time, Franz Oppenheimer (1864–1943), a Berlin doctor and sociologist who had established his first cooperative settlement in 1893 in Bärenklau in Oranienburg, was propounding his idea of such cooperatives as a social solution among Zionists. Herzl and Oppenheimer met in Berlin and together they defined the most important principles of the Zionist settlement movement.

Herzl introduced these principles at the Sixth Zionist Congress in Basel in 1903. His presentation touched on the issues of land reform, settlement and cooperative production. Then Oppenheimer explained his cooperative model and presented a detailed plan for a Jewish cooperative settlement in Palestine. A fund to support a cooperative settlement consistent with the Oppenheimer model finally was created at the Ninth Zionist Congress in Hamburg in 1909.

Two years later, Keren Kayemet Leisrael acquired approximately 320 hectares (790 acres) of land in Emek Izrael (the valley God sows) south of Nazareth, and the Berlin architect Alex Baerwald was commissioned to design the settlement.[24] Completed in 1915, it was named Merchavia (God's Expanse).[25]

Herzl's vision of 1899 also foresaw the founding of a bank to furnish capital for Jewish settlements. Baerwald completed the building for the bank, which originally was known as the Anglo-Palestine Company (APC), in Haifa in 1925.[26]

By that time, Herzl's Zionist programme for building a modern Palestine, his portrayal of an "attempt at a modern solution to the Jewish question", would certainly have become familiar to every Jew, whether Orthodox, Conservative, Reform or liberal, whether Zionist, anti-Zionist or assimilated.

Introduction

Now let us return to Europe and consider the Modernist movement of the 1920s: It did not remain confined to Germany. Similar developments unfolded in France, Holland and Switzerland. Soon the new style spread around the world, from Finland to Italy, from England to Russia and across the oceans to Japan and the USA. In 1932 the architectural critic Henry Russell Hitchcock and the architect Philip Johnson organized an exhibition at the newly opened Museum of Modern Art in New York accompanied by a catalogue titled *The International Style: Architecture since 1922* – and the term "International Style" entered the profession. The exhibition presented contemporary architecture through the works of some fifty architects from sixteen countries, among them the Europeans Le Corbusier, Oud, Gropius, Mies van der Rohe, and the Americans F. L. Wright and Neutra. Its emphasis, however, was essentially on the style and aesthetic qualities of Neues Bauen. The formal principles associated with the exhibited buildings, such as the use of basic geometric forms, ribbon windows, glass walls and rooftop terraces, were now defined as striking features of the International Style of architecture from the 1920s. The catalogue summed up: "This new style is neither international in the sense that one country's achievements are exactly like another's, nor is it so rigid that the works of its leading practitioners are not clearly distinguishable from one another."[27]

At the time of the New York exhibition, Modern architecture in Palestine had not developed sufficiently to be included in the presentation. However, buildings that were constructed during the next decade displayed forms and principles from the repertoire of the International Style, which of necessity were adapted to local climatic, environmental and economic conditions.

Inevitably, Israel's geography and climate greatly influenced the direction of its architecture. A strip of land stretching some 550 km from north to south, the country is only about 10 km wide at its narrowest points in the north and south, and about 80 km wide in between. It is located in a transitional climate zone between subtropical rainy and subtropical desert zones, and has both highland and lowland landscapes. In the mountains of Judah, 800 m above sea level lies the city of Jerusalem. Thirty kilometres to the east is the Dead Sea, 392 m below sea level – the lowest point on earth. On the Mediterranean coast, 60 km northwest of Jerusalem is the city of Tel Aviv. From November to April, average precipitation during forty to sixty days of rain amounts to 30 mm in the south and 1100 mm in the north. Waves of hot and cold weather are typical; on hot days, the temperature can reach 34°–38° C (45° in the south); on cold days the mercury in Jerusalem or Safed sinks to the freezing point. The prevailing winds, a prime determinant for housing orientation in Israel, are also variable. During hot months, the wind blows inland from the sea during the daytime, but in the opposite direction at night. The westerly wind is refreshing along the coast, but the air is warm by the time it reaches the interior. Strong, intense sunlight is the only constant throughout the country.

The architects who had emigrated from German-speaking countries were constantly considering the exceptional geophysical conditions of their new land. They all devoted themselves to intensive research and design in order to arrive at optimal orientations for their buildings. The individual solutions and specific structural elements that architects such as Richard Kauffmann, Leopold Krakauer and Max Loeb invented to provide protection from the sun's burning rays became their trademarks. Details such as the brise-soleil (sun-break) that projected as a ledge above doors and windows or extended the eaves, bands of windows shielded from the sun, balconies, terraces, rooftop terraces, and arcades and covered pergolas that created shaded zones, as well as the use of building block-like forms whose projections and recesses could catch the fresh breezes — all those elements were architectural forms appropriate to the country's climatic conditions.

Tel Aviv, view from a high-rise. Photo: M.W. 1990

Haifa, view from Mount Carmel. Photo: M.W. 1990

Haifa, Mount Carmel, gouache by Eugen Szekey, 1949

Jerusalem, view from the Mount of Olives. Photo: M.W. 1990

The construction technology was characterized by its extreme simplicity and, as a rule, was limited to the use of native materials such as stone and concrete. When buildings were not faced with stone, as in Jerusalem, the climate dictated white stucco exteriors.
Prestigious buildings and fantasy projects were neither in demand nor were they realized. Erich Mendelsohn had to temper his expressive architectural language and Oskar Kaufmann set aside his predilection for theatre architecture. Priority was given to those buildings, public institutions and settlements that would further the Zionist programme.
The architects were confronted with circumstances and building tasks that presented unusual difficulties. There was virtually no body of experience to rely on and building codes, which might have simplified the work, were only minimally adequate. A kibbutz dining hall had not just a social function, it also was supposed to be a community status symbol – it had to satisfy all members' practical and aesthetic demands and be financially feasible as well. Not only did a housing development have to be appropriately sited on the hilly terrain, it also had to be strategically planned in view of clashes with Arab neighbours. The climatic, socio-cultural, economic and political conditions in Eretz Israel during those years presented architects with highly complex architectonic challenges, ones that could not easily be resolved by dogmatic application of the forms of the International Style.
The Modernist movement in architecture that originated in Germany in the 1920s was the wellspring for the creations of the German-speaking architects in Palestine. Like the champions of Neues Bauen, they radically rejected prior architectural traditions. Their buildings, erected in the Modern style, were designed to be the expression of the new life in the new homeland. The architects were challenged to build functional and economical architecture with clarity and artistry in the Land of the Forefathers. Inspired by their ideals and fired with enthusiasm, they wanted to get Herzl's Zionist programme underway and see it realized. From the bitter experiences they endured in their homelands because they were Jewish, these men and women drew the inner strength to take on their new tasks and responsibilities.

The purpose of this book is to recall and record the names, fates and works of these architects so nearly forgotten by their profession and the world at large. They came as immigrants to Palestine during 1920s and 1930s, and their contributions during 1930s and 1940s laid the foundation for modern architecture in Israel. Sixty years later, on July 3, 2003, UNESCO recognized the import of these social-political and architectural events and designated "The White City" in Tel Aviv as a World Heritage Site. It consists of 1000 of the 3700 buildings that were designed in the Modern style between 1931 and 1948, most of them by these architects.

And the search for traces of the lives and works of others among the five hundred German-Jewish architects persecuted by the Third Reich in no way ends here. Their paths took them not only to Palestine, but also to England, Sweden and Switzerland, to the USA and Canada, Brazil and Chile, South Africa, Australia and New Zealand, as well as to the infamous concentration camps of Theresienstadt, Lodz, Riga, Majdanek, Buchenwald, Mauthausen, Sachsenhausen, and most often to Auschwitz. Some eighty Jewish architects were gassed or murdered in another way, or are listed as missing. A lexicon of the lives and works of the persecuted German-Jewish architects was published in Berlin in 2005.[28]

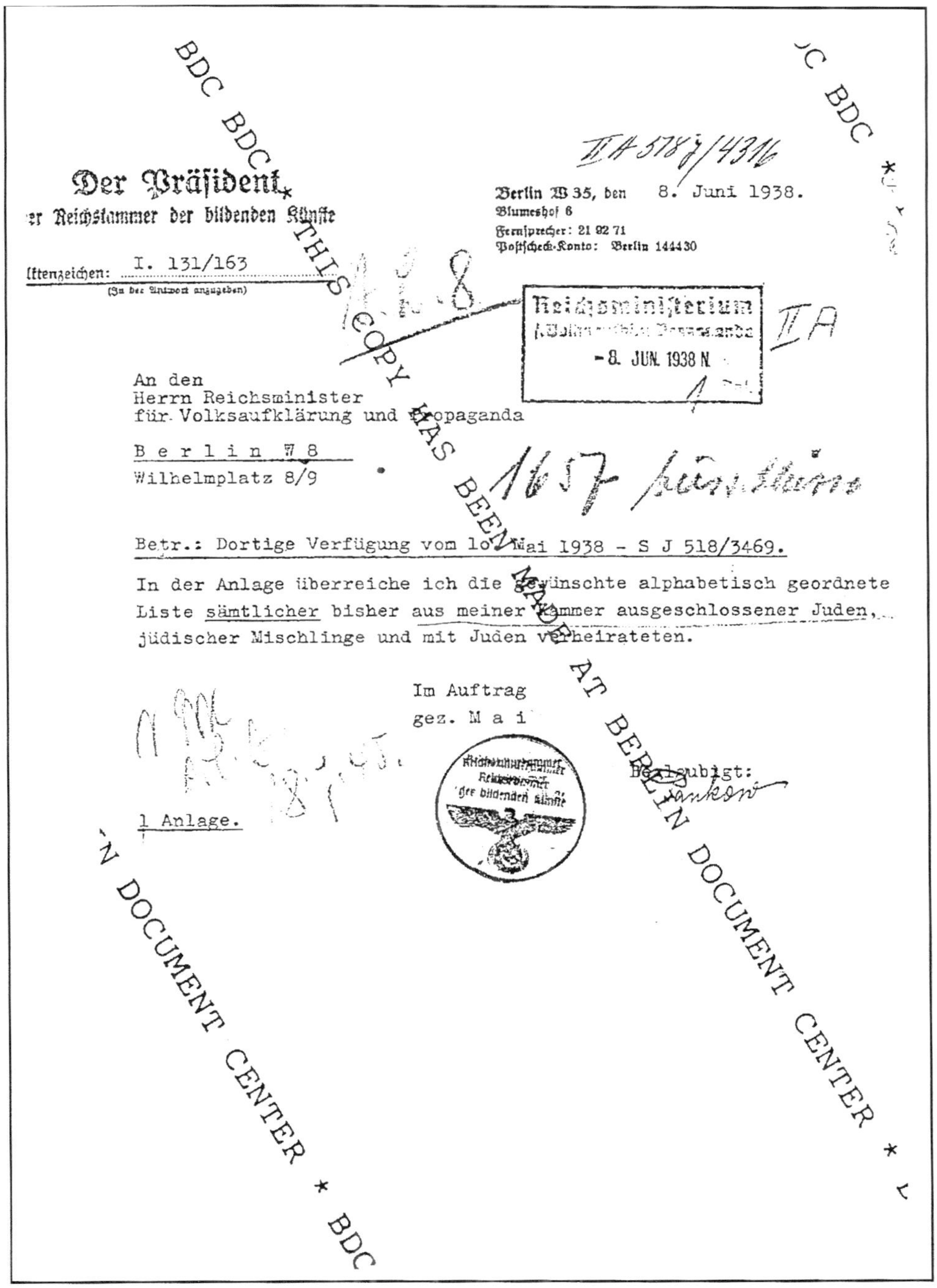

Der Präsident
er Reichskammer der bildenden Künste

ktenzeichen: I. 131/163
(Zu der Antwort anzugeben)

Berlin W 35, den 8. Juni 1938.
Blumeshof 6
Fernsprecher: 21 92 71
Postscheck-Konto: Berlin 144430

Reichsministerium
f. Volksaufklärung u. Propaganda
- 8. JUN. 1938

An den
Herrn Reichsminister
für Volksaufklärung und Propaganda

Berlin W 8
Wilhelmplatz 8/9

Betr.: Dortige Verfügung vom 10. Mai 1938 – S J 518/3469.

In der Anlage überreiche ich die gewünschte alphabetisch geordnete Liste sämtlicher bisher aus meiner Kammer ausgeschlossener Juden, jüdischer Mischlinge und mit Juden verheirateten.

Im Auftrag
gez. M a i

Beglaubigt:

1 Anlage.

Letter accompanying list of Jewish architects forbidden to practise, Berlin, June 8, 1938

1 Anatole Kopp, *When Modern architecture was not a style, but a cause*, Ecole nationale Supérieure des Beaux-Arts, Paris 1988 (French).
2 Myra Warhaftig, "Berlin 750 – Tel Aviv 75" in: *Bauwelt* 47/1984, pp. 2012–2013.
3 Dr. Max Osborn was a writer and art critic. Born 1870 in Cologne, he left Berlin for Paris in 1938 and later moved to New York, where he died in 1949.
4 Feilchenfeld 1972, pp. 89–90.
5 The travelling exhibition "Architecture in Palestine 1918–1948. The Lives and Works of German-Speaking Jewish Architects" (curator M.W.) documents the settlements, public buildings and housing built in response to each aliya. Since 1997 it has been shown in Tel Aviv, Jerusalem, Haifa and Be'er-Sheva, in Berlin, Dessau and Braunschweig, and at Columbia University in New York.
6 Myra Warhaftig, "Pionierarchitektur" in: *Basler Magazin* 44, 29.10.1988, pp. 12–13.
7 Wingler 1974, p. 5.
8 Herzl 1986, pp. 76–77.
9 Werkbund Exhibition, "Die Wohnung", Stuttgart 1927; see: Kirsch 1993.
10 Mosse 1992, p. 35.
11 Botstein 1991, p. 78.
12 Ibid., p. 82.
13 Mosse 1992, p. 46.
14 Alfons Anker and Fred Forbat fled to Sweden after Hitler's takeover, Rudolf Fränkel went via Romania and England to the USA. Ernst Freud and Arthur Korn saved their lives by going to England. Erwin Gutkind and Paul Zucker also fled to the USA. Martin Punitzer went to Chile and Erich Mendelsohn and Harry Rosenthal initially went to Palestine. Richard Neutra had already gone to the USA in 1923; see: Warhaftig 2005.
15 Hirdina 1991, p. 164.
16 Miller Lane 1986, p. 134.
17 Ibid., p. 126.
18 Campbell 1981, p. 291.
19 Quoted in Miller Lane 1986, p. 163
20 Campbell 1981, p. 298.
21 The title *Altneuland* alludes to the name of the Prague synagogue: Altneuschul; Herzl 1962, p. 46.
22 Bein 1983, p. 271.
23 Pollak 1934, p. 11.
24 See biography of Alex Baerwald.
25 Oppenheimer 1910; Myra Wahrhaftig, "Siedlungsgenossenschaft Merchavia von Alex Baerwald nach Franz Oppenheimer" in: *Architekturexperimente in Berlin und anderswo. Für Julius Posener*, Berlin 1989, pp. 164–171.
26 Since 1951 it has done business as the Israel National Bank (Bank Leumi Leisrael).
27 Hitchcock 1985, p. 27.
28 See: Warhaftig 2005.

Die Pioneers

ALEX BAERWALD

Alex Baerwald, self-portrait (drawing)

1877 Berlin – 1930 Jerusalem

The eldest of the pioneer architects, the Berliner Alex Baerwald, gave an essential artistic impetus to all their endeavours. When the 'father' of the pioneer architects was commissioned to design the Technion in Haifa in 1909, he embarked on a search for the design principles of a Jewish national architecture. His Technion buildings feature a combination of stylistic elements derived from both the Judaic symbolic world and Islamic architecture.

Baerwald was born into an assimilated Jewish family in Berlin on March 3, 1877. The term "assimilated Jews" refers to those who set aside their cultural and religious traditions and adapted to the prevailing dominant culture. From 1897 to 1901, Baerwald studied architecture in Berlin at the Technische Hochschule Charlottenburg (now the Technische Universität). He spent the summer semester of 1898 in Munich at the Königlich-Technische Hochschule.

From 1903 to 1927, Baerwald worked for the Prussian Department of Building and Finance in Berlin, first as a municipal building director and then as the head architect, while also holding the title of Königlicher Ministerialbaurat, or royal ministerial building councillor. One of his ministerial responsibilities was to supervise the construction of a new building for the Royal Library, now the Staatsbibliothek Berlin on Unter den Linden. The building in the Baroque style was built by Ernst Eberhard von Ihne (1848–1917) between 1903 and 1914.[1] On the day it was dedicated, Baerwald was decorated with the Königlicher Kronenorden IV Class.[2]

But Baerwald did not limit himself solely to his tasks as a civil servant; three articles in Berlin's professional journals in 1908 document the fact that he also carried out private commissions. Among these were proposals for the King's Colonnades at Alexanderplatz and for an apartment building renovation in Kaiserin-Augusta-Strasse.[3] In 1905 he was awarded the Schinkel plaque for his participation in the Schinkel competition to design a museum for architecture and architectural sculpture in Berlin.[4]

While he worked at the Prussian ministry, Baerwald also became involved in planning and design for projects in Eretz Israel. The welfare organization Hilfsverein der deutschen Juden (German Jewish Aid Association) had been established in Berlin in 1901 by the patrons James Simon and Eugen Landau and the journalist Paul Nathan with the aim of erecting Jewish school buildings – which were needed in Eastern Europe and the Middle East in the wake of pogroms, wars, and waves of immigration.[5] The organization's members were neither Orthodox nor Zionist. In 1909 the Association decided to build a Jewish institute for technical education in Palestine. It was suggested to Paul Nathan, the director and co-founder of the Association, that Alex Baerwald, who was as yet unknown in Jewish circles, be given the job.

As a result, Baerwald went to visit Palestine, which was still under Ottoman rule and inhabited by some 75,000 Jews and 550,000 Muslims. His encounter with Mediterranean architecture made a great impression on him and decisively influenced his style in later years.

The members of the German Jewish Aid Association decided to build their institute for technical education in Haifa. The city's advantage, in their view, was that not as many religious believers lived there as in Jerusalem, and not as many nationalists as in Tel Aviv. In addition, Haifa was not far from Syria, so that the institute's doors could also stand open to residents of that country. According to Baerwald's plans, workshops and a secondary school (the Reali School, later directed by the Berlin classicist Dr. Arthur Biram) would also occupy the same piece of property.[6]

But the Technion, as it is now known, did not open immediately after its completion in 1914 because a prolonged dispute erupted over whether the language of instruction should be Hebrew, as the Zionists in Palestine demanded, or German, as the Berlin Aid Association members wanted. Only in 1925, after the Zionists had prevailed, could the Technion open its doors.

Meanwhile, Baerwald and his wife settled permanently in Haifa and inaugurated the Technion department of architecture.[7] But only five years remained for Baerwald to convey both the Western tradition and his new experiences as an architect in the Middle East to his students. Baerwald died in Jerusalem on October 27, 1930, at the age of only fifty-three.

The public and private buildings that are the legacy of Alex Baerwald not only have a prominent place in the history of art in Israel, they also were significant for Herzl's Zionist programme of building the country. In 1915 Baerwald designed Merchavia, the first Jewish cooperative settlement, along the lines of Franz Oppenheimer's concept. In his artistic endeavour, Baerwald provided the buildings with various 'German' and 'oriental' architectural elements such as barrel-vaulted ceilings (so-called Prussian helmets), flat and rounded arches, and ventilation holes — an important element that Arabs used in their housing. Baerwald also designed the bank building for the Anglo-Palestine Company, now the Israel National Bank, in Haifa in 1925. The building was erected with reinforced concrete, but clad in limestone and decorated with Mediterranean motifs.

As he himself described it, Baerwald created his buildings "using modes of construction from the East combined with the achievements of German technology".[8] He intensively analysed the country's climatic, technical and economic conditions while searching for new forms of expression that would be aesthetically satisfying to him. Although his buildings often have the cupolas and arches typical of the East, such features also reflected his conflicted identity. Occasionally Baerwald replaced the round ventilation holes he adapted from Arabian housing with apertures shaped like the Star of David, the Jewish national symbol. In similar fashion, Baerwald used the parapets of the reconstructed Temple of Solomon as a model for the roofs of the Technion and the Reali School. Baerwald's interiors demonstrate how masterfully his architecture dealt with the blazing Mediterranean sunlight. His buildings' exterior walls were sheathed in Carmel limestone and the floors of private homes laid with patterned marble from the northern part of the country. Recently students, teachers, sociologists and art historians have made pilgrimages to many of Baerwald's buildings, including a hotel in Tel Aviv, a hospital in Afula, the Haifa residence of the Berlin painter Hermann Struck, and several other private residences.[9]

During his time in Berlin, Alex Baerwald lived first in Schöneberg and then in Wilmersdorf before moving with his wife to a country house he designed in Dahlem. The house conformed to the 1910 building ordinances, which called for two fully finished storeys and a half-finished basement and attic. The largest apartment on the ground floor had seven rooms and an inside staircase leading to office rooms in the base-

ment. A four-room apartment was on the first floor. The rest of that floor was part of a painter's duplex apartment whose studio was in the attic. In the basement, in addition to the offices, household rooms and the furnace, there was also an apartment for the doorman.
The villa was razed in 1953 and replaced by a single-storey one-family house. On the area in front of it, which previously had been a manicured lawn and a flower and vegetable garden, a four-family apartment building was erected in 1983. Only the brick entry gate and the fountain with its bench (which "was heavily used by walkers", Baerwald recorded) still remain.[10]

For almost thirty years, Alex Baerwald was an esteemed member of the Architekten- und Ingenieur-Verein zu Berlin (AIV), the professional society of architects and engineers. He even composed a long poem that chronologically recounted the Society's history as an address for its centennial celebration in 1924; the poem was printed in their commemorative publication to great acclaim. When his colleagues in the AIV learned of Baerwald's death, they decided to mount a memorial exhibition in his honour. Soon after, the plans and photographs of his architecture – the villas and apartment buildings, the Technion, the Reali School, the Anglo-Palestine Bank – as well as the entries he submitted to a large number of competitions were sent from Haifa to Berlin. The opening "with many colleagues and guests" took place on February 6, 1932, in the architecture museum of the Technische Hochschule. "The excellent memorial address was given by vice president (Benno) Kühn, who was able to bring us closer to the artist and the man Baerwald, 'always the loyal one', to whom the AIV Berlin owes a great debt."[11] Alex Baerwald's 1924 poem was reprinted, without comment, in the festschrift commemorating the AIV's 150th anniversary in 1974.[12]

1 On the occasion of the library dedication on March 23, 1914, Baerwald wrote a humorous two-page paper titled "The 8 o'clock Beer Evening News. Extra edition for the Bibulosity (!) of the Royal Library". He read the text and distributed it to guests without, however, revealing his authorship. "The editor who was responsible is long dead. Whoever might take offence had better not, for he will punish only himself." The humorous piece revealed inside details about the construction process and the persons involved, and announced satirical "rules for visitors to the Royal Library".
2 The Royal Order of the Crown was a decoration endowed by King Wilhelm I in 1861 to honour long years of contribution to the civil service.
3 Alex Baerwald, "Die Königskolonnaden am Alexanderplatz zu Berlin" in: *Wochenschrift des Architektenvereins zu Berlin* III/3, 11.1.1908; p. 12; P. Nitze, "Entwurf zu einem Garteneingang in einer Futtermauer" in: *Wochenschrift des Architekten Vereins zu Berlin* III/3, 18.1.1908, pp. 16–17. *Die Architektur des XX. Jahrhunderts*, Wasmuth, Berlin 1908, p. 18, plate 36.
4 How the design entries in the field of architecture for the 1905 Schinkel Festival competition were judged is recorded in: *Wochenschrift des Architekten Vereins zu Berlin* I/6, 10.2.1906, pp. 25–27.
5 James Simon, the prominent patron of Berlin's museums and initiator of the Deutsche Orient-Gesellschaft (1898), was born in Berlin in 1851 and died there in 1932. Eugen Landau, the financier and philanthropist, served on the board of the German National Bank for many decades; he was born in 1852 in Breslau and died in 1935 in Berlin. The politician and writer Paul Nathan was born in 1857 and died in 1927, also in Berlin; Spur/Fischer 2000, pp. 164–172.
6 Arthur Biram (1878–1967) had previously taught at the Gymnasium zum Grauen Kloster in Berlin.

7 Alex Baerwald's wife Lotte, born Eisenberg, was a painter. Her name was listed in *Dresslers Kunsthandbuch*, Berlin 1930.
8 Alex Baerwald, "Die Jüdische Anstalt für technische Erziehung in Palästina" in: *Zentralblatt der Bauverwaltung*, Berlin 10.6.1916, p. 322.
9 Alex Baerwald, "Deutsche Bauten in Haifa, Palästina" in: *Bauwelt* 51, Berlin 1928, pp. 7–8; Myra Warhaftig, "Deutsches und österreichisches Architekturerbe in Israel" in: *Kunst und Kirche* 4, Darmstadt 1986, pp. 256–257; Myra Warhaftig, "Alex Baerwald, Berlin 1877 – Jerusalem 1930" in: *Bauwelt* 32, Berlin 1990, pp. 1562–1564.
10 Alex Baerwald, "Dreifamilienhaus in Dahlem (Berlin)" in: *Zentralblatt der Bauverwaltung*, Berlin, 1913, pp. 502–504.
11 In: *Deutsches Bauwesen* II/4, 1932, p. 31.
12 Alex Baerwald, "Festspruch zum 100. Jubiläum" in: *150 Jahre Architekten-und Ingenieur-Verein zu Berlin*, Berlin 1974, p. 26.

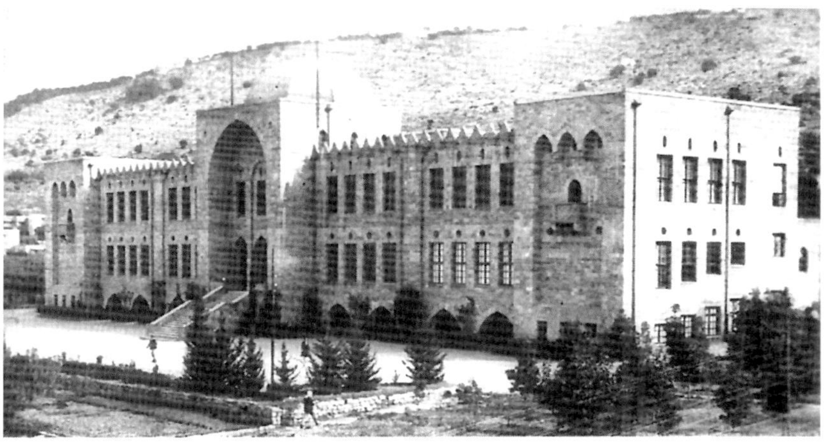

Alex Baerwald, Technion Haifa, 1914, Jewish Institute for Technical Education, Haifa

Alex Baerwald, Technion Haifa, 1914, window in the entrance hall. Photo: M.W. 1989

Alex Baerwald, 1913, secondary school, Haifa. Photo: M.W. 1989

Left page, above:
Alex Baerwald, Merchavia cooperative settlement, 1915, inner courtyard

Left page, centre:
Alex Baerwald, Merchavia cooperative settlement, 1915, living unit. Photo: M.W. 1990

Left page below:
Alex Baerwald, Merchavia cooperative settlement, 1915, grain storehouse. Photo: M.W. 1990

Right page above:
Alex Baerwald, Anglo-Palestine Bank, Haifa, 1925, entrance

Right page below:
Alex Baerwald, Anglo-Palestine Bank, Haifa, 1925

ALEX BAERWALD

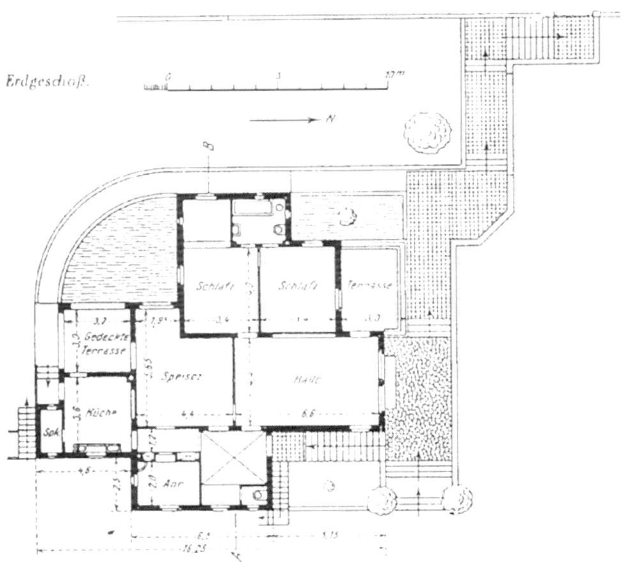

above:
Alex Baerwald, Hermann Struck residence, Haifa, 1924. Photo: M.W. 1989

left: Alex Baerwald, Hermann Struck residence, Haifa, 1924, ground-floor plan

right: Alex Baerwald, Hermann Struck residence, Haifa, 1924, nameplate. Photo: M.W. 1989

Alex Baerwald,
Baerwald residence,
Berlin-Dahlem, 1912,
garden view

Alex Baerwald,
Baerwald residence,
Berlin-Dahlem 1912,
streetside fountain
with seating, sole relic
of the Baerwald
residence.
Photo: O.W. 1989

Richard Kauffmann

1887 Frankfurt am Main – 1958 Jerusalem

Richard Kauffmann was the first architect to introduce settlement planning as a discipline and Modern architecture as a style to Palestine. He designed many urban districts and agricultural settlements as well as a number of public and private buildings. Nearly four hundred of his 644 projects were realized. These included 120 agricultural communities, some ninety urban developments, and between 120 and 160 public and private buildings. Approximately 240 of those works still survive.[1] It can therefore be said that Richard Kauffmann made the most significant contribution of any one architect to building the country of Israel.

Kauffmann was born into an assimilated Jewish family in Frankfurt am Main on June 20, 1887. From 1907 to 1912 he studied architecture at the Technische Hochschule Darmstadt, then went on to study the new field of urban planning under Theodor Fischer at the Technische Hochschule in Munich. He gained his first practical experience in Essen under Georg Metzendorf (1874–1934), who had by then designed the workers' housing on Margarethenhöhe for the Krupp firm. Kauffmann used the formal vocabulary of Neoclassicism to deal with the social requirements of Germany's first garden suburb.

When World War I broke out, Kauffmann was sent as a soldier to Verdun and then on to the Russian front. Stationed in the Ukranian city of Kovel, he experienced an East European shtetl in all its facets for the first time.[2] This experience prompted him to take part in a Russian competition to plan the garden city of Raigorod near Charkov, whose population was one-sixth Jewish. Kauffmann won first prize. His professional stature was confirmed once again when, after the war, he was selected from a field of fifty candidates for an influential position in a large architectural firm in Oslo (then known as Kristiana). Kauffmann turned down the job, however, because an involvement with Zionism had become his priority.

In 1907, at Artur Ruppin's suggestion, the Eighth Zionist Congress in The Hague decided to open a Palestine office in Jaffa as a central clearinghouse for Zionist settlement affairs.[3] Kauffmann was appointed to head the planning office and soon afterward, in August 1920, he arrived in Palestine.

Kauffmann's first architectural task there was to design an agricultural workers' community, the Moshav Ovdim Nahalal in Emek Izrael (1921).[4] The fundamental ideas for this new type of workers' settlement had been published in 1920 by the Bessarabian agronomist and labour organiser Elieser Joffe (1882–1942). In contrast to the kibbutz principle, Joffe's moshav ovdim was based on a mixed economy and independent labour. Kauffmann translated this societal model into spatial terms, creating the well-known crown-shaped settlement of Nahalal. His design was influenced by intellectual currents in European town planning and was perhaps inspired by Camillo Sitte's artistic principles, Sir Ebenezer Howard's garden city and Bruno Taut's crown city.

The subject of many publications, Moshav Nahalal is situated on a hill in the northern part of the country,

1.5 km off the main highway between Haifa and Nazareth. Its single main thoroughfare has a regular elliptical shape with access and arterial roads forming the two axes. The community buildings are on the hilltop, surrounded by a garland of land parcels for artisans. At the outer edge of the large ring road are the settlers' parcels; all the houses lie along a single line of sight, with façades and front gardens of equal width.

Parallel to the moshav ovdim form of agricultural settlement, another form of cooperative living known as the kibbutz ("to gather together") had been developing since 1910. This type of agricultural collective was based on a strictly communal way of life that required its own spatial design. Kauffmann elaborated numerous development plans for kibbutzim of various political persuasions, and proceeded logically to separate the buildings spatially according to their use. The adults' living quarters, the dining hall, the communal administration, and the children's quarters all occupied separate areas, as did the workplaces with their storerooms, cowsheds and chicken coops. The green zones that separated different areas of the kibbutz were designed to create an aesthetically unified impression. Kauffmann also paid attention to the climatic conditions by orienting the living spaces to the prevailing north-westerly breezes and situating the farm buildings on the eastern side, to minimize unpleasant odours.
Even though the social structures and economic conditions in the kibbutzim of that era varied little, Kauffmann did not develop any rigid concepts. His analysis of the ideas and desires of each new group of kibbutznikim (kibbutz members) with whom he worked, and his fundamental premise that architecture should harmonize with the landscape, continually produced new and individual kibbutz designs.

The growth of the cities of Haifa, Tel Aviv and Jerusalem, and of certain regions in the north, south, and centre of the country, presented Kauffmann with a different set of problems. Kauffmann created his first development plan for an urban garden suburb in 1921 in Jerusalem: Talpiyot ("castle built on high"). Terraced streets along the chain of hills led to the area's highest elevation, where Kauffmann foresaw public cultural buildings and schools for the eight hundred families who would live there amidst the greenery.

In contrast to Alex Baerwald, Richard Kauffmann had no affinity for Mediterranean architecture with its cupolas, arches and arcades. Kauffmann was a chalutz (pioneer) and strove to express this quality in his use of forms. His buildings respond to the conditions of climate and landscape, and are functional in design and free from any kind of historicism.
In 1926 Kauffmann built workers' housing near the Dead Sea, almost 400 m below sea level. The bedrooms on the ground floor have deep balconies on both sides that shield them from the sun's penetrating rays and also provide a place to sleep outdoors. Kauffmann erected a school in Kibbutz Degania in 1928 that has a similarly auspicious spatial design. Degania lies in the Jordan valley, one of Israel's hottest regions, and the building has a slightly pitched roof over a row of windows, enabling the warm air to constantly circulate.
Kauffmann designed Menachem Ussischkin's residence in Jerusalem (1930) with a large open balcony, so that the family could celebrate Sukkoth outdoors according to Jewish custom.[5]
The Pomeranz residence (1932) attests to the headway Kauffmann made against antiquated traditional building codes. In 1918, during the British mandate, the Englishman Roland Storrs had issued a construction ordinance specifying that all buildings in Jerusalem must be constructed using square-cut natural stone, to continue the three-thousand-year-old tradition of building in stone.[6] Kauffmann did use smooth

stone for the Pomeranz residence, but he used concrete to construct the brise-soleils and the framework supporting the windows, creating a glowing white building in the Modern style.

Richard Kauffman's contribution to the building of Eretz Israel was honoured during his lifetime. His fiftieth birthday in 1937 was the occasion for great public recognition. In honour of his sixtieth birthday in 1947, the Bezalel Museum in Jerusalem mounted an exhibition that offered an impressive overview of his work and clearly demonstrated how important a role the architect from Frankfurt had played in Israel's architectural history since the early 1920s.[7] Kauffmann was given the title "The Architect of Israel".
After the state of Israel was founded, Richard Kauffmann and his colleagues of the same generation were supplanted by the young Technion-educated architects. Commissions became fewer. Kauffmann died in the city that had become his second home on February 3, 1958.

1 Adiv 1985; Mezger-Smok 1994, pp. 260–263. Events are being planned for 2008, the fiftieth anniversary of Kauffmann's death.
2 Lotte Cohn, "Früher Städtebau in Palästina und die Bedeutung von Richard Kauffmann", Tel Aviv 1973, unpublished manuscript.
3 Artur Ruppin, economist and sociologist, prolific author, was born in 1876 in Rawicz (near Poznan, today in Poland), and died in 1943 in Jerusalem; Ruppin 1937.
4 Amitai 1971.
5 Menachem Ussischkin (1863–1941) was one of the leading Russian Zionists.
6 This ordinance is still in effect, but is often only carried out pro forma.
7 The 1947 exhibition was titled "From Reality to Planning. The Work of Richard Kauffmann".

Ha-adrikhal Street in Jerusalem, the "Street of the Architect", bears Richard Kauffmann's name in Hebrew on its sign. Photo: O.W. 1994

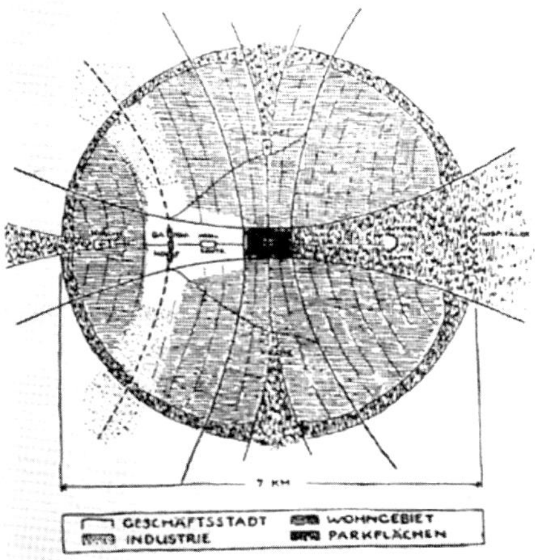

Bruno Taut, Stadtkrone, 1919

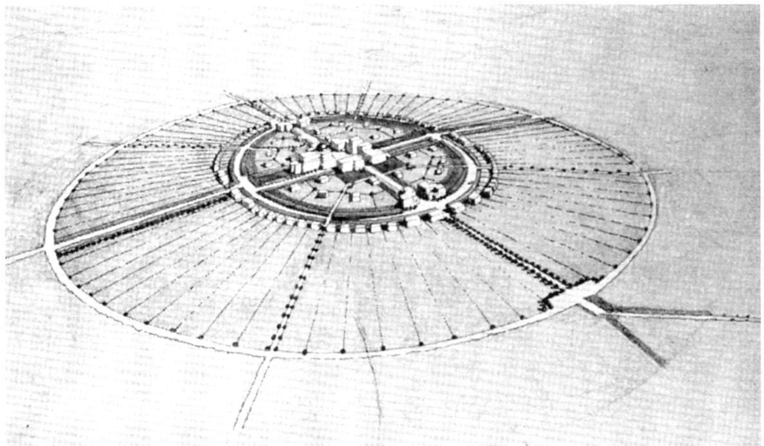

Richard Kauffmann, Moshav Ovdim
Nahalal, 1921, photograph of model

Richard Kauffmann, Moshav Ovdim
Nahalal, 1921, site plan

Richard Kauffmann

Richard Kauffmann, Moshav Ovdim Kfar Yeheskel, 1922, aerial photo

A type of moshav ovdim, designed by Elieser Joffe, 1920

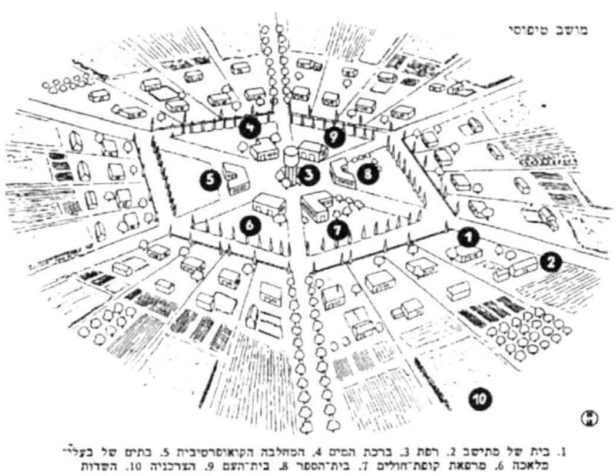

Richard Kauffmann, Moshav Ovdim Nahalal, circa 1970, aerial photo

Richard Kauffmann, garden city Talpiyot, Jerusalem, 1921, development plan

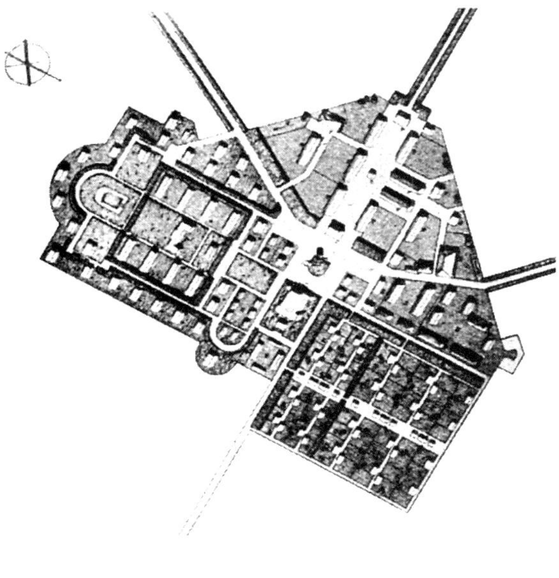

Richard Kauffmann, Kibbutz Maoz-Chaim, 1938, development plan

Left page above:
Richard Kauffmann, apartment building for employees of Palestine Potash Ltd., Dead Sea, 1930

Left page below:
Richard Kauffmann, apartment building in Kibbutz Degania, 1928

Right page above:
Richard Kauffmann, Dr. Kruskal residence, Tel Aviv, 1934 (drawing)

Right page centre:
Richard Kauffmann, Dr. Kruskal residence, Tel Aviv, 1934.
Photo: O.W. 1994

Right page below:
Richard Kauffmann, Pomeranz residence, Jerusalem, 1932.
Photo: M.W. 1990

Fritz Kornberg

1889 Bad Pyrmont – 1944 Jerusalem

Fritz Kornberg was born on November 14, 1889, in Bad Pyrmont near Hanover. At the outbreak of World War I in 1914, he broke off his study of architecture at the Technische Hochschule Charlottenburg in Berlin and was dispatched immediately to the Russian front. There he met Richard Kauffmann. Kornberg returned to the university after the war ended and received his diploma in architecture in 1920. Right after he graduated, Kornberg – a Zionist partisan since his youth – left for Palestine as a chalutz in the Third Aliya and settled in Jerusalem.
Among his first buildings were the Slonim residence and the factory of Alfred Salzmann, both in Jerusalem, and the Hofein residence in Tel Aviv.
In the matter of style, Kornberg initially was undecided whether to design functionally, like Richard Kauffmann, or in the Jewish-Mediterranean manner of Alex Baerwald. Kornberg chose a middle path, and this soon proved advantageous. After the British government decided to develop the port of Haifa into one of the most important transhipment centres for east-west trade, a series of competitions was planned. The first business centre competition was announced internationally in 1923. First prize went to a design by Erich Mendelsohn and Richard Neutra. Although Kornberg's entry was awarded only second prize, it was nonetheless realized, for its site plan adapted to local conventions and the outer appearance of his structures differed little from that of contemporary Arabian apartment buildings.[1]

Kornberg also was commissioned to oversee the initial construction process for a Hebrew university in Eretz Israel. Hermann Zvi Schapira had put forward the idea of founding a Hebrew university in Jerusalem at the First Zionist Congress in Basel in 1897.[2] His proposal to create a "general Jewish fund", two thirds of whose assets would be used to acquire land and one third set aside for "religious and moral educational institutions" in Palestine, assumed concrete form sixteen years later, at the Eleventh Congress in Vienna in 1913. It was Chaim Weizmann who introduced the resolution calling for work on the Hebrew university to begin immediately.[3] But not until 1918, after the British conquered the land, was the cornerstone laid on Mount Scopus. Finally on April 1, 1925, the first buildings that were to form the core of the planned university were officially dedicated. These were the Gray-Hill residence that, converted and expanded, became the Institute of Chemistry and Microbiology and an amphitheatre that was designed by Fritz Kornberg, and hastily constructed for the celebrations.[4]

As part of the 1913 Zionist programme, a decision was taken to build the first Hebrew college preparatory school in Jerusalem, for which an international competition was announced late in 1922.[5] The Vienna-based Verband Jüdischer Ingenieure und Techniker für den Aufbau Palästinas (Association of Jewish Engineers for the Building of Palestine) called on its members in Germany and Poland to take part in the competition and the response was overwhelming; more than 75% of the entries came from Jewish architects living in Europe. Although the jury chaired by Richard Kauffmann awarded Alex Baerwald the first prize, the winner of the second prize received the commission, and once again, his name was Fritz Kornberg. He used the basic forms of cubes in a symmetrical arrangement to constitute the building's volume and designed façades that were functional and unornamented.[6]

The Ben Shemen Youth Village, a project that continues to have great significance for the land and people of Israel, is also inextricably linked with Kornberg's name. The history of its founding goes back nearly a century. The Berlin physician Siegfried Lehmann (1892–1958) had studied Gustav Landauer's social philosophy and analysed the predicament of children living in squalor in the so-called Scheunenviertel (barn district) of Berlin-Mitte, and he was moved to found a Jewish home whose aim was to enable children to experience life in a community. Lehmann was able to open his Centre for Education and Social Work in Dragonerstrasse 22, now Max-Beer-Strasse, in 1916.[7] Two years later, confronted with the poverty and dire need of Jewish orphans of World War I in Kovno (now Kaunas, Lithuania), Lehmann decided to take the children out of Europe and bring them to Palestine.
There Lehmann made it his goal to build a self-governing children's village where youth could receive training in productive agricultural and skilled trade occupations and where they could be brought up to develop a tolerant attitude toward other peoples, parties and religions.[8] Lehmann began to realize his project in 1927, settling with the first fifteen orphans from Kovno in an area south of Tel Aviv called Ben Shemen. With the number of children rapidly increasing – three years later there were already 220 – Lehmann began to devise a spatial system whose plan called for independent residential groups, each consisting of fifty children. In addition, there were a number of community structures, such as classrooms and laboratories, workshops, a library, and teachers' residences. Agricultural facilities such as tree plantations, fields, and stalls were in the immediate vicinity. Fritz Kornberg was commissioned with the architectural planning.
The white stuccoed one- and two-storey buildings with their straight lines, horizontal or vertical bands of windows, and arcades were characteristic of Kornberg's architectural style late in the 1930s. Their hipped roofs were the only formal departure from Modernist principles. But this satisfied Siegfried Lehmann's wish to lend the place a village-like appearance.
With the onset of organized persecution of the European Jewish population, the Ben Shemen Youth Village suddenly gained enormous significance. The children of refugees found a new home there after 1933, as did the orphaned children who survived the concentration camps after 1945.[9] New buildings were needed as more and more children arrived, but Fritz Kornberg was no longer there to build them. He died at the height of his powers at the age of only fifty-four on September 28, 1944. The German-speaking architects Lotte Cohn and Chanan Heinz Pawel continued his work in Ben Shemen.[10]

Most of Kornberg's buildings either no longer exist today, or they are no longer recognizable. Plans or photographs of the buildings can seldom be found, since the architect's office was in a wooden barracks, which was twice set on fire during ongoing conflicts with the Arab neighbours. All of his drawings were burned. Kornberg's wife Zina (now deceased) preserved a few yellowed photographs of his buildings and drawings in a Jerusalem home for the aged.

Fritz Kornberg

I am very grateful to Zina Kornberg for telling me so much about her husband and for allowing me to take pictures of the only extant photographs and drawings of his buildings (1986).
I also owe thanks to Richard Levinson, who grew up in Ben Shemen Youth Village after he fled Germany. In 1987 he gave me a guided tour through the Village and also provided me with very important material. In 1997 he gave me a book, on whose editorial committee he had served, that documents the history the Village. The book was published to commemorate the seventieth anniversary of the founding of Ben Shemen Youth Village.

1 The Berlin architects Arthur Korn and Siegfried Weizmann were awarded third prize. See: Gilbert Herbert and Silvina Sosnovsky, "Urban Developments in Down-Town Haifa during the British Mandate", Technion Haifa 1984.
2 Hermann Zvi Schapira (born 1840 in Erswilki near Tauroggen, died 1898 in Cologne) was a professor of mathematics at Heidelberg University.
3 Chaim Weizmann (born 1873 in Motyli near Pinsk, died 1952 in Rechovot) earned his postdoctoral degree in 1900 while a chemistry professor in Geneva. In 1903 he was appointed a professor at the University of Manchester. In 1938 he founded the Daniel Sieff Research Institute in Rechovot, later the Weizmann Institute of Science. Weizmann was the president of the Zionist Organization (1920–1931, 1935–1946) and became the first president of the state of Israel in 1948.
4 The development of the Hebrew University on Mount Scopus is still seen as a significant event in Israel. In 1935 Erich Mendelsohn drew up a general plan for the Hebrew University, including the Hadassah University Medical Center (see biography of Erich Mendelsohn). After Mendelsohn left Palestine in 1941, Richard Kaufmann took over the planning for the university and worked out a new design which, however, was foiled by political developments: Jerusalem was divided in 1948 during the War of Independence. The Scopus building remained on Israeli territory but was under Jordanian military control. University operations in Erich Mendelsohn's Hadassah complex had to be abandoned, and a new campus was erected in the city district of Givat-Ram. Only after the Six-Day War (1967), when the entire city came under Israeli rule, did the Scopus complex eventually come to be the central focus of university activities; Katz 1997.
5 See: *Jüdische Rundschau*, Berlin, 6.4.1923.
6 In the meantime, the building has been enlarged and renovated. "Herzlia", the first Hebrew college preparatory school in Tel Aviv, was built in 1906 by Josef Barski. The Mediterranean-style building was later torn down.
7 Gustav Landauer (born 1870 in Karlsruhe, murdered 1919 in Munich) gave a lecture at the opening of the Berlin home; Landauer 1967; Naor 1997.
8 Dr. Siegfried Lehmann, *Idee und Verwirklichung*, Tel Aviv 1978. Siegfried Lehmann's concept was endorsed by Albert Einstein and Martin Buber. Elsa Einstein became chairwoman of the Berlin committee of Friends of the Ben Shemen Youth Village; Bentwich 1960.
9 Today the Village offers a home to several hundred children from different social classes and cultures.
10 See biography of Lotte Cohn and brief biography of Chanan Heinz Pawel.

Fritz Kornberg, amphitheatre, Hebrew University Jerusalem, 1923, model

Fritz Kornberg, Institute for Chemistry and Microbiology, new building tract, Hebrew University Jerusalem, 1923 (drawing)

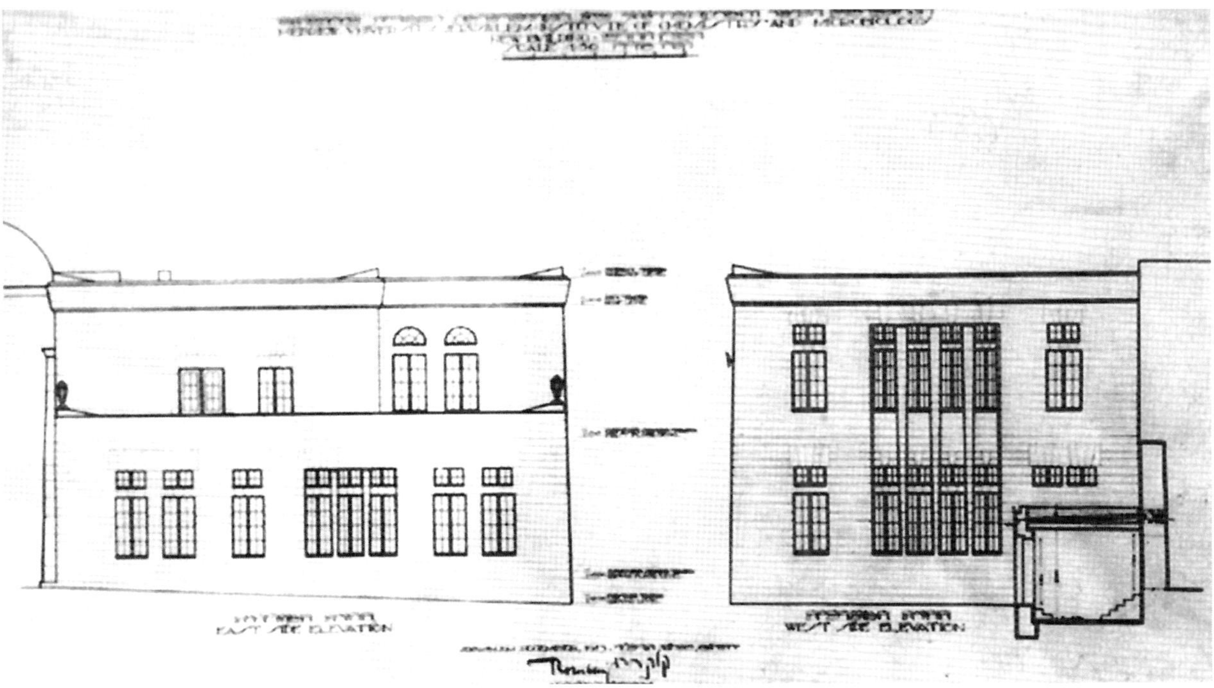

Fritz Kornberg, Hofein residence, Tel Aviv, 1921

Fritz Kornberg, Slonim residence, Jerusalem, 1923

Bruno Taut, Harkort turbine house in Wetter an der Ruhr, 1908

Fritz Kornberg, Alfred Salzmann Co. factory, Jerusalem, 1922

Fritz Kornberg

Fritz Kornberg, fantasy project for Jerusalem, 1930s (drawing)

Bruno Taut, Alpine Architecture, 1919

Fritz Kornberg, fantasy project for Jerusalem, 1930s (drawing)

Fritz Kornberg, fantasy project for Jerusalem, 1930s (drawing)

Fritz Kornberg

above:
Fritz Kornberg, youth group residences, Ben Shemen Youth Village, 1938

centre:
Fritz Kornberg, school buildings with library building in background, Ben Shemen Youth Village, 1940

below left:
Fritz Kornberg, school buildings with library building in background, Ben Shemen Youth Village, 1940 (drawing)

below right:
Fritz Kornberg, laboratory building, Ben Shemen Youth Village, 1936, perspective, floor plan and site plan

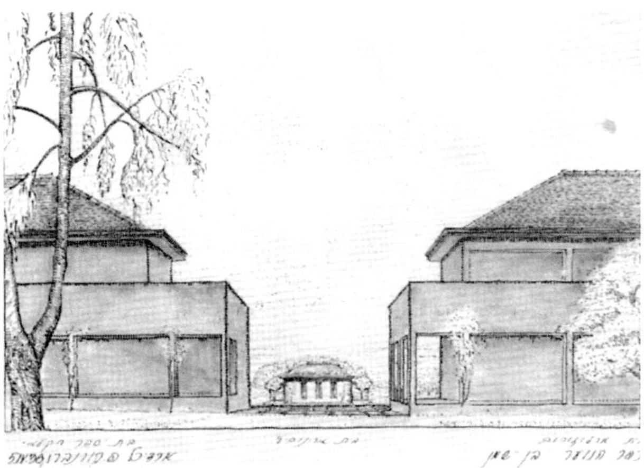

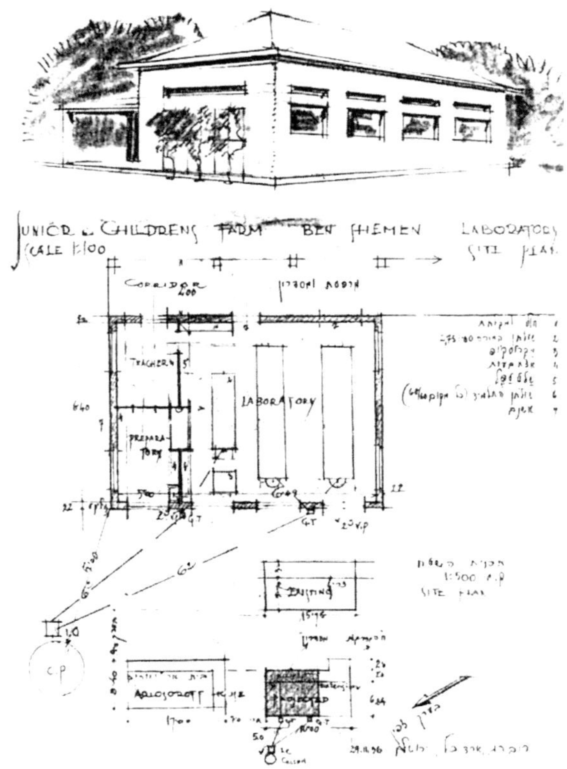

For its fifth anniversary in 1932, the Friends of the Ben Shemen Youth (Französische Strasse 32, W 56 Berlin) published a brochure that presented the Friends' achievements: Orphans from centres of Judaism around the world learned productive professions and how to live in a community.

Leopold Krakauer

1890 Vienna – 1954 Jerusalem

"Leopold Krakauer, Jewish painter in Palestine, born on March 30, 1890, in Vienna, married to the painter Grete Wolf. He first studied architecture under Friedrich Ohmann in Vienna, then turned to painting and provided several Viennese exhibitions (Bund geistig Tätiger, Hagenbund, Freie Bewegung) with works, usually abstract in nature, and with drawing cycles ("War" – 6 drawings; "Paths to Creation" – 15 drawings)."[1] When this short vitae was published in Hans Vollmer's entry for the 1956 encyclopaedia *Allgemeines Lexikon der Bildenden Künstler* (Leipzig), Krakauer had already been dead for two years. He left behind not only a large and significant collection of paintings, but also a number of buildings that have become very well known in Israel due to their especially harmonious design and originality.
Before World War I, Krakauer apprenticed for two years in his teacher Ohmann's office. He fought in the war as an officer on the Italian front. In 1919 he took part in the spring exhibition of the Vienna Museum of Art. From 1922 to 1923 he lived in Belgrade, where he helped complete the parliament building.[2]

As an enlightened member of his generation and as a Jew, Leopold Krakauer cannot have been indifferent to the smear campaign against Jews in Vienna. For national and political reasons, the development of the anti-Semitic movement in Germany had not failed to influence the Austrian situation. Anti-Semitic ideology was already part of the Christian Socialist party programme by the 1880s. Ten years later, anti-Semites gained a majority in the state parliament of Lower Austria.[3]
An exhibition on Palestine shown August 18–31, 1925, at the Vienna Konzerthaus on the occasion of the Fourteenth Zionist Congress provided Vienna's anti-Semites with an occasion to commit acts of violence. Heavy rioting resulted in scores of injuries. This incident, occurring as it did on the eve of an exhibition illustrating the many tasks involved in building the Jewish state, had a decisive impact on a number of Viennese architects. Krakauer and Jacob Pinkerfeld emigrated from Austria to Palestine that same year, and Carl Rubin followed a year later.[4] Josef Neufeld, another pioneer architect, had gone to Palestine five years earlier, and Gideon Kaminka, who visited the land in 1926 while an architecture student, also decided to go there once he had earned his degree.[5]

Leopold Krakauer first settled in Haifa and worked in the office of Alex Baerwald, but he had no affinity for Baerwald's architectural style. One year later, Krakauer moved to Jerusalem. Except for brief sojourns in Italy, he never again left the country.
The landscape of Jerusalem, with its hills and cliffs, olive trees and thistles, Arab villages – and also its beggars and Orthodox Jews – offered the artist L.K. (as his friends called him) a wealth of inspiration for his creative activity as a painter and architect.[6]
When Krakauer turned to architecture, he designed buildings that referenced the landscape's contours

through the use of geometric forms such as cubes, prisms or half-cylinders nestled inside one another. His artistry and his way of thinking, rich in fantasy yet always objective, corresponded well with the pioneer spirit in the kibbutzim. Like Richard Kauffmann, Krakauer also paid careful attention to the requirements of these working and living cooperatives in his designs. As a result, he often was commissioned to build the dining hall, the heart of each and every kibbutz.

There were already thirty kibbutzim in the country when the first dining hall designed by a professional architect was built in 1927.[7] Before that, the cooperatives had to make do without stone buildings or steel construction, since these were not economically feasible.
As membership grew, the kibbutznikim needed a permanent building for their dining hall, one that also would serve as a status symbol for the community. Attempts were made to define this type of structure more clearly and to articulate its socio-cultural and political role. The dining hall was supposed to be suitable for theatre performances and film screenings as well as for political meetings. The multiple functions finally assigned to the building necessitated the choice of an optimal site, flexible dimensions that could alter with changing populations and, above all, the use of economical materials to stay within budget. Aesthetically, an effort was made to take into account the tastes of all members of the kibbutz.
The Zionist Settlement Office tried to economize by developing only a single dining hall prototype, but this compromise proposal met with harsh criticism from the settlers, who were opposed to such undifferentiated, impersonal architecture. New European political developments meanwhile worked to the settlers' advantage, as the growing number of architects who fled fascism for Palestine in 1933 increased competition. Now each kibbutz could ask several different architects to come up with plans for their dining hall. Among the invited competitors, in addition to Leopold Krakauer, were the other pioneer architects Richard Kauffmann, Fritz Kornberg, Dov Kuczynski, Jacob Pinkerfeld, and Josef Neufeld, and the Bauhaus pupils Arieh Sharon and Shmuel Mestechkin, who possessed empathy and enthusiasm for the pioneer movement.[8]
During his years in practice, Krakauer designed fifteen different dining halls, of which seven were realized. One of his most famous is the dining hall in Kibbutz Tel Josef (1936), which has expressive features. Over a square space measuring 16 × 16 m, Krakauer set a second 11 × 11 m square, displaced at a 45° angle. Freestanding staircases at one corner of the building and the kitchen area in the opposite corner enhance the building's impact, so that it seems to have the architecture of a crystal.[9]

Haifa and Jerusalem also have their examples of Krakauer's artistic, high-quality buildings. In the Boasson residence (1940) in Jerusalem, one recognizes his affinity for Adolf Loos's architectonic approach. The main rooms of the two-storey one-family house are on different levels that follow the site's topography.
Krakauer's most elaborated building was built on one of the hills of Mount Carmel in Haifa in 1940. Adolf Rading, then the municipal architect, thought that Haifa should be developed into a resort.[10] This gave a Viennese-born Zionist woman by the name of Teltsch the idea of building a hotel on Mount Carmel. The hotel should meet "European standards" and have a "central location" that was "near the coast" with "a view to the sea and excellent air quality", the client stipulated. She gave the commission to her landsman, Leopold Krakauer.
The poet Else Lasker-Schüler (1869–1945), who was a close friend of the Krakauers, and who spent a day with the artist couple soon after the building was completed, wrote in her memoirs:

Leopold Krakauer

"Up on the sacred plateau of Carmel, the Austrian architect Krakauer, assisted by his disciple, built a resort for the hospitable parents of that talented pupil, a palace of health, which welcomed us five visitors and where we dined on a broad veranda among people from all over the world in need of recuperation. After the meal, we friends went for a walk, single file, over brooks, deeper into the woods, past shaggy, dark green-shadowed and feathery branches, to the Indian trees of Palestine."[11]
More than fifty years later, the Hotel Teltsch – meanwhile renamed Hotel Megido – still commands attention with its comfortable guestrooms, generously proportioned social rooms, and striking appearance. The dining hall and the function rooms are housed in semicircular structures supported by freestanding pillars. The guestrooms form a long block, while the ancillary rooms, administration building and kitchen are in separate cubes that connect the two main parts of the building.

In Israel, Krakauer first was known as a painter only by painters, and as an architect by other architects. But increasingly, in Israel and also abroad, interest in the synergy between painting and architecture in his life and work has been growing.[12] Leopold Krakauer died in Jerusalem on December 19, 1954. His legacy consists of 137 projects, of which thirty were realized, more than half of them in various kibbutzim.
His widow, the painter Grete Krakauer-Wolf (born 1924 in Vienna) died in 1970 in Jerusalem.

For some of the above information, I am very grateful to Leopold Krakauer's daughter, Professor Dr. Trude Dotan, Jerusalem (1986).

1 Friedrich Ohmann (1858–1927), with Otto Wagner (1841–1918), directed the master school of architecture at the Vienna Academy of Fine Arts after 1904.
2 Erlik 1987
3 Dr. Karl Lueger, who was elected mayor of Vienna in 1897, ushered in a mood of extreme anti-Semitism there; he was a true pioneer of hatred directed against Jews. After 1911 his successor continued the rabble-rousing propaganda. For instance, Jews were barred from being civil servants in the administration and were systematically forced out of their positions. Jewish students were provoked and tormented at the universities. Tirades of hatred against the "Jews from the East" became unbearable after World War I. Anti-Semitic attitudes were increasingly legalized and the ground prepared for the later influence of the Austrian fascists and nationalists.
4 See biographies of Jacob Pinkerfeld and Carl Rubin.
5 See biographies of Josef Neufeld and Gideon Kaminka.
6 Krakauer used the formats 80 × 60 cm and 60 × 45 cm. His drawings are convincing in their simplicity and spare lines, and are usually rendered in black chalk on white or yellowish paper.
7 The oldest, Kibbutz Degania, was founded in 1910. The first planned dining hall was built in 1927 by Richard Kauffmann in Kibbutz Ganigar, five years after the kibbutz was founded.
8 See biographies.
9 In 1990, for the sixtieth anniversary of Kibbutz Tel Josef in Emek Izrael, the Israeli post office issued a special stamp with a picture of this dining hall.
10 See biography of Adolf Rading
11 Lasker-Schüler 1986, p. 190.

12 Illera, 1992. Almost forty years after Krakauer's death, Christa Illera of Vienna published a comprehensive compilation of Krakauer's works in her sympathetic dissertation, thus closing a gap in the history of Israeli architecture. See also: Perry-Lehman 1996.

Leopold Krakauer, Kibbutz Beit Alpha, children's home, 1930

Leopold Krakauer

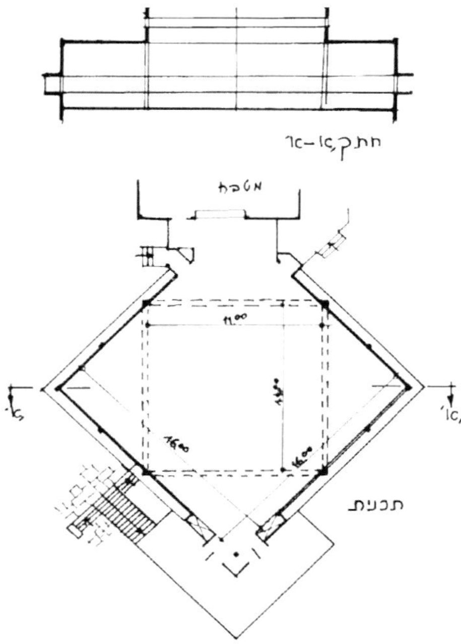

Leopold Krakauer, dining hall, Kibbutz Tel Josef, 1936, section and ground-floor plan

Leopold Krakauer, dining hall, Kibbutz Tel Josef, 1936, view from the path leading to the building. Photo: M.W. 1990

Leopold Krakauer, dining hall, Kibbutz Tel Josef, 1936. Photo: M.W. 1990

Leopold Krakauer, Bonem residence, Jerusalem, 1935. Photo: M.W. 1988

Leopold Krakauer, Sonnenberg residence, Mount Carmel, Haifa, 1937. Photo: M.W. 1988

Leopold Krakauer, Hotel Teltsch, now Hotel Megido, Mount Carmel, Haifa, 1940

Leopold Krakauer

Leopold Krakauer, thistle, no date (drawing)

Leopold Krakauer, Jerusalem beggar, 1935 (drawing)

Jochanan (Eugen) Ratner

1891 Odessa – 1965 Haifa

Buildings of national significance are not the only legacy of Jochanan Ratner; so are his many former students who went on to practise architecture in Israel and who remember his teachings well. Architect, officer, university professor, dean, commandant, diplomat and author – all were professions that Ratner pursued in various countries. He spoke fluent Russian, French, German, English and Hebrew, and painted in his leisure time.
Yevgheny (Eugen) Ratner was born into an assimilated Jewish family in Odessa on July 14, 1891. His mother died in childbirth, forcing his father, the ship-owner Dr. Efrim Ratner, to have his son raised by relatives. After the pogrom against Jews in Odessa in 1905, the father decided to move his son to safety and sent him to Mannheim, Germany where young Ratner lived with a Christian family.
In 1906 the teenager joined the Wandervogel (ramblers), a German youth movement whose communal activities made a great impression on him. As Ratner wrote in his memoirs, he felt very attached to the countryside and to the youth movement.[1] In 1911 Ratner left the Wandervogel, because the association had passed a resolution to keep itself "judenfrei".[2]
Ratner then returned to Russia to perform his year of military service. In the winter of 1912, he registered at the Technische Hochschule Karlsruhe to study architecture under Friedrich Ostendorf (1871–1915). When war broke out, Ratner felt obliged to defend his country and placed all his hopes in a military career. He did in fact serve from 1914 to 1918 as the deputy commanding officer of a Russian army division, a position unusual for a Jew – he had to conceal the fact for many years.
In February 1917, while in St. Petersburg on a military mission, Ratner was confronted with the outbreak of the Russian Revolution. He followed the events with great interest and enthusiasm, and even took an active role. At the same time, though, he also began to question his roots and his identity.
Like many of those who shared his fate, Ratner had to ask himself to which culture he belonged. On one hand, he felt attached to the Russian culture of his homeland, but on the other, he had grown up in a German cultural environment and had studied in Germany. Ratner had little contact with Jewish culture in his early years; he had been exposed only to the Christian world and had only non-Jewish friends. But his experiences with the 1905 pogrom, with the Wandervogel in 1911, and with the military legislation of 1915–16 that sent every Russian soldier of Jewish ancestry to the front, strengthened Ratner's determination to search for his Jewish identity.[3] He earned his diploma at the Technische Hochschule Karlsruhe in 1923 and soon afterward went to Palestine to have a look at the country. But the Hebrew language and culture of the Land of Israel were wholly foreign to him. The country's standard of living did not measure up to his own, nor did he see any possibility of doing creative work there. So Ratner returned to Europe, only to finally immigrate to Palestine one year later.

Haifa was the city he chose to live in. There he met Alex Baerwald, and assisted Baerwald with his Technion lectures starting in 1926. Although the two men advocated different stylistic approaches, they worked together from time to time, for instance on the plans for the Kuppat-Cholim Union Polyclinic (1929–1932). The building was adapted to Haifa's hilly topography and characterized by simplicity and functionality. The traditionalist Baerwald in this case apparently allowed some license for Modern architecture.

Jochanan Ratner's professional breakthrough came in 1928, when he participated in a competition for the building of the National Institute in Jerusalem, the site of the executive offices of the International Zionist Organization in Palestine. The jury, chaired by Josef Frank (1885–1957), who helped introduce Modern architecture to Vienna, awarded the first prize to Ratner's design and recommended that it be realized. The building, completed in 1933, was functional and unornamented in design. Its wings were positioned to create a semi-enclosed courtyard and illustrated Louis Henry Sullivan's famous maxim "form follows function". With this first building, Ratner dealt consciously and seriously with the question of what style was appropriate for the country. Like the Hebrew language, he maintained, architectural style was an element in the modern Zionist programme. In seeking a specifically Zionist architectural language, Ratner came to realize that climatic, economic and social conditions would enter into and determine its form of expression. The Star of David as an architectonic element did not yet constitute a style, in his opinion, and Ratner also was opposed to Alex Baerwald's approach. "There is an attempt to build 'Oriental' buildings, just as one built 'Gothic' or 'Renaissance' buildings at the time in Europe. The attempt fails."[4] It was both expensive and extravagant. Ratner argued further that if one looked at the distinctly modern buildings of Richard Kauffmann, Leopold Krakauer and Josef Neufeld, one arrived at the conclusion that the "Oriental" style had no future.
Jochanan Ratner maintained this architectural conviction for the rest of his life. Twenty years after his first work in Jerusalem, he built the compelling, functionally designed Faculty of Aerospace Engineering (as it is now known) at the new Technion campus in Haifa. Extending from the central entrance area, the classrooms and laboratories occupy separate wings oriented to both the compass and the site's topography. Parts of the building appear to be independent structures of different proportions and with varying window sizes and placement.

In addition to these two nationally significant buildings, Ratner's long list of works calls to mind both the history of the Israeli people and his own fate. In 1935–36, Ratner built the Jewish children's and youth home Ahava ("love" – it was named after a home that had been located on Berlin's Auguststrasse) in Kiryat Bialik near Haifa. Until 1939, children rescued from Nazi terror were brought there and cared for. The fate of Jewish children during the Third Reich is now memorialized in photographs and documents in this building.[5]
And from 1946 to 1960, Ratner and the civil engineer Mordechai Shoshani built the Beit Berl Workers' Party Central Institute in Moshav Zoffit near Kfar Saba. The extensive building complex with cultural and sport centres and a residential community was named for Berl Katzenelson (1887–1944), the chairman of the Workers' Party in Eretz Israel. Other structures that Ratner designed with the utmost economy and functionality included union buildings, synagogues, school buildings, a hotel and his own home on Mount Carmel (1935).

Jochanan Ratner was associated with the architecture department at the Technion in Haifa as both a professor and a dean from 1932 to 1962, except for brief interruptions.

At the same time, he worked for the military and was entrusted with secret missions. In 1938 he became the first commander of the Hagana underground movement; in 1949 he went to Moscow as the first Israeli military attaché; and he served as an envoy to Burma in 1955.[6]
A man of literary talents, for long periods Ratner recorded his memoirs in German, by hand. In 1978 his wife Ora published the material posthumously in Hebrew translation under the title *My Life and Me*.[7]
Ratner's social, cultural and political experiences in Russia and Germany decisively influenced and shaped his life in Israel. Few other individuals played a more significant historic role in building the country's culture and politics, architecture and strategy, teaching and praxis. Yet at the end of his life, Ratner felt despair: "The idea of making the 'Hagana' into an army had ruled my life for many years – actually since 1929, and I fought passionately and doggedly for that ... all the more so after the murder of six million Jews by a cultivated people under the leadership of Hitler.[8] I have sacrificed much and done much, but my spirit is not at peace. A personal stance? Have the accidents of my life experience shaped me into a 'citizen of the world'?"[9] Another factor was that Ratner's son David, a pilot in the Israeli army, had been killed in a training accident in 1954. Jochanan Ratner never recovered from that loss, and died on January 28, 1965, in Haifa. For his hundredth birthday on July 14, 1991, the Technion Haifa published a monograph titled *Jochanan Ratner. The Man, the Architect, and his Work* and organized a day of remembrance in his honour.[10] Professors, students, architects, friends, veterans, and government officials gathered with the Ratner family to pay tribute to the man and his work.

I am very grateful to Jochanan Ratner's wife, Ora Ratner, Mount Carmel, Haifa for information and material and, beyond that, for our close friendship of several years (1985–1991).

1 Ratner 1983, p. 17 ff.
2 Four letters from his friends exist, telling Ratner politely that they had decided to exclude him from the group because he was Jewish; private archive Ora Ratner, Haifa.
3 Ratner 1983, pp. 123–166.
4 Jochanan Ratner, "Die Baukunst in Erez Israel, Haifa dreißiger Jahre", unpublished manuscript, German.
5 Scheer 1992.
6 The Hagana (self-protection) was founded in 1920. It was the largest military organization that protected Jewish settlements in Palestine. When World War II broke out, it sided with the British government. From the end of the war to the founding of the state of Israel in 1948, it fought underground against British mandate rule. In 1948 this organization became the Israeli army.
7 Ora (Flora) née Weil, was born into an orthodox Jewish family in Mannheim in 1907. From 1926 to 1927 she attended Mary Wigman's school of dance in Dresden. She came to Palestine in 1933 and opened a dance school in Haifa, introducing modern dance to Israel; Ratner 1983.
8 In 1929, Arabs perpetrated a massacre on the Jewish population of Hebron.
9 Ratner 1983, p. 432.
10 Sosnovsky 1992.

Jochanan Ratner, Ratner residence, Mount Carmel, Haifa, 1935, front view. Photo: M.W. 1990

Jochanan Ratner, Faculty of Aerospace Engineering, Technion campus, Haifa, 1953, entrance

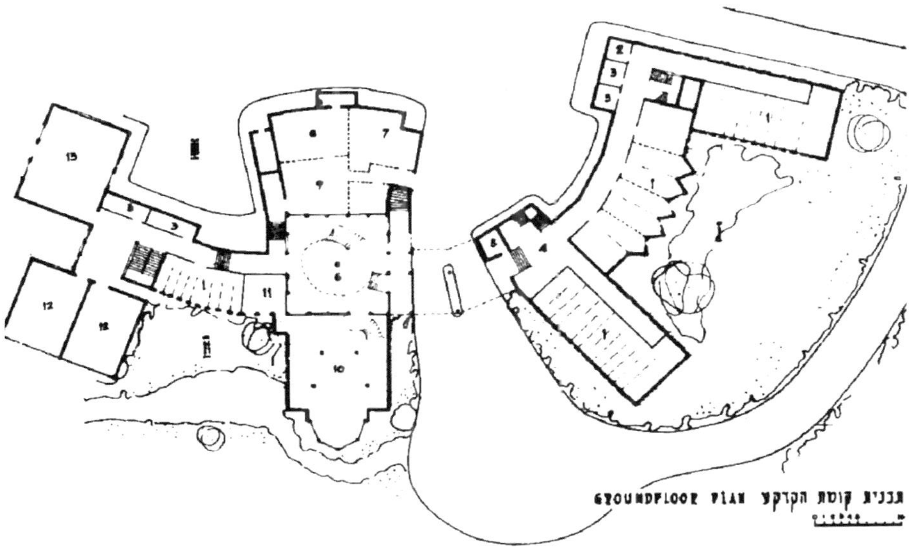

Jochanan Ratner, Faculty of Aerospace Engineering, Technion campus, Haifa, 1953, ground-floor plan

Jochanan Ratner, Faculty of Aerospace Engineering, Technion campus, Haifa, 1953, front view

Jochanan (Eugen) Ratner

Jochanan Ratner, National Institute, Jerusalem, 1933, view from courtyard. Photo: M.W. 1989

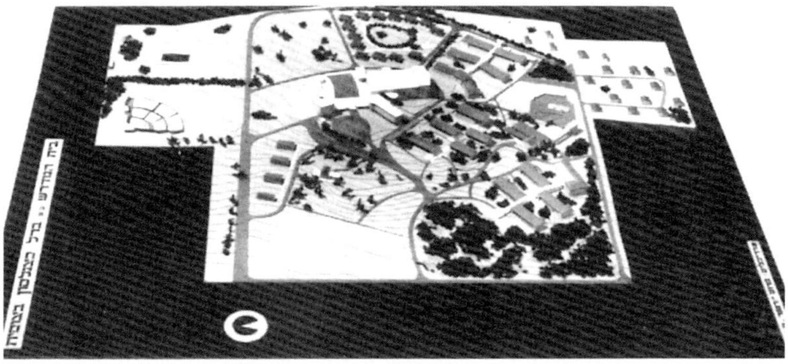

Jochanan Ratner with Mordechai Shoshani, "Beit Berl", Moshav Zoffit, 1946–1960, model of entire complex

Jochanan Ratner with Mordechai Shoshani, "Beit Berl", Moshav Zoffit, 1946–1960, student dormitories, front view

Jochanan Ratner, "Ahava" children's home, Kiryat Bialik, 1936, front view. Photo: M.W. 1993

Jewish children's home "Ahava" (until 1939), Auguststrasse 14–15, Berlin-Mitte, plaque commemorating the history of the building, dedicated November 1992. Photo: M.W. 1993

Jochanan Ratner, Union Polyclinic, Tel Aviv, 1936 (drawing)

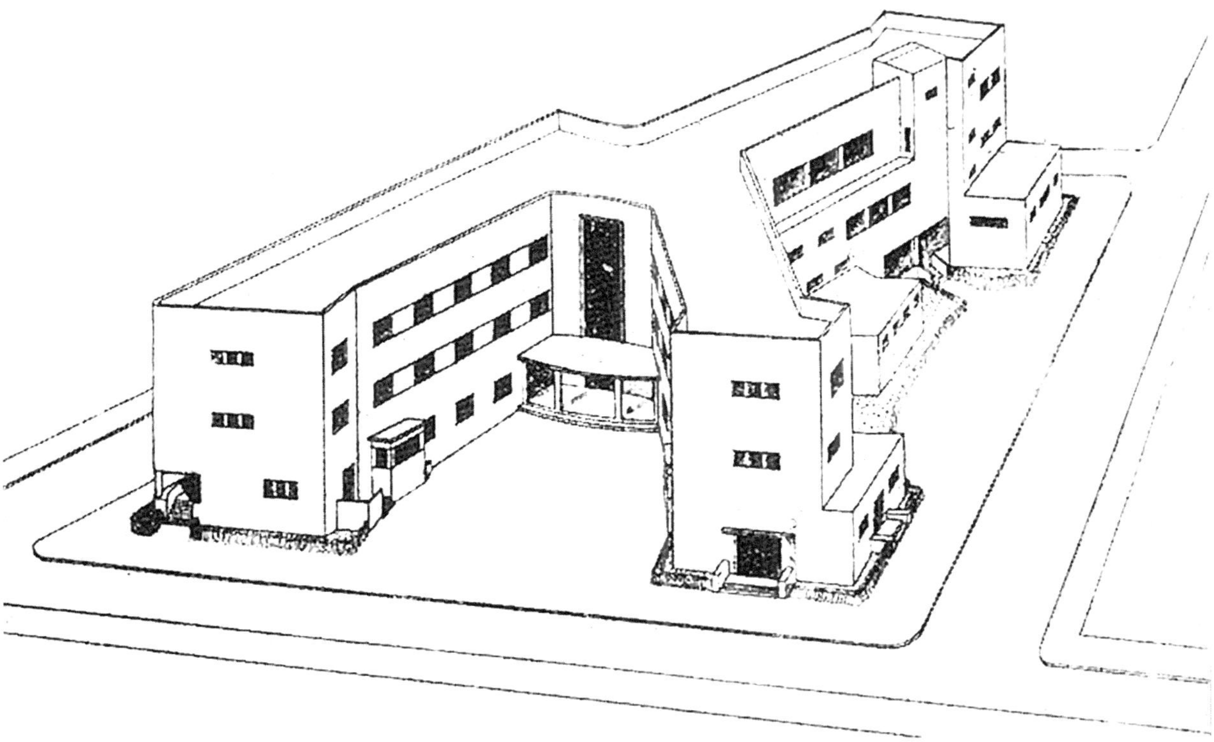

Dov (Bernhard) Kuczynski

1891 Berlin – 1980 Nahariya

Dov (Bernhard) Kuczynski was born in Berlin on October 19, 1891. Until he left Germany with his family in 1923, he lived in the district of Mitte at Invalidenstrasse 90. For forty years this building was inaccessible, because it was located directly on the border crossing between the east and west sectors of the divided city.[1]
After completing his general education, Kuczynski attended a school of applied arts and worked in various technical firms. The political events of the first two decades of the twentieth century left their mark on the family life of the Kuczynskis, who had pacifist and socialist leanings. Their great model was Rosa Luxemburg. The Kuczynski family visited her in prison and brought her food. The vivid memory of her and of her fate stayed with Dov Kuczynski for the rest of his life. A dedicated socialist, Kuczynski was also a Zionist and led a youth group in the Blau-Weiss Zionist movement in Berlin.[2] In due course, he left Germany with his wife and two young children and immigrated to the "Land of the Forefathers", Eretz Israel, in the Third Aliya. He settled in Tel Aviv, adopted a Hebrew first name, and began to seek an occupation.

During the first years, Kuczynski was employed in different architectural offices. From 1932 to 1939 he carried out independent commissions. The buildings erected using his plans show him to be an exponent of the Modern style.
Kuczynski spent the following years in the public works department that the British set up. After a long interval, he again began to work independently and to be politically active.
In 1946 Kuczynski founded an organization known as the Jewish Brigade Group for the approximately five thousand technically educated Jewish professionals who had volunteered to work for the British government in the fight against Nazi Germany.[3] This association was designed to help the engineers and architects who were returning from wartime service to reintegrate into civilian life.

Since prior to 1948 building components made of steel were quite expensive to import, Kuczynski decided to experiment and see if he could manufacture concrete girders with optimal ratio of iron to concrete. Another challenge, the country's changeable climate, later induced him to work out a typology of floor plans for apartments. He investigated a "three-bay" plan having three five-room apartments per floor, and concluded that it was impossible to create apartments suited to the climate in a building with a symmetrical form. Instead, rooms oriented in the most favourable directions should dictate the form of the building. This resulted in geometrically irregular floor plans, to which Kuczynski then added balconies so that in the end, every apartment had a rectangular shape. Kuczynski realized such a project in Jerusalem in 1936.[4]

Since Jerusalem's average summer and winter temperatures are considerably lower than those in Tel Aviv, Kuczynski designed differently for the two cities. His buildings in Tel Aviv, such as the Ashrei Bank and the Kaufmann residence, were equipped with brise-soleils, ledges projecting above the windows that offer protection from the sun's rays. But his buildings in Jerusalem, Beit Ha'histadrut (the union building) and the Zarikower residence, do not have this feature.[5]

Like Josef Neufeld, Carl Rubin, and Arieh Sharon, Dov Kuczynski belonged to the proletarian group of architects who tried to establish affordable and modern urban housing projects for workers called Meonot Ovdim.[6] He built two such attractive two- and three-storey residential communities with thirty living units each, one in Jerusalem and one in Tel Aviv. They are functional in appearance, with flat roofs, white stucco walls and no decorative ornamentation.

Dov Kuczynski was nearly ninety years old when he died on October 3, 1980, in Nahariya, 30 km north of Haifa. He spent his last twenty years in that small city, which had been founded in 1934 by German-Jewish emigrés and which for years was characterized by its German culture.

Dov Kuczynski's son Meir Kuczynski and his wife Bina, Kibbutz Ein-Gev, provided me with important information, for which I am very grateful (1986).

1 Berlin register of inhabitants 1920
2 The "Blue and White", the first Zionist association in Germany, was founded in 1913. Its aim was to train members in agriculture and trade professions to prepare them for immigration to Palestine.
3 Talmi 1977, pp. 163–164.
4 Dov Kuczynski, "Das Entwerfen von Wohnungen" in: *Habinyan Bamisrah Hakarov* 9/10, Tel Aviv, November 1936, p. 7.
5 The Israeli union Beit Ha'histadrut is the country's largest and most influential labour organization. It was founded in 1920 in Haifa, and David Ben Gurion (1886–1973) was its first secretary. At first, the union rented apartments in cities and villages for its activities. As its social role expanded, the organizers built administrative seats at each location, using the Russian model. Later the country's largest health provider joined the union, which now operates service enterprises of all kinds, from food shops to libraries. The union also publishes newspapers and books. Today every yishuv (inhabited area) has its Beit Ha'histadrut.
6 See biographies of Josef Neufeld, Carl Rubin and Arieh Sharon.

Dov (Bernhard) Kuczynski

Dov Kuczynski, Kaufmann residence, Tel Aviv, 1930s

Dov Kuczynski, Zarikower residence, Jerusalem, 1930s

Dov Kuczynski, Olitzky residence, Jerusalem, 1930s

Dov Kuczynski, Ashrei Bank, Tel Aviv, 1930s

Dov (Bernhard) Kuczynski

Dov Kuczynski, desk with chair for Mr. Levin, Tel Aviv, 1930s

Dov Kuczynski, Beit Ha'histadrut (union building), Jerusalem, 1939

Dov Kuczynski, Beit Ha'histadrut (union building), Jerusalem, 1939, first-floor plan

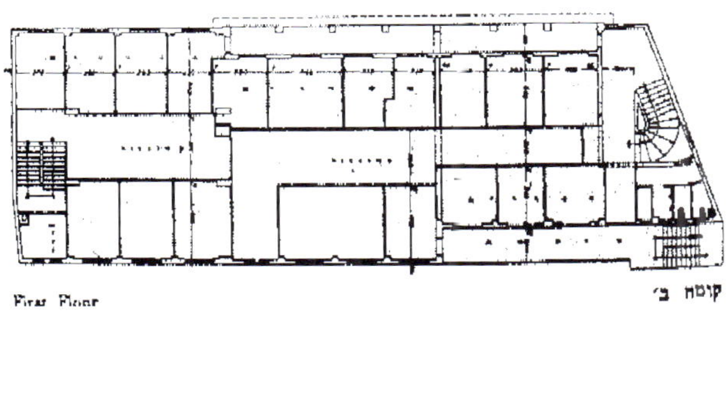

Dov Kuczynski, Beit Ha'histadrut (union building), Jerusalem, 1939, ground-floor plan

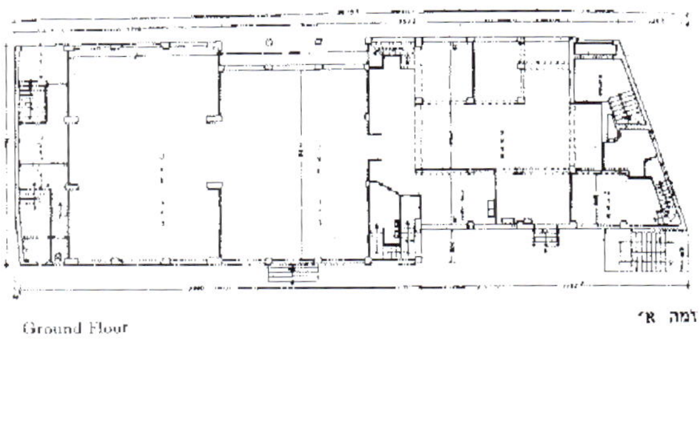

Lotte Cohn

1893 Berlin – 1983 Tel Aviv

Before he had ever met Lotte Cohn, Richard Kauffmann wrote to her in Berlin from Jerusalem on July 21, 1921: "...unbelievably beautiful work, primarily urban development, lies ahead. There are works in prospect whose dimensions, beauty, and significance for building the country joyfully compel one to unconditional, wholehearted dedication. I only hope that I continue to have the strength to cope physically and mentally with the difficult conditions here. That is primarily the people in view of our aim ... please come with some examples of model German building ordinances for cities and garden cities."[1] Cohn went to Palestine in 1921.

Lotte Cohn was born into an old, large, and established Zionist family in Berlin on August 20, 1893. She studied architecture there at the Technische Hochschule Charlottenburg and passed her exams in 1916. Before leaving Germany, she spent two years after World War I assisting in the reconstruction of East Prussia. She was also one of the few female members of the Architekten-und Ingenieur-Verein zu Berlin (AIV), the professional society in her field. She worked for six years with Richard Kauffmann in Jerusalem, and then continued to practise her profession independently in Tel Aviv for forty more years.

One of Cohn's first buildings was a small two-storey hotel with fourteen rooms built in 1929–30. The building was characteristically Modern: it had a cubic form, a flat roof, and was clad in white stucco. It was situated near the beach of Tel Aviv and was named "Pension Kaete Dan" after Kaete Danowitz, who had commissioned the project. Although the hotel was altered and expanded ten years later by Werner Wittkower, and was demolished a few years after that, it played a central role in the history of Israel's hotel industry.[2]

Lotte Cohn's plans for entire communities, her individual buildings in rural and urban areas, and her publications made her an unforgettable pioneer, particularly since she was the country's first female architect. Cohn gave advice to the Jewish farm families that left Nazi Germany for Palestine in 1933 on how to best establish their new homes. She understood how to link her concern for human welfare with her role as an architect.

In Palestine, the immigrants had to organize their lives in a completely new way. Cohn took the trouble to personally advise and motivate them. For a settlement near Nahariya, she designed a plan that incorporated different forms of spatial organization for two groups of families engaged in agriculture. One group was to carry out a communal agricultural project. The families in the other group would have their own farms and parcels of land to cultivate.[3] Cohn suggested that the families initially economize by building homes with a minimal number of rooms. Her floor plans for the Minimum One-Family House were designed so that the residents could expand the house on their own at any time.[4]

Cohn also took into account the multiple demands made on women who worked on the farm and in the home, and planned an integrated kitchen and dining room to eliminate unnecessary trips back and forth between the cooking and eating areas. The family would spend summery evenings together on a balcony as large as a room. For hygienic reasons, Cohn separated the toilet from the bath; she often preferred a shower instead of a bathtub. With German plans for one-family houses in mind as cautionary examples, Cohn warned her colleagues not to build houses of this kind, for they could lead to "a bourgeois way of life". To her, a house whose form was not consistent with its function was "a serious aesthetic mistake".[5]

Lotte Cohn wanted functional spatial concepts to be used also by those who were better-off. She and Julius Posener built "the most expensive rural one-family house in Palestine" in 1937.[6] It was equipped with an electric stove, sink, washing machine, chimney, roll-down shutters, garage, and a basement washroom. The one-storey house in the form of a "T" had a tile roof and had approximately 180 m² of living space. The bedrooms, the bath and the eat-in kitchen were in the long part of the building. The shorter tract housed the entry and a living room measuring approximately 40 m².[7] The house is in Kfar Shmaryahu near Tel Aviv. Cohn also felt that it was an important challenge to design architecture that was appropriate to the country's climate. In the Z. residence (1937) on Mount Carmel, comprised of cubic forms, the 40 m² living room had long horizontal windows located directly under the ceiling. That facilitated cross-ventilation of the pent-up heat and resulted in a comfortable room temperature.[8]
After 1952 Lotte Cohn worked with the architect Yehuda Lavie.[9] The projects they realized together included homes for the aged, apartment buildings and urban plans for Tel Aviv and Dimona, a city in the southern part of the country.

Early in the 1960s, Cohn closed her architectural office and dedicated herself to writing. Her first unpublished work bore the title: "The 1920s in Eretz Israel. A picture book without pictures. Written for the friends who lived through that time together with me." On a mere forty-five pages, Cohn describes the personal and professional experiences she had during her first ten years in Palestine. A few years later she wrote the manuscript "Early Urban Development in Palestine and the Significance of Richard Kauffmann. The Architect and Urban Planner in his Time", which she dedicated to Kauffmann's wife and two daughters. In the first section, she describes her initial impressions when she first set foot in the country of the "dilapidated cities" and the "abandoned land" with the "wonderfully changing landscape"; in the second section she pays homage to the architect, planner and person Richard Kauffmann.
Lotte Cohn thus left behind two important documents about the history of that era, written in her mother tongue. Until she died in Tel Aviv at the age of ninety on April 7, 1983, she was a lively contemporary witness for several generations of Israel's architecture students.

1 Lotte Cohn, "Früher Städtebau in Palästina und die Bedeutung von Richard Kauffmanns Werk im Städtebau des Landes", Tel Aviv ca. 1973, unpublished manuscript, p. 26.
2 See: "Yekutiel and Shmuel Federmann" and the biography of Werner Wittkower.
3 *Habinyan* 3, Tel Aviv August 1938, p. 16.
4 Ibid., p. 21.
5 Lotte Cohn, "Das Bauen in Moshav" in: *Habinyan Bamisrah Hakarov*, Tel Aviv December 1934, pp. 6–8.

6 This was the only building that Julius Posener (in collaboration with Lotte Cohn) ever built. The two remained in contact for the rest of their lives. See brief biography of Julius Posener. See also: Warhaftig 2005; Posener, Julius.
7 *Habinyan* 3, Tel Aviv August 1938, p. 25.
8 *Habinyan Bamisrah Hakarov* II, Tel Aviv November 1937, p. 13.
9 See brief biography of Yehuda Lavie (Ernst Loevisohn). See also: Warhaftig 2005, Loevisohn, Ernst.

Lotte Cohn, settlement near Nahariya, organized in part cooperatively (left) and in part individually (right), 1937, site plan

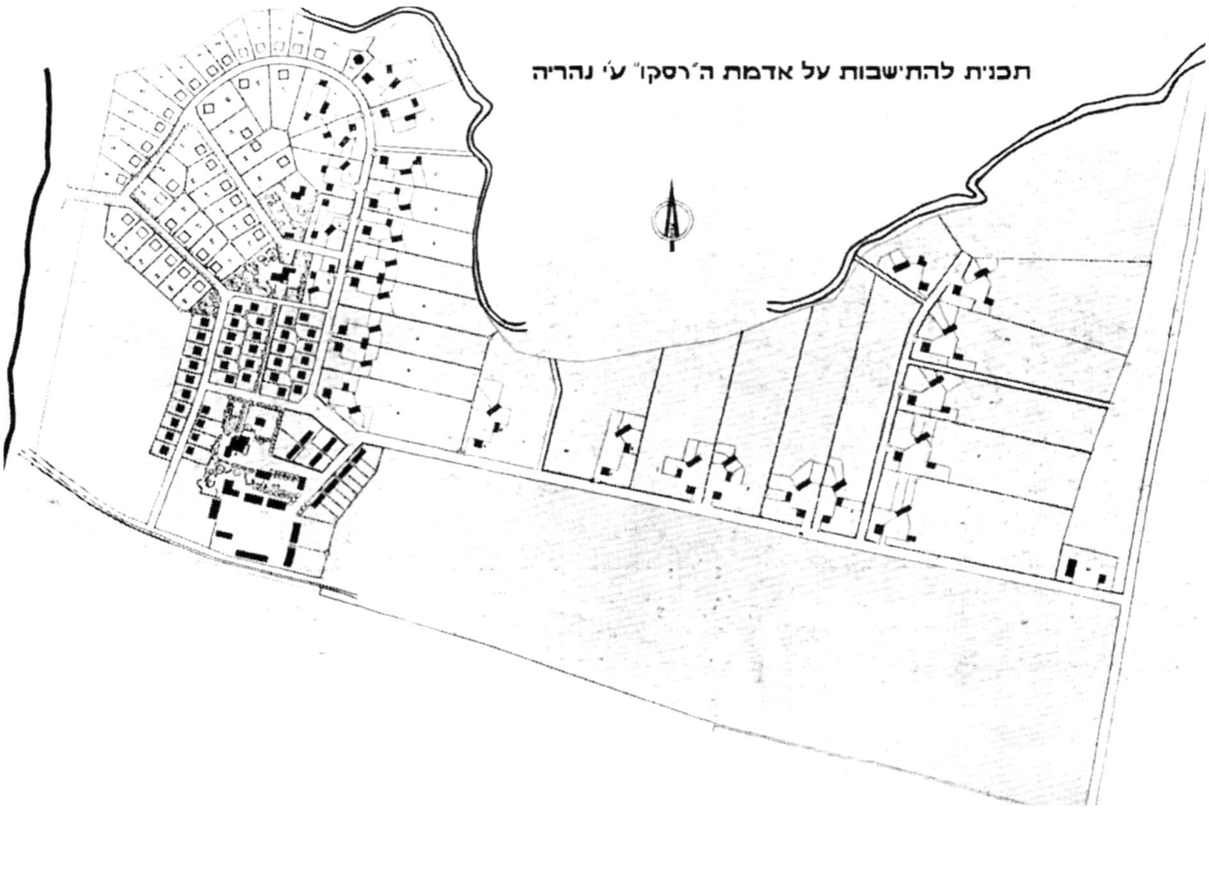

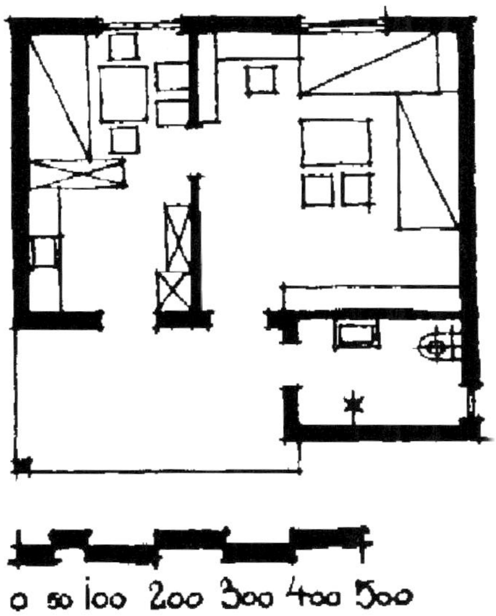

Lotte Cohn, minimum one-family house, settlement near Nahariya, 1937, ground-floor plan

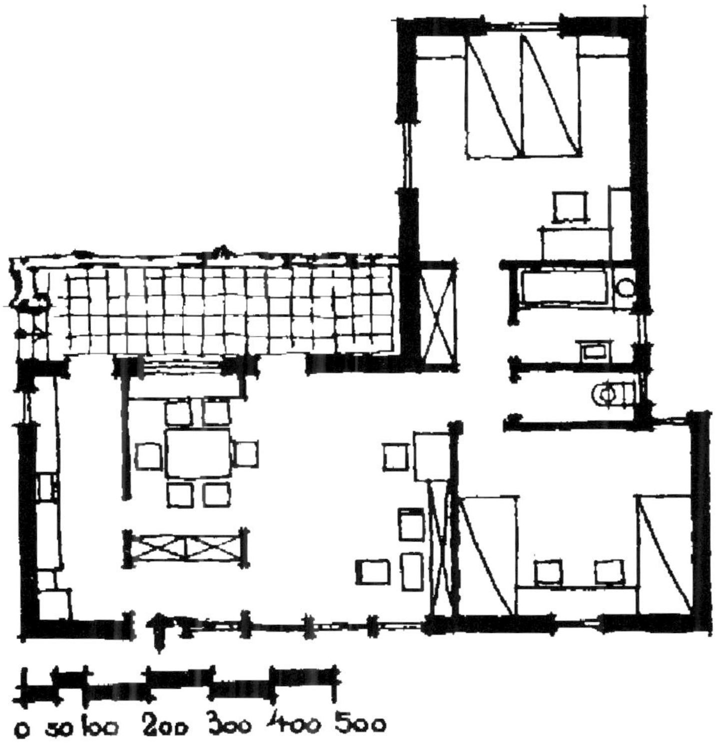

Lotte Cohn, one-family house with three rooms, settlement near Nahariya, 1937, ground-floor plan

Lotte Cohn, settlement housing for the middle class, Pardess Hanna, 1936

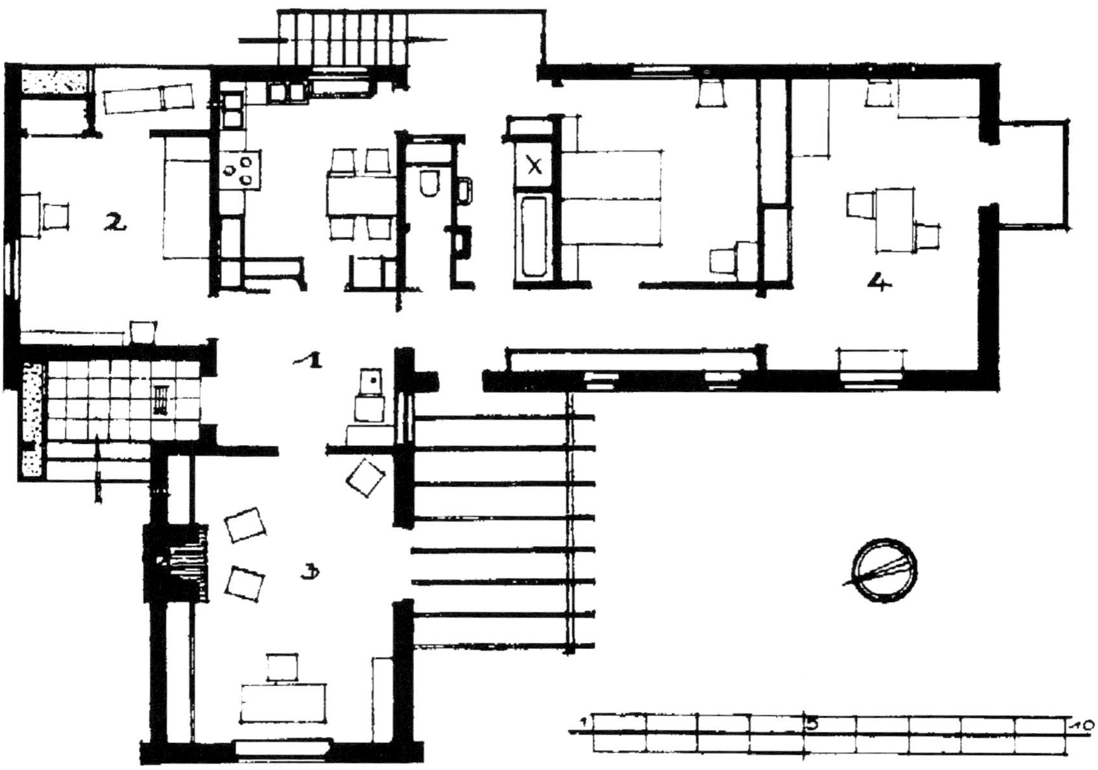
2
1
3
4
X
5
10

Left page, above:
Lotte Cohn with Julius Posener, "the most expensive rural one-family house in Palestine", Kfar Shmaryahu, 1937

Left page below:
Lotte Cohn with Julius Posener, "the most expensive rural one-family house in Palestine", Kfar Shmaryahu, 1937, ground-floor plan

Lotte Cohn, residences, Ben Shemen Youth Village, 1947, view from the courtyard

Jacob Pinkerfeld

1897 Przemysl – 1956 Jerusalem

Jacob Pinkerfeld, later called "Kuba" by his friends, was born on January 3, 1897, in Przemysl in Galicia, then part of the Austrian empire, and attended secondary school in Lemberg, today Lviv. When World War I broke out and Russia attacked Galicia, the Pinkerfeld family fled their homeland, finally ending up in Vienna. There the artistically talented young man began to study architecture at the Technische Hochschule. But soon his studies were interrupted when he was conscripted into the Austrian army; he served in World War I from 1914 to 1918. Afterward, he resumed his studies at the German University in Brno.

Without having earned his degree, Pinkerfeld, a dedicated Zionist and a member of the youth movement Ha'shomer Ha'tzair, went to Palestine with the Third Aliya in 1920.[1] There he and his young colleagues laboured to drain the country's malaria-infested swamps and make them arable. This was a very dangerous task for the enthusiastic immigrants, and many lost their lives. Pinkerfeld himself became quite ill with malaria and went to Europe for treatment. The doctors prohibited him from doing any more physical work, so he returned to his studies. In 1925 Pinkerfeld earned his diploma from the Technische Hochschule in Vienna. Immediately afterward he returned to the Promised Land.

Before Pinkerfeld opened his own office in Tel Aviv in 1930, he had amassed a variety of professional experiences, in the process discovering an interest in Jewish sacral architecture and art. In no way did he share the Jewish orthodoxy's view that there was only "art by Jews" or "art for Jews", but no distinctively specific Jewish art.[2] He made it his life's work to scientifically disprove that assertion. For thirty years, Pinkerfeld collected material and information about synagogue buildings and their sacred interior furnishings in ancient Israel, Italy, North Africa and Spain. He made trips to photograph and sketch those objects and wrote commentaries on them.

A pioneer in his field, Pinkerfeld could only sporadically publish the results of his research.[3] He had come to the conclusion that the synagogue's interior furnishings such as the Torah ark, the almemor, the women's balcony and the seating created a specifically "Jewish space". Decorative elements with motifs of ancient Israel's fauna and flora, the Star of David and the seven-armed synagogue menorah were all, to him, elements of "Jewish art".[4]

In addition to his scholarly research, Pinkerfeld was professionally active as an architect. Although he considered this work only a means to make a living, he never treated it lightly.

In 1935 Pinkerfeld built a multi-family building in Tel Aviv where he took an apartment with his family and where he set up an office. Each floor of the three-storey apartment building has two apartments on different levels. The stairwell is illuminated by a narrow continuous vertical band of windows, a characteristic design element of the period. Brise-soleils above the balconies and corner windows provided protec-

tion from the strong sunlight. The white stucco and flat roof are features of European twentieth century International Style, and the building is now under landmark preservation.
When the agricultural school for fifty girls in Tel Aviv was completed in 1935 – Pinkerfeld's design had won first prize in an invited competition – Pinkerfeld gained a reputation as an exponent of Modern architecture. The building, an assemblage of cubic forms with an arboured arcade on the ground floor and a pergola on the first floor, is an important contribution to climate-related architecture.[5] It too now is under historic preservation, one of 1000 buildings that UNESCO recognized in 2003 as part of the World Cultural Heritage.
Pinkerfeld's functionally designed buildings were an expression of his socio-political commitment. During the 1930s, he used a pragmatic formal vocabulary to design and build cultural centres, children's homes, dining halls, housing and agricultural structures in Kibbutz Revadim in the south, Kibbutz Ein Hamifraz in the north, and Kibbutz Misra in the lowlands. When he was commissioned to design the dining hall and school building in Kibbutz Merchavia in 1940, however, Pinkerfeld seemingly was left with no other choice but to relate to the design of Alex Baerwald's neighbouring cooperative settlement, so those buildings have tiled roofs.[6]

Shortly after presenting a lecture about synagogues during an archaeological congress in Jerusalem, Jacob Pinkerfeld was shot dead by a Jordanian soldier on September 23, 1956. So his life's work – to research and generate international interest in Jewish art and its historical significance – remained unfinished. The monograph he began on synagogue buildings in Spain, which was to be the next instalment of his works on synagogues in ancient Israel (1946) and in Italy (1954), remains unpublished. His documentation of the synagogues of North Africa, Tunisia, Algeria and Morocco was published posthumously in 1974. In 1957, on the first anniversary of his death, Pinkerfeld's family published a memorial book, a compilation of Hebrew translations of his articles on Jewish art that had been previously printed in Hamburg, Vienna and Jerusalem.[7]

For information and material I am most grateful to Jacob Pinkerfeld's daughter, Dr. Aya Meir, Tel Aviv (1986).

1 Ha'shomer Ha'tzair (young guards) was an international Zionist youth movement founded in 1913–14 in Galicia and Poland.
2 The Orthodox cite two reasons for this view. First, the "People of the Book" are not spiritually inclined to design forms, and the Second Commandment states "Thou shalt not make unto thee a graven image". Second, the development of an artistic tradition presupposes a settled existence, which for the Jewish people was not possible due to socio-political conditions.
3 Pinkerfeld 1946; Pinkerfeld 1954; Pinkerfeld 1957; Pinkerfeld 1974.
4 The same motifs are found in Jewish cemeteries.
5 *Habinyan Bamisrah Hakarov* 3, Tel Aviv December 1937, pp. 37–39.
6 See biography of Alex Baerwald.
7 Pinkerfeld 1974.

Jacob Pinkerfeld

Jacob Pinkerfeld, multi-family apartment building, Tel Aviv, 1935. Photo: M.W. 1989

Right page above: Jacob Pinkerfeld, school building, Kibbutz Merchavia, 1940. Photo: M.W. 1989

Right page below: Jacob Pinkerfeld, arts centre, Kibbutz Misra, 1930s

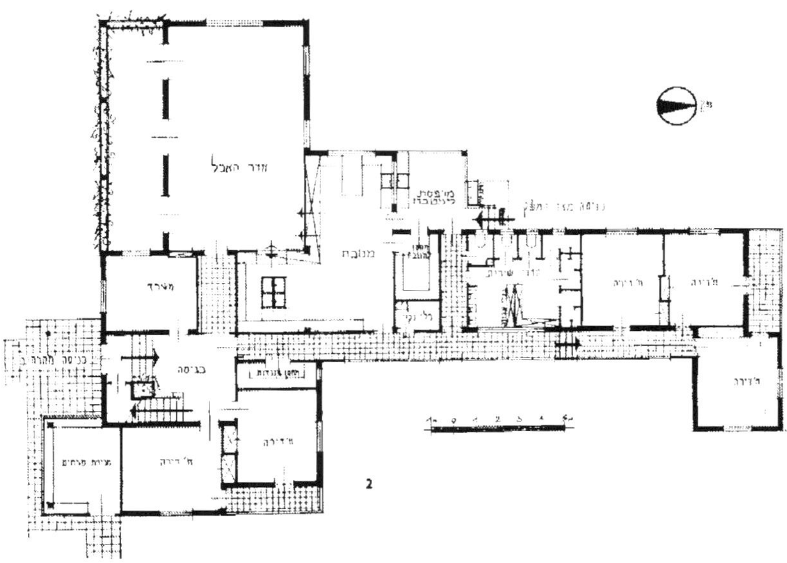

Jacob Pinkerfeld, "agricultural school for fifty girls", Tel Aviv, 1935, view from the south

Jacob Pinkerfeld, "agricultural school for fifty girls", Tel Aviv, 1935, ground-floor plan

Jacob Pinkerfeld, "agricultural school for fifty girls", Tel Aviv, 1935, view from the west

JOSEF NEUFELD

Monasterzyska 1899 – 1980 New York

Like Erich Mendelsohn, Josef Neufeld was an architect whose buildings in Israel were frequently documented over the years in both national and international professional journals. For a certain period of time Neufeld was a dedicated Socialist and Zionist, but he was a proponent of Modern architecture all his life.
Neufeld was born on February 16, 1899, in Monasterzyska, Galicia, which at the time was part of Austria. When only sixteen years old, he was conscripted into the Austro-Hungarian army in World War I; only at the end of the war, with severe injuries, did he return to his homeland, where he found himself confronted with pathologically racist anti-Semitism.[1] In response, he joined a Zionist youth organization and succeeded in reaching Palestine with the Third Aliya in 1920.
Having received a scholarship, Neufeld left the country in 1923 for Rome, where he studied for three years at the Scuola Superiore di Architettura. He continued his studies at the Akademie der bildenden Künste in Vienna in 1926, in the architecture master class of Clemens Holzmeister (1886–1983). Neufeld left Vienna with a master's degree and went to Berlin, working there from October 1927 to March 1930 in the office of Erich Mendelsohn, where he was responsible chiefly for the Mosse Pavilion at the press exhibition in Cologne.

It was very important to Josef Neufeld to work independently. He entered a competition to build a Jewish hospital in Zagreb with the Jewish architect Siegmund Ochs in 1931.[2] The two were awarded second prize, and the project was published in the trade journal *Bauwelt*.[3] This was the first in a series of hospitals that Neufeld would design in his lifetime; his crowning achievement was Hadassah Hospital (1959–60) in Jerusalem.
As he built up his practice in Berlin, Neufeld increasingly sought contact to Bruno Taut. Like Taut, Neufeld wanted to be active in building and realizing socialism. He soon had the opportunity. In 1931 Bruno Taut was invited to participate in a competition for an Intourist hotel on Ochotny Ryad in Moscow. Taut brought in Josef Neufeld to work with him on the project and the two went to Moscow in March 1932, fully confident that they would be able to realize a genuine people's architecture there. But to their disillusionment they found that the conditions in Russia did not correspond with their idea of socialism.[4] Early in 1933, Taut went back to Berlin and Neufeld returned to Palestine. Since Neufeld was no longer an unknown there, he soon received commissions. And the first project that he realized in Eretz Israel has a history that began in Berlin.

Keeping pace with the rising anti-Semitism and worsening conditions for Jews in Germany, an increasing number of young people were joining Zionist federations. In 1932 Recha Freier (1892–1984), born in East Frisia, founded a youth aliya workers' community in Berlin, to enable as many children as possible to go to

Palestine, even without their parents. Until 1939, when the Gestapo closed their office at Kantstrasse 158, Recha Freier was able to save the lives of nearly four thousand youths.[5] The girls and boys would continue their education in Palestine; some of them would also work in agriculture and learn to live in a community. For ninety of these children aged nine to seventeen, The Children's Community was built on a small hill in Kibbutz Mishmar Ha'emek, 25 km southeast of Haifa, according to plans by Josef Neufeld.[6]
The two wings of the two-storey building are slightly staggered relative to each other and have rooftop terraces. The rhythmic arrangement of the rows of windows and balcony posts picks up the horizontal lines of the landscape and lends the structure a simple but elegant appearance. Girls and boys still receive a practical and theoretical education there to this day, preparing them to be integrated into community life.
Neufeld's 1935–39 ensemble of buildings in the Meonot Ovdim (workers' housing) project in Tel Aviv also was much cited and praised in the press.[7] The total cost of the twenty-four apartments – each with two rooms, a bath, separate toilet, and a balcony, for a total living area of 55 m^2 – came in under budget. Neufeld earned high praise for preserving the single tree on the property.
The Assutah private hospital and the Kuppat-Cholim medical storage facility Neufeld designed, using a clear vocabulary of forms that generously and beautifully adapted to the landscape, were erected 1934–36 in Tel Aviv.[8] He also built the one-family G. residence in Tel Benjamin and the corner apartment building Beit Sira (known as the ship building) on a ridge in Haifa.[9]

Yet Josef Neufeld was involved not only in the practise of his profession. When his close friend Oskar Strnad, a Jewish architect from Vienna who also had worked as a stage designer for Max Reinhardt's theatre productions, died suddenly in 1935 at the age of fifty-six, Neufeld paid tribute to him in the Hebrew press.[10] He also announced that he would organize a memorial exhibition for Strnad, which was to take place in conjunction with the dedication of Oskar Kaufmann's Habima Theater in Tel Aviv, then still under construction.[11] But construction dragged on, and ultimately the new political developments in Austria made it impossible to arrange such an event.
A publication on the subject of workers' settlements, apartment buildings and public buildings in Palestine from 1920 to 1940 offered Neufeld the opportunity to be a critic.[12] Modern architecture, he wrote, which had its roots in the Western world, had not achieved its goals of creating new ways of living, for society was too beholden to traditions and unable to break with its old habits, even for good reason. But there in that tiny land of Palestine, which found itself in an "effervescent process" without tradition or legislation, countless architectonic and social experiments were being planned and also realized. Neufeld nonetheless felt the lack of a central institution that would be a forum for debate about architectural and technological ideas. He wanted more dialogue among colleagues to evaluate, among other things, the form of the cube in architecture, the form of the roof, the sizes of windows and doors as related to modern building materials, climate, the wild landscape, and the diverse ways that the country's social life was organized. Then the appropriate building ordinances could be written.

It is unclear why Neufeld left for the USA in 1941. Certainly his emigration was linked to the stagnation of the construction economy in Palestine during World War II, but there may also have been personal reasons. Possibly he had lost his belief in a revolutionary society connected with modern architecture.

Josef Neufeld

During the war years, Neufeld worked for the U.S. Department of Health in Washington, D.C. and developed functional standard floor plans for hospitals. Later he moved to New York, opened a private architectural office, and taught part-time at Yale University.

From New York, Neufeld finally was able to make an important contribution to his lifelong concern, the design of hospitals; this was his largest project of all, conceived for the country to which he always remained attached. In 1960 the Hadassah Medical Center Neufeld designed was erected in the Jerusalem district of Ein Karem, replacing the Hadassah Center building by Erich Mendelsohn, which since 1948 had been inaccessible.[13] The centre, part of the Jerusalem University, contained a hospital with eight hundred beds, a polyclinic, schools of education in medicine, dentistry, nursing and pharmacy, and an institute for cancer treatment and research. The complex is world-renowned, and not only in medical circles. Neufeld's architectonic solution that arranged hospital rooms along the outer curve of the half-oval building, with nursing stations in the inner part of the crescent, was praised in international professional journals as an example of well-thought-out, functional clinic design.[14] Last but not least, the centrally located medical centre synagogue is also an attraction: Marc Chagall created the glass paintings on the twelve windows that depict the twelve tribes of Israel.
Josef Neufeld died in New York on September 9, 1980.

For information and material I am indebted to Neufeld's wife Michiko Neufeld, Brooklyn, NY (1992). For additional photos, my thanks to Ilja Belsitzman, Tel Aviv, who was a close associate of Josef Neufeld from 1935 to 1940.

1 See biography of Leopold Krakauer.
2 See: Warhaftig 2005: Ochs, Siegmund.
3 See: *Bauwelt* 15/1931, p. 510. Architect Siegmund Ochs lived at Dörnbergstrasse 7, Berlin W-10 until he fled to England in 1935. His name was on the list of Jewish professionals who were expelled from the Reich Chamber of Fine Arts in 1933. See: Warhaftig 2005, biography Ochs, Siegmund.
4 Taut 1980, p. 109 ff.
5 *Wegweiser* 1987, pp. 240–241.
6 *Habinyan Bamisrah Hakarov* 11/12, March 1937, pp. 12–13.
7 *Habinyan Bamisrah Hakarov* 1, August 1937, p. 17.
8 *L'Architecture d'Aujourd'hui*, Paris 1937/38, p. 26; *The Architectural Review*, London July–December 1938, p. 146; Mezger-Smok 1994, pp. 310–315.
9 *Habinyan Bamisrah Hakarov* 2, November 1937, p. 17.
10 Josef Neufeld, "Oskar Strnad" in: *Habinyan Bamisrah Hakarov* 4, November 1935, p. 1.
11 See biography of Oskar Kaufmann.
12 *Twenty Years* 1940, pp. 17–19.
13 See biography of Erich Mendelsohn.
14 See: *Architectural Design*, London 1961, pp. 17–19.

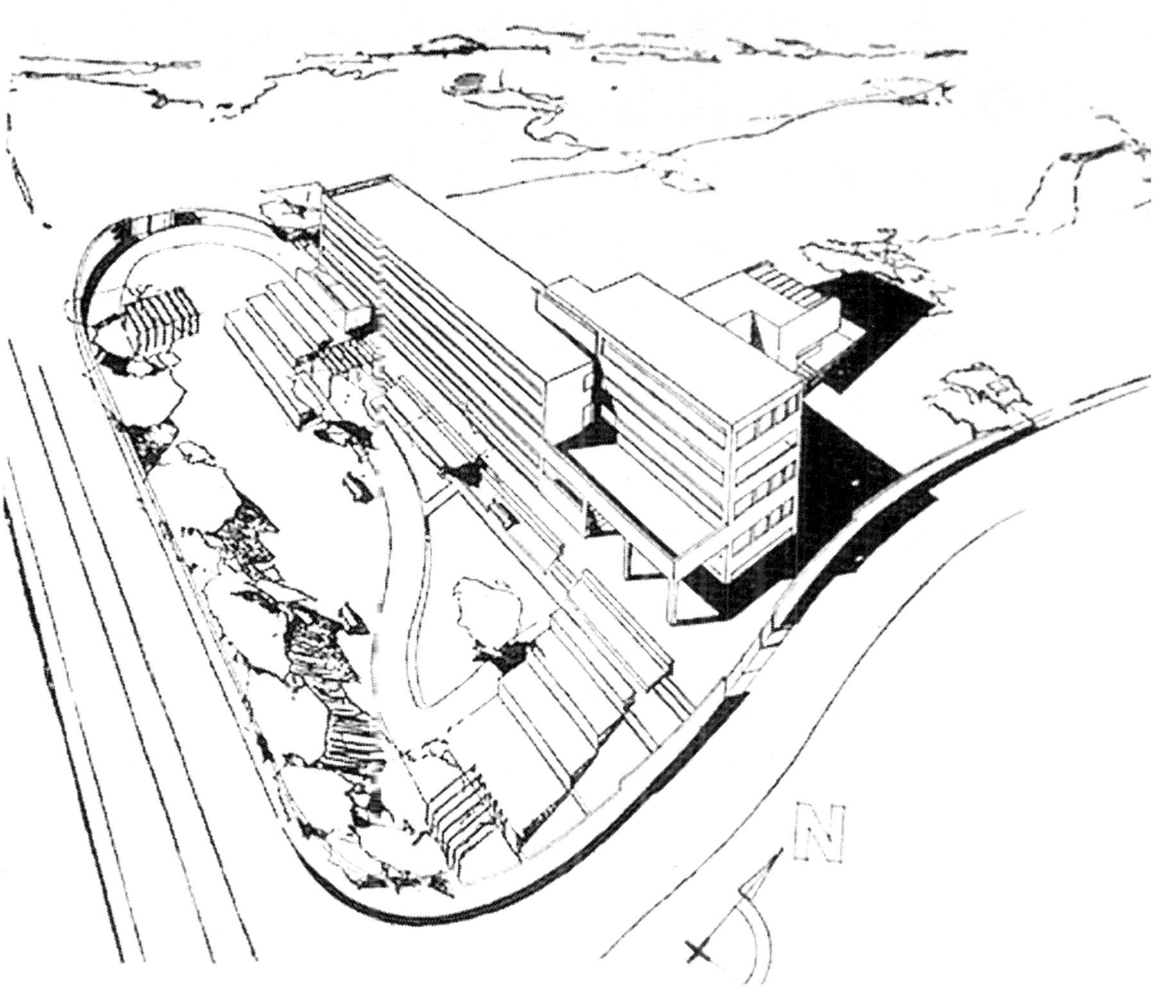

Josef Neufeld with Siegmund Ochs, Jewish hospital in Zagreb, 1931, competition entry

Josef Neufeld

Left page above:
Josef Neufeld, "The Children's Community", Kibbutz Mishmar Ha'emek, 1935, ground-floor plan

Left page below:
Josef Neufeld, "The Children's Community", Kibbutz Mishmar Ha'emek, 1935

Right page above:
Josef Neufeld, Assutah private hospital, Tel Aviv, 1935, ground-floor plan

Right page below:
Josef Neufeld, one-family residence G., Tel Benjamin near Tel Aviv, 1935

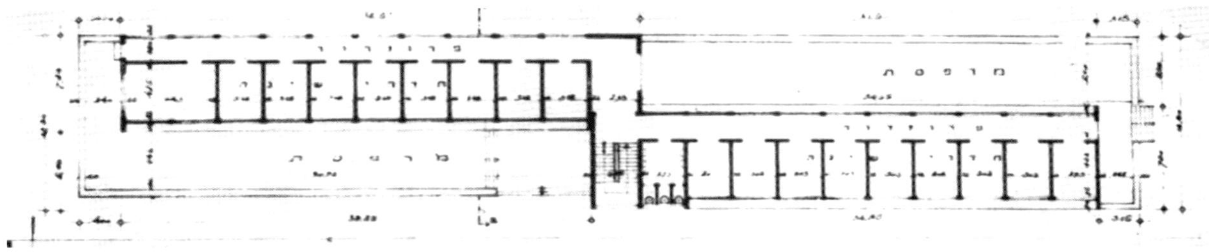

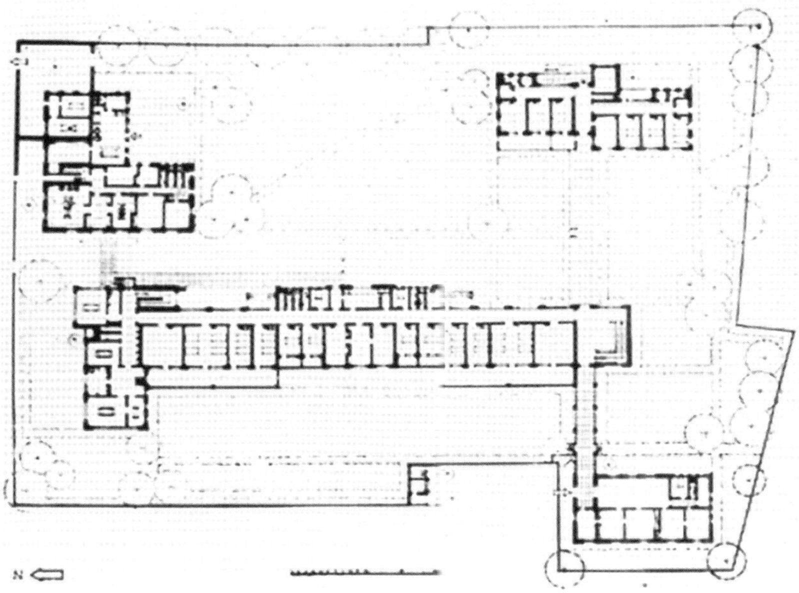

Assutah Private Hospital

Tel Aviv, Palestine. 1935.

Lay out.

1. Administration and reception.
2. Main building.
3. Isolation pavillon.
4. Main kitchen.
5. Mortuary.
6. Laundry.
7. Flower stand;
8. Surgical wing.

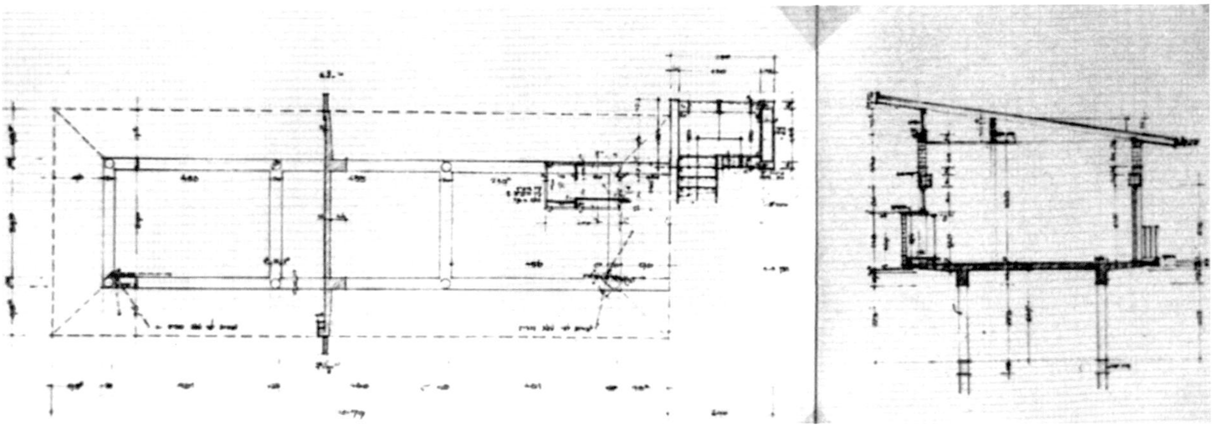

Josef Neufeld, one-family residence K., Nahariya, 1937, ground-floor plan and section. See: "Stef Wertheimer"

Josef Neufeld, one-family residence K., Nahariya, 1937. See: "Stef Wertheimer"

Josef Neufeld, children's settlement in Kibbutz Misra, 1939, residence and school unit

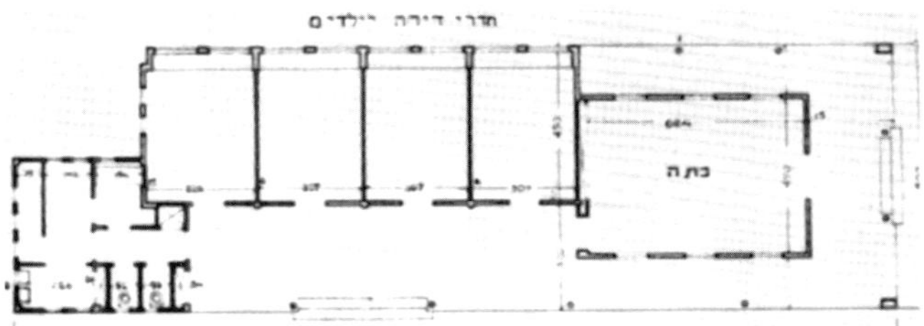

Josef Neufeld, children's settlement in Kibbutz Misra, 1939, residence and school unit, ground-floor plan

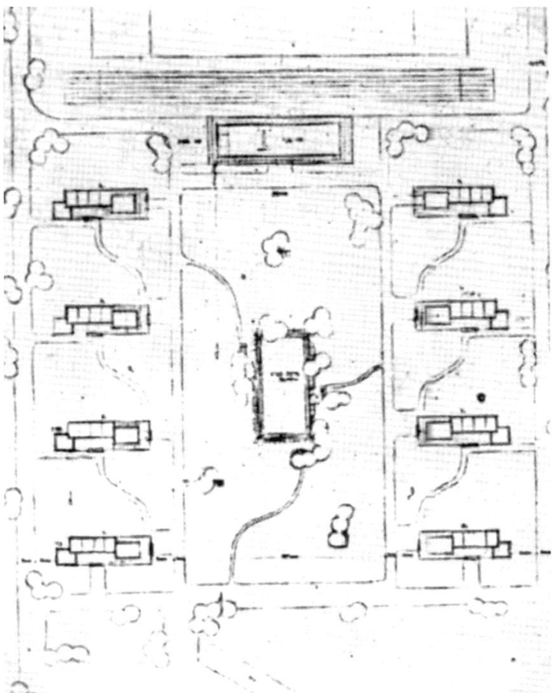

Josef Neufeld, children's settlement in Kibbutz Misra, 1939, general layout

Josef Neufeld

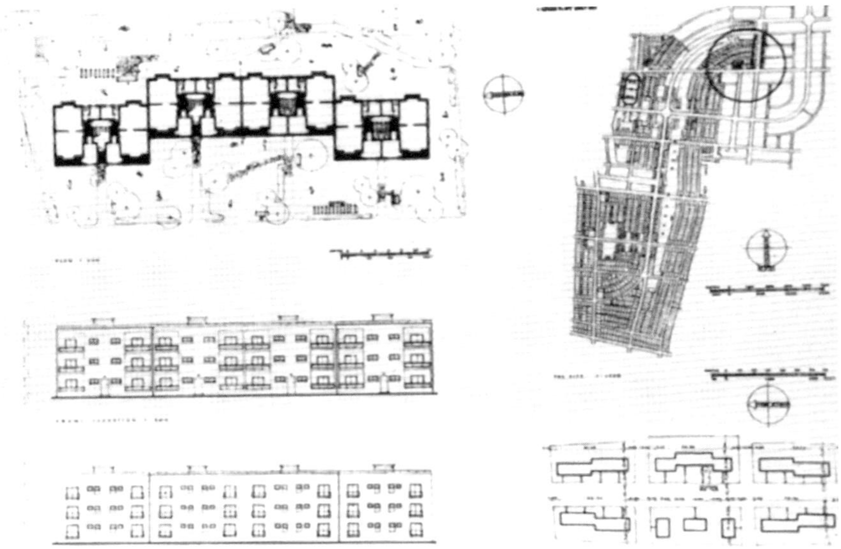

Josef Neufeld with Israel Dicker, Meonot Ovdim, workers' housing, Tel Aviv, 1935, site plan, ground-floor plan and elevations

Josef Neufeld with Israel Dicker, Meonot Ovdim, workers' housing, Tel Aviv, 1935

Josef Neufeld with Israel Dicker, Meonot Ovdim, workers' housing, Tel Aviv, 1935, ground-floor plan

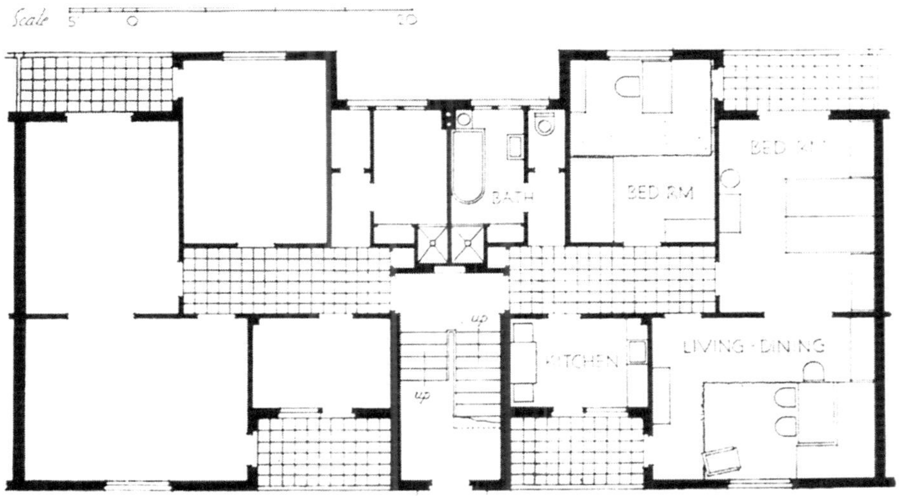

Josef Neufeld with Israel Dicker, workers' housing Ramat-Gan, 1937

Josef Neufeld

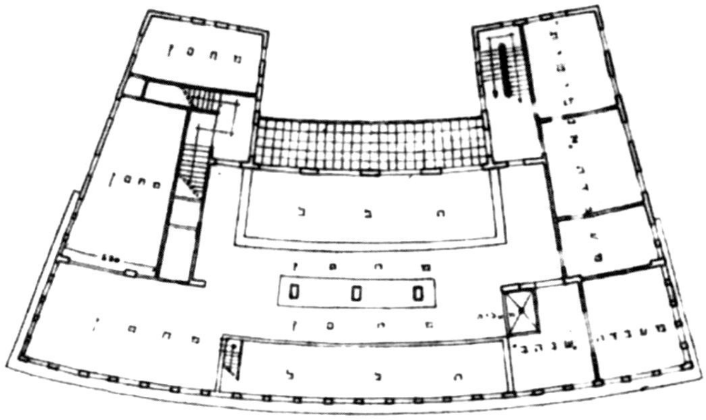

Left page above:
Josef Neufeld, medical storage facility Kuppat-Cholim, Tel Aviv, 1939, first-floor plan

Left page below:
Josef Neufeld, medical storage facility Kuppat-Cholim, Tel Aviv, 1939

Right page:
Josef Neufeld, apartment building Beit Sira (the ship building) on the ridge of Haifa, 1936. Photo: M.W. 1989

Josef Neufeld, Hadassah University Hospital Medical Center, in Ein Karem, Jerusalem, 1956–1959

Josef Neufeld, Hadassah University Hospital Medical Center, in Ein Karem, Jerusalem, 1956–1959, view of the half-oval part of the building

Josef Neufeld, Hadassah University Hospital Medical Center synagogue with Marc Chagall's painted glass windows, in Ein Karem, Jerusalem, 1962. Photo: O.W. 1993

Carl Rubin

1899 Sniatyn – 1955 Tel Aviv

Like his fellow Jewish students in Vienna's universities, Carl Rubin was both a witness to and victim of anti-Semitic rioting and attacks on Jewish students. This led him to join the Jewish student group Kadima (forward), since Jews had for decades been excluded from German student associations.[1] By joining Kadima, he could be politically active and in addition, Rubin wanted no longer to be at the mercy of his enemies. As a committed Zionist Carl Rubin was – as were his Viennese contemporaries Leopold Krakauer, Jakob Pinkerfeld, Josef Neufeld and Gideon Kaminka – guided by the idea that he would immigrate to Palestine as soon as possible.[2]
Rubin was born on June 24, 1899, in Sniatyn, Galicia. He completed his studies in architecture at the Technische Hochschule in Vienna in 1924 and emigrated two years later. He worked first in Alex Baerwald's Haifa office on the Struck residence and Anglo-Palestinian Bank projects. From there he moved to Richard Kauffmann's office in Jerusalem, where he helped design Menachem Ussischkin's private residence. In 1931 Rubin began a study trip that took him through Italy, Switzerland, France and Holland. He then went to Berlin and worked for a few months in the office of Erich Mendelsohn, an experience decisive for his future development. Rubin returned to Palestine in 1932 and worked as an independent architect in Tel Aviv until his early death in 1955.

Some eighty buildings are attributed to Rubin, among them a series of outstanding works. One of the first apartment buildings to be designed with split levels on each floor (it still stands on Rothschild Boulevard) had brought him recognition by 1935.[3] Each landing of the three-storey building leads to a four-room apartment. In view of the climatic conditions, the living rooms and kitchens in all the apartments have access to balconies, an innovation that the residents have greatly appreciated.
In 1935 Rubin's design for an office building won first prize in an invited competition whose participants also included Richard Kauffmann, Dov Kuczynski and Josef Neufeld. The Beit Hadar office building was the country's first large steel construction. The fact that Rubin based his plan on the geometric volumes of the cube and half-cylinder, and the arrangement of the windows, reveal his hidden love for Erich Mendelsohn's architecture in Germany.[4]
When Meir Dizengoff, the first mayor of Tel Aviv, died in 1936, his residence was converted into the city museum.[5] Commissioned with the renovation, Rubin was able to somewhat enlarge the structure and to design new façades. The three symmetric cubic wings now had narrow horizontal windows, and Rothschild Boulevard was enriched with yet another Modern building. Since 1948, the building has also possessed great historical significance, for it was here that Israel proclaimed statehood.

Carl Rubin was in the leading group of socially committed architects, with Dov Kuczynski, Josef Neufeld and Arieh Sharon, who built the largest workers' housing project Meonot Ovdim in Tel Aviv between 1935 and 1939.[6] In this project as well, Rubin made sure that all the rooms in each apartment, including the kitchen, had access to a balcony. He kept the design of the façades spare and functional, indebted to the so-called International Style.

Carl Rubin and Izaak Javetz, who had previously worked in Erich Mendelsohn's office in Jerusalem, also were the originators of the Museum of Jewish Antiquity, an institute for archaeological research at the Hebrew University on Mount Scopus in Jerusalem that was established in 1941. The building was realized after the design won in a competition whose jurors included Erich Mendelsohn, Alexander Klein and Salman Schocken, a university trustee at the time.[7] Erich Mendelsohn probably was quite pleased that the structure's design incorporated horizontal and vertical window slots, for these attested to his great influence.

During World War II, Rubin was stationed from 1942 to 1945 in Damascus as a military engineer for the British army. Together with an architect from Damascus, he won second prize there in a competition to design the Damascus city hall, and he was able to work on the project until construction began.
After the state of Israel was founded, Rubin was assigned to the defence department as a planner. But he could not complete this work, or the one-family houses in Herzlia, or the medical buildings and the Ort Textile School in Ramat-Gan, for he died unexpectedly in Tel Aviv in 1955 at the age of fifty-six.

For information and material, I am very grateful to Carl Rubin's nephew Dipl.-Ing. Arnon Rubin, Tel Aviv (1987).

1 Kadima, the first national Jewish network of students, was founded in Vienna in 1882 after Jews were shut out of the German students' association. It aimed, among other things, to counter assimilation and to establish settlements in Palestine.
2 See biography of Leopold Krakauer.
3 *Habinyan Bamisrah Hakarov* 9/10, November 1936, p. 8.
4 *Habinyan Bamisrah Hakarov* 3, Tel Aviv August 1935, p. 8.
5 Meir Dizengoff (born 1861 in Bessarabia – died 1936 in Tel Aviv) was one of the founders of Tel Aviv in 1909.
6 See biographies of Dov Kuczynski, Josef Neufeld and Arieh Sharon.
7 See biographies of Erich Mendelsohn and Alexander Klein.

Carl Rubin

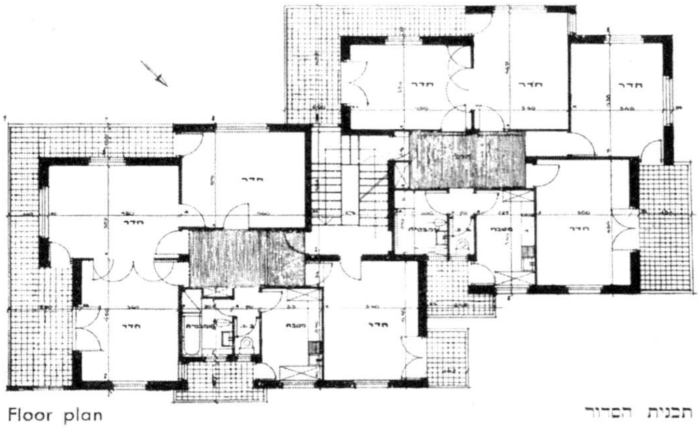

Left page above:
Carl Rubin, apartment house on Rothschild Boulevard, Tel Aviv, 1935, ground-floor plan

Left page below:
Carl Rubin, apartment house on Rothschild Boulevard, Tel Aviv, 1935

Right page:
Carl Rubin, Beit Meir Dizengoff on Rothschild Boulevard, Tel Aviv, 1936. Photo: M.W. 1989

Carl Rubin

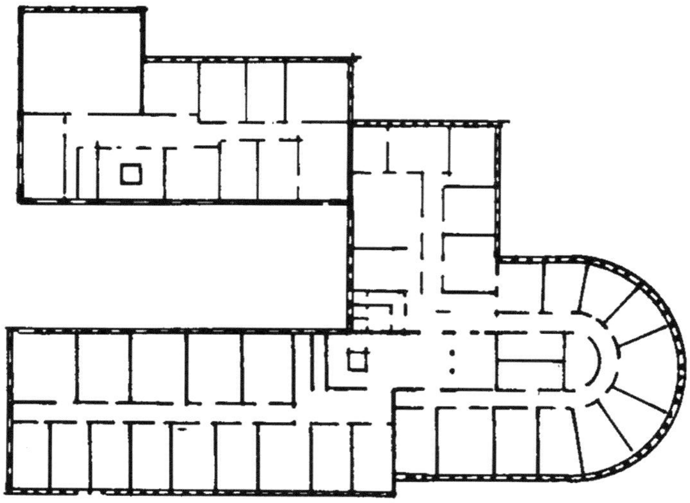

Carl Rubin, Beit Hadar office building
Tel Aviv, 1935, ground-floor plan

Carl Rubin, Beit Hadar office building
Tel Aviv, 1935. Photo: M.W. 1989

Carl Rubin with Izaak Javetz, Museum of Jewish Antiquity, Hebrew University Jerusalem, 1941, ground-floor plan (right) and first-floor plan (left)

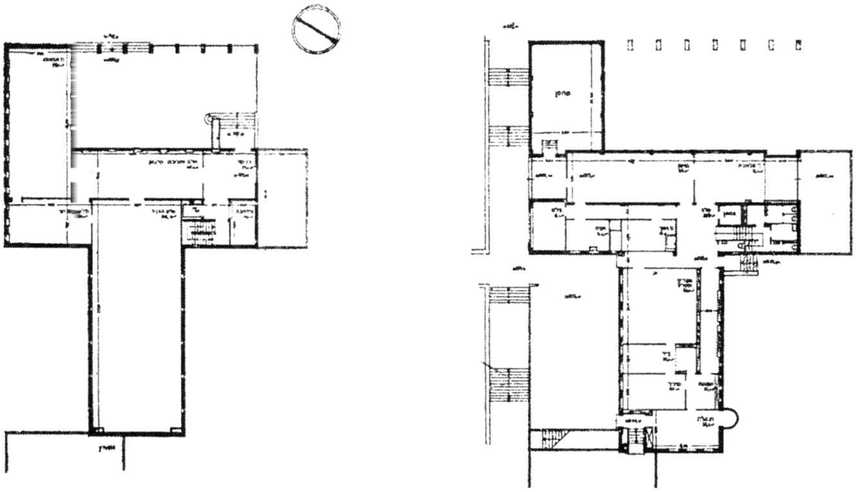

Carl Rubin with Izaak Javetz, Museum of Jewish Antiquity, Hebrew University Jerusalem, 1941

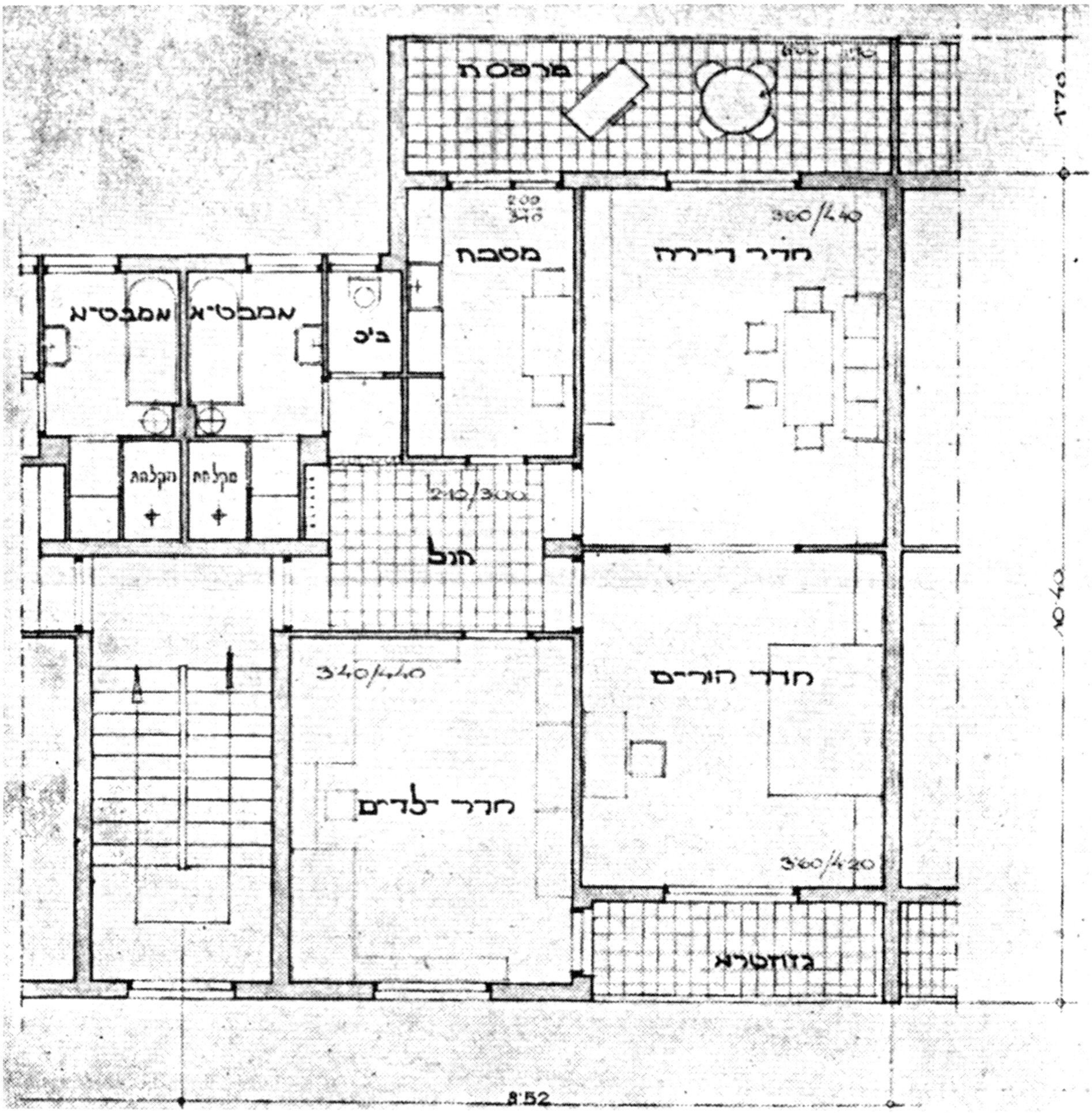

Carl Rubin, Meonot Ovdim, workers' housing project, Tel Aviv, 1939, upper-floor plan

Carl Rubin, Meonot Ovdim, workers' housing project, Tel Aviv, 1939, front view

Max Loeb

1901 Kassel – 1962 Haifa

It is thanks to Max Loeb that so many modern buildings were built in the port city of Haifa, on the ridge of Carmel, and on Mount Carmel itself.
Born in Kassel on October 29, 1901, Max Loeb studied architecture in Munich and Dresden before earning his diploma in May 1925 at the Technische Hochschule Darmstadt. Since he had grown up in a Zionist family, Loeb went immediately afterward to Palestine to see the land for himself. He returned to Germany, spending the years 1927–28 in an architecture office in Cologne. Then he moved to Palestine for good, settling in Jerusalem. He opened a practice with an engineer by the name of Danon, a Sephardic Jew (which did not escape the attention of his Ashkenazic colleagues) and immediately began to build. Among his commissions were a main branch of the Anglo-Palestinian Bank and a school building. Loeb also designed one-family houses for Professor Boneh, Dr. Hirsch and for the philosopher and Zionist from Berlin, Ernst Simon (1899–1988). The cubic forms of the functionally designed Simon residence (1932) were clad in pale limestone, in conformance with Jerusalem's building ordinance. From then on, Loeb was considered one of the pre-eminent exponents of Modern architectural style in Palestine.
Many pioneer architects were in Jerusalem during those years, including Richard Kauffmann, Leopold Krakauer, Fritz Kornberg and Loeb. They met often, for it gave them the opportunity to converse in their mother tongue.

In Haifa, although the Business Center designed by Fritz Kornberg was still under construction and uprisings repeatedly flared between Jews and Arabs, the British mandate government decided in 1930 to hold a second competition for a "New Business Center" in the harbour district.[1] None of the entries satisfied the competition's judges, however. Then Richard Kauffmann, who was a member of the municipal planning commission, recommended that Max Loeb, who had not participated, be commissioned to build the centre. Loeb's design for a building complex took a middle path between the avant-garde architecture of Erich Mendelsohn and the conservative buildings of Fritz Kornberg and immediately won over the client.[2]
In order to be on hand to oversee the construction, Loeb said goodbye to his friends in Jerusalem and moved with his partner to Haifa in 1934. Construction had no sooner been completed than he was a sought-after architect in Haifa as well. Among others, my father Noah Warhaftig, who operated one of the first printing presses in Haifa, commissioned Max Loeb to design his firm's building in 1937.
The three-storey building was erected close to the harbour, near the New Business Center. On the ground floor were the various printing presses that my father had ordered from Heidelberg; the typesetters had their workroom on the first floor, next to my parents' office.[3] Max Loeb had planned our family's private apartment for the second floor. Although my parents very much admired Loeb's clear architecture and were pleased with every detail of his design, the not entirely peaceful situation in the neighbourhood,

which was inhabited by Jews and Arabs, kept them from adopting the idea of the residence floor. The second storey was therefore also turned over to office space.
From the outside, the flat-roofed building had the clear form of a cube. But oddly enough, only the upper part of the building was clad in white stucco. The ground floor appeared to be a base made of light green imported Italian glass bricks alternating with segments of black-tiled wall. To my parents' great satisfaction, these colours and the choice of materials became the trademark of their firm.

Julius Posener had praised Loeb's architecture very early on.[4] When Posener left Nazi Germany and came to Palestine in 1935, he turned to Max Loeb and asked about employment.[5] Thanks to Loeb's connections, the immigrant soon found work in Beirut. Two years later, Posener contributed an article titled "On the Schools of Max Loeb" to an issue of the journal *Habinyan Bamisrah Hakarov* devoted to school buildings in Palestine.[6] His methodical, detailed article presented four of Loeb's schools – one in Kiryat Motzkin, two in Haifa, and an agricultural school in Pardess Hanna – with floor plans and elevations. Posener examined the one-storey school in Kiryat Motzkin and the four-storey Geula School in Haifa using a catalogue of criteria related to construction, education and hygiene. He concluded that given the country's economic, climatic and social conditions, only a low building offered the necessary positive attributes.

Max Loeb published architectural criticism as well.[7] The precondition for an appropriate architecture in the Land of Israel existed, he wrote in 1943, when there was harmony between "material, form, and landscape". He dearly loved the land, and suggested that "our architectural solutions adapt to the varied landscape of our country". He challenged his colleagues to develop a real culture of architecture, to educate the public to good taste, and not to allow unqualified people to build. Since the architectural profession was not yet regulated, engineers, construction companies and even laymen were building housing throughout the country in those days.
But above all, Loeb called for solidarity on the part of everyone participating in the building process, including the building administrators. Like Josef Neufeld, he also wanted to see new building codes implemented for tall buildings and in urban planning, for the codes then in force were faulty and inadequate.
Deeply affected by a great family misfortune, Max Loeb died on October 26, 1962, at the age of sixty-one.

If one comes across a residential building on Mount Carmel whose freestanding staircase has banisters made of tubular steel and whose eaves extend broadly, it doubtless may be attributed to the master architect Max Loeb.

For the information and material I am very grateful to Max Loeb's sister Hanna Redlich, Mount Carmel, Haifa (1988).

1 See biography of Fritz Kornberg.
2 Herbert 1984.

3 My mother was the office manager.
4 Warhaftig 2005: Posener, Julius.
5 Posener 1990, p. 245.
6 *Habinyan Bamisrah Hakarov* 11/12, Tel Aviv March 1937, pp. 14–17.
7 Max Loeb, "Architektur Wettbewerbe" in: *Journal of the Association of Engineers & Architects*, Tel Aviv June/July 1943, pp. 11–12.

Max Loeb, apartment building, Haifa, Mount Carmel, 1937. The Loeb family lived on the first floor. View of the entrance.
Photo: M.W. 1989

Max Loeb

Max Loeb, N. Warhaftig Printing Press, at the port of Haifa, 1937, interior

Max Loeb, N. Warhaftig Printing Press, at the port of Haifa, 1937, front view

Max Loeb, Simon residence, Jerusalem, 1932

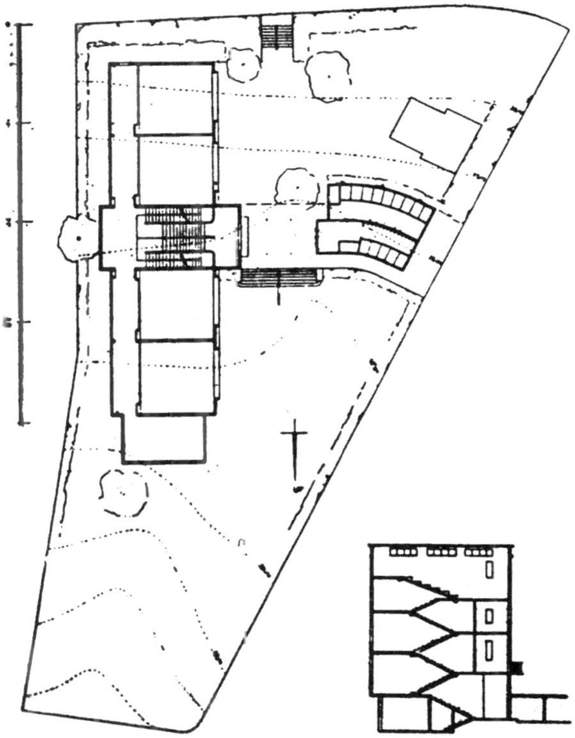

Max Loeb, Geula School, Haifa, 1937,
from left to right: north view, site plan, section
(drawings)

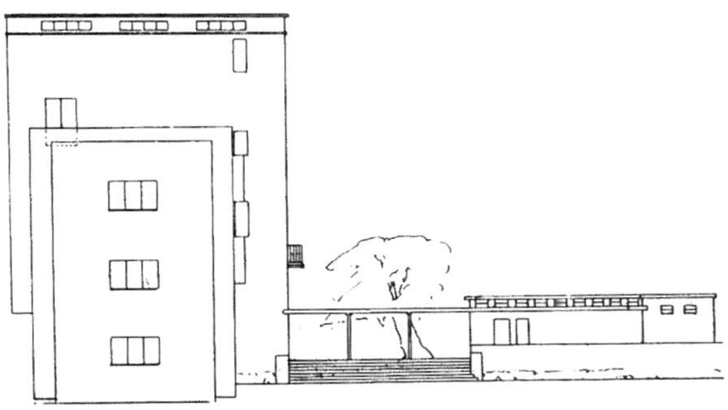

Max Loeb

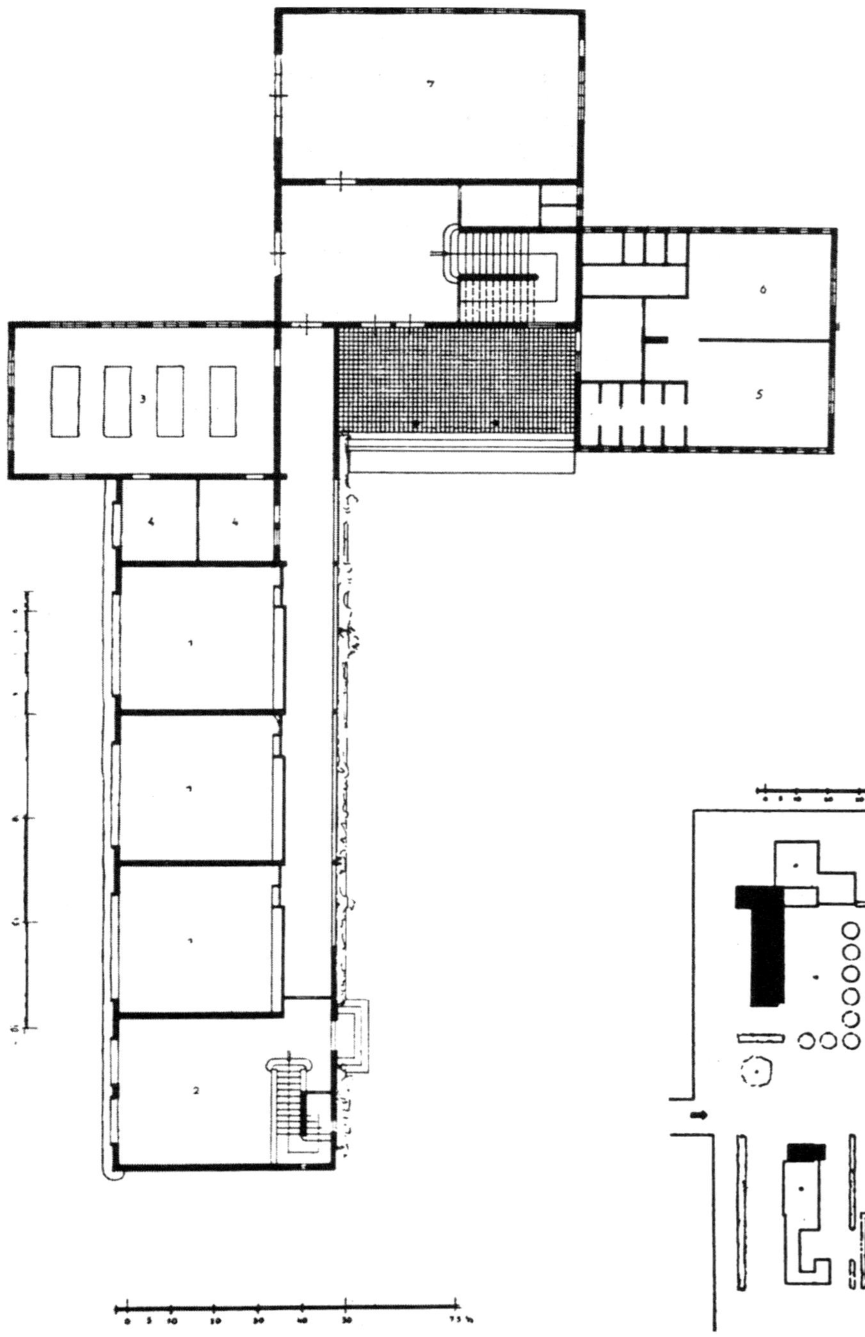

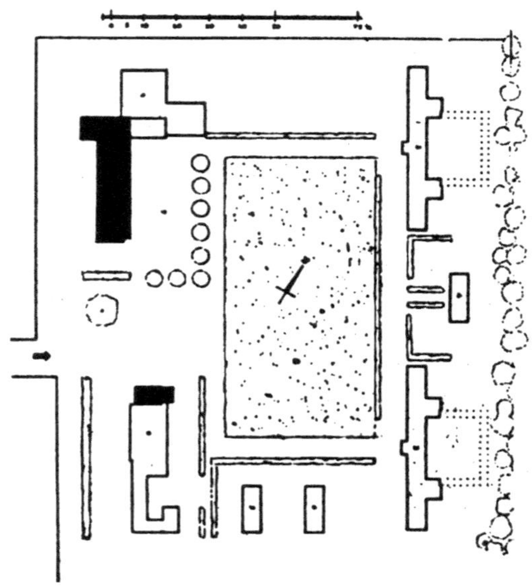

Left page above:
Max Loeb, agricultural school, Pardess Hanna, 1937, ground-floor plan of part of the building

Left page below:
Max Loeb, agricultural school, Pardess Hanna, 1937, site plan

Right page above:
Max Loeb, The Henrietta Irwell Vocational Training School for Girls, Haifa, on the ridge of Mount Carmel, 1950

Right page below:
Max Loeb, The Henrietta Irwell Vocational Training School for Girls, Haifa, on the ridge of Mount Carmel, 1950, ground-floor plan, today a secondary school

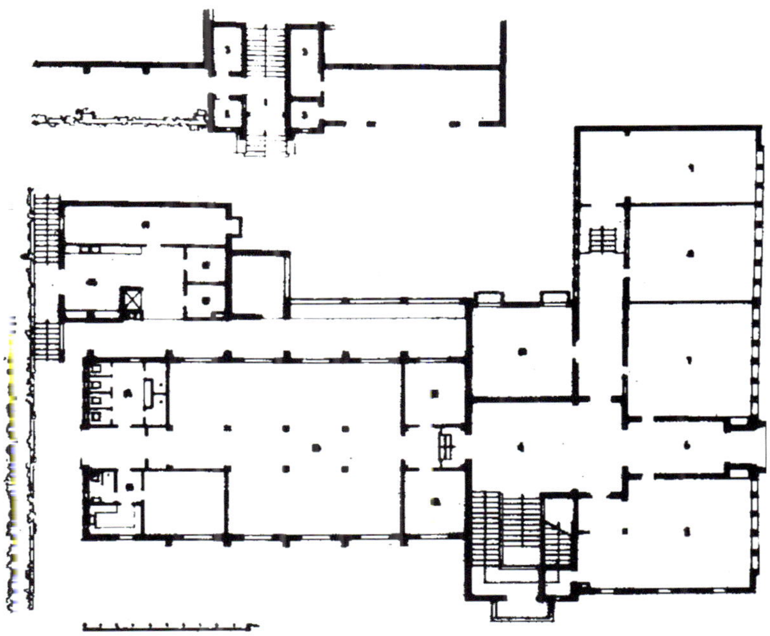

Max Loeb

Max Loeb, Milstein residence, Haifa, Mount Carmel, 1951

Max Loeb, Kogel residence, Tivon, 1940s

Max Loeb, Dr. Josef Prager residence, Haifa, Mount Carmel, circa 1938

Max Loeb, school building, Haifa, Mount Carmel, circa 1938

The Bauhaus Disciples

Arieh Sharon

1900 Jaroslaw – 1984 Tel Aviv

Arieh Sharon was a member of the Zionist-Socialist youth movement Ha'shomer Ha'tzair.[1] In 1920 he left Jaroslaw in Poland, the city where he was born on May 28, 1900, and went to Palestine as a chalutz in the Third Aliya. At first, Sharon paved the streets there with asphalt and did agricultural work. After a time, he joined the founders of Kibbutz Gan Shmuel near the city of Hadera.[2] He helped construct the facilities and worked in the apiary, took care of livestock and the silage. While working in the kibbutz residences and dining hall, his penchant for visual thinking and design became apparent. To broaden his horizons, Sharon undertook a trip to Germany, where he heard about the founding of the Bauhaus. Its new approaches in the realm of construction materials and planning processes and its experimental structures aroused Sharon's enthusiasm to such a great extent that he went to Dessau in 1926.
After one year of studying the basic concepts under Vassily Kandinsky, Paul Klee, Josef Albers and László Moholy-Nagy, Arieh Sharon became one of the first seven students in the architecture department, which was established by Walter Gropius in 1927 and headed by the Swiss architect Hannes Meyer. Sharon learned from Marcel Breuer that an apartment ought to "bear the imprint of the owner's character. The architect creates only half of a dwelling; the person who lives in it creates the other half." From Hannes Meyer, he adopted the view that the architect "must be backed by the scientist, sociologist and psychologist. Architecture is not the individual emotional activity of an artist — building is a collective activity." From Mies van der Rohe, Sharon heard the precept "less is more", which he made his own maxim.[3]
In 1929 Sharon completed his studies, receiving Bauhaus diploma Nr. 6.
Arieh Sharon then accepted Hannes Meyer's offer to work in his Berlin office and to supervise construction of a school for the Allgemeiner Deutscher Gewerkshafts-Bund (ADGB), the German federation of unions, in Bernau near Berlin.[4] After Sharon completed this task in 1931, he was offered the chance to accompany Hannes Meyer to Moscow. But Sharon decided instead to return to Palestine and contribute his knowledge and abilities to the building of that land. Kibbutz life no longer appealed to Sharon after his six-year stay at the centre of cultural, artistic and architectural life in Europe, so he settled in Tel Aviv (spring hill) with the thought that he would contribute to the design of a real cosmopolitan city.[5]

There was already a master plan for Tel Aviv, designed by the English urbanist Patrick Geddes (1854–1932), which foresaw 40,000 inhabitants in a garden city with small parcels of land, quiet streets and small public gardens. But Arieh Sharon was not ready to see Tel Aviv develop into an English garden city or into a Levantine provincial town. Rather, he dreamt that Tel Aviv would be created as the first Jewish city and develop organically and functionally along the coast, with buildings in the avant-garde style of the Bauhaus. Sharon was not alone in this view; other artists, including writers, actors and painters, also shared his vision.

The architects Josef Neufeld, Zeev Rechter and Arieh Sharon, all recently returned from training in central Europe, came together in Tel Aviv to found an architects' association called Chug, which was named after its model, the Berlin architects' association Der Ring.[6] Its aim was to promulgate the most modern design in architecture. The architects Carl Rubin, Shmuel Barkai, Julius Posener, Dov Carmi and Otto Schiller also joined this group, which reached the public through its journal *Habinyan Bamisrah Hakarov* (Building in the Near East).[7] The young architects were inspired by the prospect of creating the first Jewish city and giving it a homogeneous form. They joined the Association of Engineers and Architects in Israel (AEAI), which had been in existence since 1922, and energetically promoted their interests. They succeeded in establishing the precedent of holding architectural competitions for public buildings and housing developments. They also were able to gain representation in the municipal administration, in order to assume responsibility for construction quality and to build under the motto "modest, functional, clean, organic and modern". Their first success was in an invited competition for a Meonot Ovdim, a workers' housing development that was proposed for the city centre on the small parcels of Patrick Geddes' master plan.
In 1935, having won the competition, Sharon was able to realize his workers' housing project on Frishman Street. The housing associations and unions that funded Berlin's large housing developments of the 1920s served as the model for the financial structure.[8] Although Sharon retained Patrick Geddes's street plan, Sharon's urban concept replaced the garden city's small buildings, each containing four to six apartments, with four three-storey residential blocks that contained 150 apartments each. The ribbon development and the apartments' east-west orientation – features that characterize this housing project – were the most important requirements of the architects who practised Neues Bauen as propounded by Hannes Meyer in his Bauhaus lectures.[9] Sharon was doubtless impressed and influenced by the motif of small balconies with steel railings that Walter Gropius had used for his students' dormitory in Dessau (1926) and Mies van der Rohe used in the Werkbundsiedlung in Stuttgart (1927).

Four years later, after he had again been awarded first prize, Sharon was able to realize a second Meonot Ovdim not far from the first. In addition to the 150 apartments in each of the six housing blocks, this one had cooperative shops, kindergartens, and playgrounds in the garden courtyards. The southernmost blocks of apartments were raised on pilotis to create shady areas under the buildings. Sharon described this architectural development as post-Bauhaus. Here, too, he was able to circumvent the parcels of the Geddes plan.

In memory of the Hebrew poet Josef Chaim Brenner (1881–1921), who was murdered by Arabs in Jaffa, the trade union in Tel Aviv held a competition in 1935 for a public building that would bear his name: Brenner House. Arieh Sharon, who won first prize, created a practical and functional two-storey structure that housed a clubroom, a dining hall and offices. The dining hall, whose interior structural elements were left exposed, is reminiscent of the dining hall in the federal school of the ADGB designed by Hannes Meyer.[10]

While Sharon continued to live in Tel Aviv and endeavoured to foster the city's urban character, he also was closely connected with the kibbutz movement. From 1938 to 1949 he designed the general plans for five kibbutzim, and he built schools, dining halls and kindergartens for six others. He travelled from one kibbutz to another, mainly in northern Israel, in order to discuss the plans with his former comrades. The socio-political order of the kibbutz entailed certain ways of organising daily life, which the built space also had to reflect. Sharon understood how to translate these social structures into architectural terms. With Israel's statehood came an influx of survivors of the Shoah and other immigrants from many different countries, for whom living quarters and workplaces had to be created in the briefest time. To handle this task, a national planning office was set up within the office of the Minister President in Jerusalem. Sharon was given the leadership post, with the participation of the architects Rau, Lavie and Glikson.[11]

During his years in Jerusalem, from 1948 to 1953, Sharon had the architect Benjamin Idelson run his office in Tel Aviv.[12] As of 1954 they formed an official partnership that lasted until 1966. Several major projects resulted from their work together, including the Beilinson health insurance union's hospital in Tel Aviv, planned for five hundred beds but expanded to more than 1000 beds, which today handles over 2500 patients. A second health centre, Soroka, was built in 1959 in Be'er-Sheva, the capital of the Negev. On the campus of the Technion in Haifa, the 750-seat Churchill Auditorium and the central library were erected in 1958 and 1960, respectively.
After 1965 Sharon worked with his son Eldar, a graduate of the Technion Haifa, and extended his sphere of activities beyond the borders of Israel. He wanted to transfer the experience he had gained while building the new country of Israel to the developing nations, where he wanted to erect hospitals and university buildings. The largest project of this kind, Ife University, the main university in western Nigeria, was realized by Arieh and Eldar Sharon from 1968 to 1972. In the first decade of its existence, the university accepted 5000 students.

An overview of Arieh Sharon's forty years of creative activity was made possible when the Berlin Bauhaus Archive (then still located in Schlossstrasse in Charlottenburg) hosted an exhibition in cooperation with the Academy of Arts in 1976.[13] Sharon had already been elected a member of the Berlin Academy of Arts in 1965 and felt a close attachment to it, attending the twice-yearly general meetings.[14]
Arieh Sharon died in Tel Aviv on July 26, 1984. Almost exactly ten years later, his son Eldar died at the age of sixty-one.
The firm Arieh Sharon, Eldar Sharon, Architects and City Planners, now one of the largest in Israel with thirty-five employees, is headed today by Sharon's grandchildren Arad Sharon and Smadar Sharon.

For information and material I am very grateful to Yael Aloni, Tel Aviv (1985).

1 See biography of Jacob Pinkerfeld, note 1.
2 Kibbutz Gan Shmuel was named for the Rabbi and Zionist Samuel Mohilewer (1824–1898).
3 Sharon 1976, p. 34.
4 This building, which Hannes Meyer had designed with his Bauhaus students, had won first prize in the design competition.
5 The name Tel Aviv was the Hebrew translation of Frühlingshügel, the name of the city in Theodor Herzl's novel

Altneuland. The city was founded in 1909 in the dunes north of Jaffa as the first city to have only Jewish inhabitants. Arabs made up over 75% of the population in Jaffa.

6 Zeev Rechter (1899–1960) studied engineering at the Scuola di Ingeneria di Roma and at the Ecole nationale des Ponts et Chaussées in Paris. Influenced by Le Corbusier, he was one of Israel's most prominent architects and erected the first apartment buildings on pilotis (pillars that elevate the lowest floor of a building, leaving an open space beneath: a Le Corbusier trademark).

7 Sam (Shmuel) Barkai (1898–1975) studied architecture in Venice and Paris and worked in Le Corbusier's office before he returned to Israel. Dov Carmi (1905–1962) studied architecture in Ghent, Belgium. See biographies of Carl Rubin, Julius Posener and Otto Schiller. The journal appeared twelve times during Chug's existence between December 1934 and March 1937. Four more issues under the same name appeared between July 1937 and March 1938.

8 Examples are the large "horseshoe development" in Britz, the Waldsiedlung in Zehlencorf, Onkel Toms Hütte, the large Siemenssstadt development, and the Weisse Stadt (White City) housing project on the Schillerpromenade.

9 Neues Bauen, literally "new building", stands for the Modern style of the twentieth century.

10 Bauhaus-Archive 1989.

11 Literature about Arieh Sharon: Mezger-Smok 1994, pp. 240–253; Tuvia 1999; Myra Warhaftig, "Zum 100. Geburtstag von Arieh Sharon" in *Bauwelt*, 19–20/2000, p. 8; see biographies of Heinz Rau, Yehuda Lavie and Artur Glikson.

12 Benjamin Idelson, born in St. Petersburg, studied architecture in Ghent, Belgium.

13 Arieh Sharon, *Kibbutz + Bauhaus*, exhibition catalogue, Israel 1976.

14 He was usually accompanied by his wife Chaya, a well-known actress, and his daughter Yael Aloni. She was the child of his marriage with Gunta Stölzl (1897–1983), who studied at the Bauhaus and later was the school's renowned master teacher of weaving.

Arieh Sharon, residence Dr. H. Kupfermann, Mount Carmel, Haifa, 1936

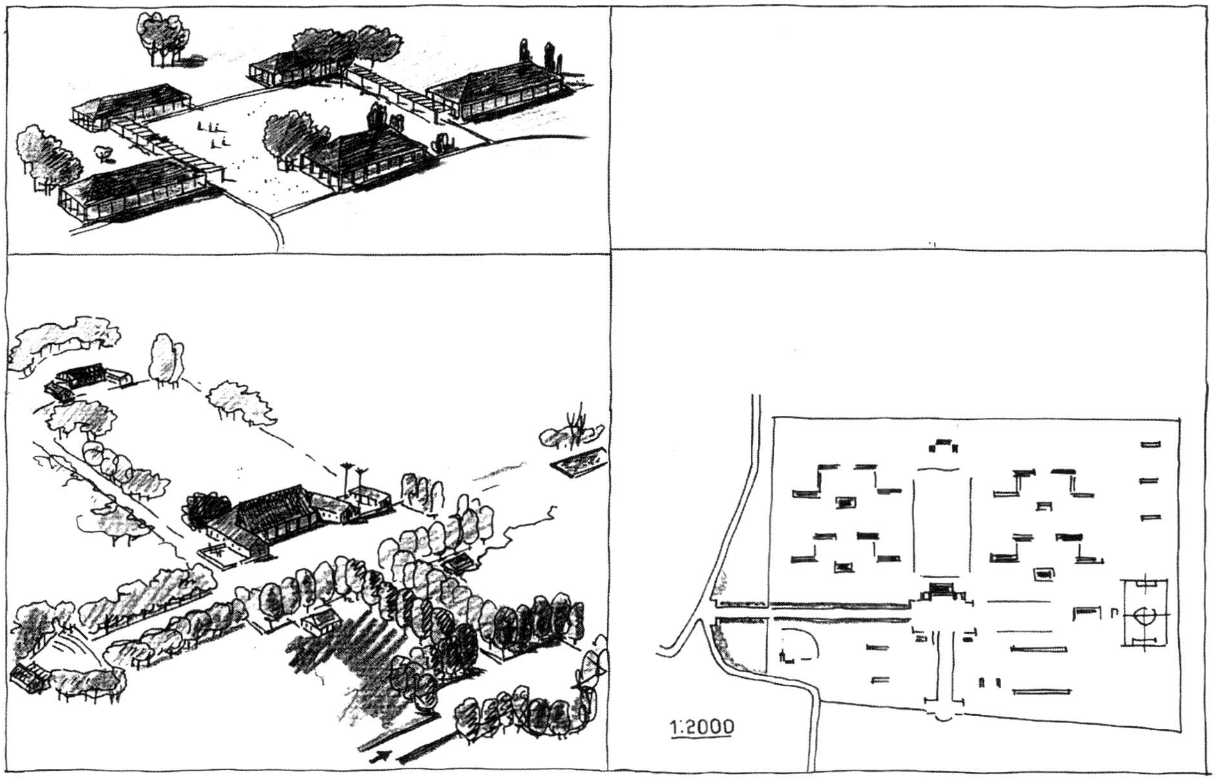

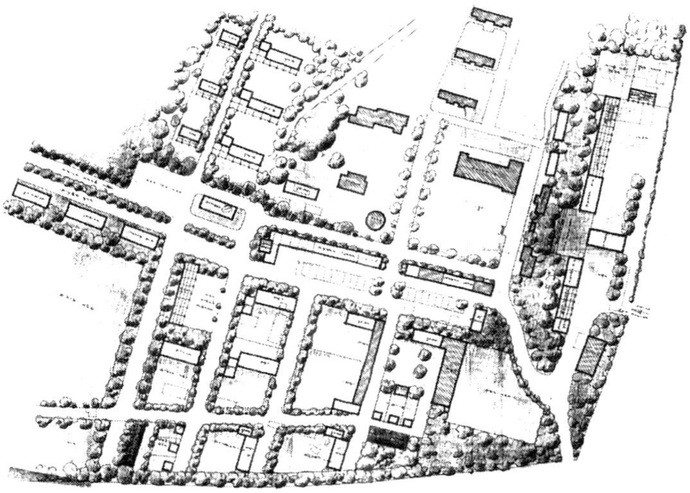

Arieh Sharon, school community, Kibbutz Beit Alpha, 1945. The five classrooms (above left), the entrance with the school's main building (below left), perspective and site plan (drawings)

Arieh Sharon, Kibbutz Maabarot, 1944, site plan

Arieh Sharon, Beit Brenner (Brenner House), Tel Aviv, 1935

Arieh Sharon, Beit Brenner (Brenner House), Tel Aviv, 1935, interior, dining hall

Hannes Meyer, federal school of the ADGB, Bernau, 1930, interior, dining hall

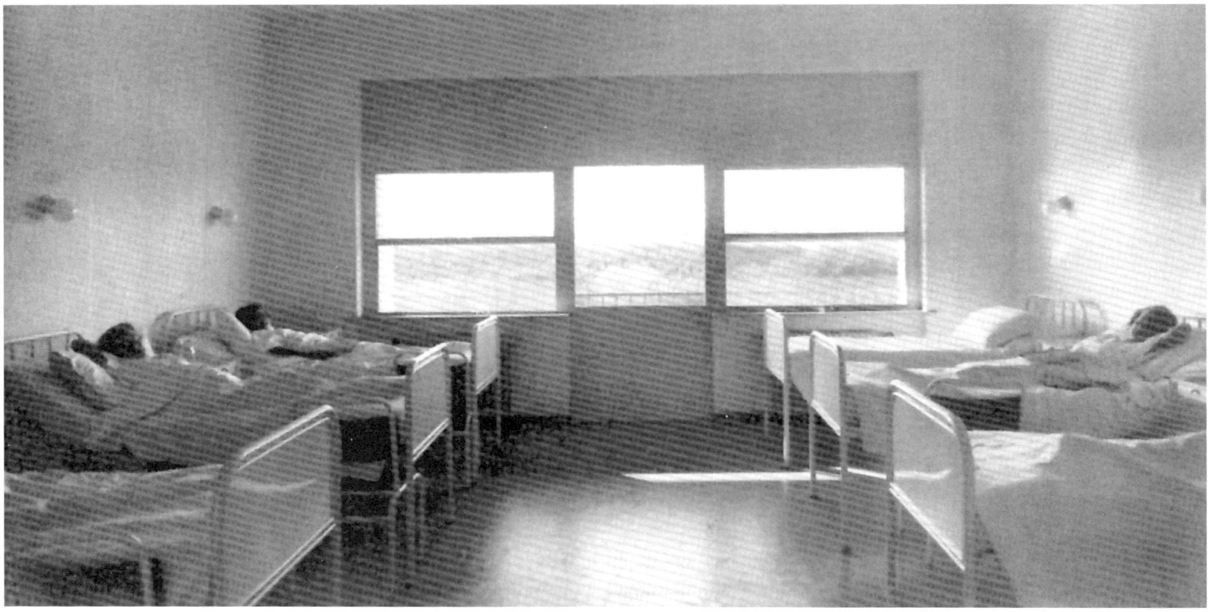

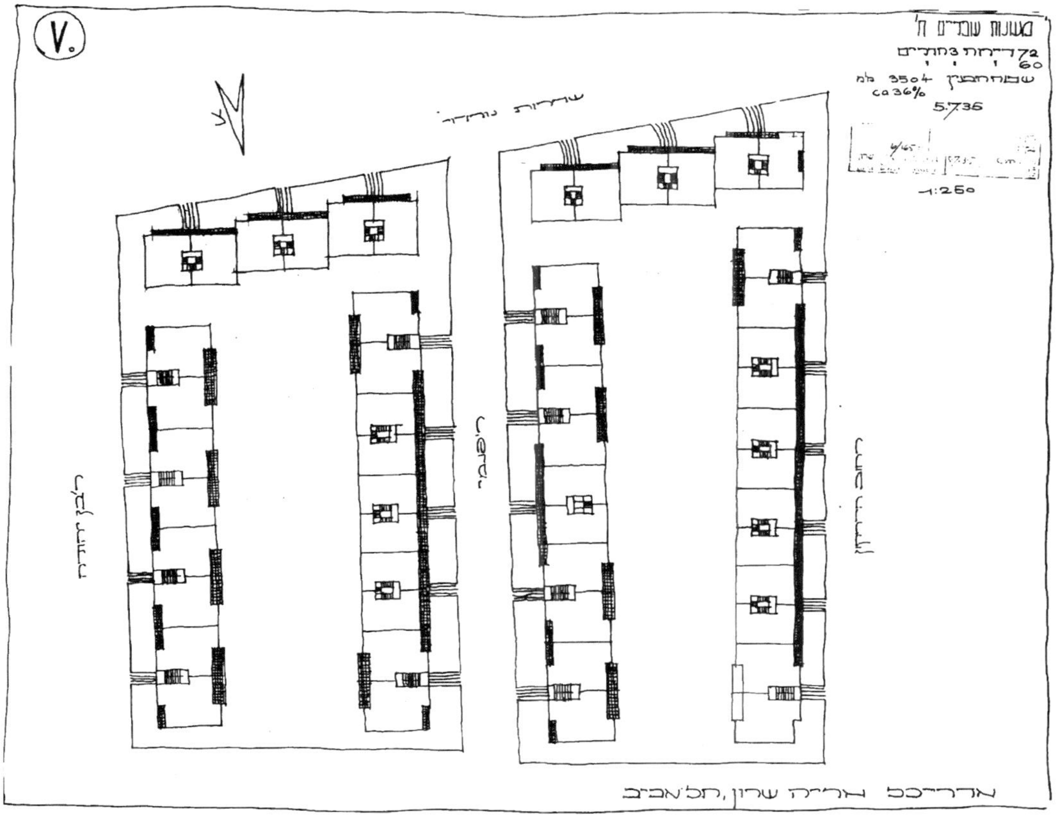

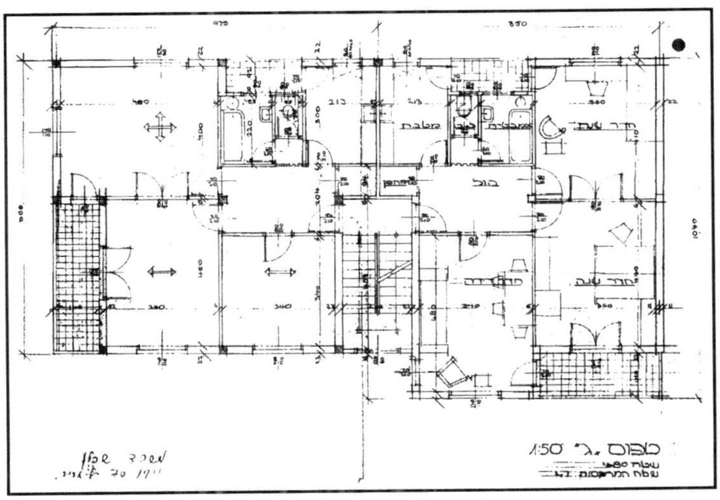

Left page above:
Arieh Sharon, Beilinson hospital, Petach Tikva, 1936, hospital room

Left page below:
Arieh Sharon, Beilinson hospital, Petach Tikva, 1936

Right page above:
Arieh Sharon, Meonot Ovdim, workers' housing, Tel Aviv, 1935, site plan

Right page below:
Arieh Sharon, Meonot Ovdim, workers' housing, Tel Aviv, 1935, ground-floor plan of the three-room apartments

Left page above:
Arieh Sharon, Meonot Ovdim, workers' housing, Tel Aviv, 1935, front view from the street

Left page below left:
Arieh Sharon, Meonot Ovdim, workers' housing, Tel Aviv, 1935, front view from the street

Left page below right:
Walter Gropius, students' dormitory, Bauhaus Dessau, 1926

Right page:
Arieh Sharon, Meonot Ovdim, workers' housing, Tel Aviv, 1935

Edgar Hed (Hecht)

1904 Kattowitz – 1956 Tel Aviv

Edgar Hed (Hecht) was born on December 16, 1904, in Kattowitz in Silesia, today Katowice in Poland. As a youth he moved to Breslau, where he attended night classes at the State Academy of Arts and earned his living by day as a decorator, sign painter and draftsman in an architectural office. Hed enrolled at the Bauhaus Dessau in the summer of 1929. During his first two semesters, he received instruction in artistic design from Paul Klee and Vassily Kandinsky. By the third semester he was allowed to attend Hannes Meyer's seminar on architecture, and from the fourth to sixth semesters he participated in the seminars on apartments and housing developments taught by Ludwig Hilbersheimer and Ludwig Mies van der Rohe.[1] Four of Hed's student assignments from their seminars on building and conversion still exist; two of them, "Southern type – two-person with garden courtyard" and "Studio housing on Stössensee", were done during his final year of study.[2] In them, the influence of Mies van der Rohe's teachings cannot be missed: liberality in the use of space, simplicity in construction, openness to the landscape by means of glass walls, and the striving toward clarity and perfection.

On August 15, 1932, Edgar Hed received Bauhaus diploma Nr. 82. There is a single notation under his name in the Bauhaus Archive card catalogue: "Edgar Hecht was an assistant to Graf Dürckheim. Hans Bellmann, 16 October 1965."[3]

Because he was Jewish, Edgar Hed was expelled from the Reich Chamber of Fine Arts on November 1, 1933, but he continued to live at Ermslebener Weg 4 in Berlin-Wilmersdorf until 1935.[4] With no prospect of work in that city, he left Germany and went to Palestine. There he Hebraised his family name into Hed (echo). Early in the 1940s he worked as an architect in the planning office of the public works department in the British mandate government. Edgar Hed died in Tel Aviv in 1956 at the age of fifty-two.

1 Hannes Meyer was fired without notice on August 1, 1930.
2 Bauhaus-Archiv 1986, pp. 61, 71, 93.
3 Dr. Karlfried Graf von Dürckheim, professor at the Psychologisches Insitut Leipzig, presented a lecture cycle on fundamentals of psychology at the Bauhaus. Hans Bellmann was also a Bauhaus pupil.
4 He was one of 323 Jewish architects who were expelled. See: Warhaftig 2005, pp. 16–18.

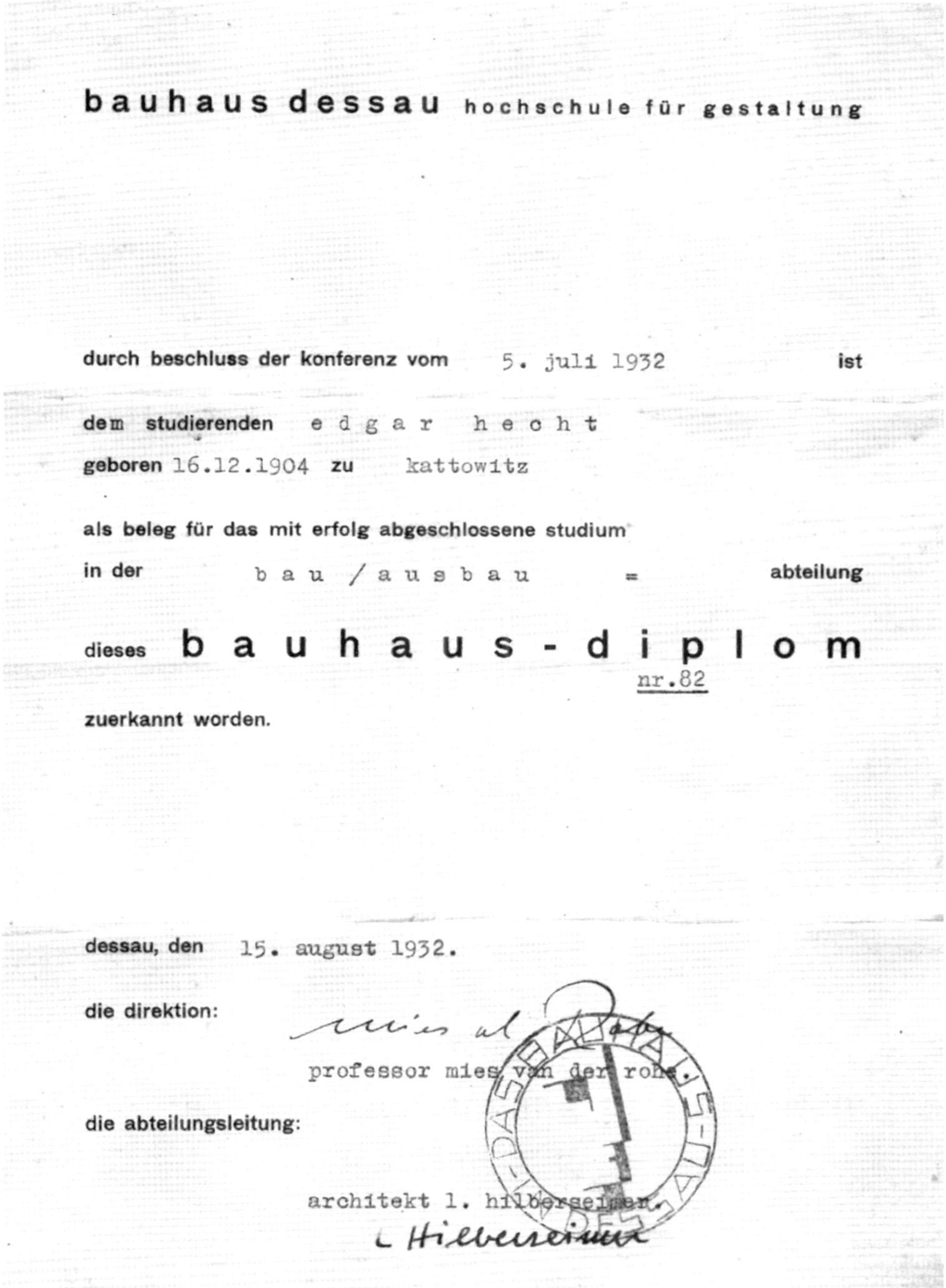

bauhaus dessau hochschule für gestaltung

durch beschluss der konferenz vom 5. juli 1932 ist

dem studierenden e d g a r h e c h t

geboren 16.12.1904 zu kattowitz

als beleg für das mit erfolg abgeschlossene studium

in der b a u / a u s b a u = abteilung

dieses **b a u h a u s - d i p l o m**

nr.82

zuerkannt worden.

dessau, den 15. august 1932.

die direktion:

professor mies van der rohe.

die abteilungsleitung:

architekt l. hilberseimer.

Edgar Hed (Hecht), Bauhaus diploma Nr. 82, Dessau, 15 August 1932, signed by Mies van der Rohe and Ludwig Hilberseimer

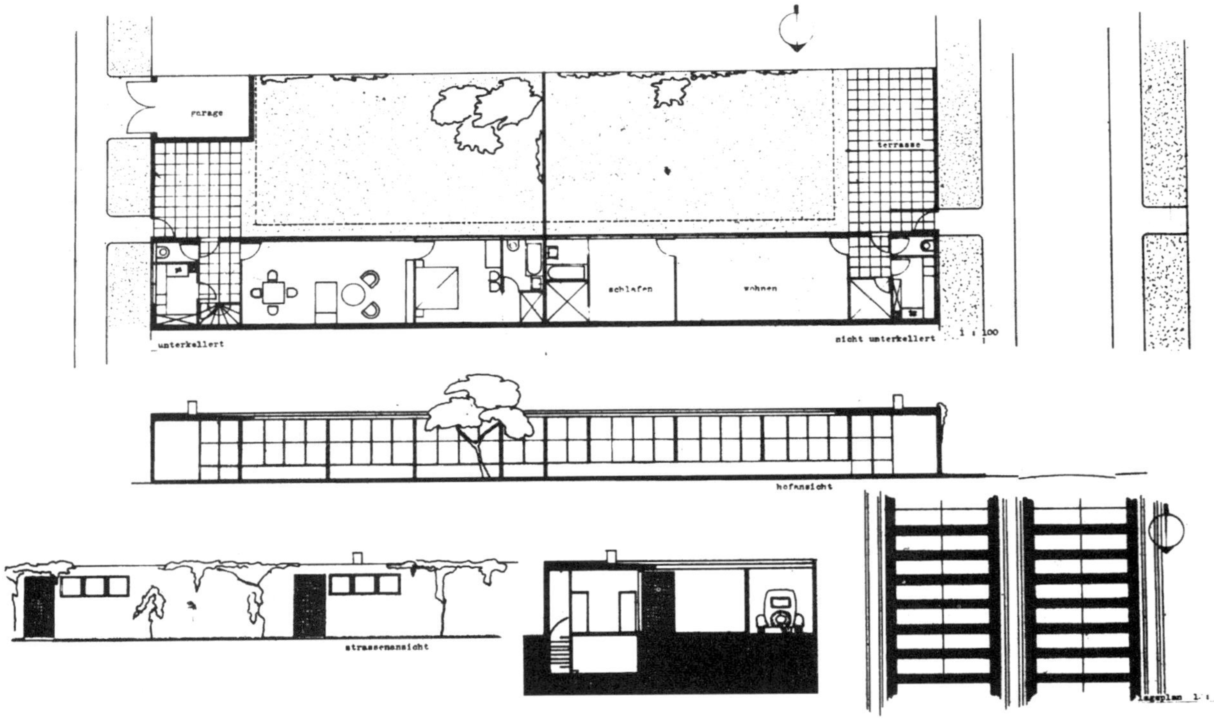
terrasse
schlafen
wohnen
unterkellert
nicht unterkellert
1 : 100
hofansicht
strassenansicht
lageplan

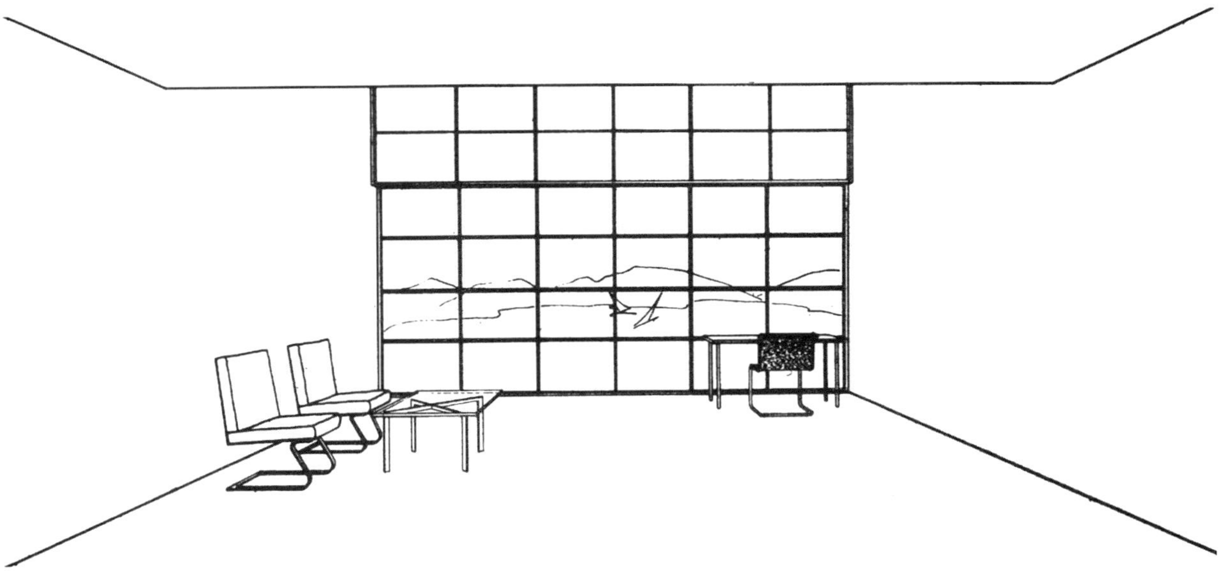

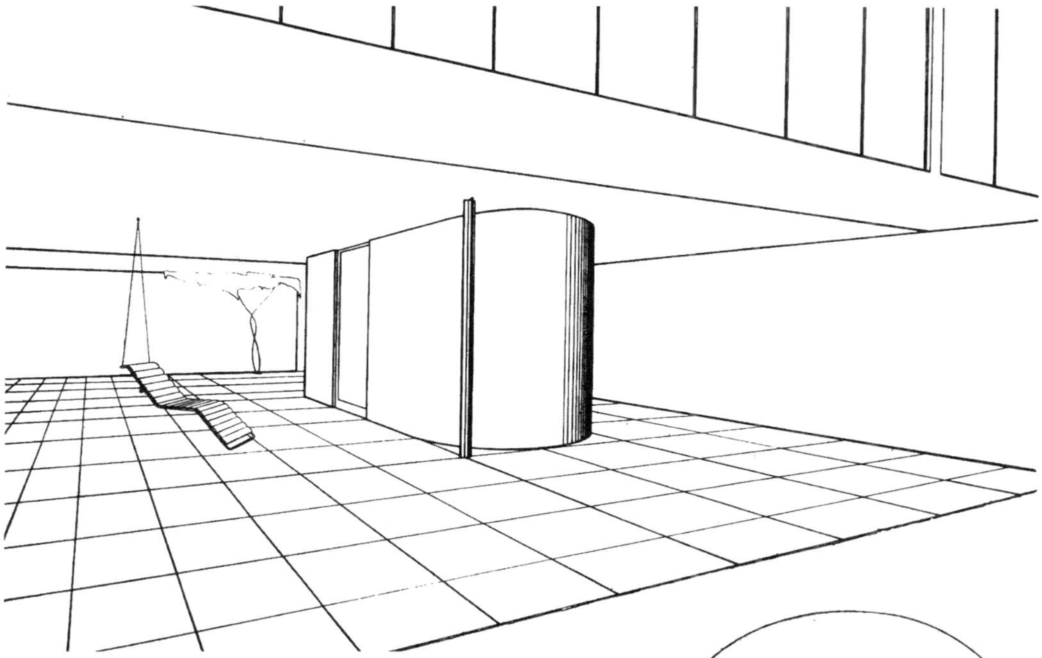

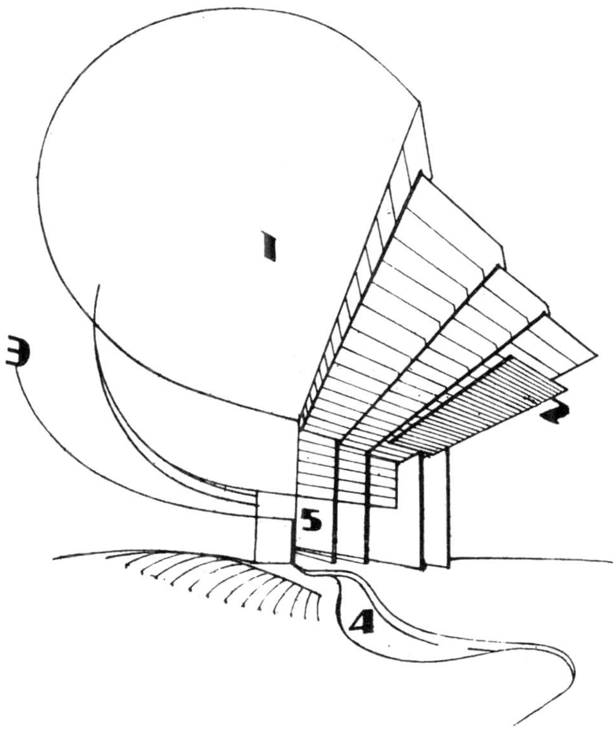

Left page above:
Edgar Hed (Hecht), "Southern type – two-person with garden courtyard", ground-floor plan, section, elevation, courtyard and front views, student project at the Bauhaus, July 4, 1931, seminar Mies van der Rohe

Left page below:
Edgar Hed (Hecht), "Studio housing at Stössensee", student project at the Bauhaus, 1931–1932, seminar Mies van der Rohe

Right page above:
Edgar Hed (Hecht), "Terrace with house entrance", student project at the Bauhaus, seminar Mies van der Rohe

Right page below:
Edgar Hed (Hecht), sketch of orientations, opera hall, Charkow, student project at the Bauhaus, seminar Mies van der Rohe

Chanan Frenkel

1905 Halle – 1957 Tel Aviv

Chanan Frenkel was born in Halle on July 22, 1905. While in secondary school, he joined a Zionist youth group in his home town and prepared himself for working life in Palestine – in Hebrew this was called hachshara.[1] In 1925 he went to Eretz Israel with the Fourth Aliya.
Frenkel had his first taste of life in a collective at Kibbutz Ein Harod in Emek Izrael. In 1928 he helped build Kibbutz Givat Brenner, south of Tel Aviv, and was among its first members.[2] Like the other chalutzim of the Third and the Fourth Aliya – Arieh Sharon, Shlomo Bernstein and Shmuel Mestechkin – Frenkel also went to Dessau, full of enthusiasm and optimism, to learn the fundamentals of building in a modern society. He commenced his studies at the Bauhaus in 1929 and received Bauhaus diploma Nr. 91 in 1932.

Frenkel then returned to Palestine and settled in Tel Aviv. During the first few years he worked in the architect Carl Rubin's office, and later moved to the office of Elsa Gidoni.[3] From 1941 to 1945, as the pace of construction slackened due to World War II, he worked in the public works department established by the English government and spent some time in Iraq working for the British army. After returning to Tel Aviv, Frenkel took a position in the office of the Russian-born architect Nachum Salkind (1895–1976). But as the years passed, Frenkel's unstable health increasingly limited his ability to work, until he died suddenly on April 30, 1957, at the age of only fifty-two.

The name Chanan Frenkel nonetheless remained significant in Israel's architectural history. The settler's house in Gedera, a village some 35 km southeast of Tel Aviv, had gained recognition in the professional literature soon after it was completed in 1938.[4]
Functional order characterized the straightforward plan of the nearly 80 m^2 three-room residence. At the client's behest, Frenkel had to put a tiled roof over the geometric structure – as frequently was the case with settlement houses of that period.
In 1948 Frenkel won first prize in a competition to design the central bus station and market halls for the town of Netanya, 30 km north of Tel Aviv on the Mediterranean coast. But war with the neighbouring Arab states meant that he could realize neither this project nor several others.

For the material he gave me about his father's works, I am very grateful to Chanan Frenkel's son, the architect David Frenkel, Tel Aviv (1986).

1 The term "hachshara" (making fit) signified the preparation for employment in Eretz Israel organized by the chalutzim movement.
2 Named for the Hebrew poet Josef Chaim Brenner. See biography of Arieh Sharon (Beit Brenner).
3 See biographies of Carl Rubin and Elsa Gidoni.
4 *Habinyan Bamisrah Hakarov* 3, Tel Aviv 1938, p. 25.

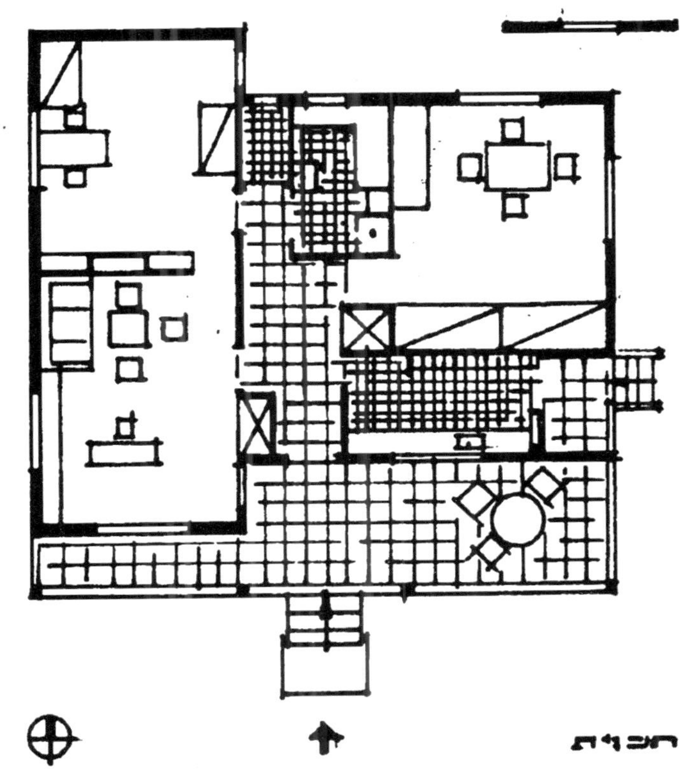

Chanan Frenkel, settlement house in Gedera, 1938, ground-floor plan

Business letterhead, S. Frenkel family, Halle an der Saale, 1920s, denotes their trade in Christmas trees and wreaths

Shlomo Bernstein

1907 Vilna – 1969 Tel Aviv

Like the chalutzim Arieh Sharon and Chanan Frenkel, Shlomo Bernstein also made the journey from Palestine to Dessau to learn about avant-garde architecture as taught at the Bauhaus so that he could introduce it back in Eretz Israel. Bernstein was born in Vilna (today Vilnius, Lithuania) on January 30, 1907.[1] He studied briefly at the Polish Academy of Visual Arts before going to Palestine at the age of eighteen, as a member of a Zionist youth movement, in the Fourth Aliya. He, too, worked first as a road builder and so contributed to the building of the country. Pursuing his artistic inclinations, Bernstein developed a strong interest in architecture.

When Alex Baerwald established the department of architecture at the Technion in Haifa in 1925, Shlomo Bernstein became one of his first pupils.[2] A friendly relationship developed between professor and student; finally Baerwald suggested that Bernstein pursue his studies at the Bauhaus in Dessau, advice that the young man followed in autumn 1931. Signatures in Bernstein's transcript by Mies van der Rohe, the director, and Wassily Kandinsky, the head instructor of painting, confirm that he was accepted as a fifth semester student on July 14, 1932. Their reasoning went: "He [Bernstein] belongs in both the architecture and painting departments because of his prior professional training." So Bernstein completed only the final two semesters at Dessau, instead of the usual six. His courses included the Mies van der Rohe seminar, urban planning with Ludwig Hilberseimer, interior design with Lilly Reich, furniture construction with Friedrich Engemann, color with Hinnerk Scheper, nude and figure drawing with Joost Schmidt, still life drawing with Josef Albers, structural engineering with Alcar Rudelt, and painting with Wassily Kandinsky.

Bernstein's sixth semester student project on the single-storey one-family house shows that he had become a devoted disciple of Mies van der Rohe. The dramatic design was clearly influenced by both Mies's Barcelona Pavilion (1928–29) and the Tugendhat House in Brno (1928–30).

On August 15, 1932, Bernstein received Bauhaus diploma Nr. 92, signed by the director Mies van der Rohe and the department head Ludwig Hilbersheimer. That same year Bernstein left Dessau and moved to Paris. There he spent a year at Le Corbusier's studio before returning to Palestine in 1933.

In Tel Aviv, Bernstein managed to make a living from private commissions until 1939. At least three multi-family apartment buildings in Tel Aviv were built under his supervision, all are unornamented and functional.[3]

Finally health problems forced Bernstein to withdraw from the competitive professional world. He joined the Tel Aviv municipal building administration, where he worked until his death on January 8, 1969.

Shortly before his death, Shlomo Bernstein, together with the painter Nissim Strick (1902–1967), was able to fulfil his wish to erect a monument in Tel Aviv to the Jews murdered in the Treblinka extermination camp.[4] In 1942–43 most of the Jews of Vilna were transported to Treblinka.

For information and material, I am very grateful to Shlomo Bernstein's wife Berta (now deceased), whom I visited in 1986, and to his son Professor Moshe Anbar, Tel Aviv (1997) .

1 Vilna was one of the most significant centres of Judaic cultural and religious life in Eastern Europe. Some 55,000 Jews lived there before World War II, constituting 28% of the population. Most of them were deported and murdered.
2 See biography of Alex Baerwald.
3 Mezger-Smok 1994, pp. 83–88.
4 Warhaftig 2005: see biography Strick, Nissim.

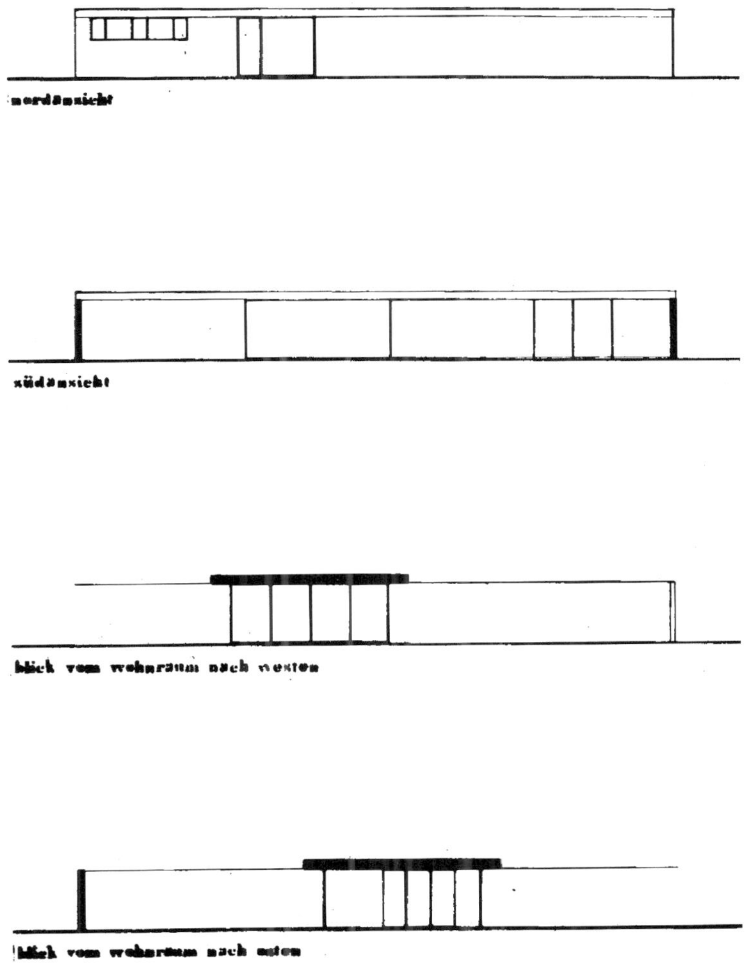

Shlomo Bernstein, one-family house, sections and views, Bauhaus student project, seminar Mies van der Rohe, 1931–1932

Shlomo Bernstein with Nissim Strick, memorial for the Jews murdered in the Treblinka extermination camp, Tel Aviv, circa 1967 (1995)

Left page above:
Shlomo Bernstein, one-family house, perspective, Bauhaus student project, seminar Mies van der Rohe, 1931–1932

Left page below:
Shlomo Bernstein, apartment building, Tel Aviv, circa 1935, front view. Photo: M.W. 1990

Shmuel Mestechkin

1908 Vasilkov – 2004 Tel Aviv

At the age of fifteen, Shmuel Mestechkin left Vasilkov, the Ukrainian city where he was born on October 25, 1908, and went to Palestine in the Third Aliya together with his family – all of whom were dedicated Zionists and Socialists. He first attended the vocational school Shearei-Torah in Tel Aviv. In keeping with family tradition, he was also politically active during his school years and was one of the co-founders of the youth workers' movement Ha'noar-Ha'oved in 1924. Afterward he joined the Ben Shemen Youth Village.[1]
Following the advice of Siegfried Lehmann, the former Berlin doctor who was the founder and director of the Youth Village, Mestechkin went to the Bauhaus in Dessau to further develop his artistic talents. He studied at the Bauhaus under Mies van der Rohe from 1931 until the institution was closed in Berlin in 1933. Mestechkin returned to Palestine late in 1933 and completed his first years of apprenticeship in Josef Neufeld's office in Tel Aviv.[2]

Starting in 1937, Mestechkin worked in Tel Aviv as an independent architect. His first building was the cultural centre for Kibbutz Ramat Ha'kovesh, ca. 30 km to the northeast. Mestechkin added a roofed pergola to the Bauhaus "flat-roofed building with courtyard" concept, adapting to the region's different climate by providing the maximum amount of shade.
One of his "most interesting buildings", as Mestechkin put it, is the Berl convalescent home, built in 1944 in Kibbutz Naan, ca. 30 km southeast of Tel Aviv.[3] He went on to note that the building was an embodiment of all the principles he learned at the Bauhaus, such as "simplicity and care with regard to proportions and forms of expression". The building has a functional arrangement of space, no ornamentation of any kind, and is adapted to the topography of the site.
Mestechkin's most published buildings are the two "Kiryati" apartment buildings (named for the client) built in Tel Aviv at the end of the 1930s. With their play of volumes, the horizontal lines of the balconies, and the rooftop terraces accessible from the stairwells, the three-storey buildings embody the aesthetic principles of Neues Bauen. Above all, Mestechkin made sure that every room in each apartment had access to a spacious balcony. It was common practice for the new immigrants, who were unaccustomed to the Mediterranean climate, to sleep outdoors.

Mestechkin worked primarily for kibbutzim and usually designed the community buildings. He always felt that it was his duty to take the knowledge conveyed to him by the Bauhaus masters and apply it in Israel. The educational goal of integrating art into life meant, to him, developing the aesthetic forms for life in a community. The social organization of the kibbutz necessitated its own unique spatial design. Mestechkin concerned himself chiefly with this political and architectonic task and it became his life's work, out of "conviction and to honour the kibbutz movement and its comrades".[4]

For over forty years after 1943, Mestechkin was the most influential architect and planner for all the kibbutzim founded by the great Zionist-Socialist youth federation Ha'shomer Ha'tzair.[5] Under his supervision, settlements, dining halls, cultural centres, schools, housing and working quarters were built in most of the organization's kibbutzim. Yet Mestechkin also felt morally obliged to contribute to the building of the country independently, apart from the Ha'shomer Ha'tzair movement. By mutual agreement with the technical division of Ha'shomer Ha'tzair, he was able to construct buildings in the vicinity of the Dead Sea, at the University of Jerusalem in Givat-Ram, and at Kibbutz Sde Boker – the collective in southern Israel where David Ben-Gurion and his wife Pola settled in 1953, and where they were buried. Mestechkin was among the first architects invited to build in these territories newly established after 1948.

An active member of the Association of Engineers and Architects in Israel (AEAI), Mestechkin became the association's chairman from 1959 to 1963, and received its honorary title declaring him first among architects in 1980.[6]

Shmuel Mestechkin continued to work as an independent architect until an advanced age. After the early death of his son Yosi (1942–2001), with whom he had worked since the 1970s, Mestechkin retired. Three years later, on June 2, 2004, he died at the age of ninety-six in Tel Aviv.

Throughout my research, which began in 1984, I remained in contact with Shmuel Mestechkin and his companion Didi. For the material and the information I am very grateful to both.

1 See biography of Fritz Kornberg.
2 See biography of Josef Neufeld.
3 Named for Berl Katzenelson, the founder and leader of the Israeli workers' party Beit Berl. See biography of Jochanan Ratner.
4 From a letter to the author in July 1990.
5 See biography of Jacob Pinkerfeld, note 1.
6 "Yakir zibur ha'adrichalim mispar echad".

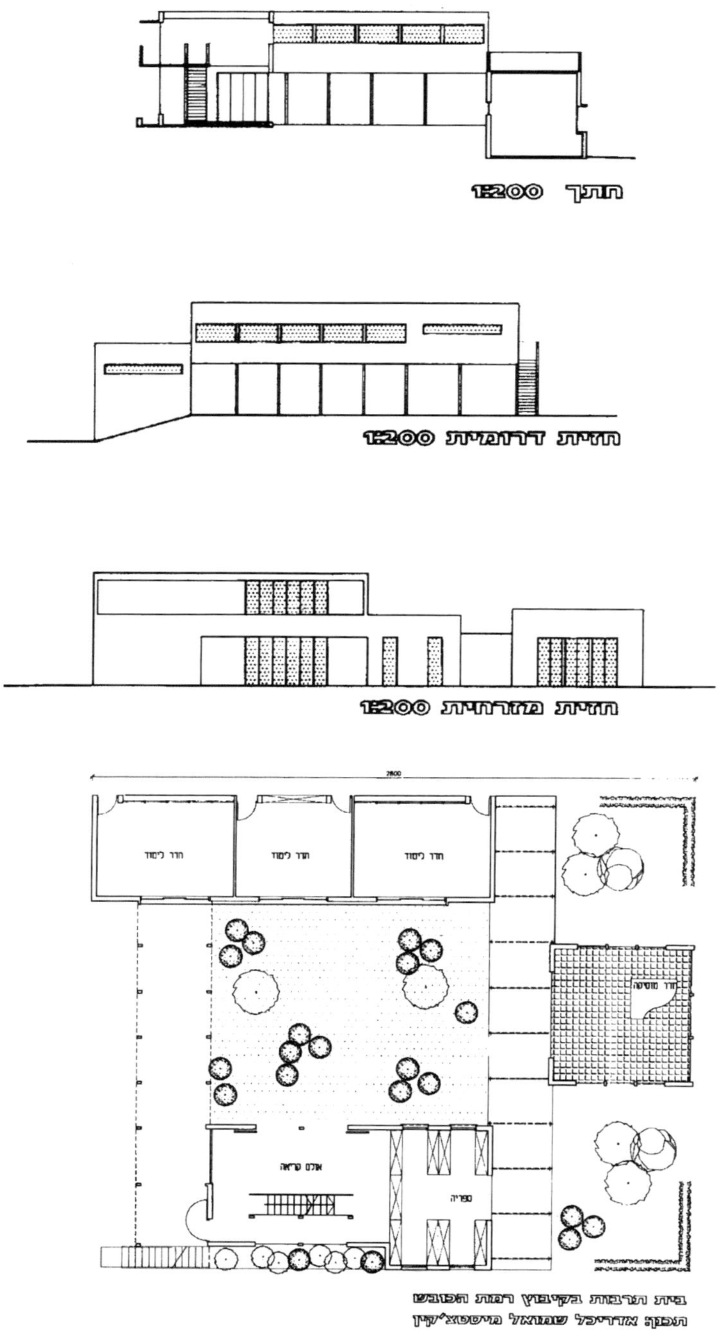

Left page:
Shmuel Mestechkin, cultural centre, Kibbutz Ramat Ha'kovesh, 1937, ground-floor plan, section, elevations

Right page above:
Shmuel Mestechkin, dining hall, Kibbutz Naan, 1937, ground-floor plan

Right page below:
Shmuel Mestechkin, dining hall, Kibbutz Naan, 1937, photo taken during construction, wooden roof

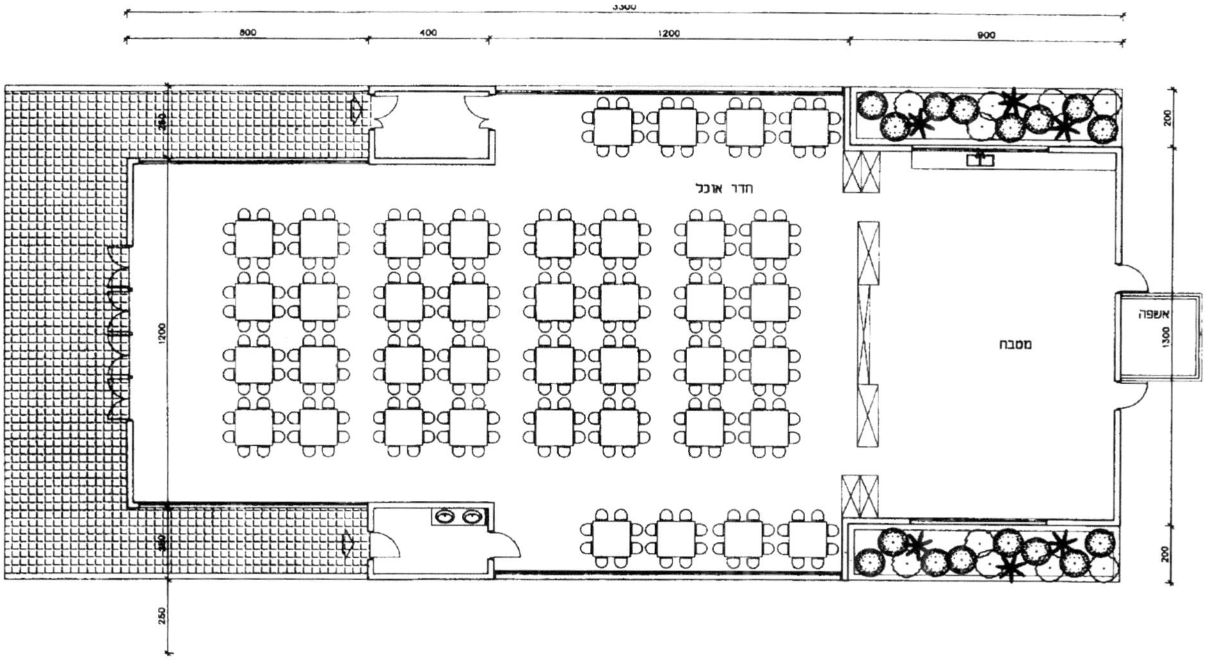
3300
800
400
1200
900
חדר אוכל
מטבח
אשפה
200
1300
1200
250

Shmuel Mestechkin

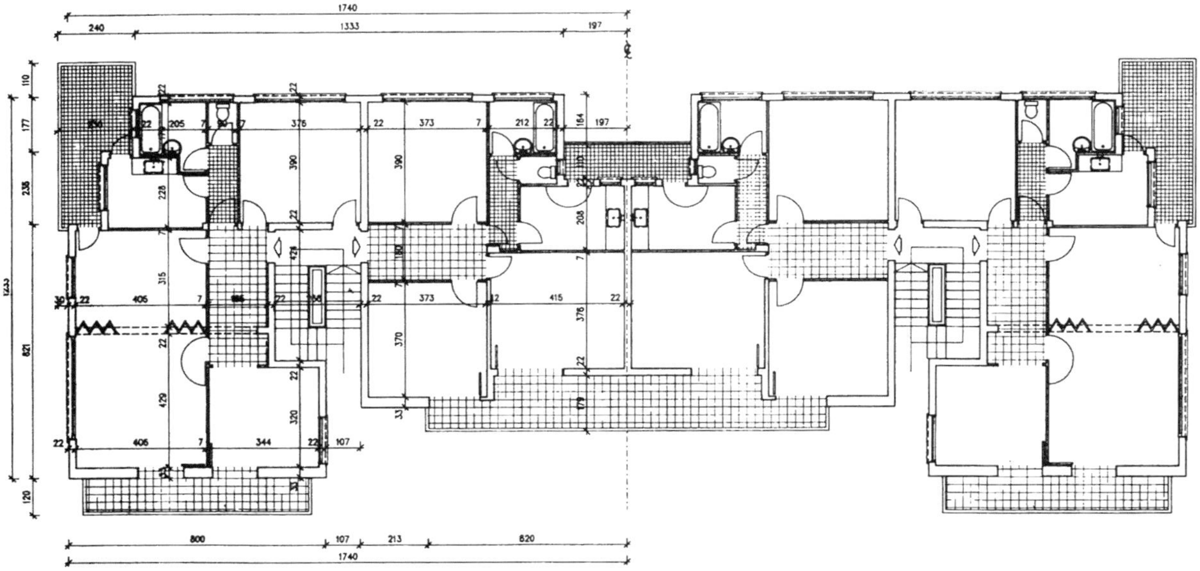

Shmuel Mestechkin, Kiryati apartment building, Tel Aviv, 1939, floor plan

Shmuel Mestechkin, Kiryati apartment building, Tel Aviv, 1939, view from the street

Shmuel Mestechkin, "Young Workers" building, Jerusalem, 1938–1939

Shmuel Mestechkin, "Young Workers" building, Tel Aviv, 1941

Shmuel Mestechkin, "Young Workers" building, Haifa, 1944–1945

M. Weinraub & Al Mansfeld

Munio Gitai (Weinraub)
1909 Szumlany – 1970 Haifa

After establishing a partnership in 1937, the two principals of M. Weinraub & Al Mansfeld Architects worked together for twenty-two years.[1] By the late 1940s their Haifa office was one of the most renowned in the country, its architecture synonymous with high quality. Young architects eagerly sought positions there, especially since both architects taught in the architecture department of the Technion in Haifa as of 1949 – Munio Weinraub as professor of interior design and Alfred Mansfeld as professor of design.

Munio Weinraub was born on March 6, 1909, in Szumlany, Poland. From 1923 to 1927 he learned the carpenter's trade in a Zionist youth organization. Since he particularly enjoyed wood detailing and furniture design, he decided to attend the Bauhaus in Dessau and took courses there during the summer semesters of 1930 and 1932. In between, Weinraub worked in Mies van der Rohe's Berlin office. He often recounted those experiences for his students during his classes.
After the Nazis came to power, Weinraub fled Germany, reaching Palestine via Switzerland in 1934 and settling in the port city of Haifa. There he met the young architect Alfred Mansfeld, who had just completed his education in Paris after being forced to break off his studies at the Technische Hochschule Charlottenburg in 1933.[2] The two soon decided to open an office together.

During their years of partnership, Weinraub and Mansfeld built many buildings of different kinds, both private and public – one-family houses, settlement buildings, factories and administration buildings – and all their architecture was clear, functional and well thought-out. Their office also tirelessly entered competitions and often met with success. In 1959 Munio Weinraub and Alfred Mansfeld dissolved their partnership. Both established their own offices and went their own ways. Munio Gitai died on September 24, 1970, at the age of sixty-one, shortly after he had Hebraised his family name.
Early in 1994 a congress on the International Style in architecture took place in Tel Aviv. For this event, an exhibition of the works of Munio Gitai titled "Munio Weinraub-Gitai. Building for a Working Society" was shown in Jerusalem's Israel Museum.[3]

Alfred Mansfeld
1912 St. Petersburg – 2004 Haifa

Alfred Mansfeld was born in St. Petersburg on March 3, 1912. The family moved to Germany in 1922 in search of work. In 1931 Mansfeld began studies in architecture at the Technische Hochschule Charlottenburg in Berlin. Two years later, when political power in Germany changed hands, Mansfeld became an "undesirable" and left the country to continue his studies in Paris at the Ecole Spéciale d'Architecture under Auguste Perret (1874–1954).[4] Mansfeld received his diploma in 1935 and went to Haifa, where he soon met Munio Weinraub. The two entered into a partnership that would last for twenty-two years.

The buildings of that era, such as the functional and unornamented union building in Haifa (1947) or the Shalon residence on Mount Carmel, with its flat roof and pergola, are not only to be classified as Modern. The influence of August Perret's architecture is clear in Haifa's cold storage plant (1946), a skeleton-frame structure with concrete walls whose ventilation holes appear to be decorative elements. Perret, the first to use reinforced concrete in buildings, often used iron construction with concrete-fill walls, for example in the Paris College of Music (1928), or decorated his buildings, such as the famous residence at 25 Rue Franklin in Paris, with flower-patterned faience.
One has the impression that Weinraub and Mansfeld were searching for a vernacular architecture in their centrally located housing development at Mount Carmel. The terraced arrangement of the two-storey apartment buildings, whose tile roofs are slightly pitched, follows the topography. To capture the cooling breezes, each apartment's long, capacious balcony is accessible from every room.
In later years Alfred Mansfeld increasingly worked with geometric forms that were determined by the functions of the respective buildings. He regarded the Israel Museum in Jerusalem, which he realized 1959–1965 together with the interior designer Dora Gad, as a successful example of this.[5] The complex consists of cubes of different sizes, arranged as required on a grid and adapted to the topography of the hill. Mansfeld's idea was that if the museum was expanded, the basic form would be preserved.[6]

Mansfeld achieved great fame and was often invited to participate in international competitions. In 1966 he was honoured with the golden plaque of the Bund Deutscher Architekten (BDA). After he was elected a member of the Berlin Academy of Arts in 1976, he regularly attended the biannual general meetings. In the winter of 1994, an exhibition of Manfeld's works entitled "Al Mansfeld: Private and Public Structures" was shown at the Israel Museum in Jerusalem.
In 2002 the Israeli Architects Association held a celebration in honour of Mansfeld's ninetieth birthday. Alfred Mansfeld died at the age of ninety-two on March 15, 2004, in Haifa. The Haifa weekly magazine *Kol Bo* then published a special issue in Mansfeld's honour titled "Man of the Cube". It presents twenty of his works in words and pictures.[7]

M. Weinraub & Al Mansfeld

I am very grateful to Al Mansfeld, who was my professor at the Technion, for the material and information. After I graduated, we met often over the years, in Haifa or in Berlin, until his death.

1 In Hebrew alphabetical order, the letter "W" (vav) comes before the letter "M" (mem).
2 See biography of Alfred Mansfeld.
3 Catalogue of the exhibition: Ingersoll 1994.
4 See: Warhaftig 2005, biography of Mansfeld, Al.
5 See brief biography of Dora Gad (Goldberg).
6 Alfred Mansfeld, "Designing for Growth and Change with Open-ended Cumulative Systems. Buildings and Projects by Al. Mansfeld, Technion Haifa 1976" in: *Bauwelt* 11/1997, p. 490.
7 *Kol Bo*, Haifa, March 26, 2004.

Left page:
M. Weinraub & Al Mansfeld, the central synagogue of Haifa, 1937, partial view, entrance

M. Weinraub & Al Mansfeld, Feitelberg residence, Kfar Shmaryahu, 1939

M. Weinraub & Al Mansfeld, Gottlieb residence, Haifa, Mount Carmel, 1941

Left page above:
M. Weinraub & Al Mansfeld, cold storage building, Haifa, 1946

Left page below:
M. Weinraub & Al Mansfeld, union building, Haifa, 1947

Right page above:
M. Weinraub & Al Mansfeld, Shalon residence, Haifa, Mount Carmel, 1947

Right page below:
Mr. Weinraub & Al Mansfeld, housing development, Haifa, Mount Carmel, 1949

The Persecuted

Kurt Reinsch, Mount Carmel overlooking the Mediterranean Sea, Haifa, 1930s, oil painting

Oskar Kaufmann

1873 Uj Szent Anna – 1956 Budapest

"Artistry in Theatre Building. A New Work by Oskar Kaufmann" — this was the headline on a leaflet distributed in January 1927 at the ceremonious opening of the Renaissance Theater. The text continued, "Berlin again has a new theatre worthy of mention. And again its creator is Oskar Kaufmann, whom the imperial capital can already thank for six theatres of noble artistic stature. Kaufmann began with the Hebbel Theater – now, under the direction of Victor Barnowsky, known as the Theater in Königgrätzer Strasse – whose exquisite, wood-panelled, dramatically accentuated space is virtually unsurpassed in its formal solemnity by any other modern stage. After the Hebbel Theater he built the mighty Volksbühne, whose interior architectonic wood-toned elegance has no peer. Just a few years later he came out in a lighter vein with the 'Komödie', etc. And each of these theatre buildings bears its individual stamp. Whoever someday records the history of the city of Berlin will have to erect a monument to the genius of this artistically full-blooded, imaginatively gifted theatre architect."[1]

By chance, Kaufmann happened to meet the essayist and journalist Max Schroeder (1900–1958), a member of the circle around the Berlin Volksbühne, almost thirty years later, in June 1956, in Kaufmann's former hometown of Budapest. The architect was extremely eager to learn something about the postwar fate of his theatres in Berlin and received the following report from his visitor: "The Hebbel Theater, in the midst of ruins, is itself undamaged; the Cinema at Nollendorfplatz is now unrecognizable. The Volksbühne has been rebuilt." Schroeder then asked, "Weren't you invited to the dedication of the Volksbühne?" Kaufmann replied, "They probably know nothing about me anymore." And Schroeder continued, "The Komödie is still standing, the most beautiful theatre in the West; the Renaissance Theater also has been preserved; the Theater am Kurfürstendamm has been rebuilt quite plainly; I haven't seen the Krolloper." Kaufmann responded, "After what went on there, the Krolloper should not be rebuilt. I no longer care for it."[2] Three months after this encounter, Kaufmann died in Budapest on September 6, 1956.

Oskar Kaufmann was born on February 2, 1873, in Uj Szent Anna in Hungary.[3] Musically gifted, he was supposed to become a pianist and commenced his studies at the Budapest Conservatory. But Kaufmann's interest in architecture soon brought him to Karlsruhe, where he graduated from the Grossherzogliche Badische Technische Hochschule in 1899. During his five years as a student, Kaufmann became thoroughly familiar with that classical city, which had been designed by Johann Jakob Friedrich Weinbrenner (1766–1826).

Kaufmann returned briefly to Budapest in 1903 to relinquish the Jewish religion and convert to Protestantism. It was only under this condition that he could marry Emma Barbara Cecilie Valburga Gönner, the daughter of the mayor of Baden-Baden. Kaufmann and his wife then moved to Berlin, where he practised for thirty years and, it is obvious, transferred his musicality to his buildings.

Kaufmann's first work, a bedroom display for the Wertheim department store in 1906, launched him into

the field of theatre-building, starting with the Hebbel Theater in 1907. It did not take long for his fame to spread far beyond Berlin. In 1909 he built the Stadttheater and Museum in Bremerhaven, in 1913 the Neues Stadttheater in Vienna, and in 1927 the Neues Schauspielhaus in Königsberg (Kaliningrad). In both his theatres and his many villas in Berlin-Grunewald, Kaufmann designed every detail of the interiors, down to the door handles. His works in all their variety were photographed, described and acclaimed in books, architectural journals and even in the tabloids.[4]
Kaufmann's close colleague – and after 1911 his official partner – was Eugen Stolzer.[5] In addition to Stolzer, his staff from the period 1907 to 1927 consisted of six architects, including Heinz Becherer, Walter Böckmann and Arthur Menge; nine sculptors, including Hermann Feuerhahn, Professor Anton Hanak, Rudolf Paul Henning and Georg Leschnitzer; and eleven painters, including Josef Bato, Professor Willy Jäckel, Lene Kaiser-Schneider and Professor Hans Meid.[6] Oskar Kaufmann was a member of the Deutscher Werkbund (DWB) and the Architekten-und Ingenieur-Verein zu Berlin (AIV) until 1933. When the Nazis came to power, Kaufmann and Stolzer were forced to liquidate their practice and flee. They soon found their way by separate paths to Palestine, where they again met and were able to continue to collaborate from time to time.

In Berlin, Kaufmann and his wife had lived in a sumptuous apartment on Neue Ansbacher Strasse 9 in the Schöneberg district. In Tel Aviv, they were able to sublet one room in an apartment. The theatre architect from Germany was well known in Palestine and soon was commissioned to build the first Hebrew theatre, for the Jewish city of Tel Aviv was intended to grow into the music and theatre capital of Palestine. The arrival of members of the Habima theatre group late in the 1920s had provided the reason to build a stage.[7] The job had been proposed to the two prominent Berlin architects Erich Mendelsohn and Oskar Kaufmann even as they were still in the process of fleeing Germany. In 1934 the decision was made to give Kaufmann the commission to build the Habima Theater.[8]

Assessing Kaufmann's architectural language before 1933, one is struck by the powerful forms he uses. His vocabulary corresponds to Jugendstil, but is simultaneously expressive, monumental, and above all theatrical. Kaufmann had a predilection for curving lines and the colour of old roses, and used costly materials modelled on the Baroque style of the seventeenth and eighteenth centuries for his interiors. Kaufmann worked closely with directors and actors. To adequately execute his many-faceted ideas, he employed not only architects, but also many sculptors and painters. The experience of a theatre visit in Berlin was doubtless memorably engraved with the exterior and interior radiance of his buildings. Indeed, the proverbial "golden twenties" would be virtually unimaginable without his contribution to the field of theatre design.

By comparison, the mood at the time in Palestine was anything but 'radiant'. The influx of political refugees from Europe aroused outrage in the Arab population. There also was a continual shortage of apartments and high unemployment. So Kaufmann's design for a complex of buildings that would include a town hall, museum, library and theatre as well as an open plaza for 25,000 people was sacrificed to the prevailing political and economic circumstances. After many proposed changes, all that remained was the design for a 1300-seat theatre. The cornerstone for the Habima Theater was laid in June 1935. But it was not until ten years later that the Habima group staged its first production in the still-unfinished building.

By then Kaufmann no longer lived in Palestine. Kaufmann's Tel Aviv theatre resembled the Berlin Volksbühne (1913–14) in appearance, though it was more modest in form. Six columns originally stood in a semicircle at the entrance to both theatres; today in Tel Aviv, the columns are visible behind a glass wall. Kaufmann left behind two works in Haifa: the 'subdued' expressively designed Cinema Ora (light) in the city centre, and the understated rose-colored Hyam residence on Mount Carmel. In Tel Aviv he was also able to erect a three-storey apartment building, with a rooftop pergola, that features rounded, outwardly curving balconies and windows. Two projecting exterior staircases emphasize the symmetry of the façade and seem to form the impressive entrance to a stage. This apartment building was possibly the last theatrical work by Oskar Kaufmann.

When World War II broke out in 1939, commissions became few. Kaufmann, accompanied by his ailing wife, went via Bucharest to Budapest, where he was again subject to persecution. In 1948, when he was seventy-five years old, Kaufmann was rehabilitated by the Hungarian Ministry of Culture and declared a "distinguished artist".[9]

For some of the information and material, I am very grateful to Oskar Kaufmann's granddaughter Julika Müller and to his son-in-law Mr. Götz (Berlin, 1986–87).

1 A chronological listing of Kaufmann's theatres up to 1927: Hebbel Theater, Berlin 1907; Stadttheater Bremerhaven 1909; Kinotheater Nollendorfplatz, Berlin 1912–13; Die Volksbühne, Berlin 1913–14; Neues Stadttheater, Vienna, 1913–14; Oper am Platz der Republik (Kroll), Berlin, 1923; Theater am Kurfürstendamm, Berlin, 1923; Die Komödie, Berlin, 1924; Renaissance Theater, Berlin, 1926; Die Tribüne, Berlin, 1926; Neues Schauspielhaus, Königsberg i. Pr. (Kaliningrad), 1927. Since 1987, theatregoers can view a standing exhibition at the Hebbel Theater, curated by Myra Warhaftig, about "The Architecture of Oskar Kaufmann (1873–1956)". The Hebbel Theater is now known as HAU I.
2 After the Reichstag fire in February 1933, Hitler convened the Reichstag at the Krolloper.
3 Today, the village lies in Romania.
4 Bab 1919; Bie 1928; Osborn 1928 (reprint 1996).
5 See biography of Eugen Stolzer.
6 See their biographies in Osborn reprint. For Leschnitzer, Georg see: Warhaftig 2005.
7 The Hebrew theatre troupe Habima (the stage) was founded in Moscow in 1916. During a tour through the USA and Europe in 1927, the group disbanded. A few in the group remained in New York, the rest went to Palestine, determined to settle in Tel Aviv and to continue to perform there.
8 Edina Meyer, "Oskar Kaufmann's 'Habima'-Theater in Tel Aviv" in: *Architektur, Stadt und Politik*, eds. Burkhard Bergius, Janos Frecot, Dieter Radicke, Gießen 1979, pp. 135–144.
9 Recent publications that include evaluations of Kaufmann's architectural style can be found in: Baudenkmale 1993; Mezger-Smok 1994, pp. 170–173; Berents 1998; Hansen 2001; Recknagel 2002; Warhaftig 2005.

Excerpt from newspaper article "New Ways of Building Theatres" by Oskar Kaufmann, Berlin 1924

Left page above:
Oskar Kaufmann, Hebbel Theater, Berlin, 1907, view from the street

Left page below:
Oskar Kaufmann, Renaissance Theater, Berlin, 1926, main entrance

Right page:
Oskar Kaufmann, Die Komödie, Berlin, 1924, main entrance

Oskar Kaufmann, B. Bechstein Company salesroom, Berlin, 1926

Oskar Kaufmann, Die Volksbühne, Berlin, 1913–1914, main entrance

FÜNFZEHN JAHRE BERLINER VOLKSBÜHNENHAUS

Haupteingangstür
(Bildhauer: Georg Sieburg)

Das Volksbühnen-Haus (Architekt: Oscar Kaufmann)

Relief am Proszenium
(Bildhauer: Franz Metzner)

Am 14. September jährt sich zum fünfzehnten Male der Tag, an dem der Grundstein zu jenem Haus der Berliner Volksbühne gelegt wurde, das sich heute stolz und schön am Bülowplatz als monumentales Zeugnis für die Kraft der Berliner Volksbühnenbewegung erhebt. Die Errichtung dieses prächtigen Theaters für 2000 Menschen bedeutete in Wahrheit einen Markstein auf dem Wege zu einer neuen Volkskunst. Zum erstenmal wurde hier der Versuch gemacht, ein Thater zu bauen, dessen Mittel nicht von einem kapitalkräftigen Unternehmer und nicht von einer öffentlichen Einrichtung bereitgestellt, sondern von einer Organisation kunstfreudiger Theaterbesucher aus der werktätigen Bevölkerung aufgebracht wurden. Zum erstenmal galt es die Errichtung eines Theaters, dessen Spielplan, dessen Programm ganz nach dem freien Willen dieser Organisation gestaltet werden sollte.

Es war ein herrlicher Herbsttag, an dem die Grundsteinlegung vor sich ging. Tausende hatten sich zu dem feierlichen Akt eingefunden. Die hohen Behörden, voll Mißtrauen gegen die Volksbühne mit ihren demokratischen Prinzipien und ihren sozialen Tendenzen, waren freilich sehr dürftig vertreten. Kaum, daß die Stadt Berlin einen Vertreter entsandt hatte. Aber das tat der gehobenen Stimmung der Versammelten keinen Abbruch. Treffliche Reden wurden gehalten: von dem Vorsitzenden der Neuen Freien Volksbühne, Georg Springer, dem Vertreter der „alten Freien", Conr. Schmidt, von Bruno Wille und anderen. Gesangsvorträge der „Typographia" umrahmten den Festakt.

15 Jahre sind seit jener Grundsteinlegung vergangen. Gestützt auf ihr eigenes Theater, nahm die Berliner Volksbühnenbewegung einen vorher kaum geahnten Aufschwung. Zählte der Verein Volksbühne, in dem sich inzwischen Freie und Neue Freie Volksbühne zusammenfanden, doch im letzten Jahr mehr als 120 000 Mitglieder. Um diesen Mitgliedern jährlich je 12 Vorstellungen, wie es den Traditionen des Vereins entspricht, darbieten zu können, reichen die täglichen Aufführungen des Hauses am Bülowplatz trotz seiner gewaltigen Dimensionen nicht aus. Aufführungen von 4, 5 anderen Bühnen müssen sie ergänzen, wobei bemerkenswert ist, daß es der Volksbühne gelang, durch ihre Beteiligung beim Bau der Oper am Platz der Republik den Mitgliedern auch gute, billige Opernaufführungen zu sichern. Aber die Vorstellungen des Theaters am Bülowplatz stehen doch im Mittelpunkt dessen, was die Volksbühne ihren Mitgliedern bietet. Und viele unvergeßliche Eindrücke wurden den Mitgliedern gerade hier zuteil. Gerade auch das letzte Spieljahr brachte wieder eine Reihe ausgezeichneter Aufführungen; es sei nur an den „Peer Gynt", an Tollers „Hinkemann", an Brechts „Mann ist Mann" und an Shakespeares „Was Ihr wollt" erinnert.

Ohne das eigene Haus am Bülowplatz wäre der Verein Volksbühne sicher nicht imstande, das zu leisten, was er heute seinen Mitgliedern bietet. Ohne diesen Besitz könnte er die Vorstellungen ganz gewiß auch nicht so billig stellen, wie es heute geschieht. Vermittelt er den Mitgliedern doch die Schauspielaufführungen bereits für einen Beitrag von 1,70 Mk., die Opernvorstellungen für 2,20 Mk., eingerechnet einen seit einiger Zeit zur Erhebung gelangenden Zins- und Tilgungszuschlag von 20 Pf. Dabei brauchen die Mitglieder bei keiner Vorstellung Kleiderablage und Programmzettel gesondert zu bezahlen. Die Plätze werden bei den Vorstellungen der Volksbühne bekanntlich ausgelost, weil alle Mitglieder gleiches Recht genießen sollen. — Möge der prächtige Bau am Bülowplatz auch weiterhin dazu beitragen, daß die Berliner Volksbühne einen gesunden Aufschwung nimmt. Und möchten recht viele durch ihren Anschluß an den Verein Volksbühne seine Macht und Möglichkeit zu gedeihlicher Wirksamkeit noch weiterhin verstärken!

Unten (Mitte):
Szenenbild aus Tollers »Hinkemann«, aufgeführt im Volksbühnen-Theater
(Photo-Schmidt, Berlin)

Links:
Grundsteinlegung zum Theater der Volksbühne (14. Sept. 1913)
Georg Springer bringt das Hoch auf die Volkskunst-Bewegung aus

Unten: Szene aus B. Brechts im Volksbühnen-Theater aufgeführten Lustspiel »Mann ist Mann« (Photo-Schmidt, Berlin)

Unten: Szene aus Brieux »Die rote Robe«, aufgeführt im Volksbühnentheater (Photo-Schmidt, Berlin)

"Fifteen years Berlin's Volksbühne Building", newspaper article, Berlin 1929

Oskar Kaufmann, the Stadttheater and Museum in Bremerhaven, 1909, main entrance

Right page above:
Oskar Kaufmann, Habima Theater, Tel Aviv, circa 1938, main entrance

Right page below:
Oskar Kaufmann, Hyam residence, Haifa, Mount Carmel, 1937, main entrance. Photo: M.W. 1986

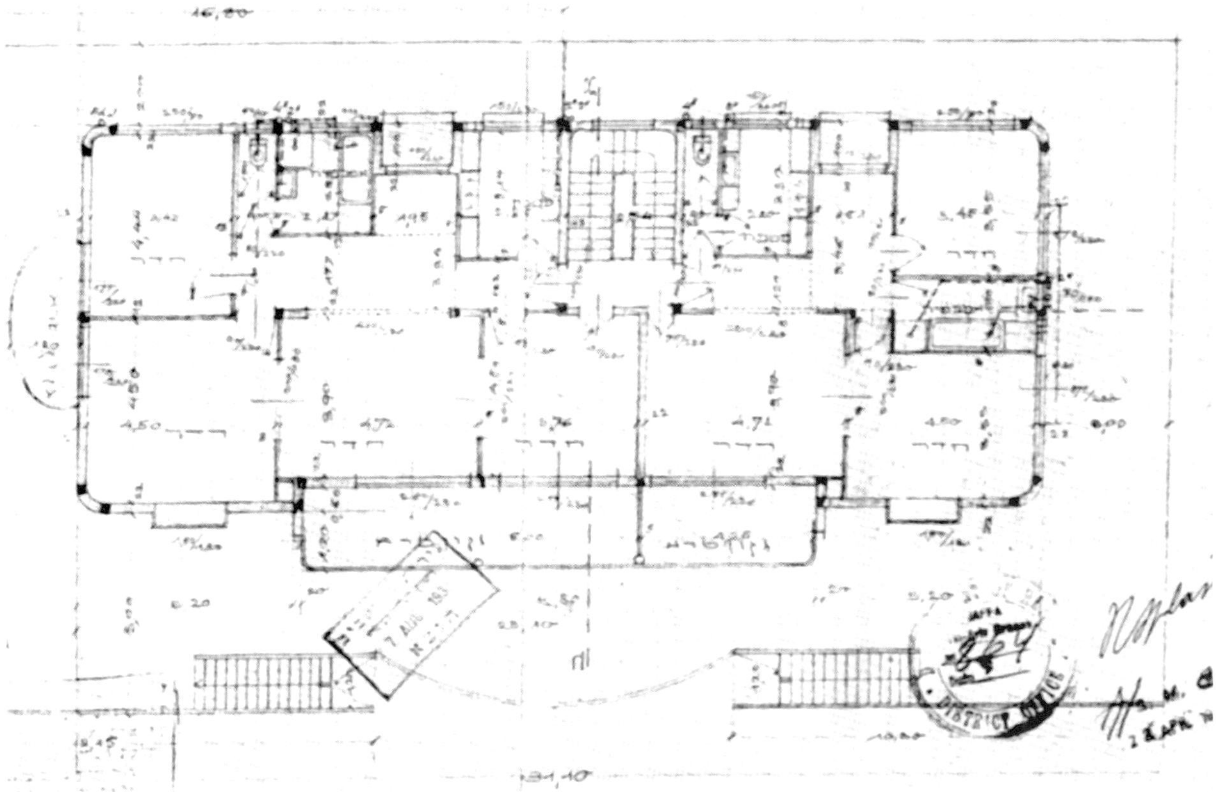

Oskar Kaufmann, apartment building, Tel Aviv, 1935, ground-floor plan

Left page above:
Oskar Kaufmann, Hyam residence, Haifa, Mount Carmel, 1937, view of the garden side, which looks out on the Mediterranean Sea. Photo: M.W. 1986

Left page below:
Oskar Kaufmann, Hyam residence, Haifa, Mount Carmel, 1937, view from garden. Photo: M.W. 1986

Oskar Kaufmann, apartment building, Tel Aviv, 1935, view from a side street. Photo: O.W. 1990

Oskar Kaufmann, apartment building, Tel Aviv, 1935, view from the main street. Photo: O.W. 1990

Oskar Kaufmann

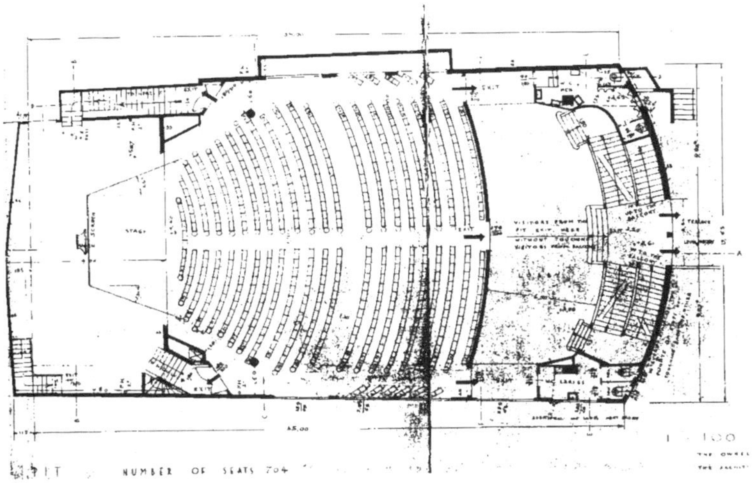

Oskar Kaufmann, Cinema Ora (light), Haifa, circa 1935, ground-floor plan of theatre

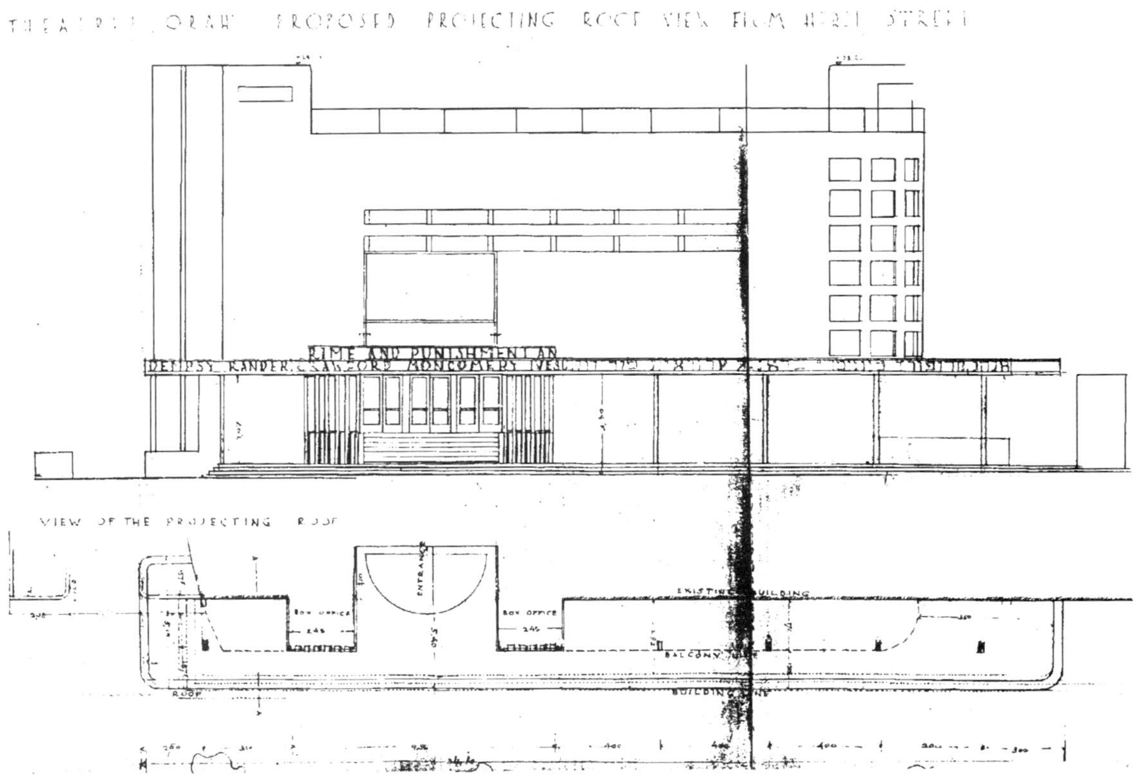

Oskar Kaufmann, Cinema Ora, Haifa, circa 1935, view from the street and proposal for a rooftop viewing platform (drawing)

Oskar Kaufmann, Cinema Ora, Haifa, 1935–1945, view from Herzl Street. Photo: M.W. 1986

Oskar Kaufmann, Cinema Ora, Haifa, main entrance. Photo: M.W. 1986

Eugen Stolzer

1886 Györ – 1958 Rome

Eugen Stolzer, photo in the *Palestine Post*, November 23, 1945

Both shared the same origin, the same profession and a similar fate, but Eugen Stolzer was thirteen years younger than Oskar Kaufmann. The two met in Berlin in 1911 and formed a professional and social relationship that lasted for nearly thirty years. They ran a large architectural office in Berlin before they were driven out of Germany in 1933. In Palestine they later had just a small office, until Kaufmann left the country.
Stolzer was born on May 12, 1886, in Györ, Hungary. As a young man he went to Germany to become an architect. He studied at the Technische Hochschule in Munich, earning his diploma in the summer of 1908. After studying interior design under Professor Friedrich von Thiersch, and gaining professional experience in the office of the theatre builder Max Littman in Munich, Stolzer's pathway into the world of theatre architecture lay open.[1] Before he entered into an official partnership with Oskar Kaufmann, Stolzer worked in Munich, Berlin and Paris. He earned a doctorate at the Technische Hochschule in Munich in 1916, then performed his year of military service as a lieutenant in the Hungarian army. His permanent residence as of 1910, though, was at Münchener Strasse 42 in Berlin-Schöneberg, near his and Kaufmann's joint office.
As an independent architect, Stolzer designed theatres and movie houses almost exclusively. His clients were the leading European theatre directors and stage technicians such as Max Reinhardt (1873–1943); Leopold Jessner (1878–1945), the writer and founder of the Renaissance Theater in Berlin; Ferdinand Bruckner, who was born Theodor Tagger (1891–1958); and André Antoine (1858–1943), the Parisian stage director and founder of the Théâtre Libre, to mention just a few. Stolzer also collaborated on all of Oskar Kaufmann's buildings except the 1907 Hebbel Theater.[2]
Stolzer reported on their experiences together before the National Socialists came to power, his flight and his first years in Palestine: "I was one of the busiest architects in Berlin until the rise of Nazism. My partner, the master architect Oskar Kaufmann, having built the Volksbühne, was listed as a Social Democratic Party candidate for the Reichstag in 1932. That lost us some clients. I could continue to do movie and theatre decoration only under an assumed name. As a Jew, it was made impossible for me to go on working in Berlin. Our clients could not and would not build with Jewish architects because they were afraid. So there was nothing left for me to do but emigrate, leaving behind everything I owned.
I auctioned my art collections and my books at Perls in January 1933. For a library of well over 1000 valuable art books, Propyläen Library and art historical works, I received 1000 Marks; for a bust by Lehmbruck, 50 Marks; for a collection of small Egyptian pieces, 80 Marks, etc. The Hungarian envoys, whose embassy I had built, helped me by providing a passport identifying me as a Roman-Catholic. Despite that, I did not dare go out on the street after April 1, 1933. By early May I could stand it no longer and left Germany with two tiny suitcases, crossing the border at Basel to go to friends in Lugano. From there I went to Palestine on October 15, 1933. In January 1934 I first contracted amoebic dysentery, which kept recurring despite med-

ical treatment and weakened me greatly. I also tolerated the heat poorly, developed rashes and prickly heat. Despite 'splendid' commissions, my modest income did not make it possible for me to regain my health. For many years I literally went hungry."[3]

In Palestine, Stolzer settled in Jerusalem. There, with the architects Meir Rubin and Alexander Friedmann, he won first prize for the Jeshurun Synagogue in 1934.[4] Stolzer designed the prayer hall in semicircular form, which gave it the character of a theatre. The semicircular arrangement of the seating also is unusual. The building, clad in Jerusalem stone, has no ornamentation. Its narrow elongated windows are appropriate to the climate and temper the effect of the harsh sunshine.

Until Oskar Kaufmann left the country in 1939, Stolzer sometimes worked with him, for instance on designs for the Habima Theater, a three-storey apartment building in Tel Aviv, Cinema Ora, and the Hyam residence in Haifa. Beyond this, Stolzer entered competitions and developed plans for several projects in Haifa, Tel Aviv and Jerusalem, but without success. He had to be satisfied with "small odd jobs" until he was able to erect Beit Ha'histadrut (the union building) in Jerusalem in 1950.[5]

Stolzer adapted the ground plan of the six-storey Israeli union building to the curving street. Contrasting elements distinguish the façade, which is faced with Jerusalem stone. Rows of small windows rhythmically contrast with rows of large windows, and a glazed entrance area breaks up the massive expanse of wall. To lend the building a garden atmosphere, Stolzer designed a pergola for the top floor. Whether at ground level or on the roof, the pergola was part of the formal vocabulary of Modern architecture as it developed in Palestine.

After the building was completed in 1957, Stolzer and his wife, the architect Judith Stolzer-Segal, left the country.[6] They had decided to return to Germany and to live near Munich, where he wanted to spend his twilight years. But the first thing Stolzer did was travel to Berlin to see the theatres that he and Oskar Kaufmann had built; a popular daily newspaper commented on the event.[7] A few months later, on December 22, 1958, Eugen Stolzer died unexpectedly during a brief stay in Rome. He was buried there in the Jewish cemetery.

1 Friedrich von Thiersch (1852–1921), one of the most important architects of late historicism in Germany. With Paul Wallot (1841–1912), he built the Reichstag building (1884–1894) in Berlin. Von Thiersch was an associate professor of interior design and perspective at the Technische Hochschule Munich. Max Littmann (1862–1931), renowned specialist in theatre construction in Germany, built the Prinzregenten Theater in Munich (1900–1901) and the Schiller Theater in Berlin (1903–1906), among others.
2 See biography of Oskar Kaufmann.
3 From Eugen Stolzer's unpublished curriculum vitae, which he wrote in Berlin a few months before his death.
4 Jeshurun is the poetic name for Israel. When the synagogue was completed after more than two decades, Eugen Stolzer no longer lived in Israel.
5 See biography of Dov Kuczynski, note 5.
6 See biography of Judith Stolzer-Segal.
7 *Bildzeitung*, Berlin July 4, 1957.

Left page above:
Eugen Stolzer with Meir Rubin and Alexander Friedmann, Jeshurun Synagogue, Jerusalem, 1935.
Photo: M.W. 1986

Left page below:
Eugen Stolzer, Beit Ha'histadrut (union building), Jerusalem, 1950–1957, general view.
Photo: O.W. 1989

Eugen Stolzer, Beit Ha'histadrut (union building), Jerusalem, 1950–1957, view of main entrance.
Photo: O.W. 1989

Josef Rings

1878 Honnef am Rhein – 1957 Honnef am Rhein

Josef Rings's significance for the history of architecture in the Weimar Republic is evidenced by the many articles about his buildings published in various architectural journals between 1906 and the early 1930s. His own writing on urban planning and his connection with the leading companies in the German coal and steel industry, especially Friedrich Krupp A.G. in Essen, also attest to his importance. Yet the housing developments that Rings designed and realized in Essen (1919–1924) became the subject of scholarly research (by Professor Gerhard Fehl of Aachen) only sixty years later.[1]

It would have been virtually impossible to reconstruct an account of Josef Rings's life without the assistance of his son Werner Rings, a journalist from Ascona, Switzerland (1910–1998). The son began late in life to take a closer look at his father's life and work. He donated copies of building plans and projects from his father's estate to the department of architecture at the Technion – Israel Institute of Technology, and wrote a curriculum vitae summarising his father's achievements.[2]

Josef Rings was born on December 20, 1878, in Honnef am Rhein. After several years of practical experience, he studied architecture from 1903–06 at the Technische Hochschule in Darmstadt. From 1907–12 he was an assistant there to Professor Friedrich Pützer in the subjects of ecclesiastical architecture, urban planning and sketching.[3] Rings also worked on city planning and on the designs for administrative buildings, schools, churches and the Darmstadt train station in Professor Pützer's private studio. At the same time (1908–12), Rings taught in Offenbach am Main at technical schools and the school of applied arts (master class). He collaborated on the planning and construction of a model workers' colony at the Hessian State Exposition of 1908.

In 1912 Rings was appointed to head a division of Krupp A.G. in Essen. There he planned and realized housing developments, factories, stores, etc. until 1919.

Then Rings opened a private practice in Essen. He planned and realized large housing estates such as the Essen-Stadtwald Siedlung, the Feldhaushof Siedlung (1919–1921) and the Essen-Kray Siedlung (1919–1923). In addition, he designed and built factory buildings, workshops, coal treatment plants, bridges and traffic installations, as well as the city of Essen's great exhibition and festival hall, which was totally destroyed in World War II.

Rings received awards for his work in fourteen public competitions. He participated by personal invitation in fifteen exhibitions in Germany and abroad, including the exhibitions of architecture, art and urban planning that took place in Brussels (1910), Gothenburg (1923), Vienna (1926), Oldenburg (1928) and London (1929), and the architecture exhibition organized by the Bund Deutscher Architekten (BDA) in Moscow in 1932.

Rings did fundamental research in urban planning; he focused chiefly on the problems caused by the precipitous growth of large modern cities and on the increasingly difficult tasks of routing traffic around and inside the city centres. At the heart of his thinking are the ideas of ribbon development and the structural scheme of the honeycomb system. That is, Rings links the ribbon city idea with the idea of residential districts arrayed in fundamentally hexagonal structures.[4] A monograph on the topic was first published by the

Duisburg Museum in 1927.[5] During his years of exile in Palestine, Rings elaborated his ribbon city plan for Netanya (1942) and Rishon Lezion (1945). He pursued his intensive inquiry into the prerequisites for solving the traffic problems that result from urbanization; his thoughts are recorded in a 1952 manuscript and in scattered notes from 1952–57.[6]

Toward the end of the 1920s, Rings had developed and patented a construction method, described as a "lighting system" that made it possible to bring daylight into the basements and central hallways of large multi-storey buildings all day long. In 1937 he patented a "Ventilation of Buildings" construction system that provided natural air conditioning for buildings in tropical or sub-tropical climates.

Rings was a member of the Bund Deutscher Architekten (BDA) the Freie Deutsche Akademie für Städtebau, the Deutsche Gesellschaft für Bauwesen (DGB), and the Deutscher Werkbund (DWB). In 1933, when Hitler assumed power, Rings turned down an offer of a university professorship in the Third Reich, adding that he was married to a Jewish woman and did not want to change that situation. In June 1934 political conditions obliged Rings to leave Germany and to transfer his field of operations to the British mandate territory of Palestine.

For fourteen years, Rings was a regional planner in various areas of Palestine. He sometimes worked with British urban planning officials, for instance as a city and settlement planner for the Rassco settlement association in Tel Aviv.[7] His task was to create housing plans for middle-class Jewish emigrants from Germany. In the fall of 1937, the cornerstone was laid for a garden community that Rings designed for two hundred unemployed families on the mountain ridge of Carmel near Haifa.[8] The site known then as Kiryat Amal – today Kiryat Tivon – has unusual topographic conditions. Before Rings began to design, he devoted special consideration to how to make the great differences in elevation manageable for the inhabitants. He succeeded in laying out streets with less than a 5.5% grade, and paths with less than a 10.5% grade. He created a stepped arrangement of land parcels, each measuring 20 m × 100–150 m, with up to 15 m of difference in elevation. The public buildings – the community centre, school, kindergarten, administrative buildings, polyclinic, synagogue, department store and small shops – were distributed throughout the site. The placement of routes among the buildings harkened back to the schemes Rings had realized in his Essen housing developments of the 1920s.[9]

Rings returned to Germany early in 1948; he had been appointed professor of urban studies at the Johannes Gutenberg University in Mainz. He taught there, for the reconstruction of destroyed German cities presented new challenges, until the end of 1949. Josef Rings died on August 7, 1957, in Honnef am Rhein, the city of his birth.

1 Gerhard Fehl, "Gartenstadtbebauung oder schematische Reihenhausbebauung? Zum Konflikt um die Bebauungsweise neuer Siedlungen ab 1918, dargestellt am Werk des Essener Architekten Josef Rings" in: *Im Grünen wohnen – im Blauen planen*, ed. by F. Bollerey, G. Fehl, K. Hartmann, Hamburg 1990, pp. 189–227.

2 From a letter to the author, November 7, 1991; Werner Rings also delivered an inventory of the archived works to the Technische Hochschule Darmstadt.

3 Friedrich Pützer (1871–1922) was an architect, urban planner and college professor at the Technische Hochschule Darmstadt.

4 Werner Rings intended to highlight Josef Rings's ribbon city concept in a planned book on the history of the ribbon city.

5 See note 2.

6 Archive Josef Rings at the Technion – Israel Institute of Technology.

7 Rassco – the Rural and Suburban Settlement Company Ltd. – was founded in 1934 with the aim of building agricultural and urban developments for immigrants who had their own means.

8 Josef Rings, "Town Planning Schemes for Kiryat Amal" in: *Habinyan Bamisrah Hakarov*, Tel Aviv August 1937, pp. 26–27; Patishi 1983.

9 Publications: Josef Rings, *Siedlungsreform*, Essen 1923; Josef Rings in: *Wasmuths Monatshefte für Baukunst*, Berlin 1925, pp. 168–172; Herrmann Ehlgötz (ed.), *Essen*, Berlin 1925, pp. 39, 210; "Siedlungen des Architekten Josef Rings" in: *Der Neubau* 6/1928, pp. 65–74.

Josef Rings, Eyhof housing estate, Essen-Stadtwald, 1924

Josef Rings, exhibition and festival hall, Essen, 1927

Josef Rings, Altenessen miners' housing, 1923, view into the curving street

Josef Rings, the first houses, Kiryat Amal, 1938

Josef Rings, building scheme for Kiryat Amal, 1937: a street “with a view” (right) instead of “a view of empty space” (left)

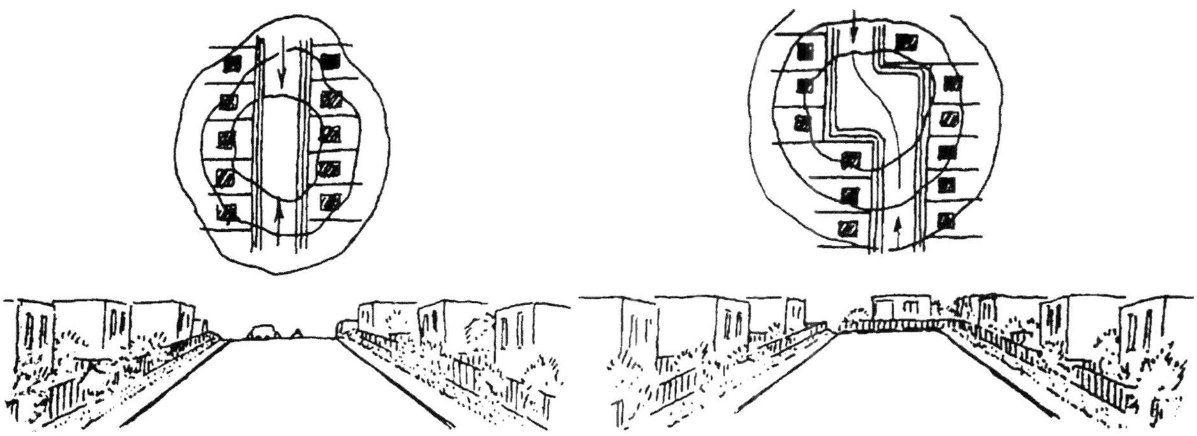

Alexander Klein

1879 Odessa – 1961 New York

Alexander Klein was one of the first, last and most consistent advocates of functionalism. Virtually no other architect dealt so intensively and seriously with the functional arrangement of rooms in apartments and with spatial economy in housing. He is credited with the careful rendering and investigation of countless types of floor plans in order to arrive at optimal solutions, both architectonic and financial. No one else dealt so thoroughly with the question of buildings and climate. And Klein was better than anyone else at translating the results of his research directly into practice.
From 1922 to 1925 Klein erected a row of buildings in the Classic style, which may best be described as semi-detached villas, on Ballenstedter Strasse in Berlin-Wilmersdorf. For about ten years, until he was forced to flee Germany, he created a wealth of designs embodying his insights for residential projects. These were realized as single apartment buildings in the Berlin districts of Wilmersdorf, Neukölln, Dahlem and Zehlendorf, and as a large housing estate in Bad Dürrenberg.

Alexander Klein was born into a prosperous Jewish family in Odessa on June 17, 1879. After secondary school he went to St. Petersburg and studied civil engineering, receiving his diploma in 1904. He entered an architecture competition as a student and won first prize. Two years later, also in St. Petersburg, he and Leonid Iljin and Alexander Rosenberg won a competition to build the Peter the Great Municipal Hospital, which he was then able to build. In 1913 Klein was named St. Petersburg's building commissioner, and in this capacity he erected hospitals, public buildings and workers' housing in various Russian locations. As of 1915 he also headed the architecture department at the Petersburg Polytechnic. In 1917 Klein went to the Caucasus, where he won first prize in a competition to design a public park in the town of Kislovodska. But he could not oversee its completion, for pogroms perpetrated against Russian Jews following the 1917 November Revolution forced him to leave the country.

At the construction site,
from left to right: Dov Patischi,
Alexander Klein,
Dr. Alexander Pinthus

And so in 1920, Klein arrived in Berlin with his wife and son. There he continued to participate in national and international competitions, in the process discovering his interest in creating floor plans for small flats. Rethinking the standard contemporary apartment plans with their dark central foyers and non-functional use of space, Klein began to develop designs that would be functional in relation to household tasks.[1] He started from two basic functional premises. First, his flats had no hallways: instead of the typical dark corridor, a large bright entrance hall adjoins the living room. Second, his spatial plan clearly divides all the rooms into two groups: the living room, dining room and kitchen form one group, the bedrooms, bath and closet/storeroom the other.
After painstaking research, Klein reached the conclusion that each type of floor plan should have "a certain depth and frontage corresponding to its usable floor space". In calculating the dimensions, the determining factor should not be the development costs but rather "the number of beds and the resulting cost per bed".[2] The results of his investigations into building depth as related to frontage and the resulting usable space and number of beds were published in a number of leading professional journals.[3]
In 1928 Klein published his "floor plans for flats without hallways".[4] The dining and living rooms were clearly separated from the bedroom group, yet all rooms could be reached by the shortest of paths. Klein was soon able to realize this type of floor plan at the Gagfah exhibition, with eighteen flats in three two-storey buildings in Berlin-Zehlendorf.[5] In 1930 Klein built a larger, more varied selection of apartments in several sizes in the large housing development at Bad Dürrenberg near Leipzig, one of the most significant residential projects of that era.[6] Klein's precise planning of construction and details for the five hundred apartments reduced the production cost, which had a corresponding effect on the rent.
When the National Socialists came to power, Klein, who was a member of the Bund Deutscher Architekten (BDA) and the Architekten-und Ingenieur-Verein (AIV), was expelled from the Reich Chamber of Culture. He was forced to suspend his professional activities and postpone publication of an encyclopaedia of city planning and residential construction. He did manage to publish the first volume in 1934: *Das Einfamilienhaus – Südtyp* (The One-Family House – Southern Type); all the other volumes remained in manuscript.[7]

Under persecution, Klein first went with his family to Paris. Then, at the invitation of the Jewish National Fund, he went to Palestine as a planning advisor for Keren Kayemet Leisrael (KKL).[8] For the next twenty-five years, Klein, along with the Frankfurt architect Richard Kauffmann, was one of the most influential protagonists in the country's urban housing and settlement programmes.[9] He was a professor in the department of architecture at the Technion in Haifa, the director of the Institute for Urban Planning and a member of the Technion Senate. In 1943 he founded Technion's Research Institute for Urban Planning and Housing and served as its director. Klein published his scholarly research in Hebrew journals of architecture after 1936. He gained new insights as he attempted to apply his Weimar-era thoughts about economical and spatially functional floor plans to the conditions in Eretz Israel.
Klein now focused not only on apartment floor plans, but also broadened his investigations to include the building's exterior design in relation to climatic conditions. His informative 1942 paper on "The Influence of Climate on the Organic Design of Ground Plan and Exterior" relates to his personal history. Since Klein had lived first in a cold climate, then a temperate one, and finally in a subtropical climate, he was able to base his comparisons on first-hand experience.[10]

Klein also continued to practise professionally. He designed both the garden city of Kiryat Bialik in 1936 and the Tivon garden estate in 1940. In 1953 the cornerstone was laid for the new Technion campus in Haifa that he planned.

In post-war Germany, it was the city of Stuttgart that remembered Klein and his work. He was awarded an honorary doctorate from the Technische Hochschule there in 1954. He was supposed to take part in Interbau, the international building exhibition in Berlin (1957), with an apartment building whose type of ground plan harkened back to the works of his Weimar Republic years. For still unknown reasons, this project was not realized.
In 1960 Klein and his family emigrated for the third time. They went to New York, where he died one year later, on November 15, 1961. Klein had passed on his practical experience in designing residential floor plans to his students at the Technion in Haifa (I was one of them). He lectured sometimes in Russian and sometimes in German, while we students for the most part understood only Hebrew. Jochanan Elon (Eichenbaum) (1914–1994), an urban planner who was Klein's assistant, translated his lectures into Hebrew for us. We sensed that Klein was a highly qualified architect and urban planner, and held him in high esteem, though he never told us anything about his professional achievements in Germany. But we students took a more sceptical look when Klein began to teach us how to arrange the furniture in various rooms so that the sunlight would not create shadows on the floor.

1 At first, Alexander Klein's research was funded by the Reichsforschungsgesellschaft für Wirtschaftlichkeit im Bau- und Wohnungswesen e.V. (Imperial Research Society for Economy in Building and Housing), founded in 1927. Later he established his own small research institute, which he maintained, along with his architectural practice, until 1933.
2 Alexander Klein, "Wirtschaftliche Grundrißbildung und Raumgestaltung" in: *Wasmuths Monatshefte für Baukunst* 10/1927, p. 539.
3 Alexander Klein, "Versuch eines graphischen Verfahrens zur Bewertung von Kleinwohnungsgrundrissen" in: *Wasmuths Monatshefte für Baukunst* 7/1927, pp. 296–298; *Zentralblatt der Bauverwaltung* 34 & 35/1928; *Baugilde* 22/1927; *Städtebau* 1/1928; *Wasmuths Monatshefte für Baukunst* 11 & 12/1931.
4 Alexander Klein, "Flurlose Wohnungen" in: *Wasmuths Monatshefte für Baukunst* 10/1928, pp. 454–461. An apartment without a hallway is still inadmissible in plans for subsidized housing today.
5 Gagfah (Gemeinnützige Aktiengesellschaft Angestelltenheimstätten) Berlin. The development built for its tenth anniversary consisted of eighty apartments designed by seventeen architects; See: *Der Neubau*, Berlin 20/1928, p. 235.
6 Adler 1931, reprint 1998, pp. 90–95.
7 Verlag Julius Hoffmann, Stuttgart 1934.
8 The KKL was founded in 1901 at the Fifth Zionist Congress. The KKL's sole purpose was to purchase land in Palestine, under civil law, as the inalienable property of the Jewish people and to create Jewish settlements on the purchased land.
9 See biography of Richard Kauffmann.
10 Alexander Klein, "Der Einfluß des Klimas auf die organische Gestaltung von Grundriß und Ansicht" in: *Journal of*

the Association of Engineers & Architects 5, Tel Aviv February/March 1942, p. 24. Additional publications on Alexander Klein: Günther Kühne, "Alexander Klein noch Zeitgemäß" in: *Die Neue Stadt* 3/1950, pp. 101–105; Serge Klein, "Arbeiten Alexander Kleins" in: *Bauwelt* 7, Berlin 1962; Matilde Rivolta & Augusto Rossari, *Alexander Klein*, Milan 1975; Ulrich-Klaus Stöhner, "Untersuchung über den Beitrag Alexander Kleins zur Entwicklung und Bewertung von Grundrissen im Geschoßwohnbau", dissertation, Berlin 1976; Myra Warhaftig, "Alexander Klein zum 110. Geburtstag" in: *Bauwelt* 23, Berlin 1989, p. 1024; Myra Warhaftig, Susanne Rexroth, Philipp Oswalt, "Gebäudeklimatische Untersuchungen von Alexander Klein" in: *Wohltemperierte Architektur*, ed. by S. Rexroth, Heidelberg 1994; Myra Warhaftig, "Wohnungen der kurzen Wege: Alexander Klein" in: *Der Architekt* 6, Köln 2000, pp. 20–22; Warhaftig 2005, Klein, Alexander.

Alexander Klein, row house villa, Berlin Wilmersdorf, 1924, Klein's residence, demolished in the 1970s

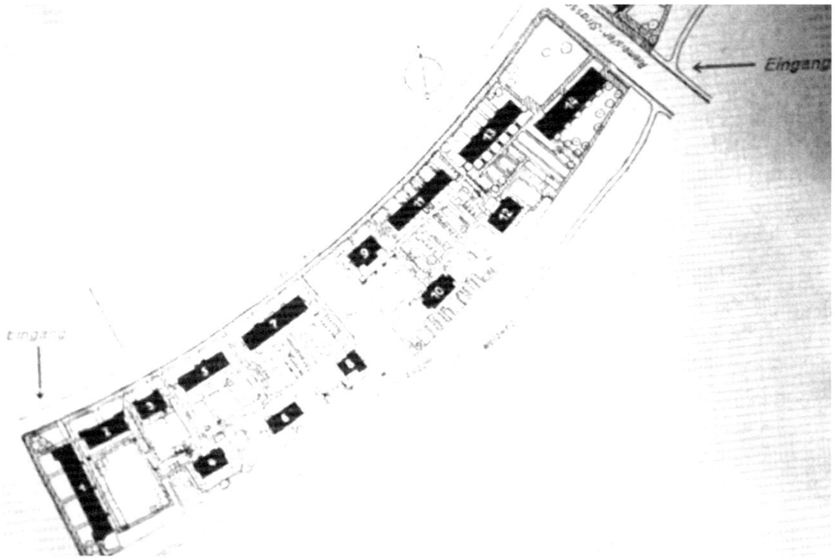

Gagfah housing estate, Berlin Zehlendorf, 1928, site plan groups 1, 2 and 3: Alexander Klein

Alexander Klein, Dr. Schulz residence, Berlin Dahlem, 1927

Alexander Klein, Gagfah housing development, Berlin Zehlendorf, 1928, floor plans of group one, (below to above): basement, ground floor and attic

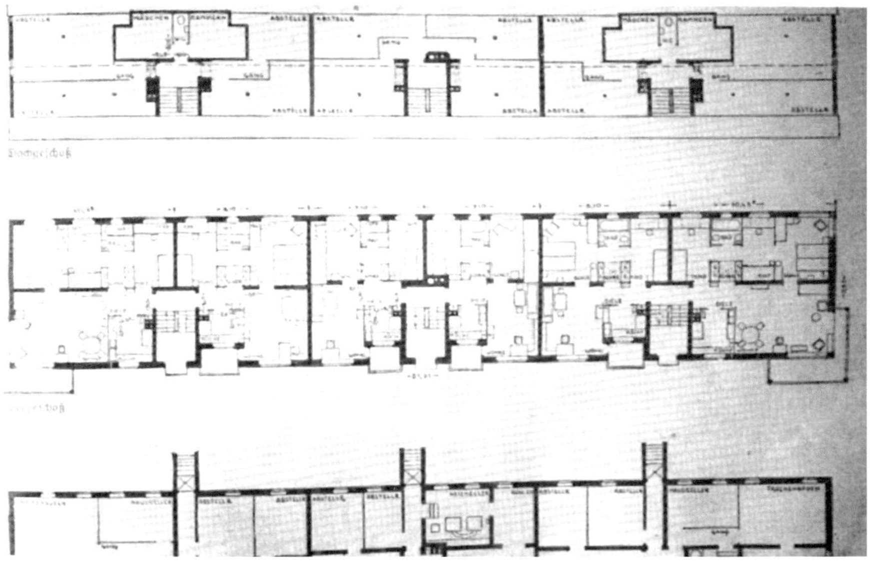

Alexander Klein, Gagfah housing development, Berlin Zehlendorf, 1928, building in group two, view from the street

Left page:
Alexander Klein, large housing estate, Bad Dürrenberg near Leipzig, 1930 (1986)

Right page:
Alexander Klein, garden city Kiryat Bialik, 1937, site plan

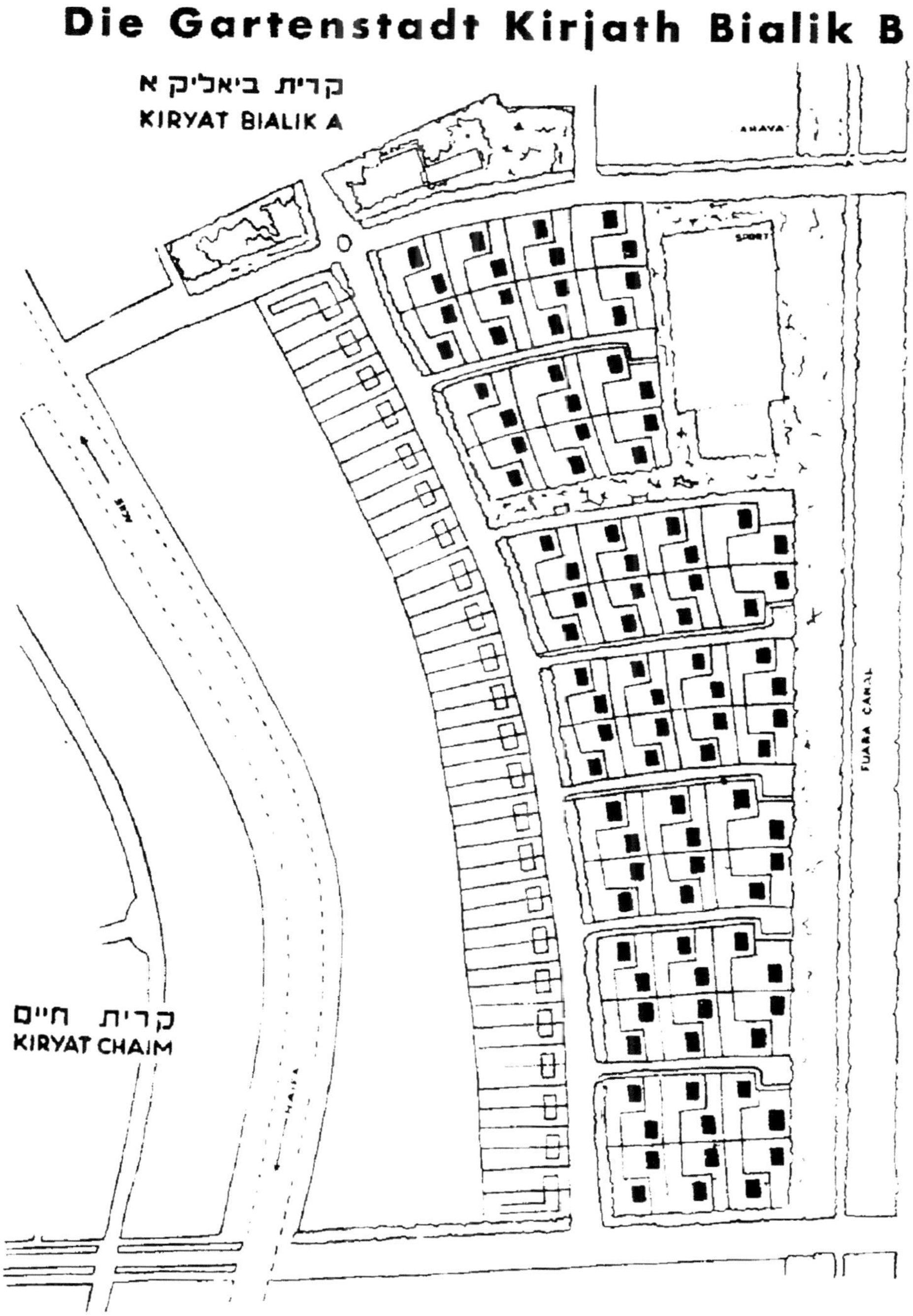

Alexander Klein

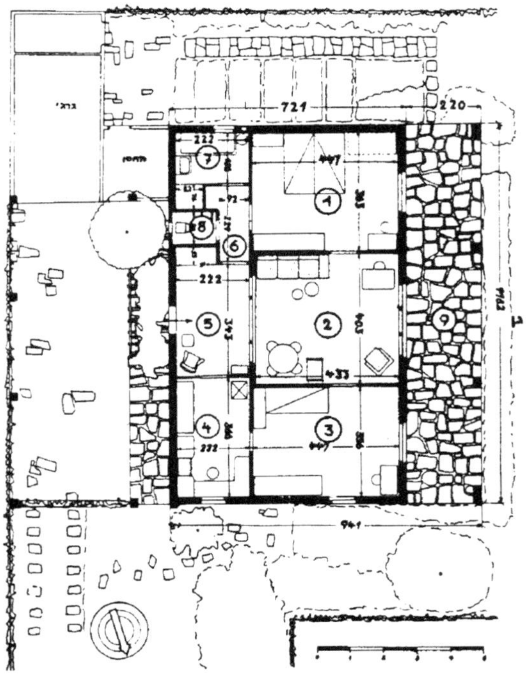

Alexander Klein, residence, Kiryat Bialik, 1937, ground plan

Alexander Klein, residence, Kiryat Bialik, 1937, view from the garden. Photo: M.W. 1986

Alexander Klein, Tivon garden community, 1940 (to 1950), site plan. The housing is loosely grouped around a "saddle"

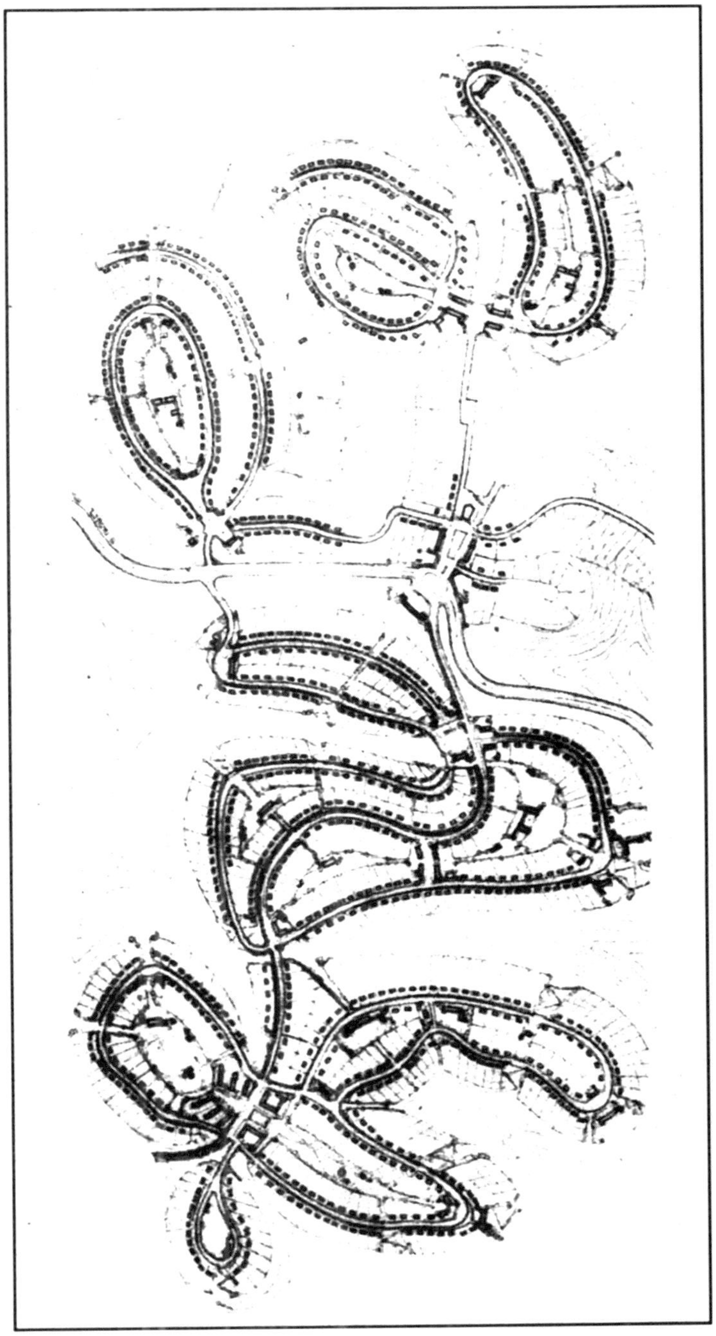

Tivon, photograph ca. 1937

Alexander Klein, garden city of Tivon, photograph ca. 1967

Alexander Klein, research 1942: the influence of climate on building design, example of apartment buildings in Haifa, Tel Aviv, Berlin and Oslo (above to below)

Alexander Klein, research 1942: the influence of parcelling and street direction on the orientation of buildings in Haifa

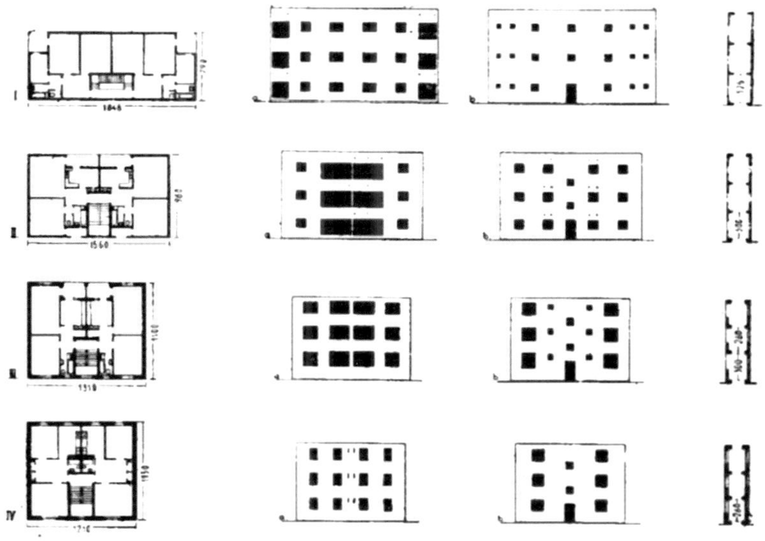

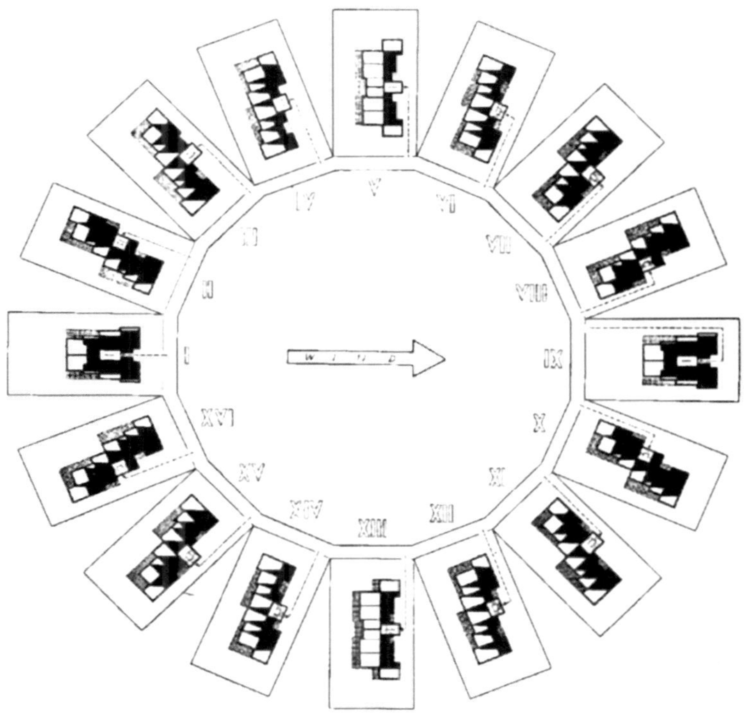

Ze’ev (Wilhelm) Haller

Ludwig Schwerin, Ze’ev Haller, Tel Aviv, 1950, oil painting

1884 Gleiwitz – 1956 Tel Aviv

Ze’ev Haller was born on June 11, 1884, in Gleiwitz, today Gliwice in Poland. He studied the building trades at schools in Dresden and Zittau and in the department of architecture at the Darmstadt Technische Hochschule (1909–1910). His first practical experience was as the head of construction in architectural offices in Breslau and Frankfurt am Main. In 1911 Haller went to Leipzig, working first in the office of Emil Franz Hänsel and then at Weidenbach & Tschammer.[1] Haller decided to stay in Leipzig and opened his own office there in 1914. He moved into an apartment at Kaiserin-Augusta-Strasse 67, where he lived until he was forced to leave Germany in 1933.

A monograph in the *Neue Werkkunst* series provides an overview of Haller’s buildings, design projects and competitions up to 1930.[2] Various rural residential housing developments in Coburg, Stendal and Weissenfels are listed as among his first realized projects. In 1926 he built a residence in neoclassical style for a wealthy family in Berlin-Wilmersdorf. However, the office building that he built in 1927 for J. J. Frank in Offenbach/Main was designed in Art Deco style.

Haller, a member of the Bund Deutscher Architekten (BDA), participated in various competitions, including ones for both synagogues and churches. Most of the projects he realized were for Jewish religious structures, such as mausoleums and war memorials, and for essential synagogue furnishings including the bimah, the Torah ark and curtain, and menorahs. Haller’s largest commissions for Jewish congregations were two cemetery buildings, erected 1926–29 in Leipzig and Halle/Saale. For the New Cemetery in Leipzig, Haller designed a soaring dome and arches with curves that came to a point, adapting oriental elements, but in the Jewish tradition. He used hipped and pyramidal roofs on the cemetery buildings in Halle, so that only the sparing use of the Star of David indicated the religious affiliation of those buried there.

If one observes Haller’s use of forms, neither a homogenous style nor one typical of that era can be discerned. He made use of Neoclassicism as well as Art Deco, and applied Mediterranean architectural forms to the tradition of his homeland. His sacred buildings combine elements of two incommensurable religions. Max Reimann, then director of urban planning in Leipzig, wrote in the introduction to the monograph on Haller: “He goes his own way here, showing that one must not affect an oriental mien, as has for so long been the rule. Haller here is thoroughly German, accommodating his structures to the forms of the German cities and countryside.”[3]

The art historian Wolfgang Hocquél wrote about the fate of the Leipzig cemetery and Haller’s artistic design: “His most remarkable achievement was the ceremonial hall of the New Israelite Cemetery in Leipzig, which was built 1926–28, and torched on the night of the fascist pogrom, November 9–10, 1938. The building complex was designed with a pale blue stucco façade and red roofs. The main hall with its stalactite vaulting within the steel-reinforced concrete dome produced a magnificent spatial effect.”[4]

Although the buildings in the Halle cemetery did survive the period of political anti-Semitism, today they are unrecognizable.

When the National Socialists assumed power, Haller went to Palestine without delay. He had long been interested in Zionism, as his 1925 design for a farm in Nahalal to be run by girls attests.[5]
In 1934, at one corner of a crossing in the centre of Tel Aviv, Haller built a three-storey building whose design no longer referenced his Leipzig architecture. Instead, it was an unornamented building whose curved balconies lent the structure an expressionistic appearance. Haller took an apartment there and established his office.
Dynamic expressive form characterizes Haller's apartment buildings of the 1930s. His formal vocabulary had become understated and resolute. In his new homeland, Haller departed from the confusing architectural pastiche of his Leipzig works and turned to Modern architecture.
Despite active participation in competitions, where he had some success, Haller was only occasionally able to build residential buildings in Tel Aviv. Without sufficient work, he had to take a job with the public works department, where he worked as an inspector in heavy industry from 1940 until his retirement.
When the state of Israel was established, Haller adopted the Hebrew first name Ze'ev (wolf) and put the name Wilhelm in parentheses. Ze'ev Haller died in Tel Aviv on May 10, 1956.[6]

In the summer of 1986, I visited Ze'ev Haller's brother, Dr. Albert Haller, and his nephew, the graphic artist Shlomo Sawady, in Tel Aviv. They generously provided me with important material for which I am very grateful to them both.

1 Emil Franz Hänsel, Hermann Georg Carl Weidenbach & Richard Tschammer ran a renowned architectural firm in Leipzig.
2 Reimann 1930. Before the Nazis stopped publication of the *Neue Werkkunst* series, the Berlin publisher Friedrich Ernst Hübsch had published more than seventy monographs on architects such as Oskar Kaufmann, Robert Friedmann and Bruno Kalitzki, whose biographies are in this book.
3 Reimann 1930, p. XII.
4 Hocquél 1990, pp. 226–227; see also: Tel Aviv 1993, pp. 106–117; Mezger-Smok 1994, pp. 66–71; Warhaftig 2005, Haller, Wilhelm.
5 Reimann 1930, p. XIII.
6 According to some sources, he went to Arizona in 1954 and died there in 1956.

Ze'ev (Wilhelm) Haller

Ze'ev Haller, Frauboes residence, Berlin-Wilmersdorf, 1926, view from the street

Ze'ev Haller, the Jewish cemetery, Leipzig, 1928, full view

Ze’ev Haller, the Jewish cemetery, Leipzig, 1928, main hall

Ze'ev (Wilhelm) Haller

Ze'ev Haller, J. J. Frank company building, Offenbach, 1927

Right page above:
Ze'ev Haller, the Jewish cemetery, Halle an der Saale, 1929, front view

Right page below left:
Ze'ev Haller, soldiers' memorial in a synagogue, Eisenach, 1920s

Right page below right:
Ze'ev Haller, Torah curtain in a synagogue, Leipzig, 1920s

עץ חיים היא
למחזיקים בה ותומכיה מאושר

Ze'ev (Wilhelm) Haller

above left:
Ze'ev Haller, Delfiner-Picker apartment building, Tel Aviv, 1934, view from the street. Photo: M.W. 1986

above right:
Ze'ev Haller, Delfiner-Picker apartment building, Tel Aviv, 1934, partial view. Photo: M.W. 1986

below left:
Ze'ev Haller, Boaz-Schwabe apartment building, Tel Aviv, 1936, view from the street. Photo: O.W. 1986

Right page
Ze'ev Haller, Boaz-Schwabe apartment building, Tel Aviv, 1936, view from the street. Photo: O.W. 1986

Moshe Gerstel

1886 Lemberg – 1961 Haifa

The famous Shuk Talpiyot market hall and the Industrial Center, both on the slope near the sea at Haifa, as well as the Kuppat-Cholim union polyclinic on Mount Carmel, were all built between the 1930s and 1940s.[1] Though they no longer stand in isolated locations, these buildings have maintained their social functions and are landmarks of Haifa. They are some of the unusual and striking buildings designed by Moshe Gerstel.
Born in Lemberg, Galicia (today Lviv, Ukraine) in 1886, Gerstel completed his architectural studies in 1914 at the Technische Hochschule in Vienna, where his instructors included Max von Ferstel (1859–1936). He served as an infantry officer in World War I and was wounded. Before moving to Romania in 1922, Gerstel was able to realize some large housing projects in Vienna, Florisdorf, St. Pölten and Amstetten. Since violent acts against Jews also were increasing in Romania by 1935, Gerstel left Bucharest, where he had spent thirteen productive years and built twenty to thirty villas. He arrived in Palestine, settled immediately in Haifa, and remained active as an architect in that city until his death on April 1, 1961.

In the vicinity of the Haifa harbour, a bazaar, or suq (an Arab marketplace of labyrinthine alleys and a multitude of small stores) had grown up since the mid-nineteenth century around the Turkish baths and the mosques, churches, and prayer rooms. The bazaar was the soul of the city and an important, attractive meeting place for adherents of every religious faith. It was in the suq that Jews, Christians and Moslems did their daily shopping, came in contact and spoke with each other.
Because of the growing number of disturbances between Jews and Arabs, the city fathers decided to spatially separate the two religious communities in 1936. The city district of Hadar, between the port area to the north and the hills of Carmel to the south, was designated for development as the shopping centre for the Jewish population. Gerstel won first prize among ninety-six entrants in a competition for a new market hall. Shuk Talpiyot was created from two axially aligned volumes – a half-cylinder and a cube – with horizontal ribbons of windows and an elliptical glass roof. Haifa now had a building in which the influence of Erich Mendelsohn's expressive use of forms was recognizable.
The polyclinic on Mount Carmel (1937) also was indebted to the Modern style. A semi-circular staircase with a vertical arrangement of windows accents the white stuccoed building, which has a rooftop terrace. Most of Gerstel's private clients were Arabs. So the residence that he built for the lawyer Channa Asfour and his family in 1937 on Mount Carmel had a floor plan that reflected his client's Middle Eastern traditions, while the building's style was European. The centrally located living room on the ground floor was both a reception area and a space traversed by all members of the family. The cubic structure was faced with smoothly chiselled stone and dominated by two curved archways on stilts that emphasized the entrance. But the semi-circular balcony projecting above the band of windows on the street-side façade obviously is not rooted in the architectural culture of the Near East.

For information and material, I am very grateful to Moshe Gerstel's son, Professor Leopold Gerstel, Haifa and Innsbruck (1987).

1 Shuk means market in Hebrew and is related to the Arabic "suq", which has the same meaning; the polyclinic was originally built as a hotel.

Moshe Gerstel, housing development, Florisdorf, Vienna, 1918–1922, overall view

Moshe Gerstel

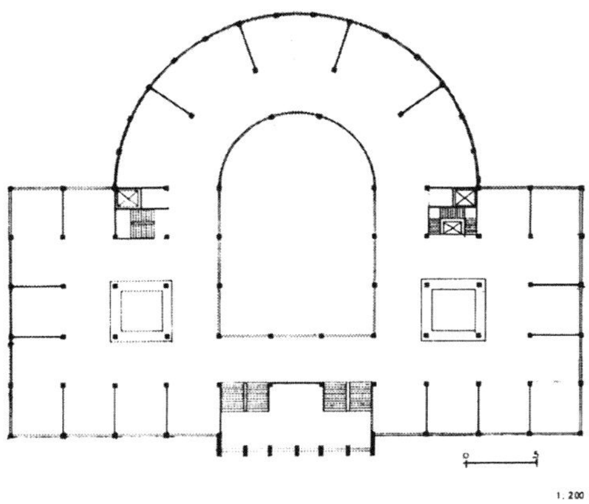

Moshe Gerstel, Shuk Talpiyot – market, Haifa, 1937–1940, ground-floor plan

Moshe Gerstel, Shuk Talpiyot – market, Haifa, 1937–1940, view of the hall

Moshe Gerstel, Shuk Talpiyot – market, Haifa, 1937–1940, view from a side street

Moshe Gerstel, Shuk Talpiyot – market, Haifa, 1937–1940, view from the main street

Moshe Gerstel, Khuri residence, Haifa, Mount Carmel, 1937

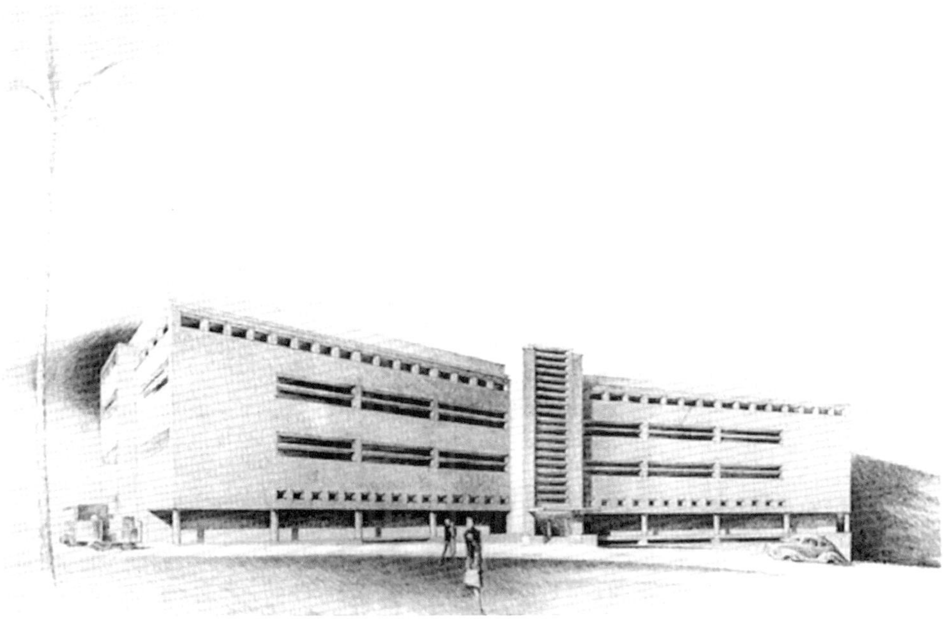

Moshe Gerstel, Industrial Center, Haifa, 1946 (drawing)

Moshe Gerstel, Kup-pat-Cholim union polyclinic, Haifa, Mount Carmel, 1936. Photo: M.W. 1986

Erich Mendelsohn

1887 Allenstein – 1953 San Francisco

Like all German Jews, Erich Mendelsohn was affected by the monstrous political events of the 1930s. He left his German homeland in 1933 and never returned. But without the recognition he had first achieved in Germany, he could not have so widely, quickly and surely conquered the world of architecture in England, Palestine and the USA, the lands of his exile.
There are many publications about Mendelsohn's life and work; therefore this biography does not attempt to present him in the larger framework of his significance as an internationally practising architect, but instead highlights his contribution to the building of Eretz Israel.
Although Mendelsohn lived in Palestine for seven years, from 1934–1941, and maintained an architectural office in Jerusalem during that time, he did not erect a very large number of buildings there, despite his powerful influence. The architectural historian Ita Heinze-Mühleib writes about this in *Erich Mendelsohn. Buildings and Projects in Palestine:* "It seems of little sense to concentrate here on a detailed treatment of those 'iconic buildings'. It also may be unfair in an individual instance to interpret every rounded corner treatment and every sweeping balcony on Rothschild Boulevard (one of the finest streets in Tel Aviv) as a copy of the 'master'. The fact that Erich Mendelsohn's German architecture exerted a powerful influence on modern architecture in Palestine is enough. Also significant is the fact that his Palestinian architecture never met with nearly the same level of response. Tel Aviv's streets display copies of the Sternefeld Villa or scaled down versions of Stuttgart's Schocken department store, but not buildings that call forth associations with the Weizmann or Schocken residences."[1]

Erich Mendelsohn was born on March 21, 1887, in Allenstein, East Prussia, today Olsztyn in Poland. He began to study architecture at the Technische Hochschule in Berlin, transferring two years later to the Technische Hochschule Munich, where he earned his degree in 1912. He was conscripted in 1915 and sent to the Russian front. Even there he worked on architecture, drawing fantasy projects in the Expressionist style. From 1919 until 1933 when, at the behest of the ruling National Socialists, he was expelled from professional associations and from the Prussian Academy of Arts, Mendelsohn lived and worked in Berlin. But his work had an effect far beyond the boundaries of his chosen city. His Berlin buildings – the Cinema Universum (today the Schaubühne), the Woga complex on Kurfürstendamm (now apartment buildings on Cicerostrasse), the main administrative building of the German metalworkers' union, his own residence am Rupenhorn and, last but not least, the Einstein Tower in Potsdam – have always been stimulating subjects for architectural historians and continue to provide architects with new inspiration. The architectural history of the cities of Nuremberg, Stuttgart, Chemnitz, Gleiwitz (Gliwice), and Breslau (Wroclaw) also are linked with Mendelsohn's name. But not all of his buildings survived destruction in World War II or have been preserved in their original form.
Mendelsohn was committed to the Jewish faith and had connections both with advocates of political

Zionism and with the movement's opponents.[2] His wife, the cellist Louise Maas, also was Jewish. Their daughter Esther (1916–2004) was named after the heroine in the book of the Old Testament.
At the invitation of Pinchas Ruthenberg, Mendelsohn visited Palestine in 1923 to design a power station for Haifa.[3] It was then that he got to know the land. After that visit, he and Richard Neutra took part in a competition for a business centre in Haifa. Only after he settled in Palestine in 1934 was Mendelsohn able to realize some of his projects. He created a total of nine building complexes during his years in the country, of which five were public buildings essential to the realization of Theodor Herzl's Zionist programme.

The Hadassah University Medical Center, one of Mendelsohn's most extensive projects, was built between 1934 and 1939 on Mount Scopus, Jerusalem.[4] The aim of Hadassah, the American Zionist women's organization founded by Henriette Szold in 1912, was to bring medical assistance to Palestine.[5] In cities and villages, Hadassah had new hospitals and polyclinics built for the country's ever-increasing number of inhabitants and also supported their operation.
The Hadassah complex on Mount Scopus consisted of a university hospital, a nursing school and a medical school and was then the largest of its kind in the Near East, covering an area of 20,000 m². After only three years of construction, some parts of the complex could be occupied. The quality of medical care and the architectonic solution soon became world famous.[6]

Not all of the young people who reached Eretz Israel from Nazi Germany during the Fifth Aliya (1933–39) wanted training in agriculture, although this was greatly encouraged at the time. So a decision was made to allow them to learn the trades as well. In 1936 Mendelsohn was asked to build a trade school with an attached boarding school for sixty to eighty teenagers aged fifteen to seventeen on Kibbutz Jagur, some 25 km southeast of Haifa. By early 1937, sixty boys from Germany were able to move into the building and begin their training.[7]
Some thirty-five years earlier, the idea of creating a credit institution to finance the settlement of Palestine had circulated. In 1903 the Zionist organization in Jaffa established the first bank, the Anglo-Palestine Company, as a subsidiary of the Jewish Colonial Trust. In addition to the central office, bank branches were opened in subsequent years in various locations around the country, often in provisional spaces. Alex Baerwald built the first APC bank institute in Haifa in 1927.[8] The largest Anglo-Palestine bank building was completed by Mendelsohn in Jerusalem in 1939.[9]

Chaim Weizmann, the scientist and president of the Zionist organization, was tireless in his efforts to promote the country's agricultural and industrial development. With financial assistance from the Sieff family of England, two academic facilities could be built according to Mendelsohn's plans between 1938 and 1941 in Rechovot, then still a small agricultural settlement with some 7500 inhabitants, 20 km southeast of Tel Aviv.
The Daniel Sieff Research Institute and the Agricultural College were part of the Hebrew University of Jerusalem.[10] Ten selected colleagues worked on research projects that ranged from problems in the citrus and dairy industries to the production of chemicals for medicine and technology. Among the scientists were former employees of the Kaiser-Wilhelm-Institut for Biochemistry in Berlin-Dahlem who had escaped persecution and found a new homeland in Palestine.

In 1944 it was decided to expand the Sieff Institute into a large scientific research centre that would bear Weizmann's name. The Weizmann Institute, inaugurated in 1949, today has twenty-one divisions and employs over 1500 researchers, engineers and technicians, including some five hundred scientists from around the world who are there for postgraduate studies.

Less political in character, but no less significant, are Mendelsohn's other buildings in Palestine. From 1934 to 1936, he erected a villa for Chaim Weizmann and his wife in the city of Rechovot.[11] During the same period, in Jerusalem, Mendelsohn built a residence and library for Salman Schocken, one of his most important clients from the Weimar Republic.[12] Mendelsohn had built department stores for Schocken in Nuremberg (1926), Stuttgart (1926–28) and Chemnitz (1928–29), which architectural historians laud as milestones in his creative development.

The only commission Mendelsohn received from the British mandate government was for the government hospital in Haifa, built in 1937–38.[13] Located at the sea among old pines and eucalyptus trees, the curving structure had an optimal site. To the north the view is toward the bay of Akko, to the south are the hills of Carmel. But one only gets a real impression of how harmonically the building complex is integrated into the landscape if one looks toward Haifa from the sea.

Despite his architectural contribution to the Zionist work of building the country, Mendelsohn did not find it necessary to remain in Israel the rest of his life. When the construction economy went into recession with the outbreak of World War II, most independent architects were forced to look for other sources of income. No new commissions were forthcoming – even for the genius Mendelsohn – that might have proved satisfying. So he decided to leave the country. In 1941 Mendelsohn went to the USA, where he died on September 15, 1953, in San Francisco.

Did the land of Palestine unleash new creative energies in Erich Mendelsohn? Julius Posener commented: "Mendelsohn was not averse to certain mannerisms in Palestine. One finds them in the houses that he built for Chaim Weizmann in Rechovot and for Salman Schocken in Rechavia. I think that one finds similar features for the first time in the metalworkers' union building on Lindenstrasse in Berlin. Now, in Palestine, these represented something like an attempt to preserve continuity, while the new environment forced him to rethink his approach in more than one instance."[14]

I am very grateful to Esther Mendelsohn Joseph (San Francisco), the daughter of Louise and Erich Mendelsohn, for telling me stories about life with her famous parents during the International Style Architecture Conference in Tel Aviv, May 22–28, 1994.

1 Heinze-Mühleib 1986, pp. 331–332.
2 Ibid., pp. 18–28.
3 Pinchas Ruthenberg (1879–1942) was born in Romny, Russia. He studied engineering and was one of the most active members of the Social-Revolutionary Party of 1905. He also took an active part in the October Revolution.

Ruthenberg went to Palestine in 1918 and founded the Palestine Electric Corporation, the project he developed to make use of water power to provide electricity in Palestine, in 1923.

4 Heinze-Mühleib 1986, pp. 201–235; see also biography of Fritz Kornberg, note 4. Hadassah (myrtle) is a bush known for its dense foliage and sweet aroma that grows in the Mediterranean region. The biblical heroine Esther originally had the Hebrew name Hadassah.

5 Henriette Szold (1860–1945), born in Baltimore, was a writer and a Zionist leader. She was the long-time secretary, vice-president and chairman of the board of the American Zionist Organization.

6 All the university buildings on Mount Scopus were cut off from Jerusalem in 1948 due to political events. Josef Neufeld (see biography) built a new Hadassah University Medical Center in the Jerusalem district of Ein Karem in the 1950s. Mount Scopus was again reunited with Jerusalem in June 1967 as a result of the Six-Day War.

7 Heinze-Mühleib 1986, pp. 236–246.

8 See biography of Alex Baerwald.

9 Heinze-Mühleib 1986, pp. 247–265.

10 Ibid., pp. 288–305.

11 Ibid., pp. 89–117.

12 Ibid., pp. 118–165.

13 Ibid., pp. 266–287.

14 Posener 1990, p. 237. Recent publications about Mendelsohn: Mendelsohn 1998; Richter 1998; Mendelsohn 1999; Huse 2000; Mendelsohn 2002; Heinze-Greenberg 2004; Posener 2004, pp. 229–235, 361–365, 400–405; Warhaftig 2005, Mendelsohn, Erich.

Left page above:
Erich Mendelsohn,
Mendelsohn family
residence, Berlin-
Charlottenburg, 1929.
Photo: M.W. 1990

Left page below:
The windmill, Erich
Mendelsohn's residence
and workplace
(1935–1941), Jerusalem

Right page:
Erich Mendelsohn, Einstein Tower, Astrophysical Institute, Potsdam, 1924

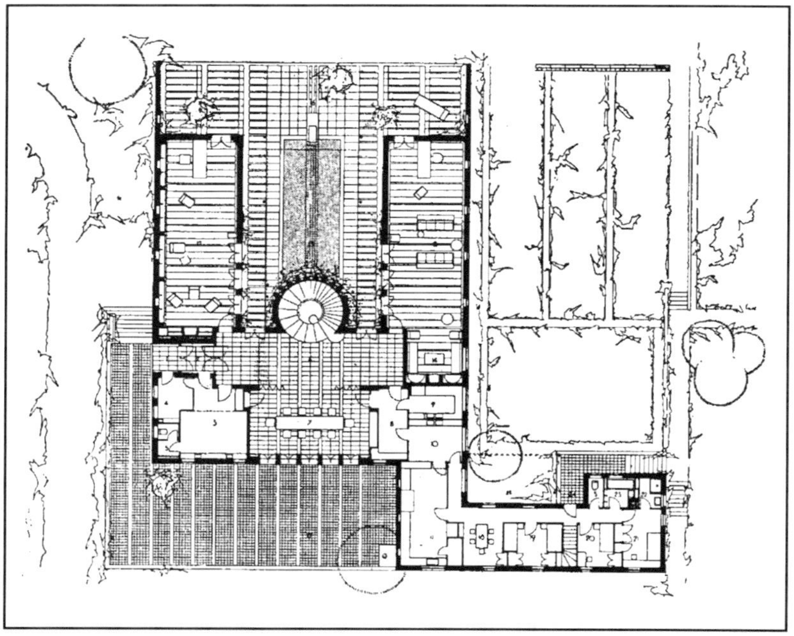

Erich Mendelsohn, Weizmann residence, Rechovot, 1936, ground plan

Erich Mendelsohn, Weizmann residence, Rechovot, 1936, side view

Erich Mendelsohn, Schocken residence, office and library, Jerusalem, 1937, ground plan

Erich Mendelsohn, Schocken residence, office and library, Jerusalem, 1937, view from the garden

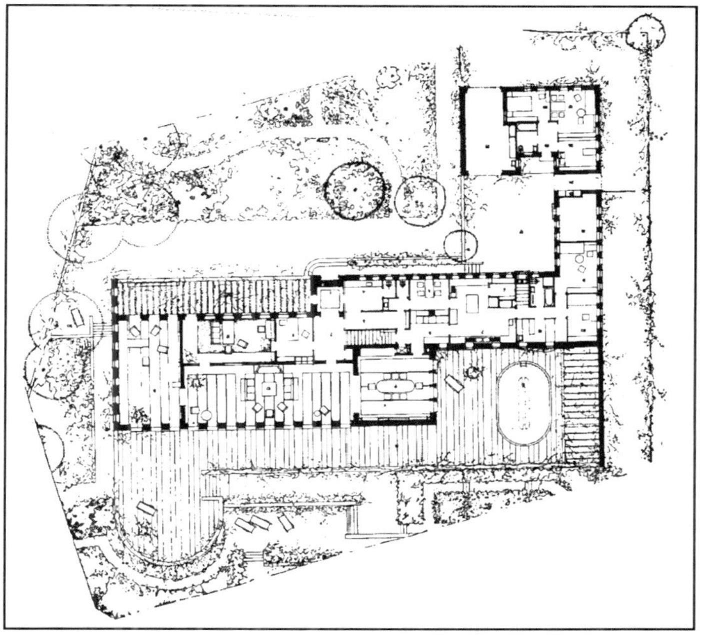

Erich Mendelsohn

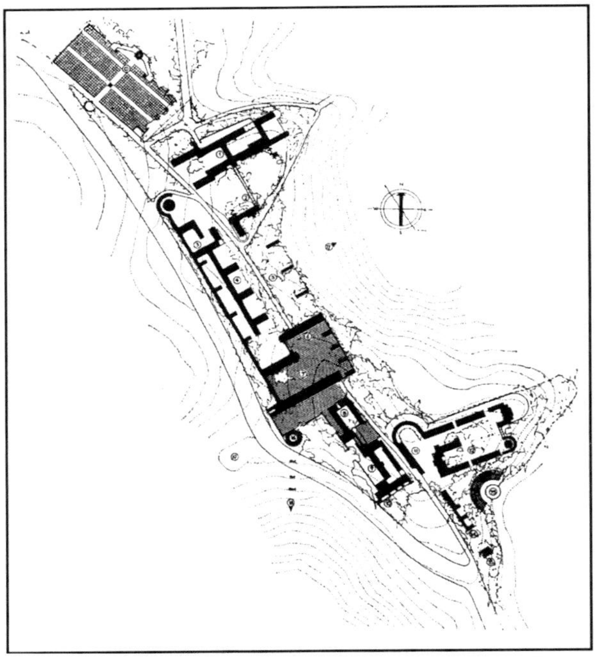

Erich Mendelsohn, Hadassah University Medical Center, Jerusalem, Mount Scopus, 1934–1939, site plan

Erich Mendelsohn, Hadassah University Medical Center, Jerusalem, Mount Scopus, 1934–1939, view of the main building

Right page:
Erich Mendelsohn, Anglo-Palestinian Bank, Jerusalem, 1939, front view

Erich Mendelsohn, government hospital, Haifa, 1938, view from the sea

Left page above:
Erich Mendelsohn, Daniel Sieff Research Institute, Rechovot, 1941, partial view of the machine room

Left page below left:
Erich Mendelsohn, Daniel Sieff Research Institute, Rechovot, 1941, machine room interior

Left page below right:
Erich Mendelsohn, Steinberg, Herrmann & Co. hat factory, Luckenwalde, 1923, machine room interior

Robert Friedmann

1888 Hamburg – 1940 Jerusalem

A white stuccoed one-family house composed of geometric volumes, with round and horizontal bands of windows, tucked behind lush plants and trees on Mount Carmel some 2 km from the beach at Haifa, spurred me to go to Hamburg to track down its creator, Robert Friedmann. I received the following information about him from the Hamburg art historian Hermann Hipp: "Along with Karl Schneider, Robert Friedmann was one of the main exponents of Neues Bauen in Hamburg in the 1920s."[1]
Born in Hamburg on February 15, 1888, and educated at the Kunsthochschule Dresden, Robert Friedmann fought in World War I in Palestine – as a German soldier on the side of the Turkish army against the English. After the war, he returned to his native city to work as a self-employed architect.
At the suggestion of Fritz Schumacher, in 1926 the Hamburg Credit Bank announced a competition for residential buildings whose foremost criteria were: ground plan features, urban grouping, architectural design and economical construction.[2] After winning the competition, Friedmann, a member of the Bund Deutscher Architekten (BDA) and the Architekten-und Ingenieur-Verein (AIV), was commissioned to build a housing block along Jarrestrasse-Hanssensweg in Hamburg. The Jarre City, developed along the lines of the prize-winning design, sustained heavy damage during World War II but later was carefully restored. Not until the 1970s was it rediscovered as a quiet revolution in architecture.[3]
In 1930 a monograph about the significance of Friedman's buildings was published in the *Neue Werkkunst* series.[4] Unfortunately, both the Haag residence (1927) with its axially arranged brick-clad façade and interior furnishings designed by the architect, and some of Friedmann's housing blocks faced with clinker brick were destroyed in World War II. However, the apartment building in the Eppendorf district with its grand and elegant floor plan, the apartment block in Barmbeck-Nord with its dark clinker brick façade, and the simply designed, white stucco apartment block in Hamburg-Winterhude were spared. All of these buildings now stand under landmark preservation.

But Friedmann's legacy consists not only of residential buildings. After winning a competition with Felix Ascher, he built the synagogue on Oberstrasse in 1931.[5] It was the Israelite temple for Hamburg and one of the last synagogues built in Germany before Hitler came to power.[6]
The synagogue was designed to hold 1200 persons; it had both a large prayer hall and a smaller room, for 130 persons, for weekly services. Instead of the Orientalism then commonly used to symbolize a relationship to Palestine, the building has features typical of the Modern style of the 1920s. Symmetrically arranged, undecorated pure cubic volumes form the temple, situated up a broad set of steps at the rear of an empty forecourt. Only the menorah above the entrance denotes the visitors' religion. It is astonishing that the building survived the 1930s and 1940s unscathed. During the war it was used as a movie theatre;

after the war, the Norddeutsche Rundfunk (NDR – North German Radio) moved into the building but made no changes to the exterior. The interior has been converted into a broadcast studio and concert hall.

After Hitler assumed power in 1933, Friedmann – forbidden to practise his profession and persecuted – emigrated with his wife and son to Palestine, settling in Haifa. There he encountered a tough competitive situation. His son Tomas Friedmann recalled, "Tiny Haifa had as many architects as greater Hamburg did back then, and my father wanted to keep on working, and was able to, but he had a very difficult time."[7] The architects who emigrated from Germany had brought with them the idea of holding competitions. So Robert Friedmann was able to win additional prizes for a synagogue in Jerusalem, for the "Engineers' Building" in Tel Aviv, and for a commercial building in Haifa. But he was only able to complete the Salomon residence on Mount Carmel in 1936 before he died in Jerusalem on September 10, 1940, at the age of fifty-two.[8]

I am very grateful to Robert Friedmann's son Tomas D. W. Friedmann (Terzorio) for information and material, and also for visiting me in Berlin (1986–1997).

1 From Hermann Hipp's letter to the author dated December 7, 1986; architect Karl Schneider (1892–1945), married to a Jewish woman, was obliged to leave Germany. He emigrated in 1937 to the USA.
2 Fritz Schumacher (1896–1945), architect and renowned urban planner, was Hamburg's building commissioner after 1909, and promoted brick architecture there.
3 Hänsel 1981.
4 Eulenberg 1930, reprint Berlin 2000.
5 Architect Felix Ascher, born 1883 in Hamburg, was on the list of Jews expelled from the Reich Chamber of Fine Arts as of 1933. He emigrated in 1933 to London, where he died in 1952; Warhaftig 2005, Ascher, Felix.
6 *Bauwelt* 13/1930, p. 439; *Deutsche Bauzeitung* 2/1931, pp. 5–8.
7 In a letter to the author dated January 21, 1987.
8 Myra Warhaftig, "Erinnerung an Robert Friedmann" in: *Bauwelt* 11/1988, p. 402.

Robert Friedmann

Robert Friedmann, housing block Jarrestrasse-Hanssensweg, Hamburg, 1928, Hanssensweg

Robert Friedmann, housing block, Jarrestrasse-Hanssensweg, Hamburg, 1928 Semperplatz corner of Semperstraße

Robert Friedmann, housing block, Jarrestrasse-Hanssensweg, Hamburg, 1928, Semperplatz corner of Hanssensweg

Robert Friedmann, Haag residence, Hamburg, 1927, view from the street

Robert Friedmann, large apartment building, Eppendorfer Landstrasse, Hamburg, 1928

Left page above:
Robert Friedmann, housing block, Stellbergstrasse corner of Starstrasse, Hamburg, 1926

Left page below:
Robert Friedmann with Felix Ascher, synagogue on Oberstrasse, Hamburg, 1931. Photo: M.W. 1986

Right page:
Robert Friedmann, Salomon residence, Haifa, Mount Carmel, 1936, view from the street. Photo: M.W. 1986

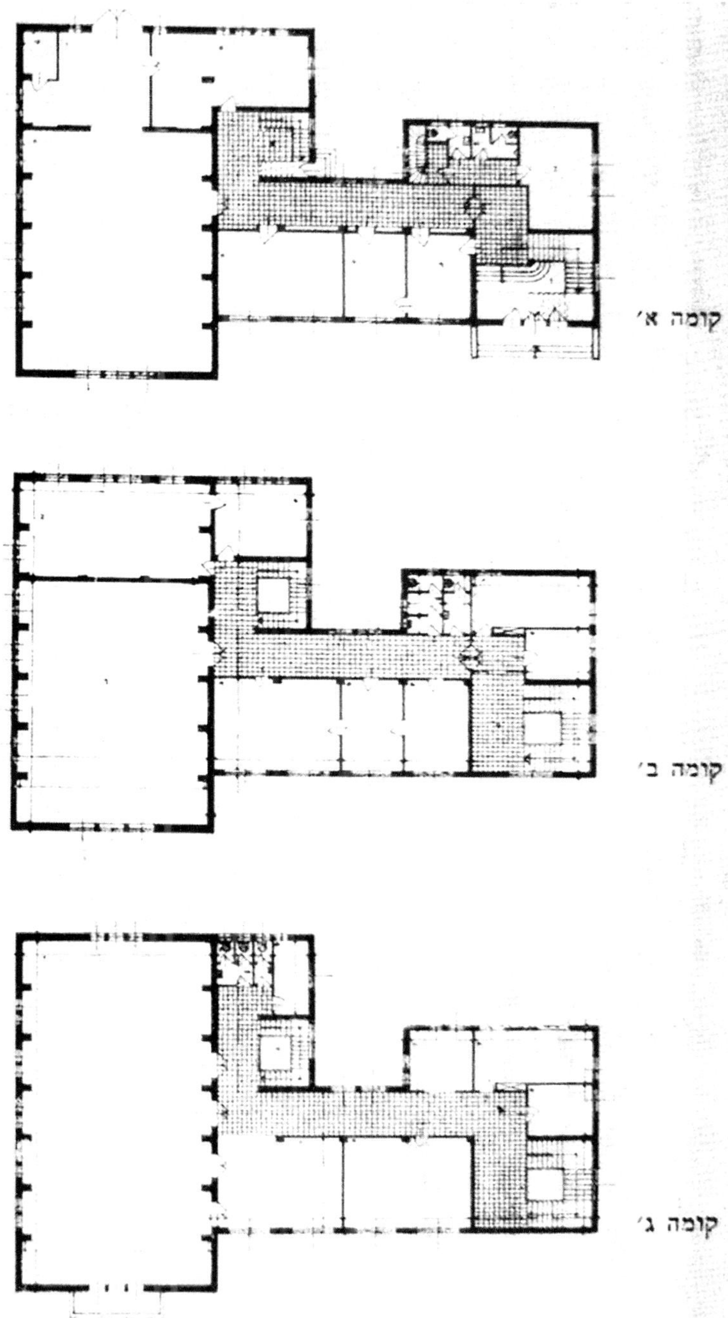

Left page:
Robert Friedmann, "Engineers' Building", Tel Aviv, around 1937, photomontage

Right page:
Robert Friedmann, "Engineers' Building", Tel Aviv, 1937, plan of ground floor, first and second storeys (from above to below)

Adolf Rading

1888 Berlin – 1957 London

His colleagues in Haifa's municipal office called him "the Professor", not just in deference to his academic standing in Germany before 1933, but rather to avoid having to address him by his first name, as is customary in Israel. They respected and admired Adolf Rading not only for his knowledge, ability and long years of professional experience, or his advocacy of Modern architecture in the country. Rading was held in high esteem because, although he was not a Jew, he left Nazi Germany and followed his Jewish wife to Palestine.
Rading lived and worked in Haifa for fourteen years. The many private homes, public buildings, squares and neighbourhoods that were built according to his plans shaped the port city and its surrounding area. In a letter from January 1946 he described his urban architectural work after 1943: "For nearly four years I was a consulting architect, and now am the architectural advisor to the municipality of Haifa. In effect, that is, I am the director of urban planning, much the same field of activity as in Germany. I plan and execute all major municipal building projects; in addition, I deal with urban problems and the city parks. One concomitant of this is that I am the fount of most financial dispensations. All in all a very interesting field of work, particularly because Haifa is a fast-growing city that today has 140,000 inhabitants."[1]

Rading was born on March 2, 1888, in Berlin. He trained as a bricklayer's apprentice and salesman before enrolling at the school for building and construction trades in Berlin. After his World War I military discharge, he worked in the offices of Peter Behrens (1868–1940) and Albert Gessner (1868–1953). Rading began to teach in 1919, and by 1923 he was a professor and director of the architecture program at the State Academy of Applied Arts in Breslau (Wroclaw). After he got to know Hans Scharoun (1893–1972), whose architecture he greatly respected, Rading arranged Scharoun's appointment to a position in Breslau in 1925. But by 1932 there were already difficulties; the Academy was shut down by emergency decree and Rading lost his job. One year later, he left Germany with his wife Else and never returned.
At first he went to southern France. Having decided to renounce architecture, Rading purchased a farm. He worked there for two years, but then he changed his mind and went with his wife to Palestine.
"Now he wants to get back to architecture here in Palestine," Julius Posener reported, after visiting Rading in Jerusalem. "The first thing I suggested was to take a walk on the Mount of Olives with the view of Jerusalem. It was the right introduction ... Seldom have I met an architect who is so completely the creative artist."[2]
Two years after the founding of the state of Israel, Rading left the country with his wife and went to London. The fact that Rading, in his third country of emigration, could so easily become a member of the Royal Institute of British Architects (RIBA), the Town Planning Institute and the Institute of Registered Architects, may surely be traced back to the distinguished reputation he enjoyed among his British colleagues during

the mandate period in Palestine. It was in London that Adolf Rading died seven years later, on April 4, 1957. Only four private residences have been identified from Rading's time in London.[3]

Rading had already been influential in Germany prior to 1933. He had been chairman of the Bund Deutscher Architecten (BDA) in Silesia, a member of the Deutscher Werkbund (DWB), the Reich Research Society for Economy in Construction and Housing, the International Federation of Housing and Town Planning (London), and chairman of the German Board of Standards for Berlin and Brandenburg. Rading was also a member of the Berlin architects' group Der Ring, along with other colleagues who championed Neues Bauen, later known as International Style, and he remained committed his entire life to its tenets – to take technology, culture, art, and society into consideration when designing built space.

In looking at what Rading accomplished in the three countries he lived in, with their different cultures and traditions, what stands out is his consistent approach to the architecture he advocated. Human living space was always the focus for him, whether he was dealing with a one-family house for a well-to-do client or with a housing project for unemployed families. Rading's intention to build economically and functionally was evident even in one of his first structures, a housing block on Oranienstrasse in Breslau (1922). When the framework of the buildings (originally intended to be one-family houses) was completed, and the need for multi-storey rental units suddenly became apparent, Rading did not hesitate to redesign his plans, for "the unusual current state of affairs justifies economy as the decisive factor".[4]
Adolf Rading was a highly respected architect.[5] His scientific and artistic gifts were evident in his one-family house for the Weissenhofsiedlung in Stuttgart (1927) and in the four-storey apartment building for the Werkbund's "Living and Working Space" development in Breslau (1929). The Ernst Rading residence (1929, Berlin-Zehlendorf) attests to his mastery of Modern style. A housing development built between 1930–33 in Berlin-Lichtenberg was apparently the last of his projects to be realized on German soil. Those apartments were built for the unemployed under a government job creation programme that hired jobless construction workers.

When Rading arrived in Haifa, he met the like-minded architect Kurt Reinsch and they began to enter competitions together.[6] In 1936 both received first prize for their plan to design the centre of Haifa.[7] This district near the harbour, with many commercial buildings, was supposed to create a connection between Egypt and Syria and to develop Haifa into a model trading city in the Near East.[8] But the unrest between Jews and Arabs (1936–1939) and the uncertain state of affairs in Europe immediately preceding World War II prevented this promising project from being realized.
Haifa's landscape of mountains, hills, and cliffs – its special geographic and topographic setting – signified a new challenge for Rading. One of the subjects that absorbed him for years was an investigation of stepped housing, whose setbacks also created rooftop terraces.[9] Since he lived on one of the hills of Mount Carmel, Rading knew that in this region, careful investigation was required to erect structures of good quality at reasonable cost. And so he designed differentiated types of housing that could be built on steep gradients of fifteen to thirty degrees. Even today, his investigations still serve as the basis for building in the region. The fact that each of Haifa's hills is a functioning district linked to the others by a well-organized transport system and that Mount Carmel enjoys a reputation as a centre for rest and recreation goes

back to Rading's suggestion that his colleagues plan with those goals in mind.[10] The squares that Rading planned for Haifa in the 1940s – Fichte Square, Masaryk Square, Moriah Square and Cyclamen Square – retain their central function and, like all his buildings, still appear contemporary.

The multi-family residence that Adolf Rading and Kurt Reinsch built for Rading's brother-in-law Walter Roth, which today lies hidden behind evergreens, eucalyptus and rubber trees, exhibits a clearly recognizable functional order in its floor plan and exterior design. The size and layout of every room and opening, both interior and exterior, exists for a purpose. The current residents confirmed this, saying that the wide balconies and the windows installed at different heights were comfortable living features.

Rading's masterpiece is actually the one-storey Frutarom chemical laboratory. The building was erected in 1944 in Haifa's industrial district. It is situated on the bay, where temperatures are unusually high in the summer. The offices and laboratories are accessible from a rectangular atrium that houses subtropical plants. A white stuccoed concrete dome, visible from all sides, indicates the main entrance.

Rading became one of the most influential and respected architects in Haifa and the region, and provided the city with stimulating ideas that have lost none of their currency. The fact that he left Israel two years after the country's founding may in large part be attributed to the behaviour of his colleagues in the municipality.

Jehoshua Prushansky, an engineer and former member of the municipal planning commission, eulogized Rading on the first anniversary of his death, and celebrated Rading and his work: "Those of us who were privileged to work at his side were deeply influenced by his rare personality, which combined the qualities of a gifted artist, a teacher of the House of Hillel and an independent thinker. [11] Contact with him always had a purifying, elevating effect. His presence within the Town Hall seemed to bestow nobility on the whole establishment and gave us the feeling that a man of great worth, 'one of the righteous men of the world's nations' was dwelling among us." Then Prushansky acknowledged in the name of his colleagues, "However, all this could not prevent his departure from the country in 1950. The sad tidings of his death in April 1957 renewed in us the burning sense of remorse for not having treated him fairly."[12]

I am very grateful to my good friends Tea (née Hirsch) and Nechemia Aharon who have lived in the Walter Roth residence, Haifa, Mount Carmel, for many years and who knew Adolf Rading. They allowed me to view their home from inside and showed me photographs of the original building. I am also grateful to Rading's niece, Miriam Dessauer (1986), who gave me his portrait, and to Jehoshua Prushansky (1988), whom I visited in Tel Aviv, for telling me about Adolf Rading.

1 Pfankuch 1970, p. 9.
2 Posener 1990, pp. 242–243.
3 Pfankuch 1970, p. 134.
4 *Deutsche Bauzeitung* 56/1926, p. 458.
5 *Der Neubau* 17/1927, pp. 197–205; *Der Neubau* 14/1929, pp. 264–284; *Bauwelt* 23/1927; Müller-Wulckow 1925–1932,

reprint 1975, pp. I, 73; II, 36, 84; III, 48, 49, 51; IV, 24, 25, 98, 111; *Bauwelt* 40/1930, pp. 54–55; Myra Warhaftig, "Deutsches und österreichisches Architekturerbe in Israel" in: *Kunst und Kirche* 4, Darmstadt 1986 pp. 258–259; Szymanski 1992; Pegels 1992; Posener 2004, pp. 282, 361; Göckede 2005.

6 See biography of Kurt Reinsch.

7 *Habinyan Bamisrah Hakarov*, Tel Aviv July 1937, p. 24.

8 See biography of Max Loeb.

9 Pfankuch 1970, pp. 96–99.

10 *Journal of Israel Association of Town Planning* 1/1950, p. 34.

11 The House of Hillel was the school that adopted a lenient, humane attitude towards mankind during the Talmudic period, as opposed to the House of Shammay, whose attitude was of a more rigorous, exacting nature.

12 Jehoshua Prushansky, "Professor Rading and his work in Haifa", unpublished manuscript, April 1958; see also: Kaminka 1980, pp. 77–78; see biography of Gideon Kaminka.

Adolf Rading

Adolf Rading, residence in the Stuttgart-Weissenhof Werkbund exhibition, 1927, view from the garden

Adolf Rading, apartment building in the Werkbundsiedlung Breslau, 1929, partial view from the east

Adolf Rading, Ernst Rading residence, Berlin-Zehlendorf, 1929, view from the front entrance. Photo: M.W. 1989

Adolf Rading, residential block, Berlin-Lichtenberg, 1933

Adolf Rading, stepped housing for Haifa, Mount Carmel, 1936 (sketch)

Stepped housing in Haifa, Mount Carmel, circa 1972, architect unknown. Photo: M.W. 1989

Adolf Rading, Maurice Gerzon residence, Haifa, Mount Carmel, 1939, view from the street. Photo: M.W. 1986

Adolf Rading, Walter Roth residence, Haifa, Mount Carmel, 1939, view from the street

Adolf Rading, Walter Roth residence, Haifa, Mount Carmel, 1939, side view

Adolf Rading, Walter Roth residence, Haifa, Mount Carmel, 1939, entrance

Adolf Rading, Frutarom chemical laboratory, Haifa, 1944, interior courtyard. Photo: M.W. 1988

Adolf Rading, Frutarom chemical laboratory, Haifa, 1944, partial view from the street, with entrance. Photo: M.W. 1988

Bruno Kalitzki

1890 Chemnitz – 1953 Haifa

Bruno Kalitzki (right) and Dov Entin (Eitan)

Bruno Kalitzki was born into a Jewish family from Chemnitz on December 8, 1890. He studied architecture from 1910 to 1914, the first two years at the Technische Hochschule Charlottenburg and then at the Technische Hochschule in Dresden. When World War I broke out in 1914 he joined the army and was not demobilized until 1918. He returned to Chemnitz and there began to practise with the architect Walter Naumann.
During the nineteenth century, Chemnitz had developed from an important centre of textile production for the kingdom of Saxony into a thriving industrial metropolis whose chief enterprise was machine construction. Kalitzki and Naumann contributed greatly to building up Chemnitz during the 1920s. They erected many factories and administration buildings, large and small department stores, and housing developments for workers and civil servants, along with villas and summerhouses in Chemnitz and the surrounding area. In 1925 a comprehensive catalogue listing the designs of the two Chemnitz architects and the projects they had realized was published by Max Hoffman's Verlagsanstalt für Architektur in Berlin-Schöneberg.[1]
In 1929 Kalitzki was able to publish a second survey, solely of his independent projects and with an introduction by W. Illing, in the multi-volume *Neue Werkkunst* series.[2] Among his most important buildings of that period were the 1050-seat Red Tower cinema, located in the city centre, and the 1200-seat Schauburg cinema. Other fields of concentration included department store renovation and construction, the Königsfeld & Co. administrative building, factory buildings and additions, housing developments, and a domicile for the Protestant community.

Kalitzki's buildings created a somewhat confusing impression at times. They were designed neither in the spirit of Neues Bauen nor according to classical models. Rather, they seemed to present a kind of bridging style. In his introduction to the 1929 monograph, Leo Adler assessed Kalitzki's use of forms and attempted to arrive at an explanation: "Bruno Kalitzki belongs to the in-between generation of architects who were educated before the World War and whose creative period came after it. This circumstance means above all that instead of being an architect who, like an alchemist, creates buildings out of the ingredients of the styles he has learned, he became a designer who contemplates the original task of all building, the creation of spaces. From the old-school architect emerged the creator whose activity is closer to that of the constructing technician and economically-thinking engineer."[3]
At the end of the 1920s, Kalitzki built himself a villa in Chemnitz-Schönau, which Adler mentions in his introduction: "The forms (of the house) have something of the moodiness that seems to me to be one of the decisive character traits of our in-between generation. And so perhaps it is precisely the architect's house that is 'real' in a special, if not to say metaphysical, sense; perhaps only in our day could it be erected in this form."[4]

In 1933 Kalitzki fled to Palestine with his Christian wife and settled in Haifa, where he lived and worked until his sudden death in 1953.[5]

In view of the compulsory monetary exchange regulations that existed in Germany after 1931 and the prohibition on taking capital out of the country, special modes of transfer – ha'avara – had to be devised.[6] So German goods needed in Palestine were bought and paid for by persons emigrating from Germany. Upon arriving in Palestine, the individuals received the purchase amount in Palestinian currency (LP) from the importer of the ha'avara. Within the scheme of this transfer system, which enabled all sorts of construction materials to be brought into the country, Kalitzki developed a new area of activity.[7]

He and Dov Entin (Eitan) began to design two- and three-storey apartment buildings that made use of the steel-frame construction system manufactured by Böhler Steel in Berlin. They sent the plans to the factory in Berlin, which did a structural analysis, produced the corresponding steel framework, and shipped it to Haifa under the terms of the transfer contract.[8] In this way, Kalitzki and his partner were able to erect six such buildings in Haifa between 1934 and 1937.[9]

The balanced style of the buildings' façades derives from the construction and makes a simple and practical impression. It is evident that Kalitzki had completely freed himself from the "moody" formal language of his Chemnitz days, meanwhile coming to favour a restrained and functional architecture. Kalitzki was convinced that the Böhler system was optimal for the climatic, economic and topographic conditions of Haifa, published all the details about it, and suggested that colleagues trust and use the system.[10] Unfortunately, political developments then blocked any further such experiments.

I was fortunate to be able to visit Bruno Kalitzki's wife Margarethe Kalitzki in her Berlin apartment five weeks before her death in 1986. She kindly provided me with a great deal of information and material, for which I am most grateful.

1 Illing 1925.
2 Adler 1929.
3 Ibid., p. VII. See also biography of Leo Adler.
4 Ibid., p. XIII.
5 After Kalitzki died, his wife Margarethe Kalitzki returned to Germany and lived in Berlin-Wilmersdorf until her death in 1986.
6 Feilchenfeld 1972, p. 38.
7 In connection with Bruno Kalitzki's work in Israel, it is necessary to provide a brief explanation of the immigration regulations enacted by the British mandate government in Palestine in 1933 to limit the influx of Jewish refugees from Germany. Immigrants were assigned to strictly bureaucratic categories according to the following criteria:
Category A: Immigrants with independent means
A1: Immigrants with at least LP 1000
A2: Immigrants – freelancers with at least LP 500
A3: Immigrants – tradesmen with at least LP 250
A4: Pensioners with monthly income of at least LP 4

A5: Those with at least LP 500 having reasonable expectations of success in their specialized professions
Category B: Immigrants with assured support
B1: Orphan children with assured support through public institutions
B2: Those with religious occupations
B3: Students in educational institutions
Category C: Immigrants with definite prospects of employment (worker certificate)
Category D: Invited immigrants
D1: Relatives of immigrants
D2: Special workers

8 Because of this regulation, in 1933–34 some fourteen copper prefabricated houses by Hirsch-Kupfer-Messingwerk Berlin, whose owner was Jewish, also entered the port of Haifa. At least four of the copper prefab houses still stand on Mount Carmel.

9 Herbert 1980, pp. B16–B18.

10 Bruno Kalitzki & Dov Entin, "Böhler-Stahlbau in Haifa" in: *Habinyan Bamisrah Hakarov*, Tel Aviv July 1937, pp. 10–11.

Right page above:
Bruno Kalitzki and Walter Naumann, administration building Gebr. Sußmann AG, Chemnitz, 1928

Right page below:
Bruno Kalitzki and Walter Naumann, factory Karl Fr. Kreissig, Jahnsdorf, 1928

KARL FR. KREISSIG

Bruno Kalitzki, Villa K., Chemnitz-Schönau, 1928, view from the garden

Bruno Kalitzki and Dov Entin (Eitan), apartment building, Haifa, Mount Carmel, 1936, construction using the Böhler system from Berlin

Bruno Kalitzki and Dov Entin (Eitan), apartment building, Haifa, Mount Carmel, 1937, construction using the Böhler system from Berlin. Photo: M.W. 1986

Bruno Kalitzki and Dov Entin (Eitan), apartment building, Haifa, Mount Carmel, 1937, construction using the Böhler system from Berlin, floor plan

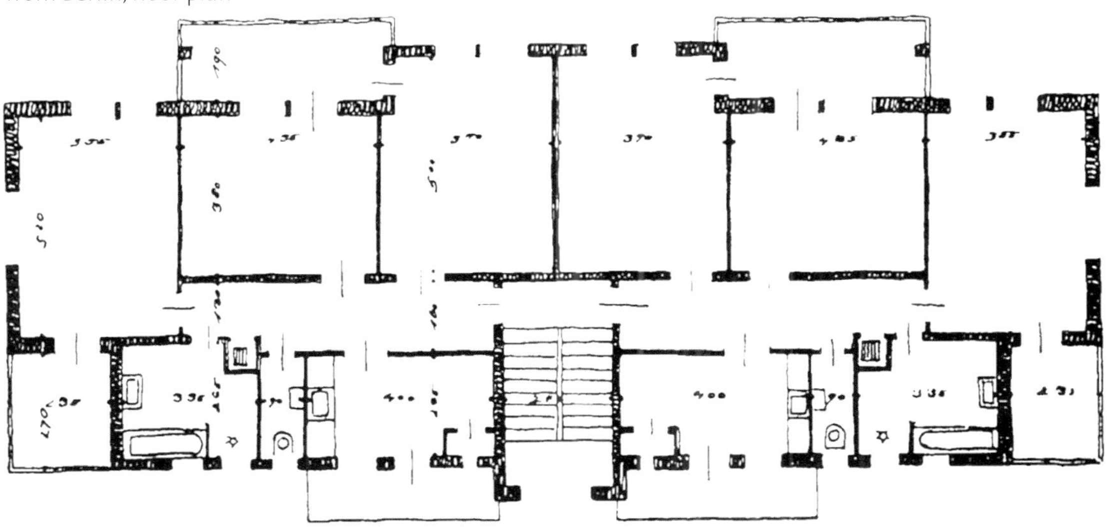

PAUL ENGELMANN

1891 Olmütz – 1965 Tel Aviv

Paul Engelmann built houses, designed furniture, published books and articles, created paintings, and wrote psychological case studies. His essays on philosophy, religion, art, and literature and on Austrian, German, and Israeli politics remain unpublished.[1] The fact that he never graduated from college was no obstacle to his endeavours.
Born on June 14, 1891, in Olmütz (Olomouc, today in the Czech Republic), Engelmann graduated from secondary school there in 1909 and then went to Vienna to study architecture at the Technische Hochschule. But he soon broke off his studies, for encounters with Adolf Loos and Karl Kraus had opened new perspectives for him, and his interest turned to philosophy and literature.
The completion of Adolf Loos's department store and apartment block for Goldmann & Salatsch on Michaelerplatz in Vienna presented Paul Engelmann with an unusual opportunity. He responded to the outrage that this functional, ornament-free new building had unleashed among conservative architects and laymen with a poem of praise, "The Building on Michaelerplatz". The poem was published in Karl Kraus's satirical magazine *Die Fackel*.[2]
When Adolf Loos founded his private school of architecture in 1912, Engelmann became his first pupil and colleague. Although the school closed after only two years, Adolf Loos's teachings so greatly influenced Engelmann that Loos's central idea of the Raumplan, denoting spatial planning in housing, remained with Engelmann for the rest of his life.[3]
For health reasons – as a youth he had a bad case of tuberculosis – Engelmann was exempted from military service in World War I. He left Vienna in 1914 and returned to his parents' house in Olmütz. There he received a visitor, a soldier stationed in Olmütz, who came at the recommendation of Adolf Loos: the philosopher Ludwig Wittgenstein. As a result of this meeting, the two men developed a close friendship that led to later professional collaboration.

After the war, Engelmann began to work as an architect. He first took on repair work that Wittgenstein steered his way, making structural alterations to the Wittgenstein residence in Neuwaldegg, where the family occasionally lived in the spring and

Paul Engelmann (left) and Dr. Max Zweig

autumn. He also carried out renovations to the family's home in the Alleegasse, today Argentinierstrasse, in Vienna's fourth district.

Early in 1925, Engelmann wrote Wittgenstein a letter in which he stated that he intended to immigrate to Palestine, an undertaking that Wittgenstein supported.[4] But this immigration plan was initially postponed, because Engelmann was given the opportunity to build a house for Wittgenstein's sister in Vienna.

At the end of 1925, Engelmann finally received a contract from Margarethe Wittgenstein-Stonborough to design a modern villa, where she intended to spend the rest of her life. In close consultation with her, Engelmann designed the plans to the construction stage during the spring of 1926. Wittgenstein, who had trained to be a mechanical engineer, designed the technical details such as windows, doors and heating, and assumed responsibility for the construction process while Engelmann was away from Vienna. Possibly Wittgenstein influenced the building's architecture in more ways than can now be determined.[5] Nevertheless, the upper-class private residence of the philosopher's sister Margarethe Wittgenstein-Stonborough, erected in 1928 at Kundmanngasse 19 in Vienna's third district, can in no way be ascribed solely to Ludwig Wittgenstein.[6] The architect Jacques Groag, also Adolf Loos's pupil in Olmütz, was responsible for the technical execution.[7]

An inconspicuous piece of paper was found in Engelmann's estate on which he had made a handwritten list of the buildings he realized in European cities from 1918 to 1933 and in Israeli cities from 1935 to 1955.[8] Among his last buildings before 1933 were the much-published Vladimir Müller residence in Olmütz (1926–28), the Villa Groß in Libenitze near Olmütz (1928), the Villa Guttmann in Mährisch-Ostrau (1929), the Villa Beckmann renovation, also in Mährisch-Ostrau (1930), as well as ten buildings in a housing development for Dr. Liebermann in Stanislav, today Ivano-Frankovsk in Poland, which were built between 1930 and 1933.

In Palestine in 1934, Engelmann met his "class comrade", the dramatist Max Zweig (1892–1992), who also had fled fascism.[9] The two rented two tiny rooms in the attic of a nondescript two-storey building in one of Tel Aviv's finest streets. There they lived extremely modestly until Engelmann's death on February 7, 1965.

Engelmann reduced his architectural activities to a minimum during the last three decades of his life in order to dedicate himself to writing. However, he still built four one-family houses, one in Haifa, one in Herzlia and two in Ramat-Gan. For three apartment buildings in Tel Aviv and the surrounding area, he supervised a renovation, an addition, and an additional storey, respectively. He also designed furniture for "The Cultivated Home", a furniture store founded in 1934 by Arthur Wachsberger, who had run a store under the same name in Cologne until 1933.[10] Engelmann designed some of the furniture together with his good friend Kurt Unger.[11] The two had taken part in a 1937 competition for "The Marketplace in Haifa". In 1947 Engelmann also designed the interiors of the Jordanian parliament and the throne hall of King Abdullah in Rabat Ammon.[12]

Engelmann built two residences in accordance with Adolf Loos's spatial concepts, one in 1928 for Vladimir Müller in Olmütz and a second one in 1936 for Dr. Yedlin on Mount Carmel, Haifa. Both were modest, with two storeys and a basement, in Loos's characteristic multi-level cubic form – the rooms being located not on traditional floors, but at different levels with ceilings of different heights within an all-encompassing spatial relationship. In addition, the street façades of both residences featured a wooden pergola. It was only the brise-soleils above the windows, the curving corner, and the thousands of plants surrounding the Haifa residence that indicated its proximity to the Mediterranean Sea. The building on Mount Carmel was demolished in 1995.

Judaism, political Zionism and the social Zionist idea of the kibbutz movement all had a significant place in Engelmann's thinking, although he was not an Orthodox Jew. At the same time, he kept the memory of his lost world, his family and circle of friends from the Olmütz period, intensely alive. The entire Engelmann family finally fell victim to the Nazi terror. His brother, known as a caricaturist under the pseudonym Peter Eng, committed suicide with his wife when the Nazis occupied Czechoslovakia. His sister Anne, whom he described as a "highly gifted children's book illustrator", was quite melancholy and lived a secluded life in her parents' apartment until all were deported.
In the months before his death, Paul Engelmann began to record the memories of his youth. He dedicated them to his mother, to whom he was very attached: "My few friends and the young people who frequented our house all revered my mother, who frequently was a listener at our evening gatherings, and actually was a highly understanding participant. Everyone felt that she deserved thanks for the unusual comfort and warmth of those evenings. Wittgenstein, who everywhere except in his Vienna family circle felt as lonesome as if he were in a desert, and who naturally would have felt that way in Olmütz, was among those in whom intense feelings of gratitude arose. Our friends called our apartment, with good-humoured irony but not behind our backs, the 'Palace on Mauritz Square'. Mauritzplatz was located in the city centre; our apartment, however, was in the rear wing and looked out on the ancient, wondrous Mauritz church. It was an area, however, in which no respectable family lived."[13]

In memory of the works of his best friends Adolf Loos (1870–1933), Karl Kraus (1874–1936), and Ludwig Wittgenstein (1889–1951), Engelmann published a series of pamphlets in German entitled *Gedanken* between 1944 and 1949. His essays in Hebrew on the works of those thinkers appeared in the journal *Prosdor*, where the Zionist philosophers Martin Buber (1878–1965), Margarete Susman (1874–1966), and Hugo Bergmann (1883–1975) also published.
Engelmann was a loner. He worked for the most meagre honorariums and wanted above all to have an influence on political and social circumstances in Israel. He warned his small, loyal circle of friends about the decline of the pioneer spirit and the loss of socialism within the kibbutz movement. Engelmann was an architect, a draftsman and also a thinker, but above all, he was a just man — a socialist, pacifist and idealist.

From 1985 until his death in 1989, I visited Yehuda Kurt Unger regularly at his apartment on Mount Carmel, Haifa. He always welcomed me with great enthusiasm, and he told me a great deal about Paul Engelmann and showed me his notes and his paintings. I am very grateful to him for the unforgettable conversations.

1 Paul Engelmann archive, Jerusalem National and University Library.
2 *Die Fackel* 317/318, Vienna February 28, 1911, p. 18; Engelmann 1967.

3 Yehuda Kurt Unger and Eugen Szekey were also advocates of Adolf Loos's architectonic concept. See biographies.
4 Engelmann 1970, p. 38.
5 Myra Warhaftig, "Deutsches und österreichisches Architekturerbe in Israel" in: *Kunst und Kirche* 4, Darmstadt 1986, pp. 260–261; Wijdeveld 1994, pp. 53–57; Bakacsy (ed.) 1999.
6 Vladimir Slapeta, "Paul Engelmann und Jacques Groag, die Olmützer Schüler von Adolf Loos" in: *Bauwelt* 40, Berlin 1978, p. 1494 ff; Gebauer 1982.
7 The Czech architect and painter Jacques Groag (1892–1961) fled in 1938 to London.
8 Paul Engelmann gave a copy of the list to his friend Yehuda Kurt Unger.
9 Zweig 1987, pp. 77, 157, 172 ff.
10 Arthur Wachsberger, PhD, art historian and interior designer, was born 1891 in Troppau, Silesia and died 1943 in Haifa. He and his family arrived in Palestine in 1933, and he pioneered a hitherto unknown lifestyle there through his furniture factory.
11 See biography of Kurt Unger.
12 From the author's conversation with Yehuda Kurt Unger in the summer of 1987. Engelmann 1967, p. 1.
13 Engelmann 1970, p. 43.

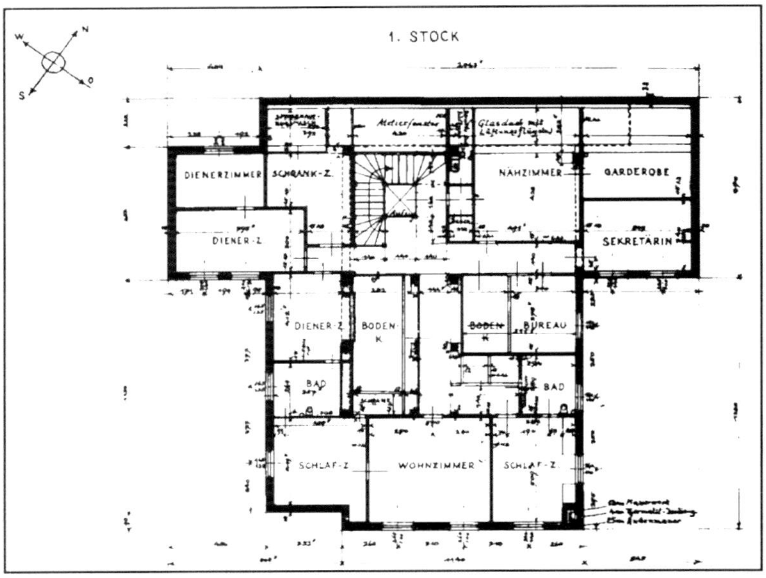

Left page above:
Paul Engelmann and Ludwig Wittgenstein, Margarethe Wittgenstein-Stonborough residence, Vienna, 1928, first-floor plan

Left page below:
Paul Engelmann and Ludwig Wittgenstein, Margarethe Wittgenstein-Stonborough residence, Vienna, 1928, view from the corner of Parkgasse and Geusaugasse (drawing by Paul Engelmann)

Right page above:
Paul Engelmann, Dr. Yedlin residence, Haifa, Mount Carmel, 1936 (demolished 1995), side view. Photo: M.W. 1986

Right page below:
Paul Engelmann, Dr. Yedlin residence, Haifa, Mount Carmel, 1936 (demolished 1995), interior (incorporating Loos's spatial plan). Photo: M.W. 1986

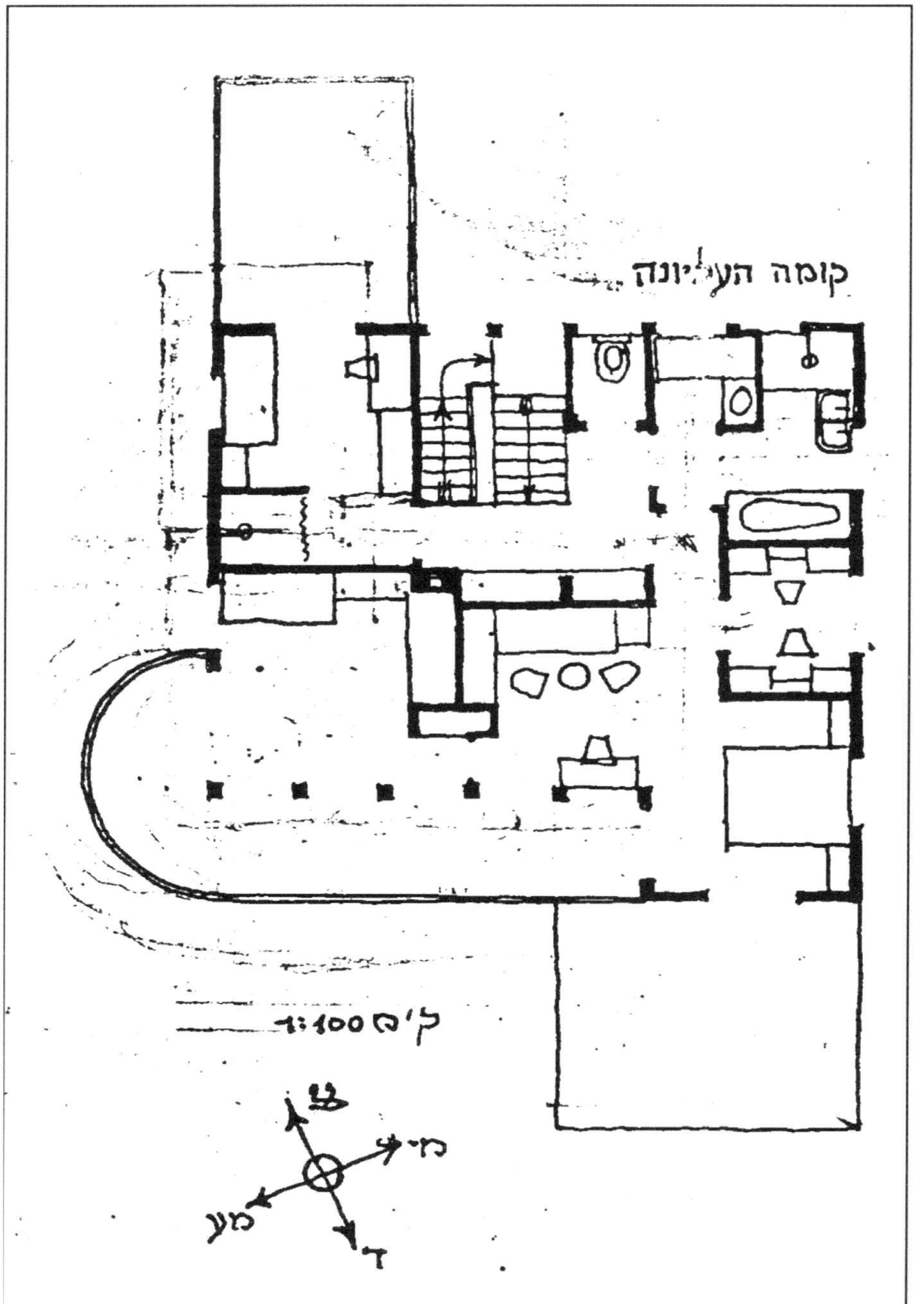

Left page:
Paul Engelmann, Dr. Yedlin residence, Haifa, Mount Carmel, 1936, top-floor plan

Right Page:
Paul Engelmann, Dr. Yedlin residence, Haifa, Mount Carmel, 1936 (demolished 1995), view from the street. Photo: M.W. 1986

סגנון אמת

לזכרו

של

אדולף לוס

הבית בככר המיכאלים בוינה, 1910

יוצא ע"י פאול אֶנגֶלמן

ויוסף שכטר

תל-אביב 1946

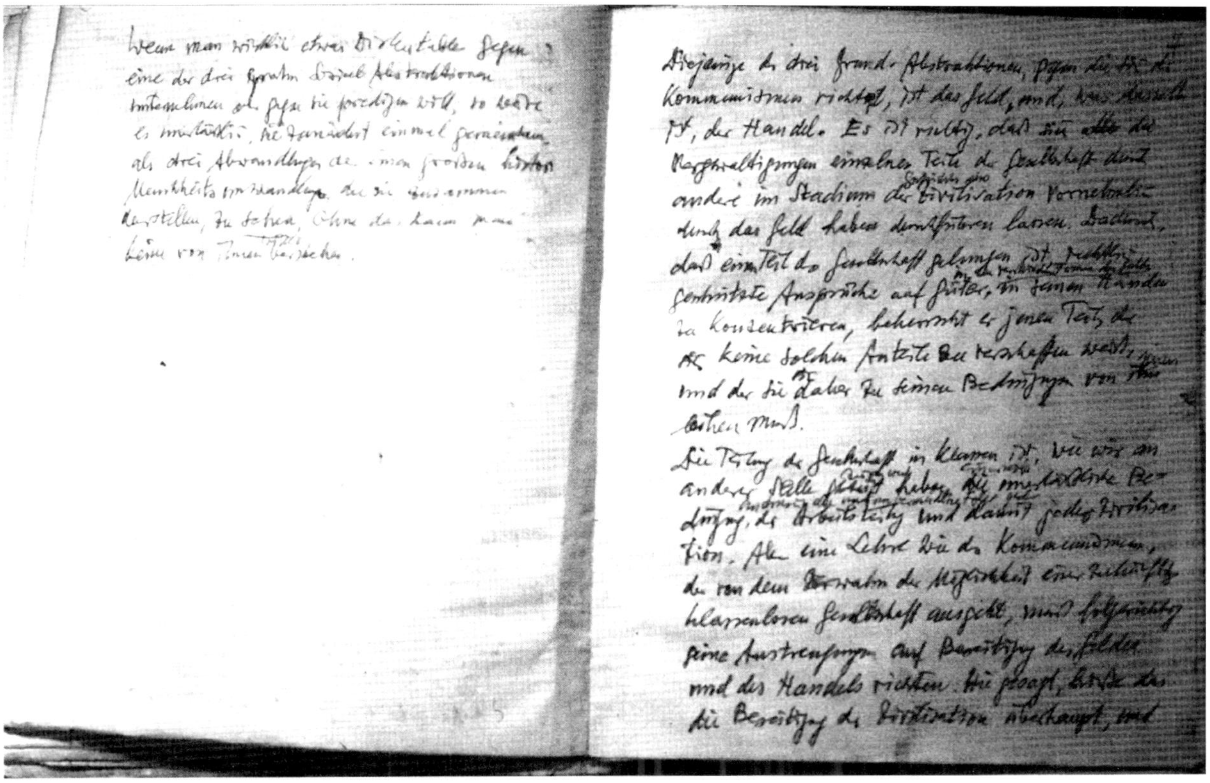

Paul Engelmann, "Die Urproduzierende Großstadt", Tel Aviv 1963, unpublished manuscript

Left page:
True Style, in memory of Adolf Loos, edited by Paul Engelmann and Josef Schächter, Tel Aviv 1946, view of the Michaelerplatz building by Adolf Loos (1910), book cover

Leo Adler

1891 Kertsch – 1962 Ein Charod

Leo Adler was born in Russia and died in Israel, but developed his scientific and artistic abilities in Berlin, where he spent his most creative years. Adler's philosophic writings were in German, although Russian was his mother tongue and Hebrew became the language he spoke every day with his children.

Leo Adler was born in Kertsch on October 8, 1891, into a family that came from Königsberg (Kaliningrad). He went to Berlin to study architecture in 1910. Late in 1912 he transferred to the Technische Hochschule in Munich, where he earned his degree. At the outbreak of World War I Adler entered the German army. After he recovered from severe injuries sustained at Verdun in 1916, Adler went to Dresden and in 1920 submitted his dissertation titled "Beiträge zu einer Entwicklungsgeschichte der Baukunst" (contributions to the history of the development of architecture).[1]

Meanwhile, Adler had decided to devote himself to architectural theory. While writing on the subject, he lived alternately in Dresden, Leipzig and Berlin. In 1926 he moved with his young family to Deidesheimer Strasse 22 in Berlin-Wilmersdorf, where he lived and wrote nearly all of his works until he was stripped of his professional memberships in the Bund Deutscher Architekten (BDA), Deutscher Werkbund (DWB) and Architekten-und Ingenieur-Verein (AIV) and was obliged to leave Germany.

Certainly the time of Adler's greatest influence was in Germany from 1920 to 1933. His most significant achievement, the four-volume *Wasmuths Lexikon der Baukunst*, an encyclopedia of architecture that he published between 1929 and 1931, remains unsurpassed as a standard reference.[2] As Adler was completing work on the final volume, Ernst Pollak, the Berlin publisher who brought out a series of six books on the subject of avant-garde architecture between 1928 and 1931, asked him to analyse the development of architecture with respect to European apartment buildings and housing developments of the second half of the 1920s.[3] Adler published the essays he collected and edited as *Neuzeitliche Mietshäuser und Siedlungen*.[4] In words and pictures, Adler sensitively and objectively pointed out the breakthrough of Modern architecture. Today, many of the apartment buildings and housing developments he described no longer exist – they were either destroyed in wartime or demolished later on. The book is consequently a priceless document about the development of Modern architecture in Europe in the 1920s.

Since at that time there was no journal devoted solely to the history and theory of architecture, Adler founded *Architectura*, a periodical to document international research that was supposed to appear six times per year. Adler was able to compile the first two issues before he had to flee. When the Koldewey Society convened in Hanover in 1933 to discuss the themes for the coming issues, Adler no longer was present. A decision was taken to publish an annual volume rather than bimonthly issues, but the first volume of *Architectura* in 1933 was also the last. During this time, Adler also wrote articles for various other journals. The major part of his intellectual legacy still lies scattered and overlooked in large German libraries.[5]

Still earlier, in 1926, Adler had published a philosophical treatise on the nature of architecture titled *Vom Wesen der Baukunst, Volume I*.[6] Due to political circumstances, he was unable to publish a second volume as he had intended. The author's copy of the first volume, with his numerous hand-written corrections and notations, is in the collection of his estate.

Leo Adler as a student

When the Nazis assumed power in 1933, Adler fled with his wife, daughter and son to Palestine. The family was able to rent an apartment in Tel Aviv, in a multi-family building that Adler had designed ten years earlier, in Germany, for his Zionist in-laws the Romanovs. The struggle for survival was difficult. Adler, the successful writer and theoretician on architecture from Germany, was suddenly no longer needed. All he had at first was the language of architecture. So he designed a factory for porcelain teeth, a three-storey office building, and two or three multi-family residences in Tel Aviv, entered some competitions, and was a judge for architectural prizes. Together with S. Steinbock, Adler was editor of the Hebrew journal *Habinyan Bamisrah Hakarov. A Palestine Periodical for Architecture in the Near East* from 1937 to 1938.[7]
Three of Adler's closest friends, who knew of his fame in Germany, encouraged him to resume his theoretical analysis of architecture. In 1948 the pamphlet *Analytische Perspektive* appeared, his first publication since 1933. In it, Adler developed a graphic system that made it possible to construct a perspective geometrically, without a vanishing point, solely with the help of right-angled coordinates. Adler's friends hoped to motivate him to reconnect with his Berlin epoch and publish additional scholarly works. But the circumstances of life in Palestine were so completely different and difficult to negotiate that Adler moved in with his daughter, who lived in Kibbutz Ein Charod, in 1952. From 1955 to 1958, he was the chief engineer in the region of Gilboa-Izrael, an area south of the Sea of Galilee encompassing twenty-seven communities – towns, villages and kibbutzim. He designed plans for these communities and documented the region's development. He also gave drawing lessons in a school. Adler died on August 6, 1962, and was buried in the kibbutz cemetery.

The multi-family Romanov apartment building in Tel Aviv, designed in 1924, remained the only building that translated Adler's analytic mindset into reality. The ground plan shows how attached he remained to the Berlin lifestyle, but the façade clearly indicates that he also reckoned with the country's climatic conditions. The three-storey apartment building is located in the old city centre. On each floor there are two 151 m^2 five-room apartments. The floor plan exhibits the spatial arrangement of an upper-class nineteenth century Berlin apartment, with only minor alterations. Facing the street are the rooms for social functions (work room, dining room and a glass-enclosed loggia). Bedrooms and baths face the interior courtyard. But a large kitchen with a pantry takes the place of the traditional so-called "Berliner Zimmer".[8] Next to it is a servant's room. All the rooms were accessible from a long, narrow, windowless hallway, as was common in Berlin. And Adler did not fail to include a delivery staircase, though there was no use for it in Palestine. However that staircase (which since has been torn down) and the rear kitchen entrances were no longer enclosed spaces, but were left open on account of the subtropical climate. To reduce the penetration of glaring sunlight into the living rooms, Adler designed the façade with a row of small windows, which he further fitted with shade-giving brise-soleils. With his use of locally-made cast-iron fencing and colourful mosaic floors, Adler employed elements that were very popular in Arabian residences of the Ottoman empire in Palestine.

I first visited Adler's daughter Vera Arnon in Kibbutz Ein-Charod in the summer of 1985. Since then we have met many times. She showed me materials from her father's estate and told me about him and the family – their life prior to 1933 in Berlin, then in Tel Aviv and later in Kibbutz Ein-Charod. At the kibbutz, I also met her daughter Nurit and some of her grandchildren. In the process, a beautiful and trusting friendship has developed, for which I am most grateful to Vera.

1 His thesis examiner was Prof. Dr. Cornelius Gurlitt (1850–1938). The second examiner was Prof. Dr. Bühler.
2 This encyclopedia of architecture is a reference on all aspects of the theory and practice of architecture; it covers construction and the history and art of architecture and contains all the important architectural biographies. Outstanding reproductions and hand-drawn details round off this standard work.
3 Ernst Pollack, a Jew born in Prague in 1893, fled Prague for Italy in 1939, after which his trail disappears. See: Warhaftig 2005, p. 33.
4 Adler 1931, reprint 1998 with an afterword by Myra Warhaftig.
5 Leo Adler, "Über das System der Künste" in: Max Dessoir, *Zeitschrift für Ästhetik und allgemeine Kulturwissenschaft* XVIII/3, 1924, pp. 258–259; Leo Adler, "Theorie der Baukunst als reine und angewandte Wissenschaft" in: *Zeitschrift für Ästhetik und allgemeine Kulturwissenschaft* XX/3, 1926, pp. 273–287; Leo Adler, "Die Notwendigkeit regelmäßiger Gestaltung des Ulmer Münsterplatz" in: *Wasmuths Monatshefte für Baukunst*, Berlin 1924, pp. 412–414. *Wasmuths Lexikon der Baukunst* I/1929, II/1930, III–IV/1931; Adler 1931, reprint 1998; Leo Adler, *Architectura*, Berlin 1933.
6 Adler 1926, reprint 2000; other publications about Leo Adler: Myra Warhaftig, Leo Adler 1981–1962, in: *Bauwelt* 93/1991, p. 2083; Warhaftig 2005, Adler, Leo.
7 See brief biography of Jehoshua Shani (Steinbock).
8 The Berliner Zimmer was a dark room with a window facing the courtyard that connected the front part of the building with the side wing. It was a typical feature of Berlin's nineteenth century apartment houses.

Leo Adler, *Vom Wesen der Baukunst*, Volume I, Leipzig 1926, book cover

Leo Adler, *Vom Wesen der Baukunst*, Volume I, Leipzig 1926, p. 58 (drawing)

Leo Adler, *Vom Wesen der Baukunst*, Volume I, Leipzig 1926, p. 59 (drawing)

Neuzeitliche Miethäuser und Siedlungen, edited by Leo Adler, Berlin 1931, book cover

Architectura. Jahrbuch für Geschichte der Baukunst, Volume I, edited by Leo Adler, Berlin 1933, book cover

Leo Adler

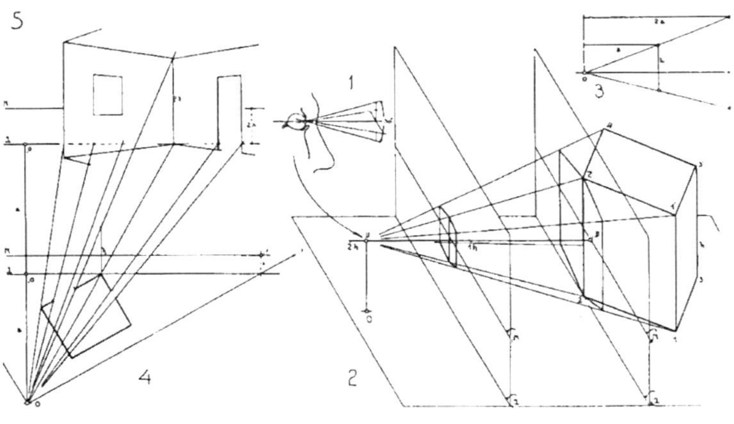

above:
Leo Adler, Romanov building, Tel Aviv, 1924, view from the street.
Photo: M.W. 1986

below:
Leo Adler, *Analytische Perspektive*, Tel Aviv 1948, table 5

Right page:
Leo Adler, Romanov building, Tel Aviv, 1924, floor with colourful mosaic.
Photo: M.W. 1986

Kurt Reinsch

1892 Burg – 1952 Haifa

It was quite difficult to track down information about the life and work of the architect Kurt Reinsch. After many conversations and extensive correspondence with various persons in Israel, I learned from an elderly woman in a Tel Aviv home for the aged that his wife's niece lived in a Jerusalem suburb. After visiting her, I was able to sketch the general outlines of Reinsch's life. The dates mentioned below are taken from his record in the archives of the registry of Haifa.

Kurt Reinsch was born into a Christian family in Burg near Magdeburg on November 2, 1892. He studied architecture and civil engineering at the Technische Hochschule in Dresden and in Darmstadt, where he received his diploma in June 1914. He was conscripted soon afterward and served as a soldier in World War I. After the war Reinsch moved to Munich, where he met the philosopher and Zionist Tony (Antonia) Gelner. They married and, acting on their convictions, immigrated to Palestine in 1923. Six years later they left the country, for they could find no work. They moved to Breslau and then to Liegnitz, where Reinsch worked as an architect for the Silesian Heimstätten-Gesellschaft. After the National Socialists came to power in 1933, they fled to Palestine and settled in Haifa, where Kurt Reinsch and Adolf Rading were brought together by their common fate. At any rate, publications indicate that the two carried out some joint projects in Haifa.[1]

Reinsch was the sole designer of the Slitzan residence on Mount Carmel, built in 1936–38 (next to Paul Engelmann's house for Dr. Yedlin). The generously proportioned one-family house, a cube faced with limestone, has two storeys over a full basement. On the ground floor (ca. 130 m^2) are a large entrance hall, the kitchen, dining room, living room and a library. Four large bedrooms and the sanitary facilities are on the first floor. A spiral staircase on the exterior wall leads to a rooftop terrace. With its sand-coloured façade and white spiral staircase, the house is striking in the midst of the lush vegetation.
According to a current next-door neighbour, Reinsch had also built two other one-family houses on the same street; one had been for himself and his wife. The one-storey building has a tile roof and is concealed by bushes and old trees somewhat below street level.[2]
Reinsch and his wife had been considered bohemians, and their home was a centre for Zionists, socialists and German emigré intellectuals such as Shmaryahu Levin, Pinchas Ruthenberg, Berl Katzenelson and Arnold Zweig.[3]
From other sources, I was told several times that there had been an excellent restaurant called "KurtTony" near the Haifa harbour, which Reinsch owned and where his wife Tony prepared fish dishes.[4] This was during the war years, when there was hardly any work for architects and philosophers. But the convivial life ceased in the mid-1940s, when Kurt and Tony Reinsch's marriage broke apart.
Disappointed, impoverished, and lonely, Reinsch died in Haifa on July 24, 1952, and was buried there in the

Christian cemetery. To pay his debts, Haifa's municipal administration offered his paintings for sale. All the paintings were sold and his debts repaid, except for two oil paintings, a landscape of Mount Carmel and a portrait of Tony Gelner, which her niece has retained as keepsakes.

I was able to compile information about the life of Kurt Reinsch from three sources: the aforementioned record in Haifa; a conversation in Jerusalem (1987) with Dr. Judith Schönberg, Tony (Antonia) Gelner's niece; and Reinsch's gravestone in the Christian cemetery. I am also very grateful to Judith Schönberg for the photograph of Kurt Reinsch and the portrait of Tony Gelner used as illustrations.

1 Kurt Reinsch, "Villa für Herrn. L., Kiryat Bialik, 1937" in: *Habinyan Bamisrah Hakarov* 2, Tel Aviv November 1937, p. 12; see biography of Adolf Rading.
2 No plan of the building was in the Haifa archive.
3 Shmaryahu Levin (1867–1935), Zionist politician and propagandist, was born in Russia and studied in Königsberg (Kaliningrad) and Berlin. He moved to Palestine in 1924. Pinchas Ruthenberg: see biography of Erich Mendelsohn, note 3; Berl Katzenelson: see Jochanan (Eugen) Ratner's biography. Arnold Zweig: see Harry Rosenthal's biography.
4 Along with his work as an architect, Reinsch was a versatile artist who played the flute and painted.

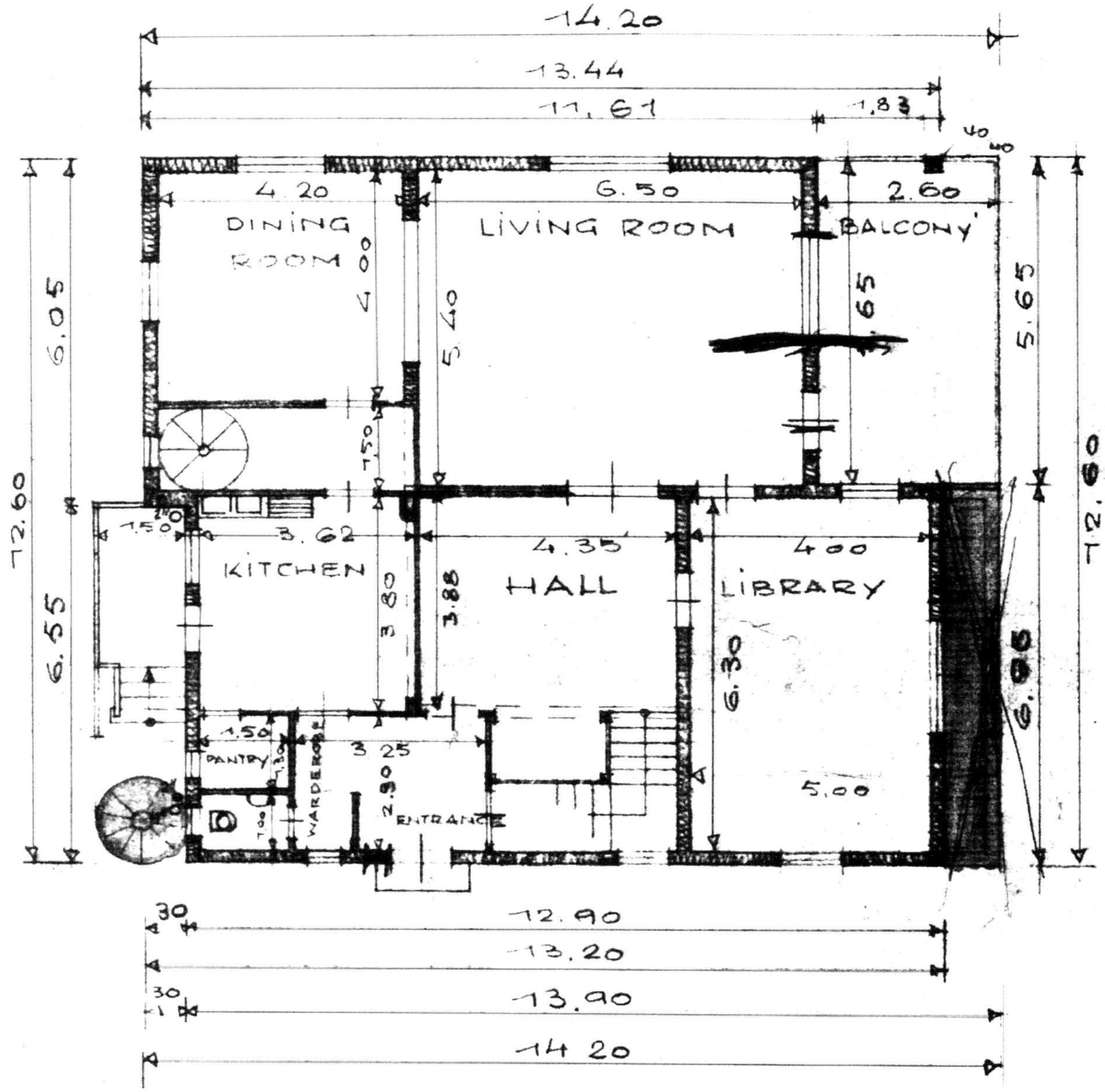

Kurt Reinsch, Slitzan residence, Haifa, Mount Carmel, 1936–1938, ground-floor plan

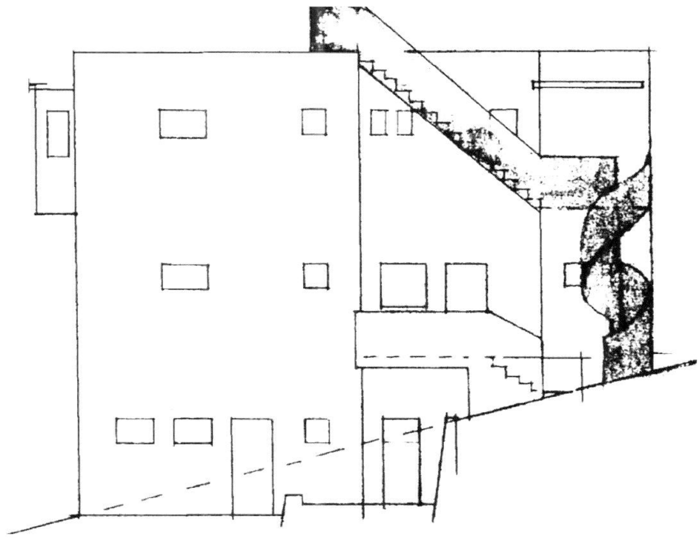

Kurt Reinsch, Slitzan residence, Haifa, Mount Carmel, 1936–1938, side view (drawing)

Kurt Reinsch, Slitzan residence, Haifa, Mount Carmel, 1936–1938, view from the street. Photo M.W. 1989

Left page above:
Kurt Reinsch (attributed), Anja residence, Haifa, Mount Carmel, circa 1935, view from the street.
Photo: M.W. 1989

Left page below:
Kurt Reinsch (attributed), Reinsch residence, Haifa, Mount Carmel, circa 1935, view from the street.
Photo: M.W. 1989

Right page:
Kurt Reinsch, Tony (Antonia Gelner), 1930s, oil painting

Harry Rosenthal

Harry Rosenthal, self portraits (drawings)

1892 Posen – 1966 London

The search for information about Harry Rosenthal's fate, which I began in the summer of 1985, lasted for many suspenseful months. Although his activities in Berlin and Brandenburg up to 1933 had been described in numerous German professional journals, and two foreign ones had published accounts of his work in Palestine up to 1938, I could find no indications whatsoever about the subsequent course of Rosenthal's life or the whereabouts of his estate.[1] Until I learned one day from Eugen Szekey's widow in Haifa that Rosenthal had lived in London after 1939.[2] Then I turned to the Royal Institute of British Architects (RIBA). Although Harry Rosenthal was not registered there, the director of the Institute's library, Ruth H. Kamen, gave me the address of a Mrs. Marjorie Rosenthal (ca. 1905–1993) in London in the hope that this might be of help. It turned out that this woman was Harry Rosenthal's widow, whom he had married in London after the war. She was very touched when I asked her about her husband, and about what had happened to him and his works; it was the first time that anyone had inquired about him since his death. She invited me to London and made her husband's estate available for my research. Later she visited me in Berlin and at my suggestion, she bequeathed her husband's estate to the Berlin Academy of Arts.[3]
Harry Rosenthal was doubtless instrumental in shaping and influencing modern architecture in Berlin. Prior to 1933, professional journals within Germany and abroad paid great attention to the formal attributes of his residential buildings, the organization of his floor plans, and the furniture he designed. The list of his publications is long, and renowned critics such as Max Osborn, Arnold Zweig and Julius Posener held his works in high esteem.

Harry Rosenthal was born on May 3, 1892, in Posen, Prussia, today Poznan in Poland. His study of architecture at the Technische Hochschule in Munich was interrupted when he was conscripted into World War I in 1914. At Verdun he sustained serious injuries from which he suffered for the rest of his life. Discharged early from military service, Rosenthal resumed his studies at the Technische Hochschule Charlottenburg (Berlin), earning his diploma in 1919. Before he opened his own office in 1922, he gained two or three years of practical experience in the firms of Hans Poelzig and Bruno Taut. Among Rosenthal's works in Berlin are one-family and multi-family residences as well as studios and weekend homes, whose interiors he often designed as well.
The residence and office that Rosenthal built in 1923 in Berlin-Wilmersdorf for his brother, the physician Dr. Ernst Rosenthal, created many problems for him at the time. Because the symmetrically designed building had a flat roof, Harry Rosenthal was unable to get a construction permit. But he remained persistent and did not hesitate to mobilize Hans Poelzig and the boards of the Bund Deutscher Architekten

(BDA) and the Werkbund (DWB) and bring them into the discussion. In the December 18, 1924, issue of the *8 Uhr Abendblatt* he brought the matter to public attention, citing the reason given by Wilmersdorf's construction authority in its written statement: "The building in its proposed form would contrast disturbingly with its surroundings and thus offend any eye that appreciates aesthetic form."
Hans Poelzig disputed that and formulated his protest: "In no way does the design give cause for any aesthetic misgivings, in my opinion. The building is restrained and clearly structured, and the arrangement of flat roofs and projecting concrete slabs is as much a part of contemporary artistic expression as steeper roofs were for a bygone era." After a further heated exchange of letters, the building authority permitted the building on Westfälische Strasse 85 to be erected as intended in its Modern form, if only so as not to exacerbate the already high rate of unemployment in the construction trades.[4] When construction was completed in 1929, Rosenthal and his brother moved in. The two lived and worked there until they were forced to emigrate in 1933.

Most of Rosenthal's buildings were destroyed during the war.[5] The brick villa in expressive form erected in Berlin-Wilmersdorf in 1924, which belonged to the banker Eugen Bab, still stands, although its striking zigzag gable ends have been partially removed. The building originally had formal rooms richly decorated with art, as well as several bedrooms and auxiliary rooms, a swimming pool and even a private synagogue for the Bab family. The prayer room, sheathed in travertine and dedicated "to the memory of my blessed father Moritz Bab", also was designed by Rosenthal. From the sculptor and architect Paul Rudolf Henning (1886–1986), Bab acquired a ceramic frieze, "The Other Dance Song", a figuration after Nietzsche's *Thus Spake Zarathustra*, for the oval vestibule of the house. The intertwined dancing figures and the words of Nietzsche were united under the same roof with the Magen David, the symbol of Judaism. Today the building contains ten different apartments, several shops and a school of dance.
The Modern style of the 1927 Eisner house in Berlin-Grunewald was discarded and changed after 1933, as evidenced most of all by the tiled gable roof. The thoroughly Modern studio that Harry Rosenthal built in 1930 for the writer and cultural philosopher Arnold Zweig (1887–1968) in Berlin-Eichkamp also was the victim of nationalistic cultural barbarism. The building, which Arnold Zweig called his "work cottage", was cubic in form, partially prefabricated, and made of wood; it had a 45 m^2 workroom and a kitchen and dining area on the ground floor as well as a bedroom and terrace upstairs. Since Zweig had a visual impairment, the house was designed with a lot of glass. In 1933 Zweig fled with his wife and two sons to Palestine and his house was Aryanized. By 1938, the glass surfaces had been walled over, new openings put in, and the flat roof replaced by a gabled one.
The only Rosenthal work in Berlin that survives in its original form is the multi-family Simon apartment building in the Schmargendorf district. The three-storey structure with three staircase entrances is characterized by an expressively designed façade. Narrow windows along the long axis are arranged increasingly close together toward the outward-sweeping crest of the balcony, the interval then grows larger again, and the rhythm again swells and recedes with the second and third balconies.
Another work by Harry Rosenthal that was minimally altered is situated on a forested hill above a lake, the Scharmützelsee, in Bad Saarow. Ironically enough, it was the 1925 studio of Josef Thorak (1889–1952), the sculptor and favourite of Hitler, which survived both National Socialism and Communism. Thorak is supposed to have produced his colossal figures in the approximately $7 \times 5 \times 5$ m studio. The white stuccoed

building with a straw roof in expressive style looks toward the lake, hidden among pine trees and bushes, giving no hint of its history or the client. The sculptor Bruno Krauskopf (1892–1960), whose art the Nazis declared "degenerate", had Rosenthal erect a similar studio building for him in Bad Saarow.

Harry Rosenthal, a member of the Bund Deutscher Architekten (BDA) and the Berlin Werkbund (DWB), had to flee when Hitler assumed power. He reached Palestine and lived in Haifa until he left the country in 1939. During that time he earned a living from small commissions for one-family houses or from doing interior design for apartments and shops. Rosenthal must have had a good reputation as an architect in the village of Pardess Hanna, which lies on the road between Haifa and Tel Aviv.[6] Many Jews who fled Germany after 1933 gravitated to that settlement, and he erected several one-family houses and an amphitheatre there.

Rosenthal understood how to bring the forms used in Modern architecture in Berlin into appropriate relation with the social and climatic conditions in Palestine. He proved to be a functionalist, arranging the number and form of the openings in his buildings not just according to aesthetic considerations. To achieve optimal air circulation in the apartments, he planned the rooms, doors and windows to take advantage of the prevailing wind direction.

Since Rosenthal could not tolerate the subtropical climate due to his health, he moved to London at the outbreak of World War II. But there had been a drastic increase in the number of architects from Central and Eastern Europe who had fled fascism and sought refuge and employment in Great Britain since early 1939. And RIBA, the British association of architects, had annoyingly bureaucratic procedures as a prerequisite for acceptance, to which Rosenthal did not want to submit. So for twenty-seven years, until his death in London on January 19, 1966, Rosenthal's existence was a struggle. He worked on plans for a highway, designed innovative toys, lectured on architecture in London's college preparatory schools, designed piece after piece of furniture with an eye toward patent rights, and was a painter and portraitist. But even though, in 1957, the architect Vassily Luckhardt, the art historian Professor Erwin Redslob, and the architect and president of the Berlin Academy of the Arts Professor Hans Scharoun provided Rosenthal with written recommendations citing his contributions to Berlin's Modern architecture of the 1920s, that unfortunately was not sufficient, either in Germany or in England, to enable him to practice his profession ever again.

1 Some of the essays appeared in: *L'Architecture d'Aujourd'hui* 1/1934, pp. 44–45; *Die Baugilde* VI/10, Berlin June 2, 1924, pp. 127–130; *Bauwelt* 13/1924, p. 243; *Bauwelt* 27/1926; *Bauwelt* 37/1931, pp. 13–24; *Haus Hof Garten* 40/1926, p. 459; *Haus Hof Garten* 31/1931, pp. 378–379; *Innendekoration*, Darmstadt May 1926, pp. 170–186; *Das Kunstblatt* 27/1927, p. 249; *Kunst und Kirche* 1/1927, p. 13; *Het Landhuis* 7/1932, pp. 283–290; *Het Landhuis* 1/1933, pp. 13–18; *Moderne Bauformen* 11/1928, pp. 421–434; *Der Neubau* 9/1930, pp. 161–178; *Viviendas* II, Madrid 1933, p. 69; *Wasmuths Monatshefte für Baukunst* 7/1927, pp. 292–293; *Wasmuths Monatshefte für Baukunst* 3/1932, pp. 101–108; Müller-Wulckow 1925–1932, reprint 1975, p. II, 24, 52; IV, 60; *L'Architecture d'Aujourd'hui* 8/1937, p. 21; *Das Werk* 9/1938, p. 267; Warhaftig 2005, Rosenthal, Harry; Claus 2006.

2 See biography of Eugen Szekey.
3 In 1988 Marjorie Rosenthal engaged the art historian Charlotte Benton of Cambridge to catalogue the estate before bequeathing it to the Akademie der Künste in Berlin.
4 See Landesarchiv Berlin, Rep. 209, Acc. 1578, Nr. 1781.
5 Myra Warhaftig, "Fast unkenntlich geworden" in: *Bauwelt* 10/1986, p. 330. Myra Warhaftig, "Die Künstlerhäuser des Harry Rosenthal für Arnold Zweig und Josef Thorak" in: *Bauwelt* 40–41/1989, pp. 1962–1963.
6 Pardess Hanna was founded as an agricultural settlement in a region of orange groves in 1928. The town's charter enabled German families to build inexpensive one-family houses and to farm there.

Harry Rosenthal, Bab residence, Berlin-Wilmersdorf, 1924, view from the street, main entrance

Harry Rosenthal, Bab residence, Berlin-Wilmersdorf, 1924, private synagogue

Harry Rosenthal, Bab residence, Berlin-Wilmersdorf, 1924, hallway with staircases

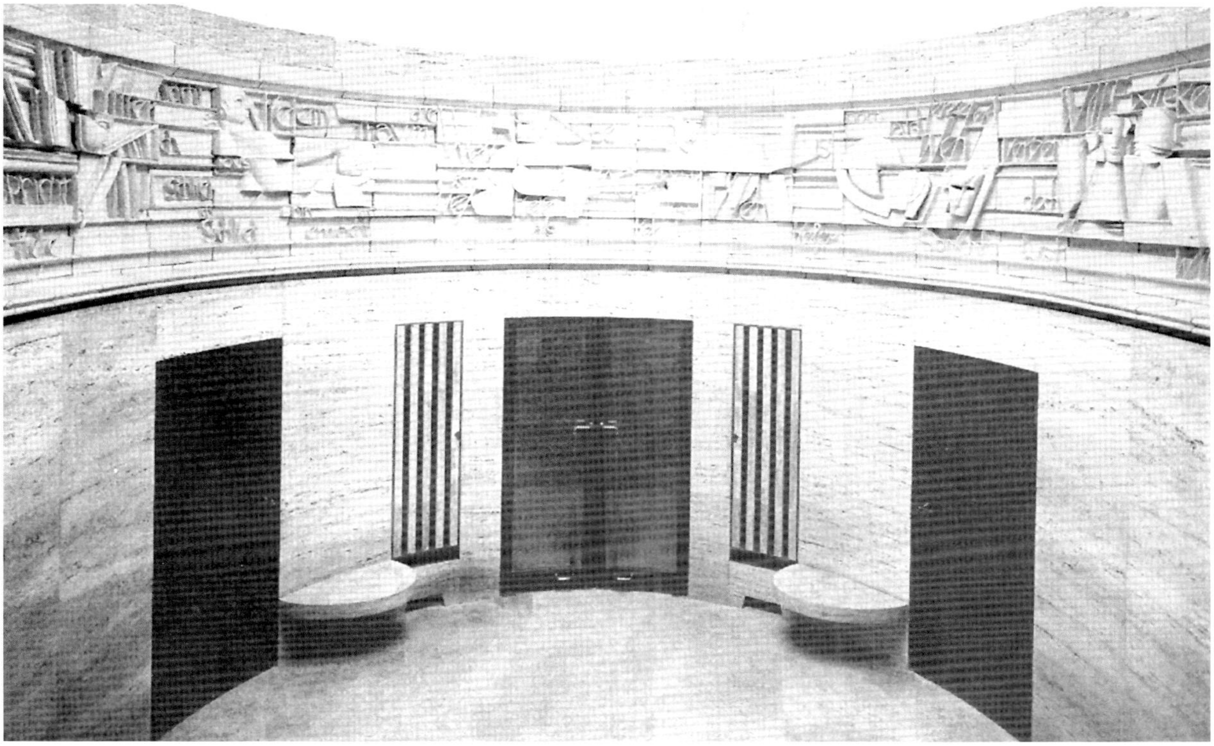

Harry Rosenthal, Bab residence, Berlin-Wilmersdorf, 1924, entrance hall with ceramic frieze by Paul Rudolf Henning

Harry Rosenthal, Bab residence, Berlin-Wilmersdorf, 1924, dining room

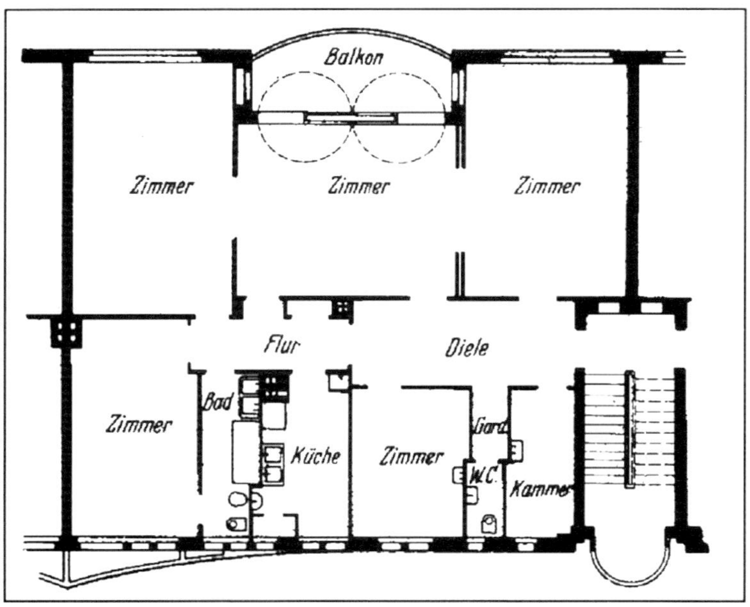

Harry Rosenthal, Simon housing block Berlin-Schmargendorf, 1927, partial view from the street

Harry Rosenthal, Simon housing block Berlin-Schmargendorf, upper-floor plan, segment

Right page:
Harry Rosenthal, lamp in a private synagogue, Berlin, circa 1924

נר לרגלי

Harry Rosenthal, Eisner residence, Berlin-Dahlem, 1927, south view

Harry Rosenthal, Bruno Krauskopf studio, Bad Saarow, 1925

Harry Rosenthal, Arnold Zweig studio, Berlin-Eichkamp, 1930, view from the garden

Harry Rosenthal, one-family house, Pardess Hanna, 1935, ground plan

Harry Rosenthal, one-family house, Pardess Hanna, 1936

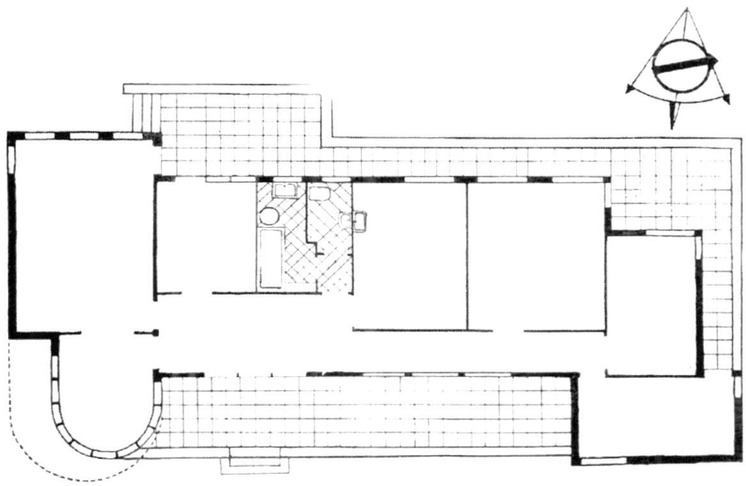

Harry Rosenthal

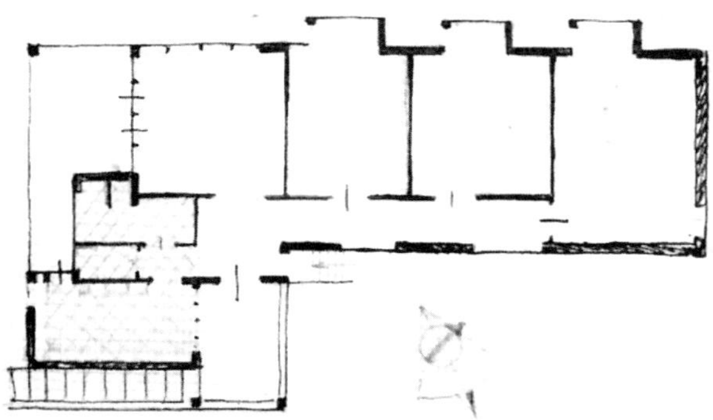

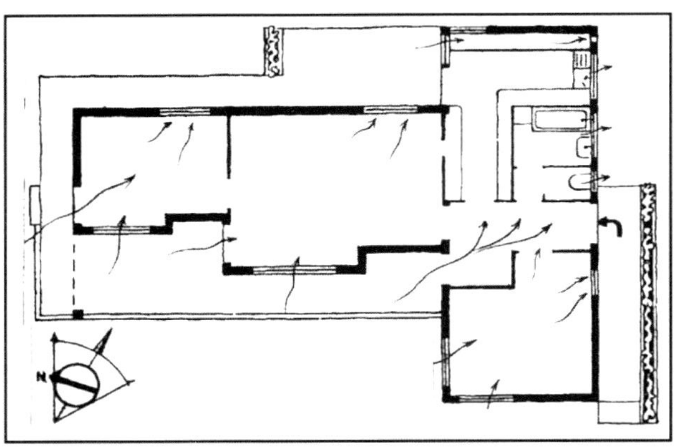

Harry Rosenthal, one-family house, Pardess Hanna, 1937

Harry Rosenthal, one-family house, Pardess Hanna, 1937, ground-floor plan

Harry Rosenthal, one-family house, Pardess Hanna, plan according to the wind direction, circa 1935

Harry Rosenthal, amphitheatre, Pardess Hanna, 1933–1936, during construction

Arthur Abraham Schragenheim

1893 Berlin – 1981 Tel Aviv

Arthur A. Schragenheim came from a German-Jewish family whose ancestors had lived in Rethem (Aller) since the beginning of the eighteenth century. The Schragenheim family tree went back five generations; they lived chiefly in Berlin, Hamburg and Frankfurt am Main until Hitler came to power in 1933. Most were strictly observant Jews. Only a few members of the extended family were able to flee Germany in the 1930s and survive the persecution and extermination of World War II; today most of them and their descendants live in Israel. Schragenheim was born in Berlin on July 5, 1893. He studied architecture there at the Technische Hochschule Charlottenburg, earning his diploma in 1920. Soon after, he opened a private office at Potsdamer Strasse 22a in Berlin-Tiergarten with the Berlin architect Walter Kretschmer.[1] The projects they realized, primarily in Berlin, included private and public buildings, plans for housing developments, synagogues, and interiors. Schragenheim, a member of the Orthodox Jewish congregation Adass Jisroel, also designed gravestones for its cemetery.[2]

Schragenheim and his partner Kretschmer were professionally active outside Germany as well. Along with other like-minded members of the bourgeoisie, they engaged in efforts to ameliorate the wretched living conditions of Jewish populations in the cities of Eastern Europe, making their contribution through architecture. In 1927, at a time when some 50% of the inhabitants of the Polish city of Bialystok were Jews, they built a sanatorium there for children with tuberculosis.[3] Built on the foundation of an old building, the new structure was an unornamented and functional cube whose setbacks created space for rooftop terraces.

Schragenheim and Kretschmer's second work outside Germany, also published in *Bauwelt* in an article about the works of German architects abroad, was the medical building in Kovno (today Kaunas), the capital of Lithuania.[4] In 1929 Jews made up circa 30% of the population there, a culturally significant number. Nonetheless most lived in poverty; epidemics, diseases and a high death rate contributed to their daily misery.[5] Jewish doctors in Russia had founded the Society for Protecting Jewish Health (OSG) early in the 1920s, with the aim of creating appropriate institutions to educate people about hygiene and provide free out-patient treatment and health care in centers of proletarian Jewish populations. The OSG announced a competition in Kovno for a medical building, the first of its kind.[6] Kretschmer and Schragenheim won both first and second prizes. Oskar Kaufmann chaired the jury. The cube-shaped building with a flat roof was striking in its symbolic colours: it was painted white, the windows and doors were painted blue. The reinforced concrete construction was erected by a German firm in 1928–29. Upon its completion, it was considered the first modern building in Lithuania and the institution quickly proved to be irreplaceable. Thousands of school children used the outpatient clinics, which were available to the general public regardless of their religion.

Soon after being expelled from the Reich Chamber of Fine Arts in 1933, Schragenheim left Berlin and settled in Tel Aviv. After 1938 he worked with his wife Bela, also an architect from Kovno; they realized many projects together over the next thirty years. The work in Israel also was multifaceted, encompassing synagogues, health and sport centres, bank buildings, shopping centres, subsidized apartments, cinemas, and schools, as well as interiors. The project closest to Schragenheim's heart, the one he was most proud to see built, was the Orthodox Bar-Ilan University in Ramat Gan, named after the head of religious Zionism, Meir Bar-Ilan.[7] From 1952 to 1957, Schragenheim planned the entire campus and supervised the construction of the first buildings.

The biblical commandment "Thou shalt not make unto thee a graven image, nor any manner of likeness" (Exodus 20, 4) generated no inner conflict in Schragenheim as an Orthodox Jew and architect. As he noted, his creative powers came from the biblical verse "Teach me good discernment and knowledge; For I have believed in Thy commandments" (Psalm 119, 66).[8]

After almost seventy years of professional activity, Schragenheim died in Tel Aviv on April 29, 1981.

After his death, his wife Bela Schragenheim moved to the town of Raanana, north of Tel Aviv, and devoted herself successfully to painting. I am very grateful to her for providing me with information and material (1986).

1 Until 1933 Walter Kretschmer lived at Kastanienallee 22 in Berlin-Charlottenburg. Both his parents were Jewish, so according to the Nuremberg Laws, he was a "Volljude" and on the list of artists expelled from the Reich Chamber of Fine Arts in 1933. His fate is unknown; see Warhaftig 2005, Kretschmer, Walter (II)

2 Offenberg 1986.

3 Bialystok, today a Polish industrial city known for its textile industry, grew during the nineteenth century to be one of the most important centers of Russian Jewry. Since the Holocaust, there has no longer been any Jewish life there.

4 "Arbeiten deutscher Architekten im Ausland" in: *Bauwelt* 8/1930, pp. 230–231.

5 There too, no Jewish life survived the Holocaust.

6 The health building was funded by donations.

7 Meir Bar-Ilan, formerly Meir Berlin, was born in Woloszyn, Russia in 1880, and died in Jerusalem in 1949. He was a rabbi, a politician and the president of the Mizrachi World Center. He lived in Berlin from 1910–14 and was the editor of the weekly newspaper *Ha'ivri*.

8 From an unpublished manuscript by Arthur A. Schragenheim, September 1967.

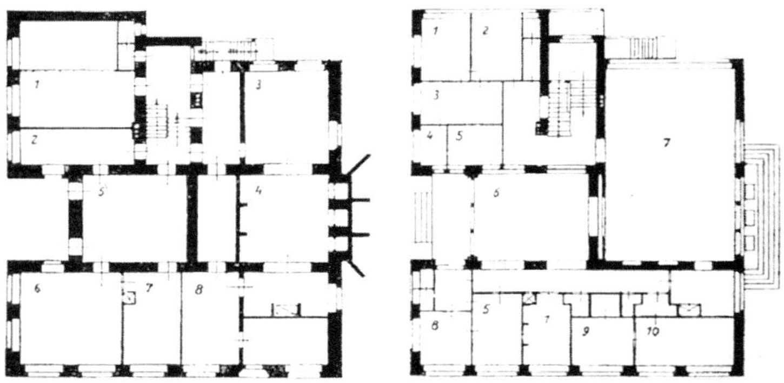

Kretschmer and Schragenheim, children's sanatorium, Bialystok, 1927, basement (left) and ground-floor plans

Kretschmer and Schragenheim, children's sanatorium, Bialystok, 1927

above left:
Arthur A. Schragenheim, gravestone of Markus Burin, Cemetery Adass Jisroel, Berlin, 1927

above right:
Arthur A. Schragenheim, gravestone of Bernhard Schragenheim (1891–1957), Jewish cemetery in Berlin-Weissensee

below right:
Arthur A. Schragenheim, gravestone of Simon Schocken (1874–1929), Cemetery Adass Jisroel

Arthur Abraham Schragenheim

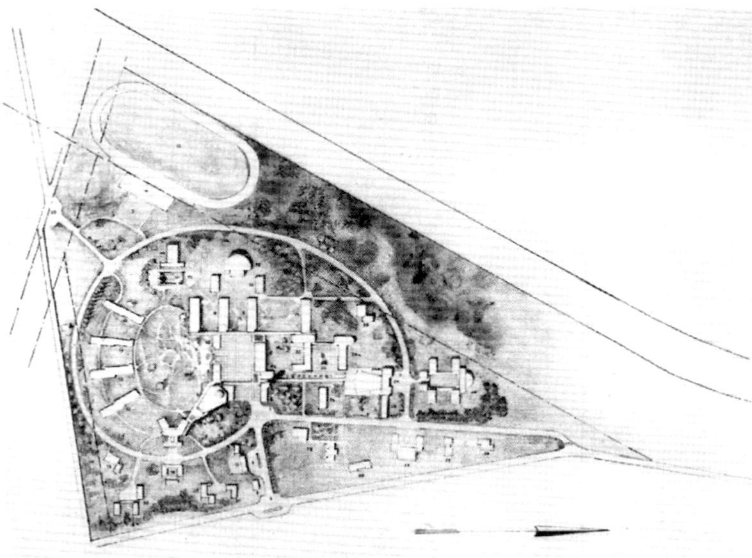

Arthur A. Schragenheim, Bar-Ilan University, Ramat-Gan, 1952–1957, site plan

Arthur A. Schragenheim, Bar-Ilan University, Ramat-Gan, 1952–1957, dining hall

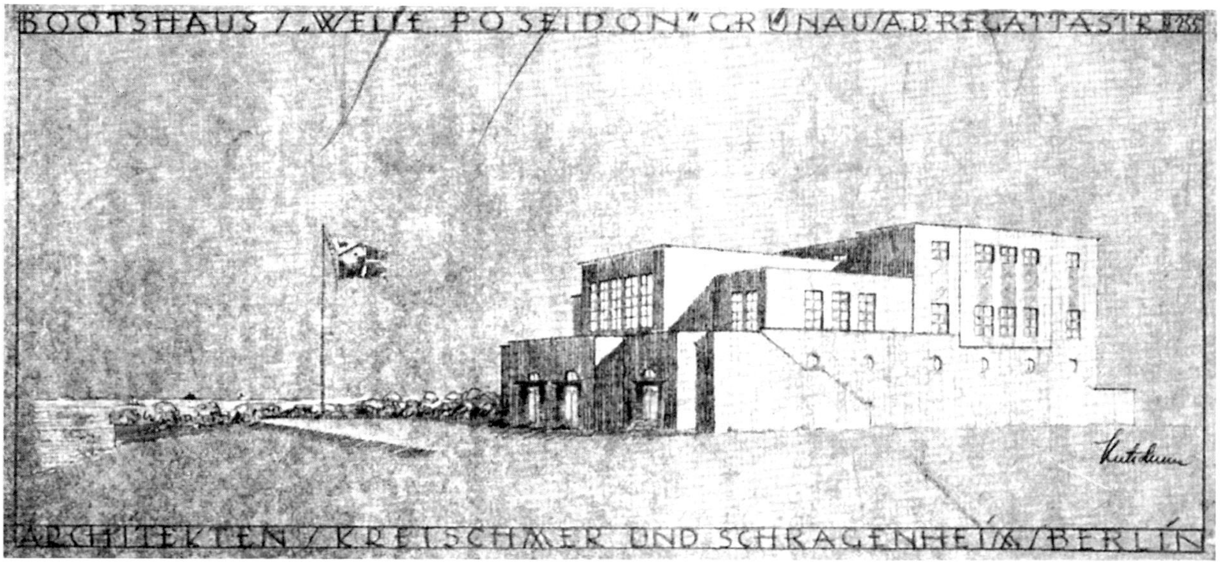

Kretschmer and Schragenheim, Boat house "Welle Poseidon", Grünau near Berlin, 1924

Joseph Ossip Klarwein

1893 Warsaw – 1970 Jerusalem

Joseph Klarwein (centre) in Fritz Höger's office, Hamburg

Joseph Klarwein was born in Warsaw on February 6, 1893. With pogroms being perpetrated against the Jewish population in Russia and Poland following the failed Russian revolution and the Polish uprising, the Klarwein family left Poland in 1905 and settled in Germany. Artistically talented, Joseph Klarwein matriculated at the Technische Hochschule in Munich, where he took courses in the architecture department from the winter semester of 1917–18 to the winter semester of 1918–19. He spent 1920 in Hans Poelzig's master class in studio architecture at the Prussian Academy of Arts in Berlin. Shortly afterward Klarwein left for Hamburg, where he became a close associate of the architect Fritz Höger for more than ten years.

Fritz Höger (1877–1949) had made a name for himself chiefly in northern Germany as an exponent of Expressionist architecture, and had secured his place in architectural history with his red brick buildings. Young Klarwein found Höger's architecture immediately convincing, and a harmonious collaboration ensued. This may be inferred from a letter written by Höger's former colleague, the architect Ernst-Erik Pfannschmidt, on June 29, 1977, in which he discussed Klarwein's role in the Hamburg office: "The chief architect was Ossip K., who lived near Schwanenwyck on the Alster and earned a salary of over 1000 RM. Klarwein's designs were then usually rendered in a chalk perspective by Müller. ... This had the following relation to the church in South Hamm: In his office, Klarwein created the drawing for the church competition according to his own ideas. Höger saw the design and cried out, 'that is plagiarism!' He was speaking of a design by Luckhardt and Anker, frequently published as a photographic model ... Klarwein angrily packed up his design, finished it at home over the weekend, and submitted it under Fritz Höger's name. (The terms of his contract specified that he could not submit designs under his own name.) The work was awarded first prize and Höger then showed it to visitors as his best work."[1]

The same firm also built the church on Hohenzollernplatz in Berlin-Wilmersdorf between 1931 and 1933. Klarwein came to Berlin shortly before construction started and lived at Joachim-Friedrich-Strasse 47 in Halensee, some 150 m from the church. His presence in Berlin at that time leads to the assumption that he also supervised the building's construction. Later, Klarwein confided to his friend in Tel Aviv, the architect Yehuda Lavie, that both this church and the Hamburg church in South Hamm were, in fact, realized from his own designs.[2]

In 1933 Klarwein fled Germany and went to Palestine. He stopped using his Slavic first name Ossip and called himself Joseph, and he opened an architecture office in Haifa. There he was busy, compared to other colleagues. He was able to earn a steady living by constructing apartment buildings for German emigrants on Mount Carmel, some of very high quality, and he also took part in many competitions. He won first prize

in at least four of those competitions and was able to realize the projects. His public buildings are located chiefly in the major cities of Haifa, Tel Aviv and Jerusalem. They are still linked with his name.
In 1937 Klarwein was awarded first prize for his design for a business centre in Haifa. The complex, with stores and offices, extends along Herzl Street, Haifa's main boulevard, from Gideon Kaminka's "clock building" in the east to Alex Baerwald's Technion campus in the west.[3] The structure, simple and functional in appearance, is composed of two quadrilaterals of unequal lengths and a semicircular volume and, like Baerwald's neighbouring buildings, it is clad in chiselled limestone. But Klarwein expressly opposed Baerwald's orientalising style, reasoning: "It goes against the Zeitgeist."[4] The triangular piazzetta between the buildings and the street is equipped with a fountain, lampposts and plantings. A bus stop in front of the building livened up the area.
The Dagon silo complex at the port of Haifa, with a capacity of 20,000 tons, is visible far off on Haifa's horizon.[5] Early in the 1950s, Klarwein was commissioned to design an artistic exterior for the silo, which then stood alone with no buildings nearby and looked like a grounded U-boat. Klarwein had ornamental patterns engraved in the concrete exterior walls, which resemble the walls of the clinker-brick hospital building that Fritz Höger built in Delmenhorst, near Bremen, in 1925.

The small city of Nahariya, north of Haifa, a prime area of settlement for Jewish emigrants from Germany during the 1930s, also is linked with Klarwein's name. There he built the first Modern one-family house in the form of a cube, with white stuccoed walls and a flat roof. Nahariya's residents called the building "the palace" because of its conspicuous appearance.[6] Klarwein was also commissioned to build Nahariya's city hall. Like the University of Jerusalem Law Institute he built in the 1950s, it shows Klarwein's interest in functional and restrained architecture.
But the Israeli parliament's Knesset building, for which Klarwein won first prize in a 1957 competition, marks a turning point in his use of forms. He designed the building after the model of an ancient temple, with columns all around and a square core measuring 84 × 66 m.[7] One small and two larger interior courtyards provide lighting and ventilation for the two-storey building, which also has two subterranean levels. Yet Klarwein could not really feel happy that the design had succeeded in winning first prize because of the strong public opposition to its realization. It took eleven years for the building to be completed, in altered form, in collaboration with the architect Dov Carmi.[8] Soon after, on September 9, 1970, Klarwein died in Jerusalem.

For information and material about Joseph Klarwein, I am very grateful to his son-in-law, Professor Dan Hoffner, Ramat-Gan (1986).

1 The letter was addressed to Dr. Eckhart Berckenhagen, who at the time was planning an exhibition at the art library in Berlin on the occasion of Fritz Höger's hundredth birthday; Brüder Luckhardt and Alfons Anker were well-known Berlin architects, indebted to the Modern style, during the Weimar Republic. See: Warhaftig 2005, Anker, Alfons.

2 From a conversation with Yehuda Lavie in Tel Aviv, summer 1985. See brief biography of Yehuda Lavie (Ernst Loevisohn); see also: Warhaftig 2005, Loevisohn, Ernst.
3 See biographies of Alex Baerwald and Gideon Kaminka.
4 Joseph Klarwein, "Eine kurze Erläuterung zu meinem Entwurf auf dem Technion Gelände" in: *Habinyan Bamisrah Hakarov* 4, Tel Aviv November 1935, pp. 13–14.
5 See "Edith and Dr. Reuben Hecht".
6 Elkin 1991, p. 3.
7 Including the roofed-over columns, it measures 96 × 78 m.
8 See biography of Arieh Sharon, note 7.

Joseph Klarwein, business centre, Haifa, 1938, ground floor

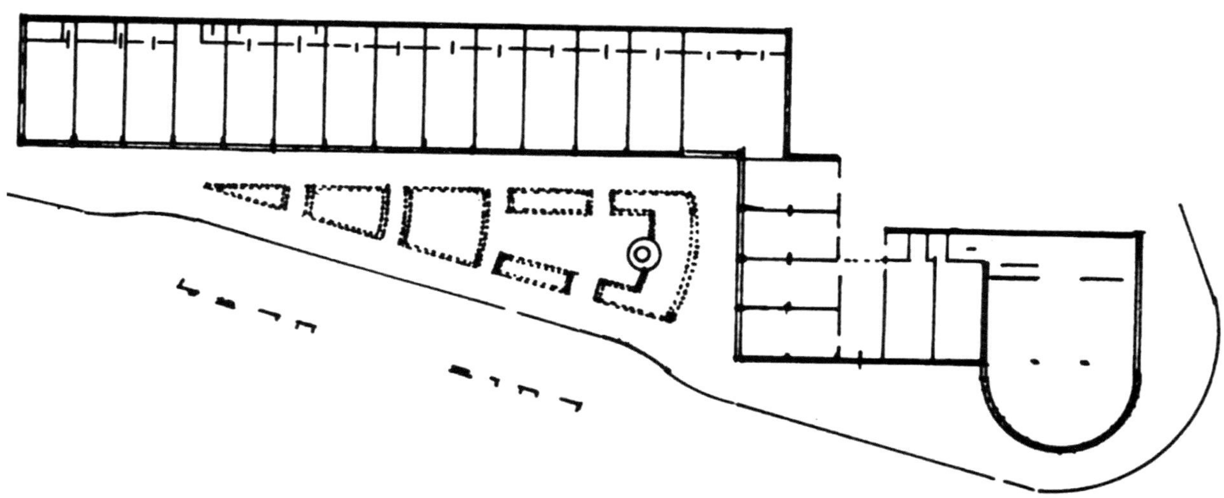

Joseph Klarwein, business centre, 1938, Haifa. Photo: M.W. 1989

Joseph Klarwein, apartment building, Haifa, Mount Carmel, 1937, partial view from the street. Photo: M.W. 1989

Joseph Ossip Klarwein

Fritz Höger, hospital, Delmenhorst, circa 1928, partial view

Joseph Klarwein, Cinema Hod, Nahariya, circa 1950

Joseph Klarwein, Dagon silo, Haifa, 1953. See "Edith and Dr. Reuben Hecht"

Joseph Klarwein, the Knesset, the Israeli parliament, 1957, competition, first prize, model

Joseph Klarwein, the Knesset, the Israeli parliament, after collaboration with Dov Carmi, 1968. Photo: M.W. 1990

EUGEN SZEKEY (SZÉKELY)

1894 Budapest – 1962 Haifa

The second architect (Paul Engelmann was the first) to use Adolf Loos's spatial plan as an architectonic concept for housing in Palestine, albeit in more modest form, was Eugen Szekey.[1]
Szekey was born in Budapest on August 3, 1894. A lieutenant in World War I, by the end of 1915 he had already been awarded a bronze service medal by the Imperial War Ministry in Vienna. Early in the 1920s, after passing his second state examination in tall building construction at the Technische Hochschule in Graz, Szekey went to Berlin. Like Joseph Klarwein before him, he was in Hans Poelzig's master class in architecture at the Prussian Academy of Arts in Berlin. Szekey earned his diploma in engineering at the Technische Hochschule Charlottenburg in 1923, while he completed practical training as a site manager. He went to Athens in 1924 to work for the Tekton Company. Three years later he returned to Graz and practised independently until he decided to leave Austria in 1935, in view of the increasing anti-Semitism there.
During his years in Graz, Szekey realized many buildings in that city and neighbouring ones: a hundred-bed sanatorium in Eggenberg, the employment office and a swimming pool in Graz, a second swimming pool in Pernegg, the employment office in Voitsberg, and a housing development with forty-two homes for the middle class in Schoenau.[2] Szekey received the Austrian State Prize in 1927 for his artistic work, and was awarded the State Gold Medal and named deputy president of the Graz Sezession in 1928. He also was a member of the Association of Austrian Architects and the Werkbund.
As recently as a few years ago, the man who, prior to 1938, was recognized as the leading exponent of Modern architecture in Austria had been completely forgotten. Szekey is now at last being rediscovered, but the majority of his buildings are no longer standing.[3]

The Austrian architectural historian Friedrich Achleitner wrote an appreciation of Szekey's work in his multi-volume history of twentieth century Austrian architecture: "The facility (a group of cabins), now unfortunately partially demolished, was among the most beautiful baths in the Steiermark in its refined modesty and aesthetic as well as practical economy. Szekey was a central figure in the Graz avant-garde of the 1920s and 1930s; his designs display an intelligence and cultivation reminiscent of Josef Frank (1885–1967). From the standpoint of materials alone it is regrettable that his baths (such as the Margarethenbad in Graz) did not survive. It would be most worthwhile to rebuild them in his spirit."[4] Achleitner's suggestion has not yet been acted upon.

In Haifa, Eugen Szekey had to be satisfied with small commissions. These included apartment interiors and a workers' housing project in nearby Kiryat Benyamin. After he met the Jewish textile engineer Hans Moller, who also had found refuge in Palestine, Szekey's professional situation immediately improved. Until 1934 Moller had owned a textile factory in Brno, with administrative offices in Vienna, and had lived at Starkfriedgasse 19 in Vienna's eighteenth district in a house built for him in 1928 by Adolf Loos.[5]

In Palestine, Hans Moller strived to replace the loss of his business and private property. In the 1940s he established ATA, Israel's first and largest textile factory, in Kiryat Ata, 12 km east of Haifa.[6] The complex included factory halls, an administrative building, workers' housing, and the new Moller residence (1947). The architectural tasks were entrusted to Szekey. The client wanted the architecture to conform as much as possible to Loos's concepts. As a result, the ground plans of the two Moller residences, one in Vienna and the other in Kiryat Ata, have almost identical proportions.

The later residence, however, has two instead of the previous four storeys, and only one differentiated level within, instead of the three in the Vienna residence. Szekey designed exterior views that were as rational and functional as those of his Vienna colleague, but also adopted traditions from the new country, such as the use of limestone as a construction material and the wooden shutters on the windows. Only the tubular steel banisters are identical in both houses.

When I spoke with Mrs. Moller in the summer of 1986, she admitted that she was not much enamoured of the spatial plan in her home. Yet it had been very important for her husband, now deceased, to sense Loos's spirit daily in their home in Kiryat Ata.

Eugen Szekey died in Haifa on November 13, 1962.

I am very grateful to Eugen Szekey's widow, Annelise Szekey, Mount Carmel, Haifa, for information and material (1986).

1 See biographies of Paul Engelmann and Yehuda Kurt Unger.

2 Steirische Jubiläums-Kunstschau, Graz 1928; *Österreichische Kunst* 4/1933, pp. 11–15; Myra Warhaftig, "Österreichisches Architekturerbe in Israel" in: *Kunst und Kirche* 4/1986, pp. 259–260; Gerhard Gruber, "Eugen Szekely – Freibad Pernegg", seminar on landmark preservation, Graz 1989; Eleonore Rieser, "Öffentliche Industrielle und Gewerbliche Bauten der Ersten Republik in Graz", dissertation, Innsbruck 1990, pp. 180–182.

3 "It is very difficult to find out anything about Eugen Szekey. Very few papers still exist and these have many gaps. Unfortunately, it is worse with his buildings. Since most were built of wood, they did not survive the long period since they were built – and if they were built of more durable materials, most were damaged or destroyed in the war." Letter from Dipl. Ing. Daniel Kampus, Graz to the author dated July 18, 1994.

4 Achleitner 1982, pp. 286, 339–342.

5 Gravagnuolo 1982, pp. 194–198.

6 ATA is the abbreviation for "Arigei Totzereth Artzeinu", Hebrew for "clothes made in our land". The factory, designed by the Haifa engineer Ernst Grunewald, who came from Vienna, was demolished in 1984 to make way for a housing development.

Eugen Szekey (Székely)

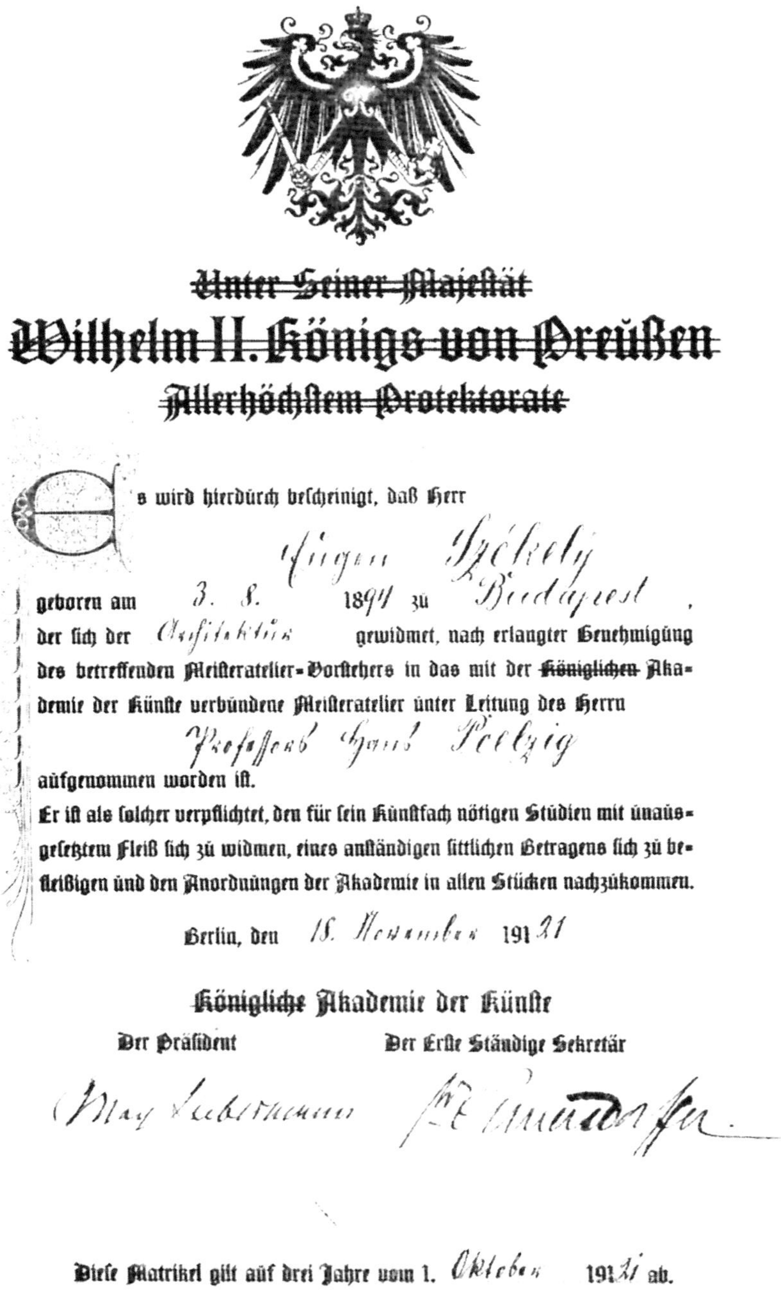

~~Unter Seiner Majestät~~
~~Wilhelm II. Königs von Preußen~~
~~Allerhöchstem Protektorate~~

Es wird hierdurch bescheinigt, daß Herr

Eugen Székely

geboren am 3. 8. 1894 zu Budapest,
der sich der Architektur gewidmet, nach erlangter Genehmigung des betreffenden Meisteratelier-Vorstehers in das mit der ~~Königlichen~~ Akademie der Künste verbundene Meisteratelier unter Leitung des Herrn

Professor Hans Poelzig

aufgenommen worden ist.
Er ist als solcher verpflichtet, den für sein Kunstfach nötigen Studien mit unausgesetztem Fleiß sich zu widmen, eines anständigen sittlichen Betragens sich zu befleißigen und den Anordnungen der Akademie in allen Stücken nachzukommen.

Berlin, den 18. November 1921

~~Königliche~~ Akademie der Künste

Der Präsident — Max Liebermann

Der Erste Ständige Sekretär — Amersdorffer

Diese Matrikel gilt auf drei Jahre vom 1. Oktober 1921 ab.

Left page:
Academy of Arts Certificate for Eugen Székely, Berlin, November 18, 1921

Right page above:
Eugen Szekey, Hans Moller residence, Kiryat Ata, 1947, partial view. Photo: M.W. 1986

below left:
Eugen Szekey, Hans Moller residence, Kiryat Ata, 1947, ground-floor plan

below right:
Eugen Szekey, Hans Moller residence, Kiryat Ata 1947. Photo: M.W. 1986

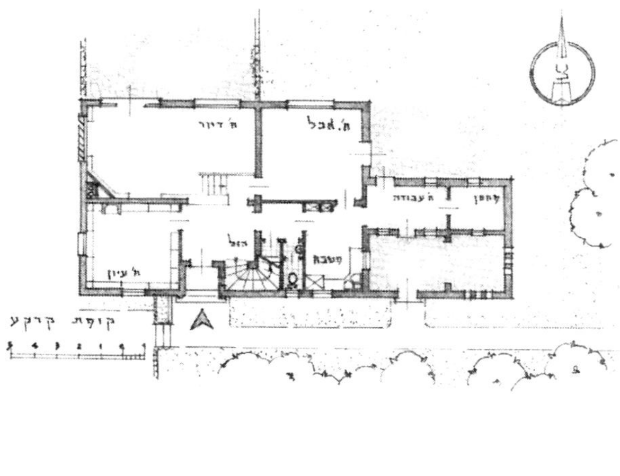

Eugen Szekey (Székely)

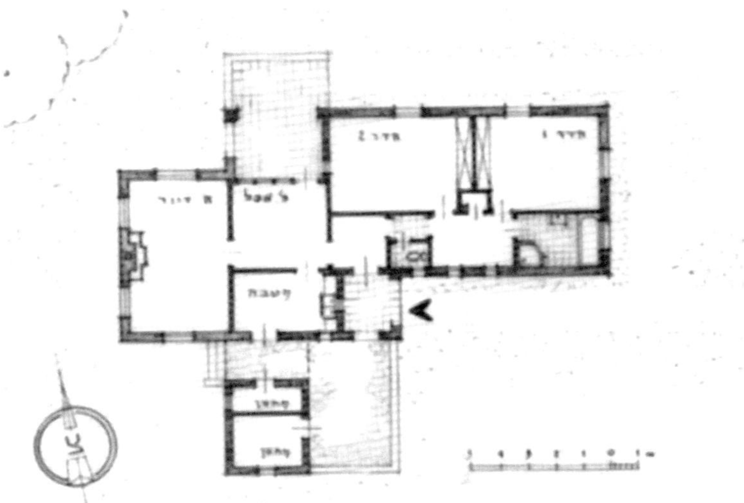

Eugen Szekey, house type for workers, textile factory housing project, Kiryat Ata, 1947, ground plan

Eugen Szekey, house type for workers, textile factory housing project, Kiryat Ata, 1947. Photo: M.W. 1986

Eugen Szekey with structural engineer Ernst Grunewald, Hans Moller textile factory, Kiryat Ata, 1947–1960 (photo circa 1960), demolished 1984

Heinz Rau

1896 Berlin – 1965 Bad Teinach

"Heinz Rau ... was a Berlin kid, a child of Wedding", Julius Posener wrote in his obituary for Rau, who had died suddenly in Bad Teinach in the Black Forest in 1965.[1] Born in Berlin on November 10, 1896, the son of a Jewish doctor, Rau, unlike most of his seven brothers and sisters, never graduated from college. He apprenticed himself to a cabinetmaker at the age of fifteen. Rau was conscripted after the outbreak of World War I and was not discharged from the military until the war ended.
From the winter semester of 1919–20 to the winter semester of 1923–24, Rau studied at the academy of the Kunstgewerbeschule (School of Arts and Crafts) under Alfred Grenander (1863–1931) and later under Bruno Paul (1874–1968), in whose studio he acquired his first professional experience. Then Rau started his own business. He entered into association with the interior designer Heinrich Schaefer, and they set up a studio together in the Kunstgewerbeschule's building on Prinz-Albrecht-Strasse 8. In April 1933 this became the address of the infamous headquarters of the secret state police (Gestapo).[2]

Rau and Schaefer were intensely concerned with the issue of living space. Their designs for private clients ranged from individual pieces of furniture to complete interiors. The collaboration achieved enviable success and was covered extensively by various periodicals. The first published article in a trade journal evaluated their functional workroom in a Berlin apartment (1928): "Corresponds to the new lifestyle, redesign of a long room with the simplest of means: pulling together a window wall with curtains and a work table; free space to move around in."[3]
In 1929 the two architects published their New Kitchen, with which they surpassed the Frankfurt Kitchen designed in 1925 by Grete Schütte-Lihotzky.[4] Their Berlin kitchen was one-third larger in area and had an additional door that led directly to the dining table. Rau and Schaefer aimed to design a kitchen that would "make housewives' work simpler and easier". The German trade press lauded the Berlin Kitchen and called upon the architects to use that kitchen scheme in the new housing development they were planning. Ernst Neufert's internationally-known handbook *Bau-Entwurfslehre* (Building and Design) cited the Rau and Schaefer floor plan for the kitchen/living/dining room as the model for a "kitchen with an ideal working pattern" from its first edition in 1936 through the thirty-second edition in 1984.[5]
Before Heinz Rau had to leave Germany, he was able to present one more prize-winning architectural idea to the public. At the 1931 German Building Exhibition in Berlin, Rau and Schaefer supplied the section called "The Apartment of Our Time", which was headed by Ludwig Mies van der Rohe, with design prototypes for two types of student dormitory rooms. The desk in one room was equipped for students in the humanities, the desk in the other for students in technical disciplines. The rooms' size stood in proportion to the then current monthly rent of thirty marks.[6]

Rau went to Palestine via Italy in 1933. He spent the first two years in Richard Kauffmann's office in Jerusalem, and then opened his own office there in 1935.
Rau was greatly inspired by Jerusalem's two-thousand-year cultural history. He knew how to design buildings in harmony with that environment, how to construct them using practical forms and how to draft floor plans that would correspond with their users' needs. As for materials, he had previously shown outstanding ability in dealing with wood as a furniture material; now Heinz Rau proved that he could work with equal sensitivity in steel and stone. He also employed Mediterranean forms, which he interpreted in a rational and elegant manner.
On a steep hill in the Jerusalem district of Rechavia, Rau built a multi-family apartment building for Heinrich Benjamin, a businessman who had emigrated from Germany in 1938. The client's private duplex apartment faced the street. Behind it, and conforming to the topography, Rau located five other rental apartments, each of which was accessible via a separate set of stairs. In keeping with the climate, the façades have relatively small windows. The entrance gate and banisters are decorated with interwoven latticed bars pierced with holes, a popular Middle Eastern motif found in old buildings in Jerusalem. The structure is clad in Jerusalem stone.
At the same time, Rau also was building seven rental apartments nearby for Max Rosenbaum, a banker from Germany, that were designed in a special way: they are arranged in a pattern that rises in three steps to adapt to the hillside topography. The white stuccoed building, with its flat roof and strongly jutting eaves, was the first Modern building in Jerusalem to make use of such stepped design. Rau's formal vocabulary was highly indebted to the International Style, yet adapted to the climate, topography and building materials of the country. The apartments' interior design features many built-in closets that add to living comfort.

Rau also built exemplary residential buildings in the cities of Haifa, Tel Aviv, Tiberias and even in Gaza. After the founding of Israel in 1948, he was able to engage in a broader range of architectural activities. With Arieh Sharon and Artur Glikson, he designed Jerusalem's urban development scheme and also was asked to advise the building administration on important decisions. This led to an interest in the field of urban planning; Rau investigated the field and published the results of his research.[7] Yet Rau continued to devote himself to architecture. In the late 1950s and early 1960s, his last three major public buildings in Jerusalem were built: the Institute of Mathematics and the synagogue of the Hebrew University in Givat Ram (the latter in collaboration with the architect David Reznik), and the Hebrew Union College.

After a while, the Israeli landscape was no longer of such central interest to him, so Rau accepted an offer from the University of Manchester in 1962 to pursue teaching and research as a Senior Fellow at the Institute of Town and Country Planning. There he discovered the field of regional planning and developed visionary projects for England, including a ribbon city on both sides of the Pennine Range in northern England that was designed for a planned population of ten million persons by the year 2000. At his own request, Rau cut short his university teaching duties and went to Bad Teinach in Germany, where he died soon afterward, on February 13, 1965.
Three weeks before his death, Rau had visited the Berlin Werkbund, participated in a board meeting, and indicated his readiness to once again become a member of the association. A few days later he was award-

ed the Rechter Prize in Israel for his Jerusalem synagogue.[8] Heinz Rau's buildings from the 1930s to the 1960s are still standing.[9] They still look modern and show no signs of age. Nor have they undergone additions, renovations, or conversion.

I am very grateful to Jutta Oesterle-Schwerin, Ulm, for the photographs of the Hebrew Union College in Jerusalem (1985).

1 Julius Posener, "Architekt in drei Ländern" in: *Bauwelt* 23/1965, pp. 656–657.
2 The street was renamed Niederkirchnerstrasse.
3 Müller-Wulckow 1925–1932, reprint 1975, p. IV, 42.
4 Heinz Rau und Heinrich Schäfer, "Die Neue Küche Berlin" in: *Bauwelt* 17/1929, pp. 402–403.
5 Neufert 1984, p. 203.
6 Deutsche Bauausstellung Berlin 1931, *Amtlicher Katalog und Führer*, Berlin 1931, p. 172. For his achievement, Heinz Rau received an honorary award from the jury of the German Building Exhibition in Berlin in the form of a 300 g bronze coin, 10 cm in diameter.
7 Heinz Rau, "Landschaftsplanung – nur in Entwicklungsländern?" in: *Bauwelt* 46/1962, pp. 1281–1284.
8 Named for the architect Zeev Rechter. See biography of Arieh Sharon, note 6.
9 Walter Münz, "Bauten von Heinz Rau in Israel" in: *Deutsche Bauzeitung* 5/1962, pp. 379–386.

Heinz Rau and Heinrich Schaefer, "Pictures of a Modern Kitchen", Berlin, 1929

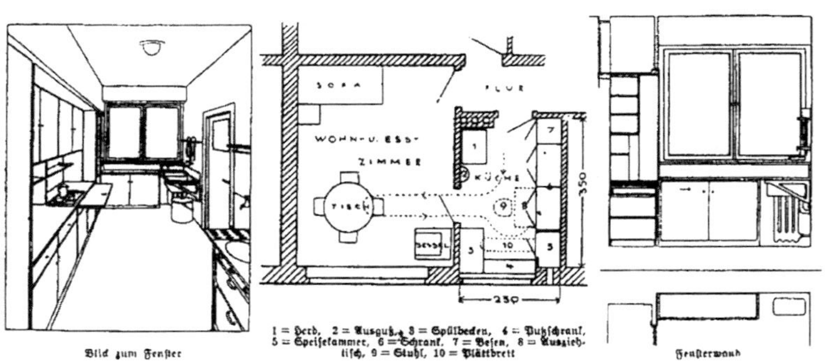

Heinz Rau, Max Rosenbaum apartments, Jerusalem, 1938, side view. Photo: M.W. 1988

Heinz Rau, Max Rosenbaum apartments, Jerusalem, 1938, view of the entrance area. Photo: M.W. 1988

Heinz Rau, Heinrich Benjamin residence, Jerusalem, 1938, partial view. Photo: M.W. 1988

Heinz Rau, Heinrich Benjamin residence, Jerusalem, 1938, view of the entrance area. Photo: M.W. 1988

Heinz Rau and David Reznik, synagogue of the Hebrew University in Givat Ram, Jerusalem, 1957. Photo: O.W. 1989

Heinz Rau and David Reznik, synagogue of the Hebrew University in Givat Ram, Jerusalem, 1957, inside staircase. Photo: O.W. 1989

Heinz Rau and David Reznik, synagogue of the Hebrew University in Givat Ram, Jerusalem, 1957, view to the landscape. Photo: O.W. 1989

Heinz Rau, apartment building, Tel Aviv, 1945, view from the street. Photo: O.W. 1989

Heinz Rau, Hebrew Union College, Jerusalem, ca. 1960, partial view

Heinz Rau, Hebrew Union College, Jerusalem, ca. 1960, general view

Yehuda (Karl Ludwig) Bienheim

1900 Duingen – 1967 Haifa

Drawing, artist unknown

Yehuda Bienheim was born on March 19, 1900, in the village of Duingen, 30 km south of Hanover. After graduating from secondary school, he was not spared military service in the final year of World War I. Bienheim's talent as a painter and his love of country life shaped his professional career. In 1919 he began studies in architecture at the Technische Hochschule in Hanover; he transferred to the Technische Hochschule in Stuttgart and earned his diploma from the Technische Universität in Braunschweig (then known as the Technische Hochschule Carolo-Wilhelmina zu Braunschweig) in 1925. His thesis "Design for a Manor" was deemed "very good".

Bienheim went to Berlin one year later and took an apartment on what was then Hindenburgstrasse 80 in the Wilmersdorf district. He soon met the architect Herbert Kuhn; their collaboration, which lasted only three years, was not without success. They published two of their projects in *Bauwelt* in 1927. The first article reviewed their competition-entry designs for three different types of weekend houses measuring 24, 31 and 50 m^2 respectively. The architects fulfilled their basic requirement that the homes could be owner-built using energy-saving materials.[1] Their second article concerned the rationalization of agriculture.[2] The task was to design a self-sufficient country estate whose layout of residence and working quarters would rationalize its activities. Various publications show that the estate in Honersdorf near Schöningen was built according to Bienheim and Kuhn's plan.

From 1928 to 1931, Bienheim worked for the Prussian government as an expert for agricultural and garden communities in Germany. He was also a regional planning advisor, with Professor Alfred Lagotz, in rural areas of eastern Germany. Although Bienheim sought an academic post during this period, his applications were repeatedly rejected. Carl Mühlenpfordt, who had been his professor at the Technische Hochschule in Braunschweig and with whom he was friendly, gave him a letter of recommendation whose last paragraph stated: "I was able to follow Bienheim's subsequent career. He soon returned to agriculture and to working on housing developments. I was especially impressed by the fact that he quickly became accustomed to being economical when it comes to building, which is necessary here, but not easily understood by architects. Bienheim's abilities in this specialized field are beyond question. His clear understanding and his sense of what is essential make him suited for a position in the teaching profession, for which I recommended him a few years ago in Germany, without success at that time. Should this now meet with success, I would be pleased. He will certainly be a good teacher."[3] But being Jewish, Bienheim could make no further use of the letter dated August 30, 1934. Immediately afterward, he fled to Palestine and settled in Hadera, then a small town between Haifa and Tel Aviv.[4]

Bienheim set up his office in the centre of the community of roughly 6000 inhabitants. The sign on his unprepossessing house was in Hebrew and English: "K. L. Bienheim, Architect, Expert on Agricultural Buildings". This professional announcement, with its reference to the country's development policies, achieved

Yehuda Bienheim, agricultural school, Pardess Hanna, 1935, general view

positive results. In the scattered settlements between Tel Aviv to the south and the Israeli border to the north, agricultural buildings and housing testify to Bienheim's abilities.

The farmers' association perceived the danger that Palestine would eventually be overrun by urbanization and decided to found a third agricultural school whose goal was to encourage "farmers with national and Zionist awareness".[5] Bienheim was given the architectural commission. In 1935 on an area of approximately forty-four hectares of fields and arable land in Pardess Hanna, north of Hadera, he was able to realize his longed-for project.[6] He located the school's facilities in separate buildings; these included a boarding school for one hundred students, apartments for the personnel, a dining and reading room, classrooms, a milking parlour, and barns for cows, horses and chickens. He designed the site in a double-U form, similar to the double-U form of the mechanized agricultural estate designed by Bienheim and Kuhn in 1927. The buildings' roofs also had their corresponding earlier models; one part of the building has a raised double roof that also was used in the Berlin project. The other buildings had hipped roofs in the style of the old church in Duingen.
But Beinheim's influences were not limited to the traditional styles of his homeland. Under the influence of Modern style, he also erected a series of one-family houses with cubic forms and flat roofs. These include the Cohn residence in Pardess Hanna and the Jaacob residence in Hadera. Because of local building ordinances, a tile roof was required on the Jacobson residence in Yokneam. Often the floor plans of these houses were generous, but sometimes they were modestly proportioned and therefore functional; the "House of an Intellectual Worker" in Hadera is typical of the latter. It resembled the 1927 weekend houses by Bienheim and Kuhn in its use of space.

When the state of Israel was founded, Bienheim dropped his German first name and adopted the name Yehuda (thanks be to God). In 1950 an old wish was fulfilled when he was named Professor of Agricultural Building and Settlement Design at the Technion – Israel Institute of Technology in Haifa. In 1956 Bienheim initiated the United Nations Study Group on Problems of Individual and Group Settlement for Europe and became internationally known. He left his teaching post at the Technion in 1960 to become an advisor to the International Institute of Agriculture in Wageningen, the Netherlands. He was appointed visiting professor at the Technische Hochschule Stuttgart in 1961, but left in 1962 for Peru, where he established the first professorship of agricultural planning in South America. Bienheim returned to Haifa in 1963 and died there four years later on April 19, 1967.

For the information and material, I am very grateful to Yehuda Bienheim's son, Dipl.-Ing. Rafi Bienheim, Munich (1991).

1 Bienheim and Kuhn, "Wochenendhäuser von 24 bis 50 qm Grundfläche" in: *Bauwelt* 15/1927, pp. 389–390.
2 Bienheim and Kuhn, "Industrielle Landwirtschaft" in: *Bauwelt* 27/1927, p. 14.
3 Architect Carl Mühlenpfordt (1878–1944) was suspended from his teaching position in 1934. He was rehabilitated by the Technische Universität Braunschweig in January 1946, on the second anniversary of his death.
4 Hadera was founded in 1891 and was among the first agricultural settlements in Israel. It was incorporated as a city in 1948. See biography of Judith Stolzer-Segal.
5 The first agricultural school for girls was designed by Lotte Cohn in 1931 in Nahalal, the second by Jacob Pinkerfeld in 1935 in Tel Aviv. See their biographies.
6 See biography of Harry Rosenthal, note 6.

The old church of Duingen, partial view showing the hipped roof

Yehuda Bienheim, agricultural school, 1935, Pardess Hanna, cowshed

Yehuda (Karl Ludwig) Bienheim

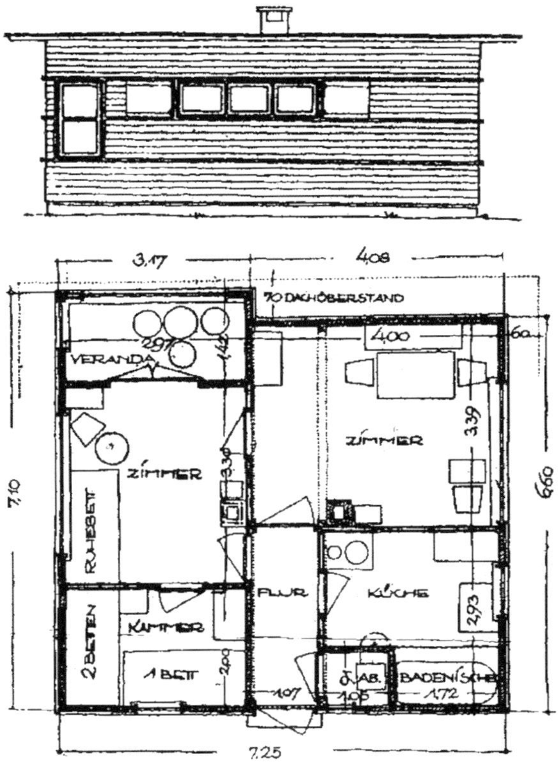

Karl Ludwig Bienheim and Herbert Kuhn, 50 m² weekend house, competition, Berlin 1927, floor plan, section and views

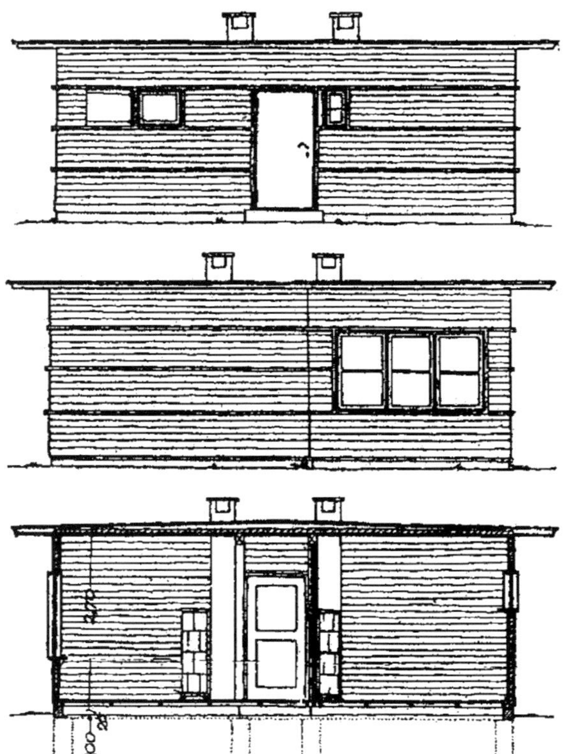

above right:
Yehuda Bienheim, house for a childless couple, Hadera, 1951, side view

below left:
Yehuda Bienheim, house for a childless couple, Hadera, 1951, ground-floor plan

below right:
Yehuda Bienheim, "House for an Intellectual Worker", Hadera, 1949. The spatial configuration is similar to that of Bienheim and Kuhn's weekend houses from 1927

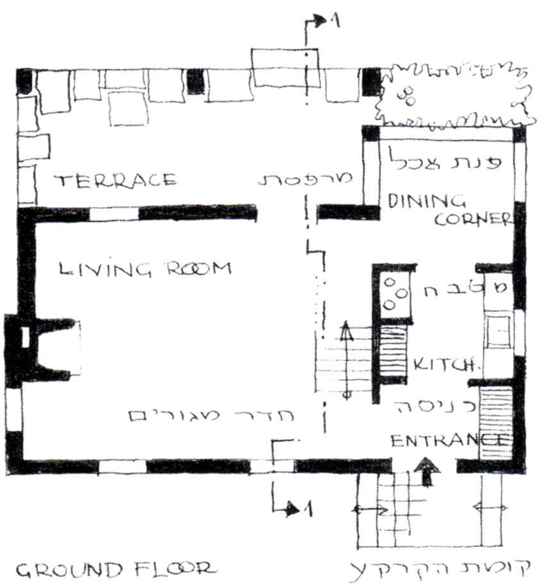

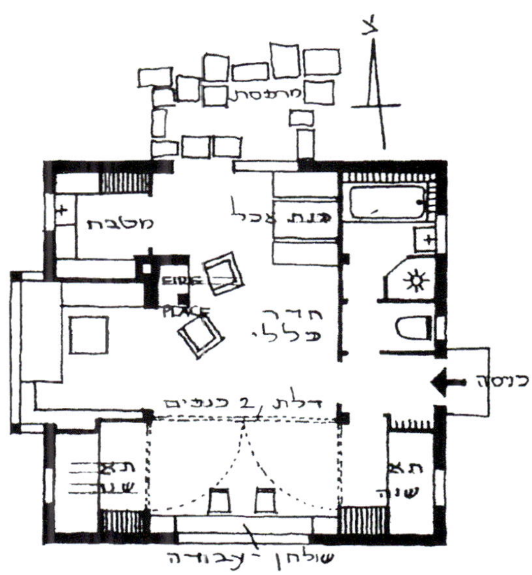

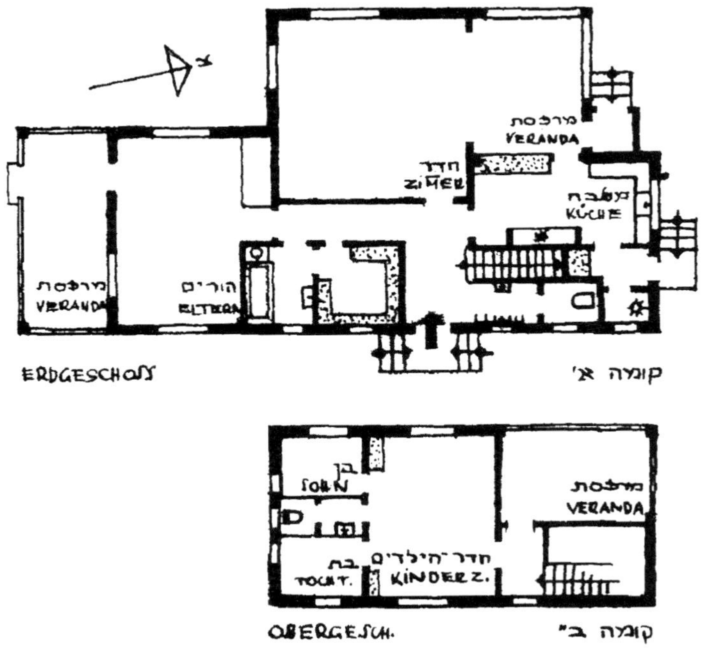

Yehuda Bienheim, Jacobson residence, Yokneam, 1936, plans of ground floor and first floor

Yehuda Bienheim, Jacobson residence, Yokneam, 1936

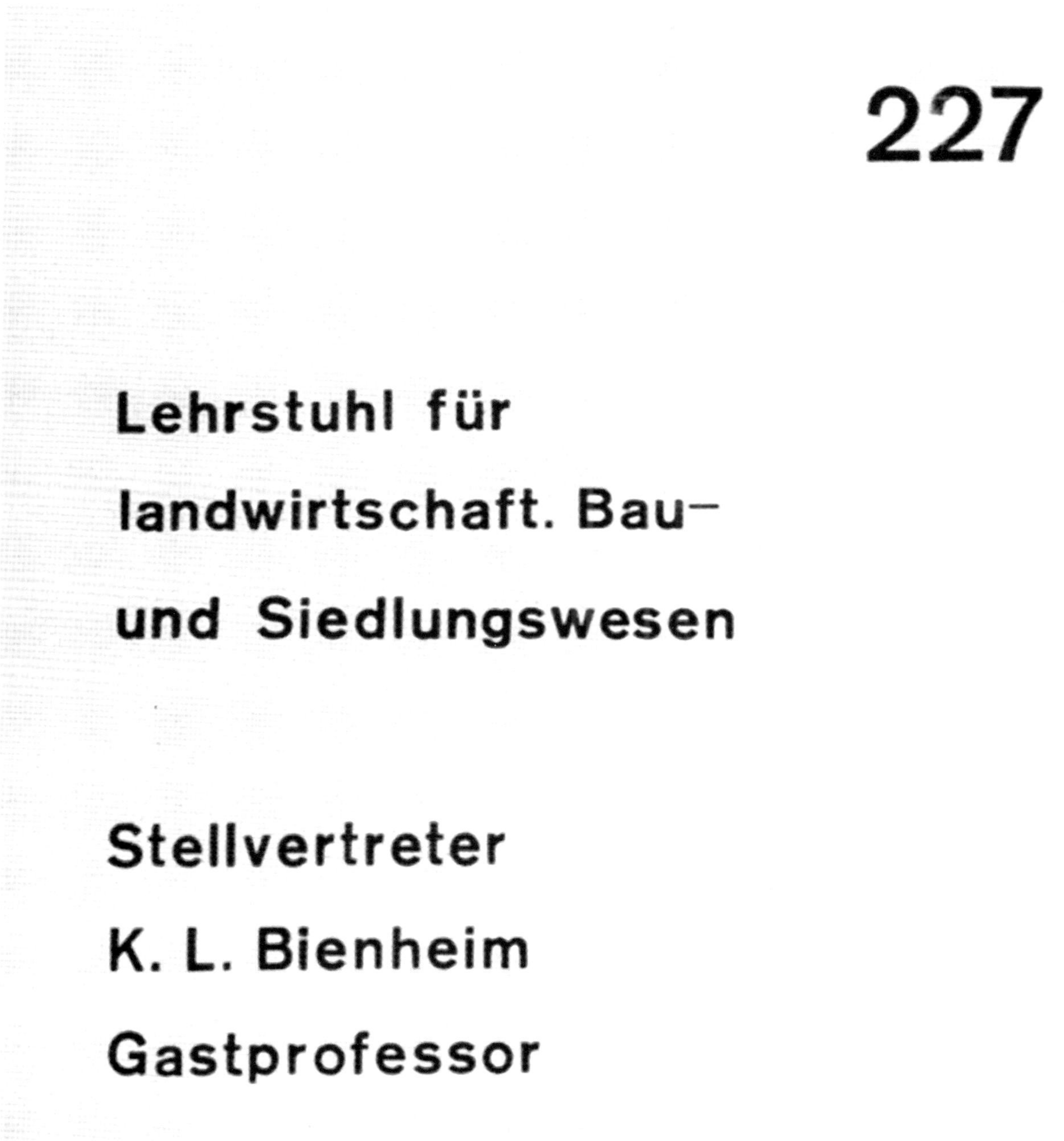

K. L. Bienheim, visiting professor at the Technische Universität Stuttgart 1961–1962. Sign on the door of room 227

David (Wilhelm) Pienaker

1900 Krenowitz – 1984 Tel Aviv

When strolling today down Tel Aviv's oldest streets, lined on either side by the apartment buildings designed by the pioneer architects Kuczynski, Neufeld, Rubin and Sharon, one discovers a number of buildings in the so-called Bauhaus style located close to each other.[1] Most of the four-storey buildings date to the 1930s and stand on small parcels of land measuring about 500 m^2.[2] Their effect is one of unparalleled intensity; the impressions of the apartment buildings in the eclectic-Mediterranean style of the 1920s fade in comparison.
What is unusual about these buildings is how they came to be built. The architects were not all graduates of German universities; sometimes they were not even trained architects. Among them were construction engineers, site managers, and clients who had come to Eretz Israel with the Third, Fourth or Fifth Aliya from countries in Central and Eastern Europe. But their shared model was the language of Modern architecture typically used by graduates of German universities.
The buildings' exterior appearance is characterized by right angles, although at street intersections their corners are sometimes gently, sometimes more markedly, rounded. Each of the buildings typically has windows of the same size placed side by side or over each other at rhythmic intervals. Behind the loggias or balconies are doors and windows of various sizes. The longer the loggias or balconies are, the more 'expressive' the building's feel. Thermometer windows that reach as high as the attic ensure that the staircases are bright and also highlight the entrances. Staircases with round windows also can be found; therefore the buildings are often compared with ships — after all, Tel Aviv is a coastal city. Originally the apartment buildings were stuccoed in white and had rooftop terraces. Today these apartment buildings are in a rather desolate state. Some have not survived the intervening years in good condition, others fell victim to the Zeitgeist. Loggias were equipped with the most disparate kinds of shutters and turned into rooms. Attics were converted into apartments. The air conditioners arbitrarily mounted on the façades do not enhance the aesthetics at all. Yet when the buildings have received fresh coats of paint, one recognizes a culture of architecture whose origin doubtless was in the German-speaking area.
Some of the architects of these buildings could build only a single building; others, however, realized several, just as it was possible for some trained architects to make a name for themselves in Israeli architectural history while others remained unknown.

One of the persons responsible for some of the buildings described above was David Pienaker. Although he was a professional architect, and Tel Aviv can thank him for several modern buildings, he was not in the architectural limelight. Little is known of his biography.
He was born on November 22, 1900, in Krenowitz, Moravia, today the Czech Republic. Later the family moved to Vienna; his last address before 1933 was Mariahilfer Strasse 76 in the seventh district. Pienaker earned his diploma in architecture at the Technische Hochschule in Vienna. Until his emigration in July

1933, he worked for Atelier Gutsch in Vienna's fourth district. After he arrived in Tel Aviv, Pienaker opened an office with the construction engineer M. Goldenberg. Together they erected at least eight apartment buildings and two office buildings. David Pienaker died on April 30, 1984, in Tel Aviv.

For information and material, I am very grateful to David Pienaker's son, Josef Perri, Kibbutz Nir David (1986).

1 The subject here is meonot ovdim, on which the architects Jonathan Shlain and Israel Dicker also worked. See biography of Arieh Sharon.

2 The parcels correspond to the garden city plan of Patrick Geddes. See biography of Arieh Sharon.

Atelier Gutsch, Vienna, circa 1932. David Pienaker: first row, third from left

DAVID (WILHELM) PIENAKER

David Pienaker with M Goldenberg, engineer, apartment building on Reines Street, Tel Aviv, circa 1936

below left:
David Pienaker with M. Goldenberg, engineer, apartment building, Tel Aviv, circa 1936, plan of a typical floor

below right:
David Pienaker with M. Goldenberg, engineer, Robinson building on Ha'hashmonaim Street, Tel Aviv, 1930s (drawing)

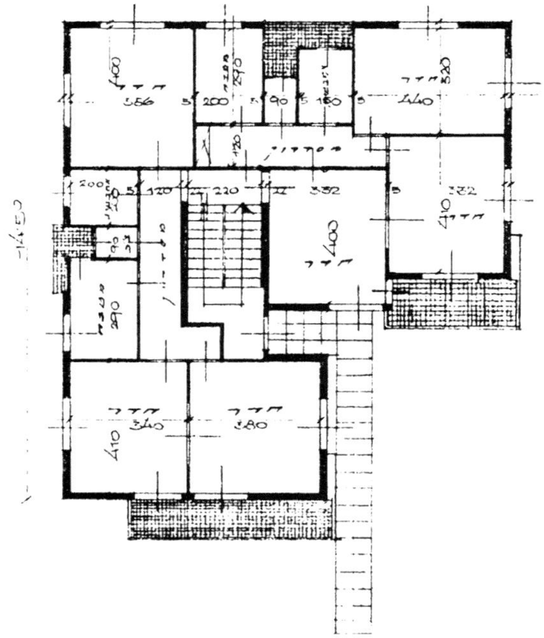

David Pienaker with M. Goldenberg, engineer, A. Mizrachi residence, Givat Rambam, 1930s, ground-floor plan

David Pienaker with M. Goldenberg, engineer, A. Mizrachi residence, Givat Rambam (drawing)

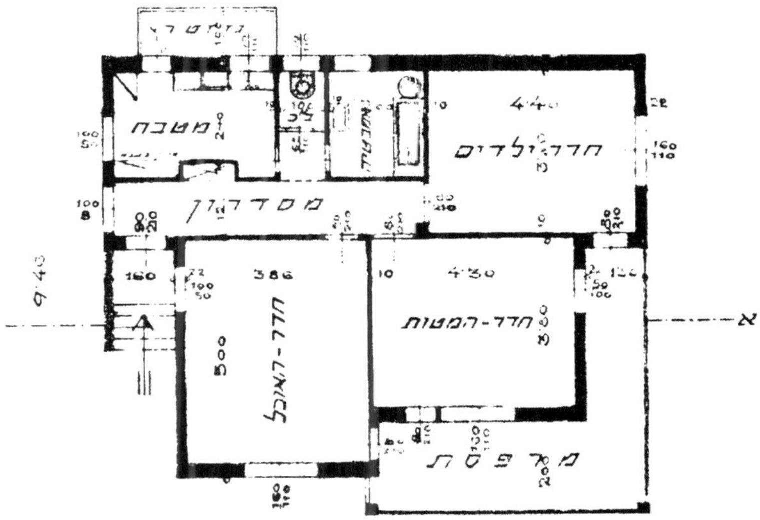

Elsa Gidoni-Mandelstamm

1901 St. Petersburg – 1978 New York

Elsa Gidoni-Mandelstamm was born in 1901 in St. Petersburg. She attended the art academy there, and continued her studies at the Technische Hochschule Charlottenburg in Berlin.[1] From 1929 until 1933, when she had to leave Berlin due to racist persecution, her home and her office for interior design were located at Landshuter Strasse 7 in Berlin-Schöneberg.

A number of publications contain references to Gidoni-Mandelstamm's career, but her creative strengths can best be appreciated in pictures of her works. A 1930 Berlin magazine article and a series of articles in architectural journals in Tel Aviv (between 1934 and 1937) and New York (1948) deal with her creative work in Germany, Palestine and the USA.[2]

The German home magazine published Gidoni-Mandelstamm's "Modern Cupboard". Its editorial commentary on the five-door, 3.2 m-long unit noted that the "especially practical cupboard contains all the different compartments for glass, silver and porcelain. The compartment where the everyday table linens hang over rods to keep them smooth is noteworthy". Photographer Lili Baruch took the pictures for the article; the Deutsche Werkstätte executed the design.[3]

After she arrived in Palestine in 1933, Gidoni (the name she used from then on) opened her own office and proceeded to make a name for herself as an architect. She designed the Swedish pavilion for the Orient Fair (organized by the British mandate in Tel Aviv in 1934) in the form of a modern basilica. Narrow bands of windows extended along the high nave and lower side aisles, and all three volumes had flat roofs.

Early in 1935, Gidoni and the pioneer architects Pinkerfeld, Neufeld, Rubin and Sharon were asked to participate in an invited competition for the House of the Women Pioneers in Tel Aviv. Gidoni's work was singled out, praised as having "the most suitable floor plan", and she was commissioned to execute the project in collaboration with Al Zeisler, who probably was the civil engineer. The building complex consisted of five right-angled structures of various sizes; three were interconnected. Classrooms, storerooms and offices, the library, dining room, kitchen and lecture hall were located on the ground floor. Accommodations for twenty-five chalutzot were located on the top floor of two of the buildings. Each room had access to a generously proportioned roof terrace with pergola – an appealing and convincing solution in view of the climate.

Another of Gidoni's buildings that attracted attention was completed in February 1936 in Nachlat-Yitzhak, a rural suburb of Tel Aviv, also in collaboration with Al Zeisler. The design of the Zionist Women's Union School of Domestic Science included a cooking school, dining hall, workrooms and classrooms, administration, library and accommodations for fifty students and four teachers in an L-shaped two-storey building. Here, too, Gidoni arranged the upstairs living spaces so that they had access to a long balcony facing west. The architect's modesty and political commitment are evident in her comments about this commis-

sion: "I would like to emphasize, though not to be praised, the fact that, although I gave special attention to developing the construction plans, this building should in no way be considered luxurious."[4]
Shortly before Gidoni left Palestine in 1938 and moved to the USA, she again won first prize in an invited competition for Beit Shalva (house of calm), a sixty-bed nursing home in Ramot Ha'shavim, 20 km north of Tel Aviv.[5]
During her five-year stay in Palestine, Gidoni enhanced her reputation as a practitioner of Modern architecture, a style the architect employed in passionate service of social and educational aims.

Gidoni continued to be active in New York. She worked in the office of Fellheimer & Wagner and designed chemical engineering buildings until the end of World War II. Afterward she entered into partnership with the New York architects Ely Kahn and Bob Jacobs.[6] She became a member of the American Institute of Architects (AIA). In 1948 she was listed as one of the eighteen most successful women architects in the USA (there were 1119 altogether), and she and her works were profiled in the *Architectural Record*.[7] In 1977 her works were shown in the exhibition "Women in American Architecture: A Historic and Contemporary Perspective", which travelled to several cities in the USA. Elsa Gidoni died in 1978 in New York.

1 In conversation with architect Abraam Erlik (died 1991), Tel Aviv 1985.
2 *Haus Hof Garten*, Berlin August 23, 1930, p. 412; *Habinyan Bamisrah Hakarov* 1, Tel Aviv December 1934, p. 1013; *Habinyan Bamisrah Hakarov* 3, Tel Aviv August 1935, p. 10; *Habinyan Bamisrah Hakarov* 8, Tel Aviv August 1936, p. 12; *Habinyan Bamisrah Hakarov* 9/10, Tel Aviv November 1936, p. 10; *Habinyan Bamisrah Hakarov* 1, Tel Aviv August 1937, p. 46.
3 Lili Baruch was a well-known architectural photographer of interiors until 1933.
4 *Habinyan Bamisrah Hakarov* 3, Tel Aviv August 1935, p. 10.
5 It was probably not realized.
6 Mies van der Rohe later built the Seagram Building with Kahn & Jacobs (1954–1958).
7 *Architectural Record*, vol. 103, New York March 1948; Warhaftig 2005, Gidoni, Elsa.

Elsa Gidoni, the Swedish Pavilion, Orient Fair, Tel Aviv, 1934

Right page:
Elsa Gidoni with Al Zeisler, House of the Women Pioneers, Tel Aviv, 1935, competition, first prize, perspective

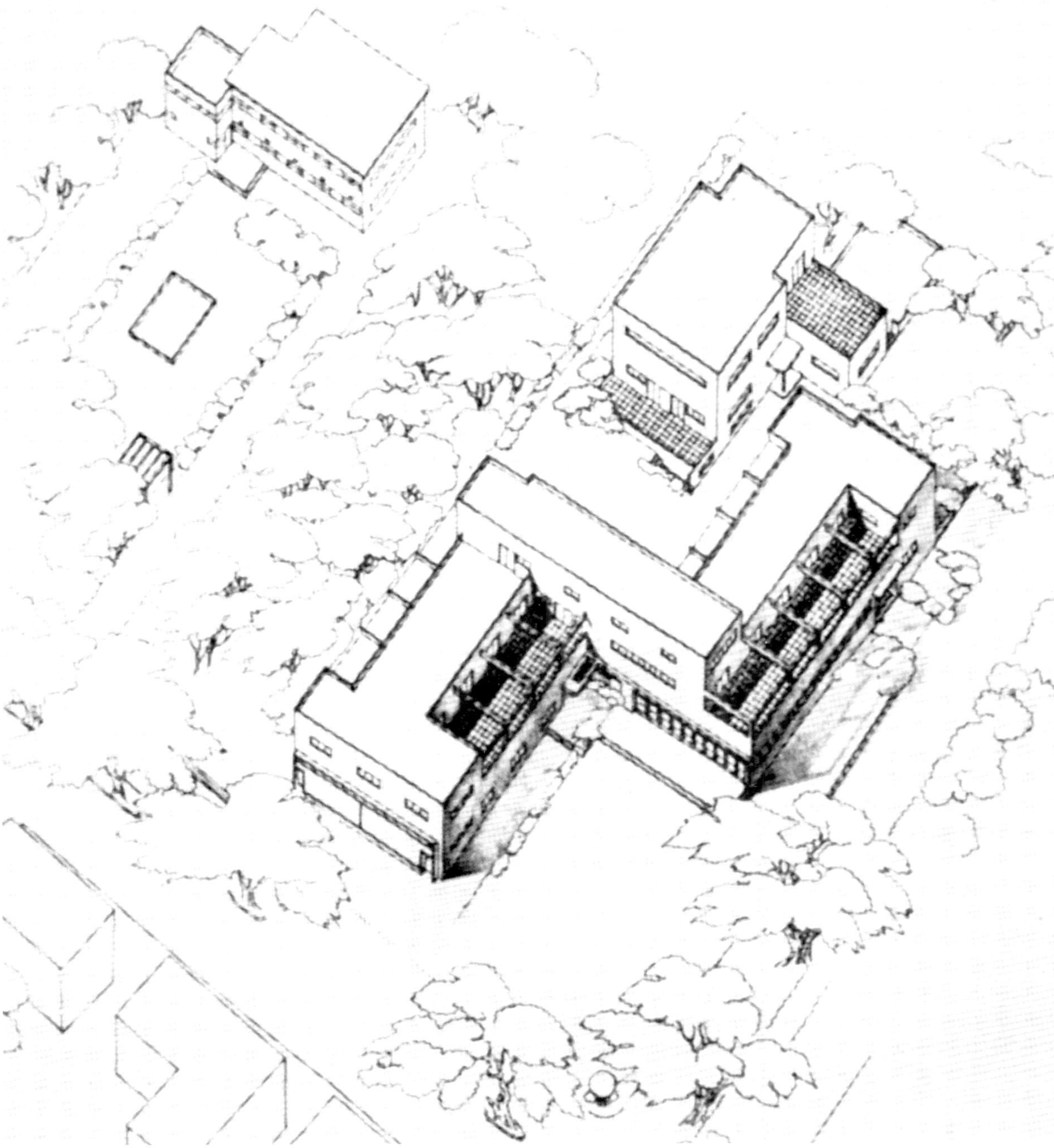

Elsa Gidoni with Al Zeisler, House of the Women Pioneers, Tel Aviv, 1935, general view

Elsa Gidoni with Al Zeisler, School of Domestic Science of the Zionist Women's Union, Tel Aviv Nachlat-Yitzhak, 1936, view of the courtyard

Elsa Gidoni with Al Zeisler, apartment building on Reines Street, Tel Aviv, 1936. Photo: M.W. 1990

Elsa Gidoni, one-family residence for Dr. and Mrs. M. Lenz, New Rochelle, New York, 1940s (drawing)

Werner (Joseph) Wittkower

Werner J. Wittkower (right) at the dedication of the Jewish orphanage in Bad Saarow, 1930

1903 Berlin – 1997 Tel Aviv

Werner Wittkower provided a telegraphic description of his "family background" in a letter to me dated June 10, 1986: "An old, long-established Berlin Jewish family; descendant of the house of Ephraim (the 'Jewish financial broker' for Friedrich the Great; Ephraim Palace in Berlin), typical 'bourgeois' family; two sons, two daughters. Both sons, one daughter university graduates. My brother, Rudolf W., famous art historian."[1]

Wittkower was born in Berlin on May 12, 1903. After graduating from secondary school, he went to Heidelberg to study archaeology and art history. Then he moved to Stuttgart and changed his focus to architecture. The well-known German architects Paul Bonatz (1877–1956) and Paul Schmitthenner (1884–1972) were his teachers. Wittkower gained professional experience in Stuttgart in the office of the architect Richard Döcker (1894–1968), with whom he also corresponded after 1933.[2]

Wittkower returned to Berlin from Stuttgart in 1927 and established what he termed a "small architectural practice" there. Before he had to leave Germany in 1933, he witnessed the dedication of two small, functionally designed buildings – a one-family residence near Heerstrasse in Berlin-Charlottenburg and a Jewish orphanage on Scharmützelsee in Bad Saarow near Berlin. An article about the orphanage was published in an issue of *Bauwelt* whose theme was "children's homes and youth hostels".[3] The building, a cube measuring some 10 × 8 m, had two storeys and two dormitories with five or six beds each, washrooms, a kitchen, dining room, staff room and a covered porch on the ground floor.

Wittkower's decision to immigrate to Palestine after Hitler came to power was not made on the spur of the moment, for he had been confronted with the hatred directed toward Jews since his youth, as he himself wrote:

"Pre-Nazi anti-Semitism

In the first year of college preparatory school (Sexta; age nine years) only two of some thirty children were Jewish. Both of us were soundly attacked by the other children, so that wild boxing matches ensued and we came home almost every day bloodied and with torn clothing. My mother complained to our teacher. He told her that he alone of the thirty teachers was not an anti-Semite, and he advised my mother to take me out of the school. – I went to another school; there anti-Semitism was forbidden! A great bit of luck for a Jewish child![4]

Youth movement

I was a member of the 'free German youth movement' (Deutscher Wandervogel – German rambler), and had many contacts and friends among Christian youth and, obviously, the 'Jewish problem' was a constant subject.[5]

Zionism
It became more and more clear to me: If I remain in Germany, I will be a second-class citizen. All this led me to join the Zionist Jewish youth movement Blau-Weiss shortly before I began to study at the university; I certainly didn't want to be a second-class citizen![6]
Nazi anti-Semitism
In 1933, when anti-Semitism began to develop the first insane forms of the Hitler era, we (I had married in the meantime) decided to emigrate. April 1, 1933 was announced as 'Jewish Boycott Day' — on the night of March 31–April 1 we crossed the border to Switzerland."

Soon afterward Wittkower arrived in Palestine and settled in Tel Aviv. He reports on his initial experiences and the emotions they evoked, and on his rise in the profession:

"*The Beginning*
We were very young – everything was wonderful. Right after we arrived, it was still summer 1933, we could make a living. The country seemed like paradise to us. There were no locks on the apartment doors in Tel Aviv (a city of approx. 40,000 inhabitants, even then). If a beggar came and knocked, and no one opened the door, he went in, and there found 10 cents (intentionally placed there for him); he took it and left 9 cents change. There was also work for a young architect in this 'paradise', although Palestine was then a British mandate territory in which only some 160,000 Jews lived. But many European Jews immigrated.
My first works in the country 1933–1940
A small private hospital in Ramat-Gan (at that time a suburb of Tel Aviv); apartment interiors, usually quite simple; 1935–36 small (at the time, 'larger') new hotel construction: Hotel Gat-Rimon in Tel Aviv, twenty-six rooms; 1937, with the architect Salkind, first prize in the competition for Tel Aviv's central bus station, building completed in 1938–39.[7] The same year, erected the Eden Hotel's new building in Jerusalem; also: several apartment buildings in Tel Aviv; several small villas.
Works 1940–1948
Renovation of Hotel 'Kaete-Dan' in Tel Aviv.[8] Small industrial building 'Blumenthal's Printing Press'; additional villas – now to a higher standard (in Ramat-Gan; in Gedera); additional apartment buildings; designed the first Sheraton Hotel (200 rooms)."

After the founding of the state of Israel, Wittkower was named chief architect in the "settlements" department of the newly established governmental planning office, and he designed many residential communities throughout the country.
The hotel Accadia, known today as "Dan Accadia" in Herzliya, and the villa for Dr. Reuben and Edith Hecht on Mount Carmel that Wittkower designed at the beginning of the 1950s are closely linked with the stories of the Federmanns and the Hechts.[9] But Wittkower earned his reputation with his general plan for Tel Aviv University, which includes the Museum Ha'aretz, and with the 1959 Glass Museum in the city centre, still considered one of Israel's most sophisticated buildings.
Along with his practical work as an architect, after 1936 Wittkower began intensive study of climate as it related to construction in Israel. He carried out fundamental measurements with the help of the government's newly established meteorological service (at the time, the government was English, headed by Mr.

Feige) and of professors Goldberg (a physicist, formerly with Zeiss-Jena) and Strauss (a hygienist, formerly at the university in Berlin). The research was published in several international journals.[10]
As of 1950, there were about ten architects working in Wittkower's office. In 1974 two long-standing members of the office became associates, and the firm was renamed W. J. Wittkower, A. Adiv, I. Stein, Architects Ltd. Throughout the years, the firm was located some 500 m from the beach in Tel Aviv, and Wittkower ran it until he retired at the age of ninety in 1993.
He died four years later, on December 11, 1997.

On December 1, 1986, Werner J. Wittkower visited me at my studio in Berlin. On this occasion, he gave me copies of two letters (dated August 1, 1933 and September 2, 1933), addressed to him by Richard Döcker, whom he highly esteemed. Disgusted by the political developments in his homeland and deeply despairing about the new rulers' stance vis à vis Modern architecture, which he championed, Döcker expressed his great apprehension. He called on Wittkower to use all his powers to further the architectural culture of the avant-garde in Palestine and to make the new land into a "model of culture".

1 Rudolf Wittkower (1901–1971) earned a degree in architecture at the Technische Hochschule Charlottenburg. He fled to London in 1933. There he became a professor at a London university. After 1956 he taught at Columbia University in New York. His books, which have been published in many countries and languages, include *Architectural Principles in the Age of Humanism* (1962) and *Art and Architecture in Italy, 1600–1750* (1964).
2 Dr. Richard Döcker was one of the leading exponents of Neues Bauen in Germany. He was responsible for the technical management and execution of the buildings in the Werkbund exhibition's Weissenhofsiedlung in Stuttgart (1927) and also was represented with two of his own apartment buildings.
3 W. Wittkower, "Kinderheime und Jugendherbergen" in: *Bauwelt* 8/1931, p. 1.
4 This was in 1912.
5 See biography of Jochanan (Eugen) Ratner.
6 See biography of Dov Kuczynski, note 2.
7 Nahum Salkind (1895–1976) was born in St. Petersburg and studied there at the Academy of Art and Architecture. He lived in Berlin in the 1920s. He fled to Palestine in 1934.
8 See "Yekutiel and Shmuel Federmann"; see also biography of Lotte Cohn.
9 See "Yekutiel and Shmuel Federmann" and "Edith and Dr. Reuben Hecht".
10 W. J. Wittkower, "Städtebau- und Wohnungsbaubestimmungen in Erez Israel" in: *Journal of the Association of Engineers & Architects*, Tel Aviv October 1943, p. 14; Werner Joseph Wittkower, "Climate-adapted Building in Israel. How far has our knowledge influenced Building Practice?" in: *Energy and Buildings* 7, The Netherlands 1984, pp. 269–280.
Further publications on Werner Wittkower: Agassi 1993; obituary in *haaretz*, Tel Aviv January 9, 1998.

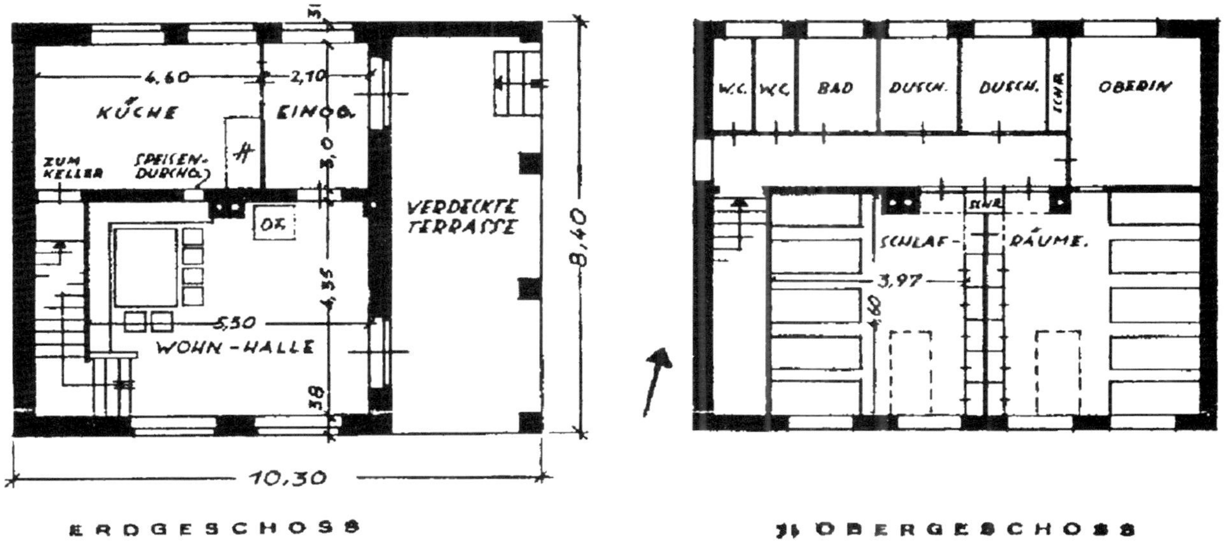

Werner J. Wittkower, Jewish orphanage, Scharmützelsee, Bad Saarow, 1930, plans for ground floor and first floor

Werner J. Wittkower, Jewish orphanage, Scharmützelsee, Bad Saarow, 1930, view of entrance

Left page:
Werner J. Wittkower, Villa Rojek, Berlin-Charlottenburg, 1932, partial view

Right page above:
Werner J. Wittkower and Nahum Salkind, central bus station "Eged", Tel Aviv, 1938–1939

Right page below:
Werner J. Wittkower, villa, Gedera, 1939–1940

ZE'EV (WILHELM) BRUCK

1904 Cottbus – 1973 New York

Ze'ev Bruck was shaped by two important figures in architectural history: he studied under Hermann Jansen at the Technische Hochschule Charlottenburg and worked as an architect in Erich Mendelsohn's Jerusalem office.[1] These two teachers, one a master of modern urban planning and the other of expressive architecture, undoubtedly influenced the course of Bruck's professional career.
Bruck was born in Cottbus on January 4, 1904. He went to Berlin to study architecture in 1922, earning his degree at the Technische Hochschule Charlottenburg in 1926. At that time he lived at Wielandstrasse 14a in Berlin-Schöneberg and worked as an architect for the Reichsbahn (German railway). From time to time he also assisted his uncles, the architects Paul and Richard Ehrlich, who had an office in Breslau.[2]

Bruck left Berlin, under persecution, in 1933 and soon arrived in Palestine. When Erich Mendelsohn established his Jerusalem office in 1934, Bruck became his first colleague. His primary responsibility was to plan the Hadassah University Medical Center on Mount Scopus.
In the summer of 1940, Palestine was drawn into the theatre of World War II and construction ceased. As a result, Mendelsohn found it necessary to dissolve his firm in 1941. Bruck then took a position in Damascus, probably working for the British mandate. From a letter that Erich Mendelsohn sent Bruck from New York on May 25, 1944, it can be inferred that Bruck and his family had already returned to Jerusalem by early January of that year.[3]
In this two-page letter, written by hand in English, Mendelsohn first recounts his Russian war experiences during the winter of 1917–18. He then reports on his professional activities, which at the time consisted solely of writing letters, lectures and books. The last sentence, "I hope to see you with me when the projects heaping up become realities" conveys the impression that Bruck had written Mendelsohn a letter in January asking about the possibility of a new collaboration. But this did not materialize.

Bruck was able to work independently for only a short time. In 1947 he erected a 160-bed hotel with a garden, terrace, shops and a private beach in Tiberias, which lies on the west bank of the Sea of Galilee.[4] Dr. Erich Kempinski, who also worked in Mendelsohn's office between 1934 and 1941, did the structural analyses. The Galei Kinnereth Hotel was one of the city's first modern buildings and much renowned in its day. Situated at the foot of Mount Galilee, the three-storey hotel building is made up of cubic forms. With its striking features, especially the long rows of horizontal apertures in its massive wall surface, the building fit superbly into the landscape. It is quite reminiscent of Mendelsohn's government hospital in Haifa, and clearly illustrates Mendelsohn's influence on Bruck.

During the 1948–49 War of Independence, Bruck made himself available to the Israeli army for security missions. He took this occasion to change his first name from Wilhelm (he was named for the German emperor and King of Prussia) to Ze'ev (wolf).

After Tiberias incorporated as a Jewish city, Bruck was named its building director in 1950, and worked in this capacity until he retired in 1969. He also accepted architectural commissions during his time in office and built the main post office and the city hall. In the spirit of his mentor Hermann Jansen, he dealt with urban planning and left a legacy of highly respected work in this discipline, including a map of Tiberias that illustrated the city's development from its beginnings to the present.[5] Using historical and archaeological sources, he documented the spread of Tiberias eastward from the Sea of Galilee and indicated the holy sites of the Jews, Christians and Moslems in chronological order. This historical overview has been essential to the city's development.
Ze'ev Bruck died during a trip to the USA on September 21, 1973.

For information and material, I am very grateful to Ze'ev Bruck's daughter Dipl.-Ing. Architect Hanna Bruck, Tel Aviv (1986).

1 Hermann Jansen (1869–1945), architect and urban planner, was especially involved in the design of a master plan for greater Berlin and also designed plans for housing developments and buildings in many of the areas later incorporated into that city.
2 Architects Paul and Richard Ehrlich were deported to Theresienstadt in 1933 and murdered early in 1943. See: Warhaftig 2005, Ehrlich, Paul und Ehrlich, Richard.
3 Private archive, Hanna Bruck, Tel Aviv.
4 After renovations, the original hotel building is today unrecognizable; Avissar 1973, p. 210.
5 Tiberias is one of Israel's four holy sites, along with Jerusalem, Zafed and Hebron. It has had a turbulent history, which will be outlined here in connection with Bruck's work. Tiberias was founded by Herodes Antipas in 18 A.D. in honour of the Roman emperor Tiberius. Talmudic sources and relics from synagogues and ceremonial objects found there verify that it had already been a Jewish settlement in still earlier times. Because of the gravesites there, Jews had long avoided the place. Only in the third century did Tiberias become a centre of Jewish spiritual life, and the major part of Talmudic literature was written there. In subsequent centuries, until the founding of the state of Israel, the city underwent severe disruptions. In the seventh century the Arabs conquered it. During the Mamluk era from the twelfth to fifteenth centuries, it was destroyed. In the sixteenth century, an attempt to revive the city failed. In the eighteenth century the Bedouin sheikh Dahir al-Omar finally rebuilt the city with a wall and a citadel to protect it from attacks. He also probably had the chief mosque, today known as Al-Omari, built in 1734. A severe earthquake struck Tiberias in 1837, followed by epidemics, floods and attacks. Only at the end of the nineteenth century, when the first Jews settled in nearby lower Galilee, did Jewish life again thrive to a significant extent. The city lies about 200 m below sea level, so it is often very hot there, with summer temperatures between 33° and 38° Celsius. In addition to its significant archaeological treasures, such as the grave of Moses Maimonides (1135–1204), Tiberias is also famous for its hot springs, which are used for healing purposes. Today the city is home to many modern spas and hotels; Avissar 1973.

Ze'ev (Wilhelm) Bruck

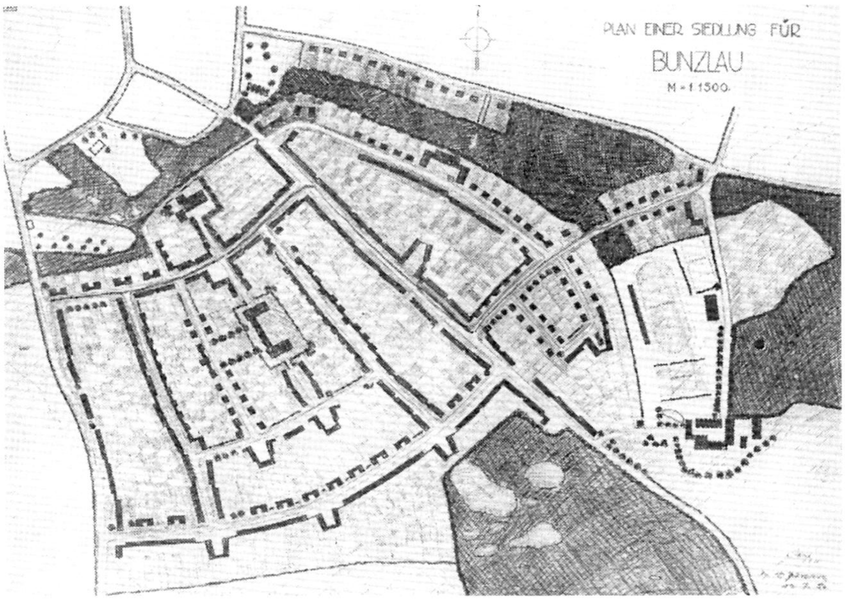

Wilhelm Bruck, "Bunzlau", student project under Prof. Hermann Jansen, Technische Hochschule Charlottenburg, Berlin, 1926

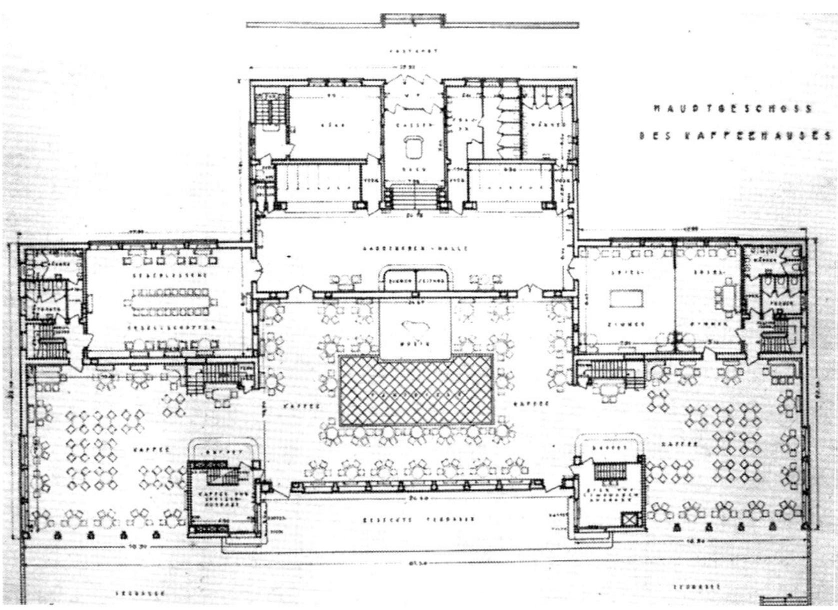

Wilhelm Bruck, "Kaffeegarten in einem Park", student project, Technische Hochschule Charlottenburg, Berlin, 1922–1926, ground plan

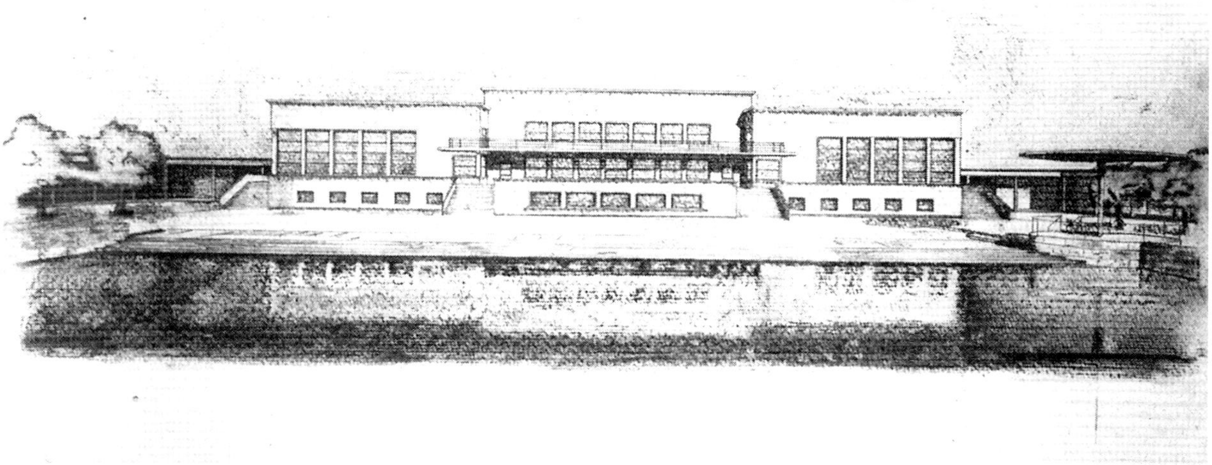

Wilhelm Bruck, "Kaffeegarten in einem Park", student project, Technische Hochschule Charlottenburg, front view (drawing)

Ze'ev Bruck, Galei Kinnereth Hotel, Tiberias, 1947

Judith Stolzer-Segal

1904 Prischib – 1990 Munich

Judith Stolzer-Segal grew up in a Russian-Jewish milieu, while Eugen Stolzer had a Hungarian-Jewish background.[1] Both went to Germany at different times to study architecture. They left Germany at the same time and found refuge in Palestine, where they met and married. Yet despite their marriage and their common fate and profession, Judith Stolzer-Segal shaped her professional career independently of her husband's. She participated in competitions, was awarded first prizes, and was also able to realize her social and cultural projects. In publications about her work, she is known as Judith Segal. Eugen Stolzer took the photographs of her buildings.

Segal was born on May 4, 1904, in Prischib, Russia. The family immigrated to Germany a few years later. After her father completed his rabbinical training in Giessen, the family decided to live in the far more attractive metropolis of Berlin and moved into a grand apartment in the Wilmersdorf district. When World War I broke out in 1914, the Segal family – like all Russian emigrants – had to leave Germany. Judith Segal finished secondary school at the Hebrew high school in Kovno (Kaunas) in the mid-1920s, then earned a degree in architecture at the Technische Hochschule in Danzig (Gdánsk) where her father meanwhile had become the head of the Jewish community. Segal, now a qualified architect and dedicated Communist, went to Berlin at the end of the 1920s to practise her profession. When Hitler came to power, she was briefly put in jail. Upon her release, despite her anti-Zionist convictions, she set off for Palestine.

In 1935 Segal achieved an important success when she won first prize in a competition for the Central Synagogue in Hadera.[2] She approached the double challenge of designing a building to be used for both sacred and strategic purposes with great sensitivity, bringing the opposing functions into harmonic balance. Demonstrating her awareness of the site's history, she based the synagogue building on the Chan, the place where Hadera's first settlers had found shelter in 1891.
Hadera was the scene of bloody struggles between Jews and Arabs during the 1930s. For this reason, Segal planned a fortress-like synagogue with a watchtower, inside of which the women's gallery was located. In case of an attack, the courtyard could offer protection for up to two thousand persons. The façades feature vaulted entrances and semi-circular windows, Mediterranean architectonic elements that could also be seen in nearby cowsheds. The synagogue nonetheless does not conceal its Modernity. It is composed of symmetrically arranged geometric forms and has an economical and functional floor plan.
Members of the jury chaired by Dov Kuczynski praised the project, yet were very embarrassed when they found out that the competition winner was a woman.[3] The rabbis on the jury at first refused to entrust the building to a female. But since Segal was able to demonstrate her close tie with the Jewish religion – her father himself being a rabbi – she faced no further difficulties.[4]

An experimental middle-income housing development (1937) was the second project for which Segal was awarded first prize. The Kiryat Meir development, in a district in the old centre of Tel Aviv, contains approximately 170 two- and three-room apartments in a configuration reminiscent of the garden city model.[5] Organized in seven pairs of rows, the buildings rise two storeys above the ground floor. The first and last rows are raised on pilotis and sited so as to form a gateway to the development, creating a threshold of sorts between public and semi-private space. Flat roofs, ribbons of balconies with an east–west orientation, and white stuccoed exterior walls are external features of the buildings. The interior design allots a spacious kitchen and dining area to each apartment, and Segal designed the adjacent balcony to serve as a second dining area during the hot season. The residents' accolades for the project also alerted the specialist publications, which then acknowledged the unusual urban and architectonic conception of the development.[6]

In 1957 Judith Stolzer-Segal and her husband left Israel. After his sudden death, she moved to Munich in 1958. One day in 1984, while crossing the street, she was hit by a car and injured so severely that she remained bedridden until her death on December 1, 1990. In 1986 I visited Stolzer-Segal in the Saul Eisenberg Jewish Home for the Aged in Munich. She was delighted to tell me her life story. In return, she asked me to tell her about the latest political developments in Israel. A single picture hung over her bed: the fourth graduating class of the Hebrew secondary school in Kovno, 1924.

1 See biography of Eugen Stolzer.
2 On Hadera, see biography of Yehuda Bienheim, note 4.
3 See biography of Dov Kuczynski.
4 Conversation with Judith Stolzer-Segal, winter 1986.
5 Named for the first mayor of Tel Aviv, Meir Dizingoff (1861–1936).
6 Judith Segal, "Kiryat Meir Quarter, Multi-Family Houses of Kuppat-Am Bank, Tel Aviv" in: *Habinyan* 1, Tel Aviv August 1937, pp. 18–19.

Cowshed with the Mediterranean apertures that were typical in Judith Segal's synagogue design, Hadera, circa 1900. Photo M.W. 1989

Judith Segal, Central Synagogue, Hadera, 1935, front view. Photo: M.W. 1989

Judith Segal, Kiryat Meir development, Tel Aviv, 1937, site plan

Judith Segal, Kiryat Meir development, Tel Aviv, 1937, main entrance to the development. Photo: M.W. 1989

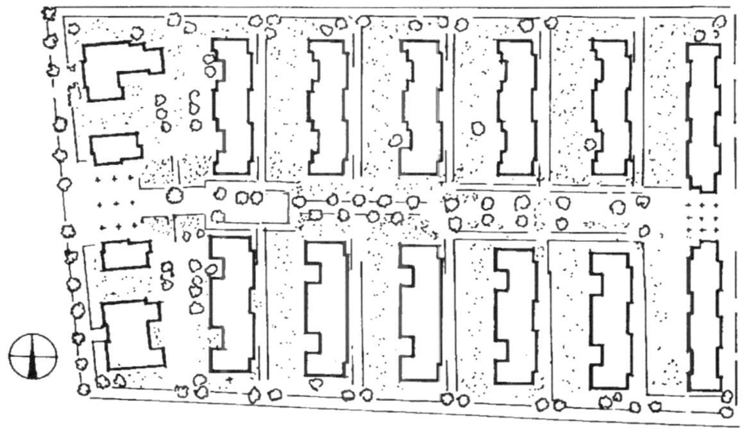

Left page above:
Judith Segal, Kiryat Meir development, Tel Aviv, 1937, partial view from the street, main entrance. Photo: M.W. 1989

Left page below:
Judith Segal, Kiryat Meir development, Tel Aviv, 1937, view from the street. Photo: M.W. 1989

Right page:
Judith Segal, Kiryat Meir development, Tel Aviv, 1937, partial view from the "semi-private street". Photo: M.W. 1989

Gideon Kaminka

1904 Vienna – 1985 Tel Aviv

Gideon Kaminka visited Palestine for the first time to form his own impression of the land as a twenty-two-year-old in 1926. Three years later he took a second trip there, this time to assess the professional scene. In 1933 he returned to the country for good. He settled in Haifa and was immediately able to realize his first building – a commission he received aboard ship on the way to Palestine.

Kaminka was born on July 30, 1904, in Vienna. His father, who had been born in the Ukraine and trained at the Jewish Orthodox rabbinical seminar in Berlin, had been appointed to head the Israelite Alliance in Vienna in 1900.[1]

Young Gideon Kaminka's confrontation with the hate campaign directed at Jews and his encounter with political Zionism made him an activist. Like Dov Kuczynski and Werner Wittkower, he joined Blau-Weiss, the Jewish Zionist youth organization whose aims were to convince young men and women to immigrate to Palestine and to prepare them for work in the trades and agriculture.[2]

Kaminka, who had literary gifts but was clumsy working with his hands, had difficulty choosing a profession that would be of benefit to Zionism. So he went to Berlin in 1923 to get advice from Alex Baerwald, whom he did not know personally but whose attention-getting buildings in Haifa had greatly impressed him.[3] Soon after, Kaminka began to study architecture at the Technische Hochschule in Vienna. The coursework did not especially engage him, however. He thought the teaching profession was rather conservative, and viewed the Wiener Werkstätten (Vienna workshops) led by Josef Hoffmann (1870–1956) as an ascetic version of the German Bauhaus. Kaminka learned purposefully, albeit with difficulty, consoled by the fact that it was all part of hachshara.[4] The political atmosphere at the university also was disappointing, oppressive and even threatening, as Gideon Kaminka recounted in his memoirs:

"The 'Tech' was a stronghold of Aryanism.[5] There were only a few Jews, barely a dozen were 'in architecture'. Our relationship to teachers and colleagues was collegial and impersonal. But Radau anti-Semitism, the rowdy and violent strain, was on the rise in the mid-1920s and spreading to Viennese universities, and the slogan 'out with the Jews' also entered the department of architecture, but only as an idea, for the students did not come to blows. When the two or three of us Jews in the drafting hall heard the sounds of beatings taking place elsewhere in the building, we initially continued our work, despite discreet warnings from other Aryan colleagues. But when the first troublemakers materialized, we very calmly and deliberately took our things and left the room, which was located on the ground floor. Silently and staring straight ahead, we calmly and slowly moved past the Teutonic line-up that had taken up position in the entrance hall and left the building. They didn't touch us, at any rate. Outside, where they weren't needed, stood the police. Even if they had wanted to, they could not have intervened, for the university had autonomy and they were not permitted to enter the building. My reaction stayed with me for a long time: rage over what I had been forced to do and anger that louts could simply take away my right to study, acquired when I matriculated. The anti-Semitism demonstrated in front of my eyes affected me the least. These guys didn't love me? I didn't love them either! They wanted me to get out of their country? As a Zionist, I myself wanted to leave. Just give us enough time and behave more or less properly, that didn't seem too much for me to ask of them. Over the years I returned to this reflection time and again and preached it to others, unfortunately without very much success. Probably I can consider myself personally very, very lucky that Radau anti-Semitism – not to mention Hitlerian – affected me directly only this once, and only in this literally bloodless way."[6]

Kaminka received his diploma and went on to earn a doctorate in 1930 with a thesis on "The Regular City Plan in Thirteenth Century East Austria". This thorough study of urban development in some fifteen cities and markets had little relevance to Zionism, however.

Kaminka gained professional experience in the offices of Josef Franks (1885–1967) and Oskar Wlachs (1881–1968) in Vienna. With Hitler's men already in power in Germany, and Nazi party adherents gaining strength in Austria, Kaminka left the country.

In 1936 Kaminka's first building was erected on Herzl Street in Haifa, within view of Baerwald's Technion complex. The three-storey corner building has shops on the ground floor, offices on the first floor and apartments featuring small balconies on the top floor.[7] It became a city landmark known as Beit Ha'shaon (the clock building) because of the two large clocks high on the corner façades. The Snir ice cream parlour located on the ground floor, whose interior was designed by Harry Rosenthal, is still an unmistakable meeting place for all Haifa residents.[8] The building has sacrificed nothing of its function or its functional appearance over time. Air conditioners now mounted on the façades are the only indication of the technological progress over the years. For five decades, Kaminka and his family lived in one of the second floor apartments and he maintained his office on the first floor.

Kaminka was well known among the German-speaking upper class as the architect of the Haifa doctors' building and the home for the aged for emigrants from Central Europe, but he also became known for his political activities. After 1939 he was among the leaders of the Jewish district of Haifa, where he came in contact with Adolf Rading.[9] The arguments between Kaminka the pragmatist and Rading, who in Kaminka's opinion "tended to the Romantic style", frequently were heated and even conducted in public.[10] After 1944 Kaminka chaired Haifa's planning commission and in 1950 he became a member of the city council and an independent liberal party representative, positions he held for twenty-eight years.

In his second autobiographical work, published five years before his death, Kaminka summed up the inner conflicts engendered by his professional activities, politics, Zionism and Judaism: "I came from the country of my birth, Austria, to Palestine nearly fifty years ago, out of an inner drive to live here as a free person and as a Jew. I felt drawn to the land through history and tradition, and was a Zionist politically, but it was not easy for me to become accustomed to the barren, but also rich, hot southern landscape and to its people. I participated in the achievements and failures of building the country. In contrast to other new arrivals, who valued their new 'homeland' from the day they arrived, I became a patriot via a slow and difficult path, proud of what had been gained by dint of sweat and blood and proud of the nation's rebirth. I needed to have an answer for my European friends, and more for the Jews than for the non-Jews among them. In their eyes, the efforts expended on national issues, during an era that tended toward the supra-

national, signified a step backward. Yet I am convinced that it is good that there are different peoples, including the Jews. I can think of nothing more annoying than the blurring of national characteristics in favour of a standardized general sort of humanity. I find it good that great diversity exists and that there are different worldviews and languages, among them the newly resuscitated Hebrew language. It is a joy that we have the bible, Shakespeare and Goethe, Anatole France and Thomas Mann and our new Hebrew authors. But I don't believe that patriotism is a virtue in all cases. The phrase 'my country right or wrong' is suspect, in my view. It often conceals injustice that the state perpetrates on its own citizens or that one people misuses against another. I have the greatest respect for nationalist sentiments and feel them myself, along with the utmost revulsion for egocentric chauvinism. I never want to relinquish insight and conscience as the ultimate arbiters of my behaviour.
Some reproach the Jews for their tradition as the chosen people, which supposedly indicates national arrogance. According to Jewish tradition, however, this in no way signifies recognition for existing achievements, but rather the obligation to maintain exemplary conduct in one's own house — Jews were never encouraged to violent proselytising. It corresponds to the spirit of Judaism that, from biblical times to the present, prophets and admonishers have time and again risen from the people to remind them of their original obligation. The religious philosopher Martin Buber, one of the recent admonishers, voiced the thought that the Israeli people are forever, yet always conditionally, connected to their country – namely under the condition that, during the periods when they inhabit the land, they work on the humanitarian task set forth for each generation. 'Because of our sins we were driven out of our country', it says repeatedly in Jewish prayers. I contrast Buber's moral and religious thinking with the statement made by our chief rabbi Goren – that the current third return of the Jews from exile is the final return, and that appropriation of the whole land at the expense of long-standing Arab residents is God's will – and I stand on Buber's side. The meaning of my life, in my view, lies in taking my place in the generation that is building the country. I have been a builder both as an architect on construction sites and as a politician on the city council. People around the world are unable to resolve their political and moral questions. I don't believe that we will be able to master the challenge set forth for my generation in Buber's sense. What is important is that we always strive to do so."[11]

Late in August 1985, I visited Gideon Kaminka at the Ramat Chen Home for the Aged in Tel Aviv, where he had moved some years before. We agreed to meet at his apartment in Haifa on September 11, so that he could give me copies of his books. But he died three days before, on September 8, 1985.
I am very grateful to Gideon Kaminka's daughter, Michel Katzenelson, who sent me copies of both books a year later.

1 Dr. Esriel Hildesheimer (1820–1899) founded the Jewish Orthodox rabbinical seminar in Berlin in 1873. It was shut down by the Gestapo on November 10, 1938.
2 See biographies of Dov Kuczynski and Werner Wittkower.
3 Julius Posener also visited Alex Baerwald in his Dahlem apartment, at the recommendation of the sociologist

Franz Oppenheimer, his uncle by marriage. But Posener wanted to learn about architectural training at the Technische Hochschule Charlottenburg. See: Warhaftig 2005, Posener, Julius.

4 Hachshara, the Hebrew term meaning "suitability, fitness", denoted the preparation of young Jews for immigration to Palestine.

5 He is referring to the Technische Hochschule Vienna.

6 Kaminka 1977, pp. 42–43.

7 See biography of Arieh Sharon.

8 See biography of Harry Rosenthal.

9 See biography of Adolf Rading.

10 Kaminka 1980, p. 77.

11 Ibid., pp. 185–187.

Gideon Kaminka, *Schwieriges Israel*, Zurich 1980, book cover

Gideon Kaminka

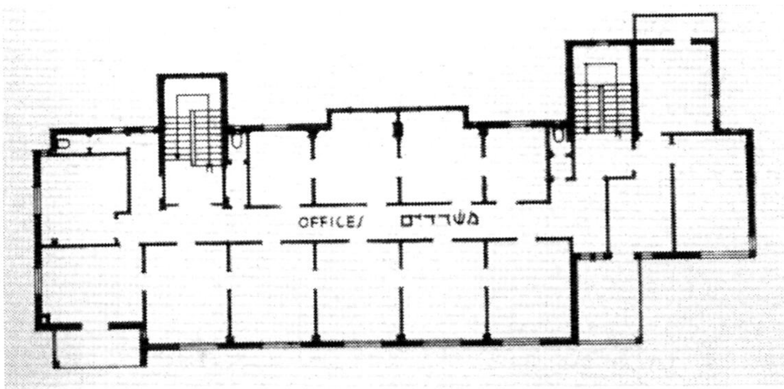

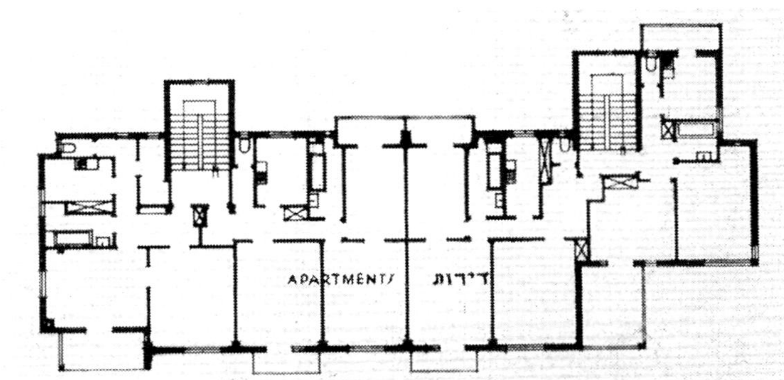

Gideon Kaminka, Beit Ha'shaon (the clock building) on Herzl Street, Haifa, 1936, first storey: the offices

Gideon Kaminka, Beit Ha'shaon (the clock building) on Herzl Street, Haifa, 1936, second storey: the apartments

Gideon Kaminka, Beit Ha'shaon (the clock building) on Herzl Street, Haifa, view from the intersection of Herzl and Balfour Streets

Gideon Kaminka, one-family residence, Haifa, Mount Carmel, 1937, ground-floor plan

Gideon Kaminka, one-family residence, Haifa, Mount Carmel, 1937, view from the garden

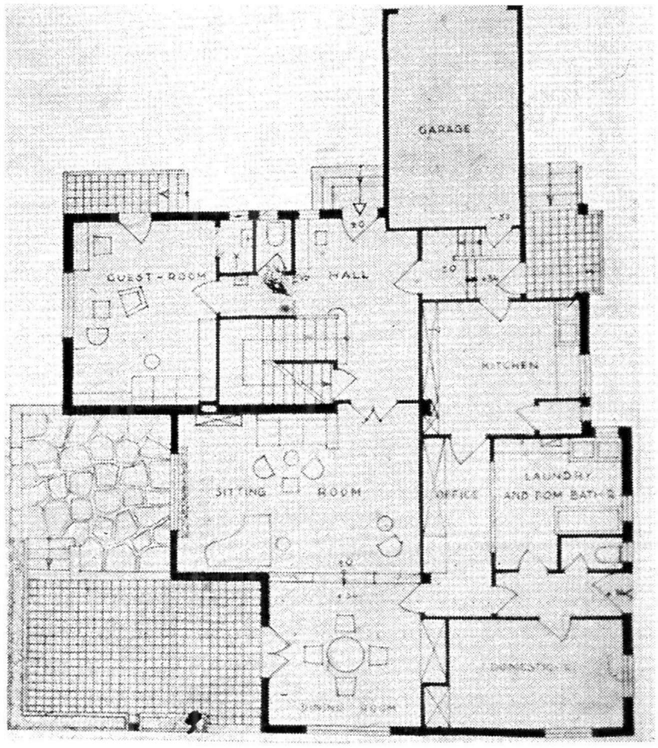

Theodor Menkes

1906 Niedernondorf – 1973 Haifa

Haifa residents have said for over six decades that the city's most beautiful building stands on Bar Giora Street on the ridge of Mount Carmel.[1] They are talking about a three-storey apartment building that has become known as "the Glass Building" due to its transparent staircase constructed of steel and glass.[2] The building's creator was Theodor Menkes.

Menkes was born on March 6, 1906, in Niedernondorf in Waldviertel, Lower Austria. He earned his degree in architecture at Vienna's Technische Hochschule on March 14, 1929. His diploma shows that he received grades of "good" in ten subjects, "very good" in eleven subjects and "excellent" in engineering science, the study of monuments, and design.

Unfortunately, information about his career prior to 1934 – when he fled fascism and arrived in Palestine – is lacking. However, papers in his estate include sketches he made of a tower in Nuremberg and photographs of the Weissenhofsiedlung in Stuttgart, testifying to travel through German cities before 1933. His photographs also indicate that he had come to favour the Modern style in housing.

Menkes settled in Haifa. There he erected housing that harmonized with the mountainous landscape and met ecological demands. He insisted that residents have views of the sea and the mountains from their apartments, and that his buildings not block the views of other residents. His first project, the three-storey Abramson apartment building (1938), also on Bar Giora Street, has balconies that jut out on four sides, creating a very dynamic effect. Each apartment is set off from the others by half a floor, with the top floor being one and one-half storeys high. From its tall vertical window there is a view of the sky above Haifa.

The Glass Building (1940–41) was originally planned as a guesthouse. Each of the fourteen living units, measuring between 30 and 35 m², is accessible from an arboured entryway. The residents had a rooftop tennis court and a courtyard swimming pool at their disposal. Glass brick walls let light into the kitchens and baths. Menkes came up with a clever and elegant idea for the ventilation: "Ventilation of the bathroom and w.c. is achieved by using the principal of gravity. The fresh air streams in through a window that extends to the floor, is warmed, and moves toward the window in the entresol."[3] Practical considerations dictated that the rain gutters be located directly above the window boxes.[4]

Menkes, who typically worked out the plans for his buildings down to the tiniest detail, was well known among his German-speaking colleagues for his "pedantry in building". Ossip Klarwein often made fun of Menkes's architectural perfectionism, saying that Menkes had even thought of a place for kitchen matches in his plans.[5] A wall cabinet designed by Menkes hung in their family kitchen. It had many small compartments, and one of them was indeed designed to hold matches.

Theodor Menkes lived and worked in Haifa for almost forty years, until his death on October 15, 1973.

For information and materials I am very grateful to Theodor Menkes's widow Ida Menkes, Haifa (1986). For photographs of the Abramson apartment building in Haifa, I am grateful to his son Arodi Ayalon.

1 Simon Bar Giora led the Jewish freedom fighters in the war against the Romans 66–70 A.D.
2 After its broken windows were not replaced for many years, the steel construction was unfortunately torn down when the staircase was renovated in 1992.
3 A Collection of Students' Work, Technion Pub. 2, Documentation of Architecture in Haifa, Haifa 1981, Project 28, Sheet 2.
4 Water is scarce in Israel.
5 See biography of Ossip Klarwein.

Theodor Menkes, the Glass Building, Haifa, 1940–1941, the rooftop terrace with view of the Haifa harbour

Theodor Menkes

Theodor Menkes, the Glass Building, Haifa, 1940–1941, side view

Theodor Menkes, the Glass Building, Haifa, 1940–1941, view from Bar Giora Street. Photo: M.W. 1989

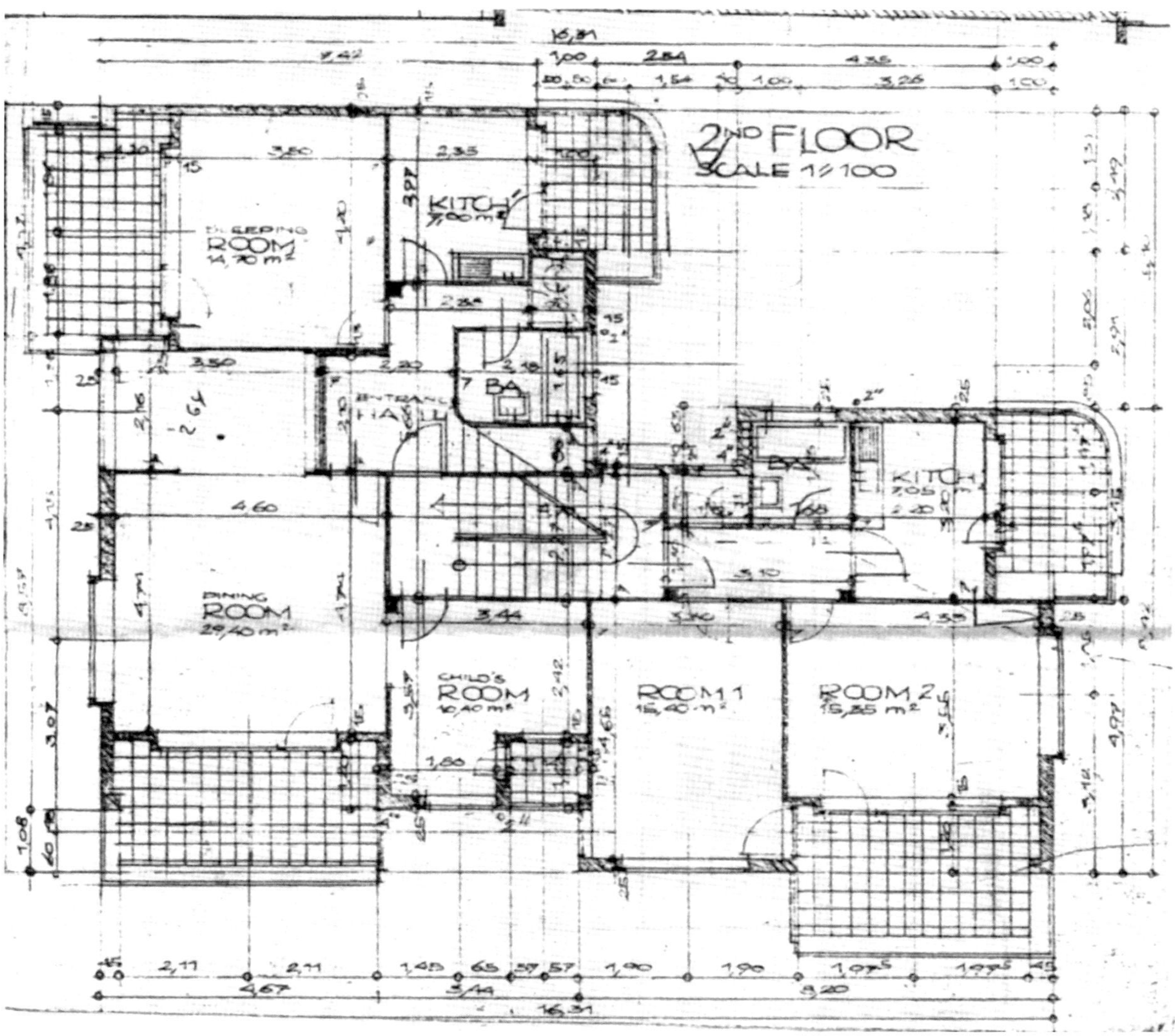

Theodor Menkes, Abramson apartment building, Haifa, 1938, second-floor plan. Archive Arodi Ayalon

Theodor Menkes, Abramson apartment building, Haifa, 1938, view from Bar Giora Street. Photo: archive Arodi Ayalon

Theodor Menkes, housing development on a ridge, Haifa, Mount Carmel, 1945

Theodor Menkes, apartment building, Haifa, Mount Carmel, circa 1935 (drawing)

Uriel (Otto) Schiller

1907 Pressburg – 1992 Tel Aviv

Otto Schiller, Vienna, 1933

Among the persecuted architects, one of the last to remain professionally active, from the 1930s to the early 1990s, was Uriel Otto Schiller, a pupil of Peter Behrens.

Born on March 14, 1907, in Pressburg, today Bratislava in Slovakia, Schiller earned his diploma at the Akademie der Bildenden Künste in Vienna in 1933. When the Schiller family sought to escape fascism in 1934, they faced the choice of going to Russia, where there were jobs and where many of their relatives had already gone, or immigrating to Palestine, though they were anti-Zionist. They chose the latter.

After three years of professional experience in Josef Neufeld's firm in Tel Aviv, Schiller opened his own office.[1] His projects over five decades ranged from private to public buildings, from single structures to settlement complexes in kibbutzim, villages and cities across the whole country, from north to south. Schiller also accomplished a great deal of political work in his field. The architectural journal *Habinyan Bamisrah Hakarov*, which he co-founded, was an important contemporary publication.[2]

Schiller also was a member of numerous professional committees and urban planning commissions.

In the spring of 1985, my visit to his office on the ground floor of an apartment building on one of Tel Aviv's most elegant boulevards provided the architect with the occasion to review his professional career. He presented me with 2.5-m-long roll of paper, on which he had made a handwritten list of all his buildings and professional activities in chronological order.

Schiller died in Tel Aviv on January 11, 1992.

Uriel Schiller, Tel Aviv, 1985

1 See biography of Josef Neufeld.

2 The Hebrew-language journal *Habinyan Bamisrah Hakarov* (Building the Near East) appeared sporadically from the end of 1934 to the middle of 1938 and a second journal *Habinyan* (Building) was published from 1937 to 1938. Both are the most important publications from those years about architecture in the land of Israel.

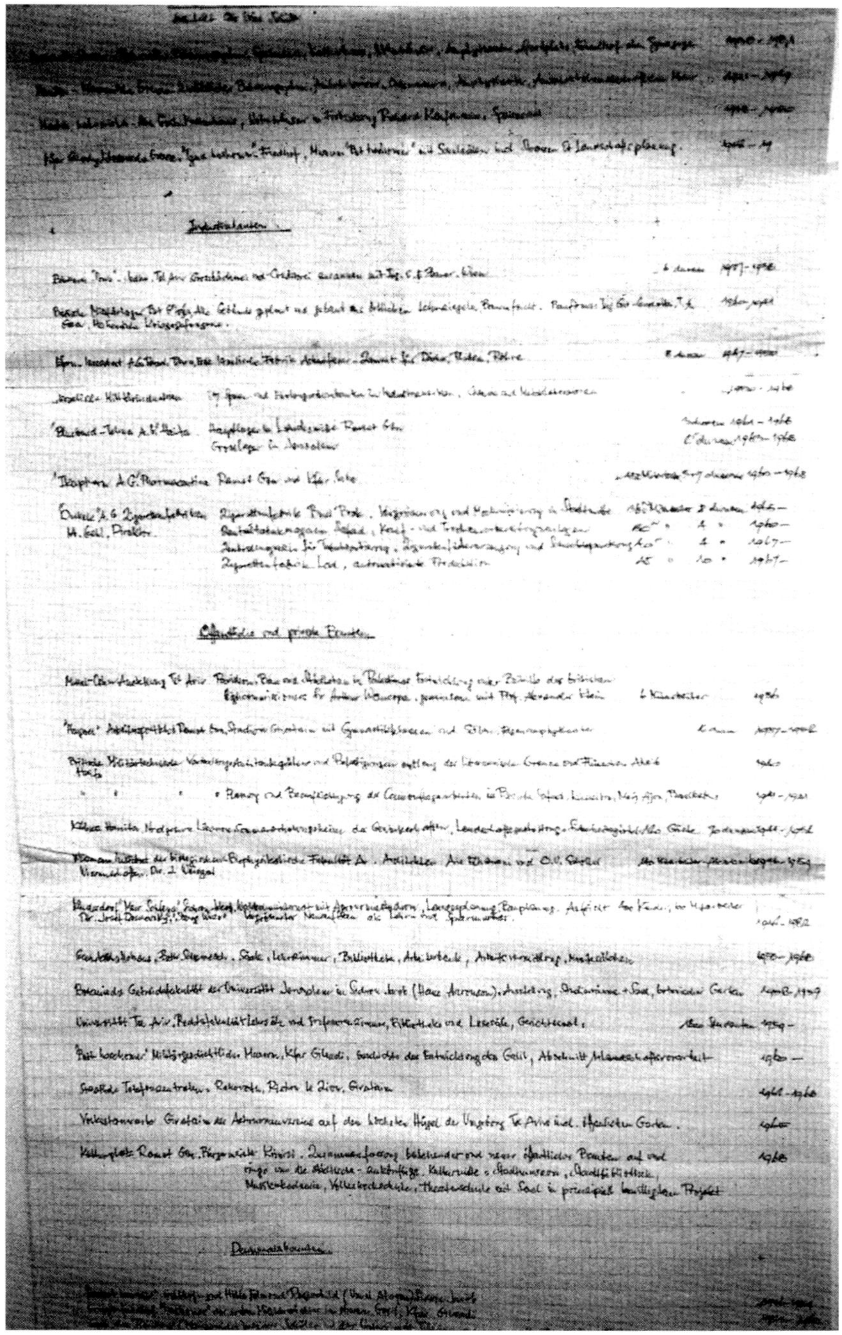

Uriel Schiller's handwritten account of his professional career on a roll of paper 2.5 m long, excerpt

Yehuda Kurt Unger

1907 Falkenau – 1989 Haifa

Yehuda Kurt Unger was the third architect to advocate the use of Adolf Loos's concept of spatial planning in housing in Palestine.[1] The weekly journal *Bauwelt* devoted an issue to Loos to mark his 111th birthday on December 10, 1981. Former co-workers and colleagues of Loos contributed articles. "My Apprenticeship under Adolf Loos" by Y. Kurt Unger was a subtle account of their encounter, which took place during Unger's last year of study at the Deutsche Technische Hochschule in Prague, 1930:

"... my uncle, who lived in Pilsen, invited me to visit one day; he wanted to have the architect Loos redesign one part of his apartment, and wanted me to meet him. I needed no further encouragement and appeared punctually at the appointed hour. The details of my first meeting with L. are no longer fresh in my memory, but it was probably arranged beforehand that I would be his assistant on this job. L. was by then almost deaf, and to communicate he used a megaphone – I would call it more of a speaking hose – which he held to his ear while one spoke into it. His instructions were brief, clear, and direct. I was able to see all his interiors and renovations in Pilsen and they made a deep impression on me.
Some of my university professors were 'historical', some 'Jugendstil', some 'moderately Modern'. We students naturally attempted to be as 'Modern' as possible in our designs, but we all lacked a clear direction. Our inspiration came from magazines. But now I felt as if I was someone who had never dared to go into the water and suddenly found that I could swim. During the course of the project, perhaps even while I was preparing drafts of the design, I received high praise from L. (or so I wanted to interpret it, at any rate): 'Unger, you understand me.' From the first day I worked with L., I learned new things. Materials: wood, textiles, leather etc. Standardization in planning and execution.
In April 1931 I received a letter from Claire Loos in Juan-les-Pins asking me to come there, since there were certain prospects for a project on the Riviera. She wrote further: 'You pay for your trip, and we'll take care of you here! We don't live as luxuriously as we did in Vienna, but it is much more beautiful here.' Their apartment consisted of two rooms, a kitchenette and a bath with a toilet (inside and unventilated!). I was given the second room. And so I lived in Juan-les-Pins together with L., his wife Claire, and Beau-Beau the Pekinese from the end of April until about the middle of June 1931. The project, to renovate the Hotel Cap d'Antibes, had by then unfortunately fallen through.
During this period, before I was conscripted into the Czechoslovakian army in autumn 1931, I was often in regular contact with L.: he had returned to Central Europe (Vienna, Prague, Pilsen, Karlsbad, St. Johannistal) in the meantime. The villa for Dr. Fleischner, a Prague physician who wanted to immigrate to Palestine and had already purchased a lot there on Carmel in Haifa, was his most important project. My task was to rework the 1922 plans for the country house of a doctor in Gastein (which was not built) for the new conditions. What is remarkable is that L. insisted that the house be oriented to the north, at a time when all the

architects in Palestine oriented their houses to the west to exploit the sea breezes for ventilation. That proved to be a mistake, and today there has been a return to the north-south orientation where possible. Dr. Fleischner immigrated to Palestine around the same time I did, but settled in Jerusalem and did not build the house in Carmel. Among the projects that I also worked on was the 'penthouse' for Jordan in Brünn, which naturally was only a preliminary project.
While I was in the military, I almost completely lost contact with L. The last meeting with my mentor, to whom I owe so much, (not only in my profession, but also in many other areas!) remains in my memory as a sad event. I used a short vacation to travel from my garrison in Prague and visited L. in a guesthouse, where he lay sick in bed, alone, with only one caretaker (Claire had already left him long ago), complaining that no one would come to see him in his mattress tomb."[2]

Unger made it his mission to advocate Loos's architectonic spatial planning in his own professional life. But despite all his efforts, he was able to realize only one building in the spirit of his mentor. This was his parents' house in Falkenau on the Eger (1935).[3] The property was somewhat higher on the street side than on the garden side, which was conducive to the spatial concept. The tile-roofed residence presents two storeys to the street and three to the garden. Inside, the living room is the largest room in the house, and also has the highest ceiling. A low-ceilinged open dining room is at a somewhat higher level. Since the living room is connected with the narrow, lower-lying entrance, that smallish area becomes magnified in effect. "That was the best house I ever built, even if it is not typical," Unger told me in the summer of 1985, while recounting his fifty-year career.
Unfortunately, a thoroughly planned project from 1936, a twelve-storey apartment building with forty-eight duplex apartments, accessible through an arbour on every third storey, could not be realized, since violence against Jews was already being strongly felt in Czechoslovakia. As a result, Unger fled to London. Unable to get on his feet there, he moved to Palestine in 1937. He settled in Haifa on Mount Carmel, correctly supposing that the terrain would be suitable for building according to Loos's "Raumplan" concept of interlocking spaces across levels. Much to Unger's disappointment, no commissions were forthcoming.
In 1941 Unger volunteered for the British army and served as a soldier until the end of World War II. After returning to Haifa he worked as a private architect, primarily in interior design. He found satisfaction in equipping his clients' apartments

Yehuda K. Unger (left) with Adolf Loos, Cannes, June 3, 1931

with a practical piece of furniture, a new fabric or a refreshing colour. He also cultivated a friendly relationship with Paul Engelmann, whose good nature and talent greatly impressed Unger.[4] They carried out projects together, including design for "The Cultivated Home", a furniture factory/store in Tel Aviv.[5]
The offer of a teaching post in the architecture department at the Technion in Haifa raised Unger's hopes that he could generate enthusiasm for Loos's architectural concepts, at least among his students. But at the time, those students wanted to develop their own ideas concerning building and living in Israel. Since Unger felt unable to cope with the teaching situation, he resigned his post at the Technion after only a few years. Unger was my professor at the Technion Haifa, and when I began my research early in 1985, he was one of the first persons I went to see, in his apartment on Mount Carmel. He showed great interest in my project. At his request, I visited him regularly during my trips to Israel, until his death four years later. One day he told me that, in a fit of depression, he had given all the drawings of his unrealized projects to a paper factory, reasoning that at least the paper would serve a purpose by being recycled – a deed that he later deeply regretted.

Unger was born with the first name Kurt on June 3, 1907, in Falkenau, today Sokolov in the Czech Republic. Because of the horrendous Nazi crime against Jewry, he decided to adopt the name Yehuda ("thanks be to God") in front of his first name. Yehuda Kurt Unger died on September 13, 1989, one year after the death of his wife, whom he had cared for during her long illness.

1 See biographies of Paul Engelmann and Eugen Szekey.
2 *Bauwelt* 42, Berlin 1981, pp. 1882–1892.
3 Kurt Unger, "Haus Dr. Unger, Falkenau a.d. Eger" in: *Der Monat* 1, Brünn 1937, p. 12.
4 Unger's wife, born in Olmütz, had been close with the Engelmann family back in their homeland.
5 See biography of Paul Engelmann.

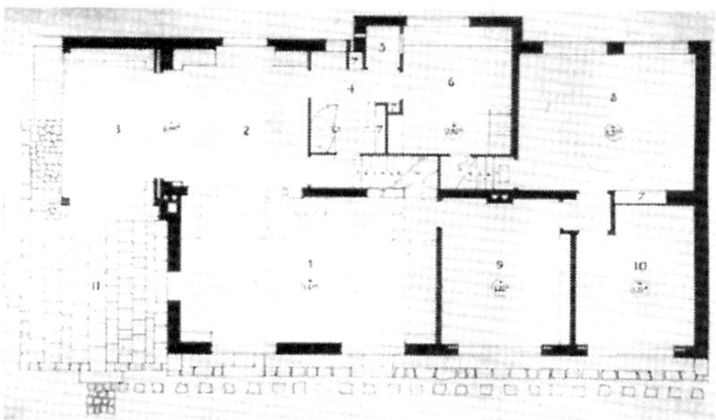

Yehuda K. Unger, residence of Dr. Unger, Falkenau on the Eger, 1935, floor plan of living area

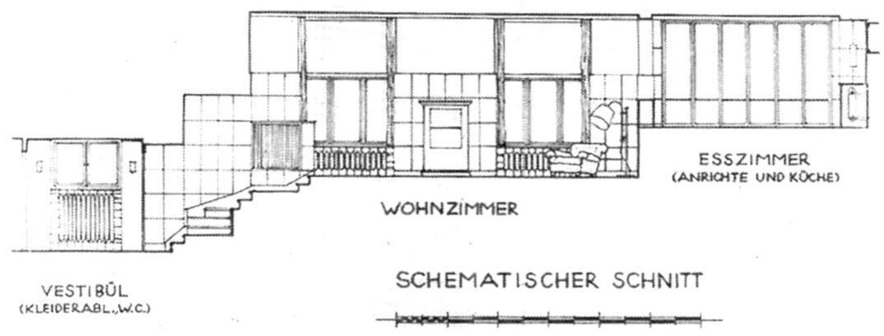

Yehuda K. Unger, residence of Dr. Unger, Falkenau on the Eger, 1935, schematic section

Yehuda K. Unger, residence of Dr. Unger, Falkenau on the Eger, 1935, view from the garden

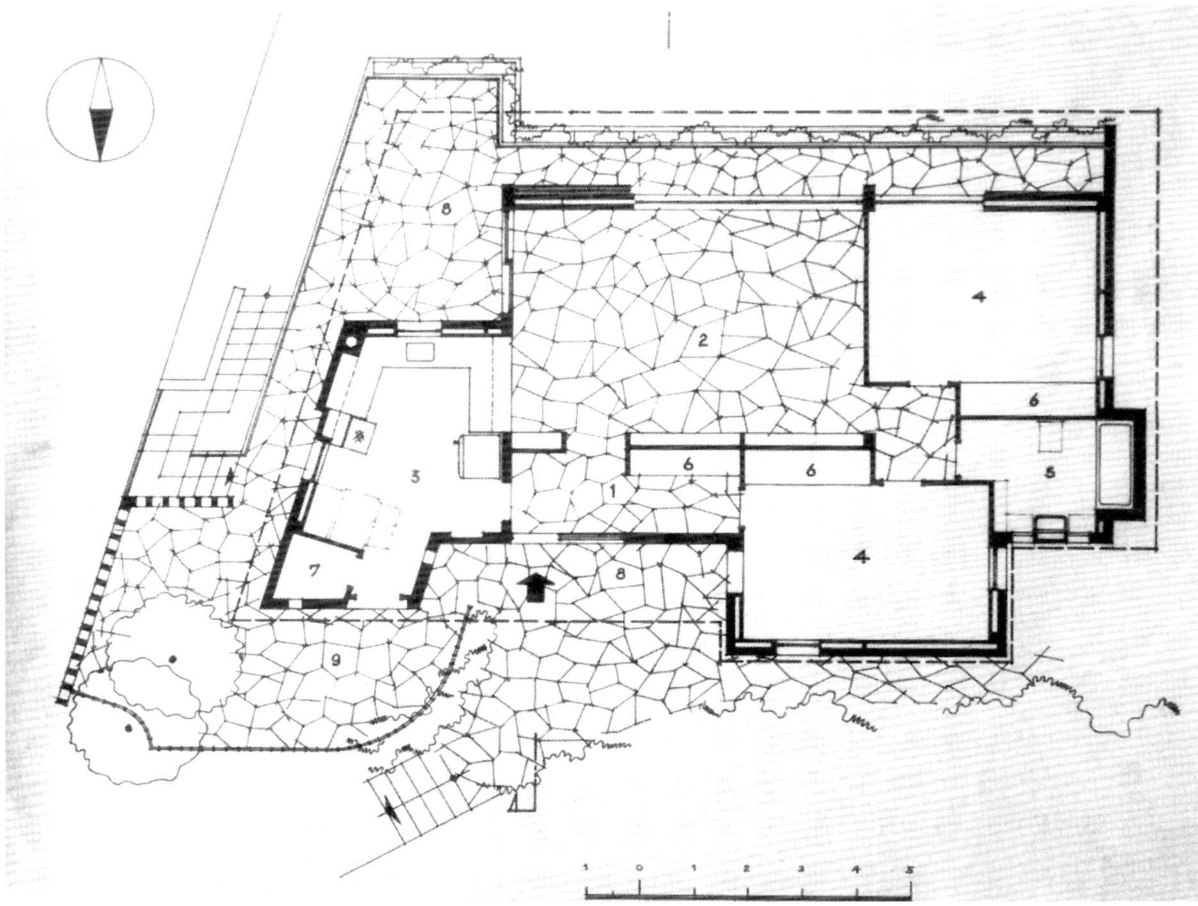

Yehuda K. Unger, Bermann residence, Haifa, Mount Carmel, 1956, ground plan of the main entrance

Yehuda K. Unger, Bermann residence, Haifa, Mount Carmel, 1956, section

Yehuda K. Unger, Bermann residence, Haifa, Mount Carmel, 1956, view from the garden

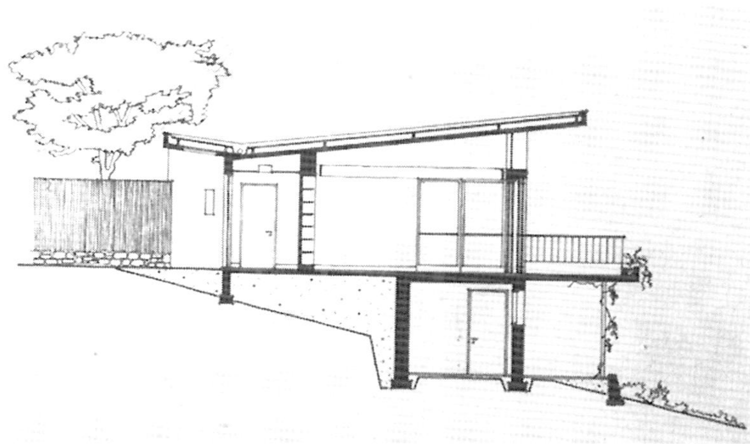

ARTUR GLIKSON (GLÜCKSOHN)

1911 Königsberg – 1966 Tel Aviv

Two months before his sudden death at the age of only fifty-five, Artur Glikson wrote to the organizer of his lecture series in Salisbury, England: "Since foreign lecturers may be entitled to some privilege ... may I ask you to keep publicity on a professional matter of fact level? For in that spirit I shall try to give my talk to your society."[1]
Glikson (the phonetic spelling of his family name was very important to him once he arrived in Palestine) was an internationally known, highly regarded architect and regional planner, admired not only for his professional talents but also for his warm-hearted personality. Glikson was born on August 11, 1911, in Königsberg, East Prussia, today Kaliningrad, Russia. After graduating from secondary school, he visited Palestine, the Land of the Forefathers, to see how he could reconcile his feelings for the Land with practical Zionism. He went to Berlin in 1930, matriculated at the Technische Hochschule Charlottenburg and became a loyal disciple of Hans Poelzig. In 1935 – his Jewish comrades had fled long before and immigrated to Palestine – Glikson was completing exams for his diploma.[2] Immediately thereafter he followed his friends.

During his first years in Palestine, Glikson worked in various capacities and also entered competitions. He had to be content with undemanding tasks during the war years; like many of his colleagues he was able to find a job in the public works department, even if that proved unsatisfying. The time was not fully lost, however, for he began to think about and make notes on the relationship between human beings and the environment and the relationship of ecology and sociology to architecture, whether of an apartment, a city, or a region. The ideas he arrived at from reading the works of the English city planner Patrick Geddes, the American architectural critic Lewis Mumford and the German bio-philosopher Ernst Fuhrmann were written down in English.[3]
Glikson's first independent position as an architect and planner was in the administrative planning department of Petach Tikva, an ancient town near Tel Aviv.[4] He drew up the first comprehensive town plan and all the detailed plans for the street network, public squares, and public buildings such as schools and clinics.
With the founding of the state of Israel in 1948, Glikson became the driving force in a working group in the regional planning office in Jerusalem headed by Arieh Sharon. The group's task was to develop the logistics for lodgings and workplaces in more than twenty new cities for the more than one hundred thousand refugees arriving annually from European camps and from other countries. It was Glikson who now introduced the country to the concept of regional planning. To create humane and hospitable surroundings, his theory went, it is necessary to have a command of the many professional disciplines encompassed by regional planning, such as biology, anthropology, sociology, geology, geography, economy and even statistics.

The largest and most significant project that put Glikson's theory into practice was the town of Kiryat Gat. This principal centre in the Lachish region lies some 50 km south of Tel Aviv. It is one of a group of towns cre-

ated after 1948 to integrate hundreds of thousands of immigrants, survivors of concentration camps, refugees from Europe, Turkey, North Africa and the Middle East. Originally, the town was planned for 10,000 residents and provided them with jobs in agriculture and agricultural industry. Contrary to all predictions, Kiryat Gat underwent rapid development and by 1965 it already had 20,000 inhabitants. As a result, the town had difficulties and had to make a political decision without delay. Glikson was entrusted with the task of setting new priorities for urban development and working out the corresponding plans. First he set up a multidisciplinary team of sociologists, economists, ethno-demographers, architects and construction engineers. The working programme he gave them had a planning goal that called for the creation of a city for 40,000 residents in the 1970s and for 80,000 to 100,000 inhabitants in the coming century.
Kiryat Gat's population structure was characterized by its heterogeneity. Immigrant families who had come from Islamic and Christian countries lived there alongside the "native" Israelis. One of the project's most important goals was to build settlements in which the most diverse groups could live side by side. Glikson and his scientific team proceeded from the assumption that neighbourhoods that consisted of different social and economic milieus not only enriched the community but also offered hope for the city's satisfactory development. The team began its work on October 1, 1965. One year later the comprehensive plan for Kiryat Gat was adopted and approved, three months after Glikson's unexpected death.
The city was built step by step according to Glikson's plans. A certain district that had various types of residential buildings as well as a shopping centre, a school, a kindergarten and cultural buildings was planned as a model experimental district. After its completion, it was observed, researched, and evaluated by representatives of the various disciplines. In the process, Glikson's most important predictions were confirmed. The model district was subsequently named the Glikson Quarter. The results of this unique social and architectural experiment had an enormous effect on how other cities in the country were built.[5]

Glikson was a notable college professor at the Technion Haifa – Israel Institute of Technology. He often participated in international conferences, where he reported on his theoretical and practical experiences with Israeli projects. His lecture series at the Institute of Social Studies in The Hague was published in an English edition by the Netherlands Universities Foundation for International Cooperation.[6] Glikson regularly published reports on the development of rural regional planning in Israel in the Tel Aviv *Journal of the Association of Engineers and Architects*. The articles were translated and published in English, French and German journals as well.[7]
In addition to Kiryat Gat, Glikson worked on several other projects. Low-income apartment houses in Tel Aviv, Ashdod in the south and Karmiel in the north, as well as school buildings in Petach Tikva and Be'er-Sheva, capital of the Negev, and a shopping centre in Kiryat Motzkin, a district in Haifa, were built during his lifetime. Glikson also left behind a full set of detailed plans for the Mesarás region on the Greek island of Crete, a commission he received in 1965.
After thirty years had gone by, Glikson was offered the opportunity to see Berlin once again. He was invited by the members of Team X to a meeting at the Academy of Arts on Hansaplatz.[8] He died soon afterward on July 3, 1966, in Tel Aviv.
Artur Glikson's early death greatly shocked all who knew him. His last work, *The Ecological Basis of Planning*, was published posthumously in 1971. Lewis Mumford, Glikson's long-time close friend, wrote the introduction, which concludes: "His premature death was a bitter loss; but it will be redeemed if the coming

generation understands the lesson of his life and work."[9] Among Glikson's numerous unpublished manuscripts are several poems that he wrote in German during his early years in Berlin.

Artur Glikson, who had been my professor at the Technion, asked about my career as an architect when he visited me in Berlin shortly before his death – a meeting that remains unforgettable. I am very grateful to colleagues in the municipality of Kiryat Gat and above all to Avigail Shefer, Tel Aviv, for material and information about Glikson's life and works (1992).

1 From Artur Glikson's unpublished letter. Private archive.
2 The comrades referred to here were David Anatol Brutzkus, Yehuda Lavie and Alfred A. Mansfeld. See brief biography of Brutzkus and biography of Alfred Mansfeld; Warhaftig 2005, Loevison, Ernst and Mansfeld, Al.
3 On Patrick Geddes, see biography of Arieh Sharon; Lewis Mumford (1895–1992), writer and social critic. Ernst Fuhrmann (1885–1956) author of biological–philosophical texts.
4 Petach Tikva (gate of hope), the first Jewish agricultural settlement, was founded in 1878. Today it is a city with over 195,000 residents.
5 Glikson 1978, pp. 70–107.
6 Glikson 1955.
7 A selection of Glikson's publications (except for articles in Hebrew): "Artur Glikson, Gedanken über Architektur und Gesellschaft" in: *Adolf Loos*, ed. by Paul Engelmann, Tel Aviv 1946, pp. 27–32; Artur Glikson, "Fragen der Stadt- und Landesplanung in Israel" in: *Das Werk*, Zurich April 1958, pp. 114–118; Artur Glikson, "L'Unité d'Habitation Intégrale" in: *Le Carré Bleu* 1, Paris 1962, p. 25; Glikson 1964.
8 Team X was a group of architects, including Jacob Berend Bakema, Georges Candilis, Aldo van Eyck, Peter and Alison Smithson, and Shadrach Woods, who attempted to free CIAM from its outdated ideas.
9 Glikson 1971, p. XXI.

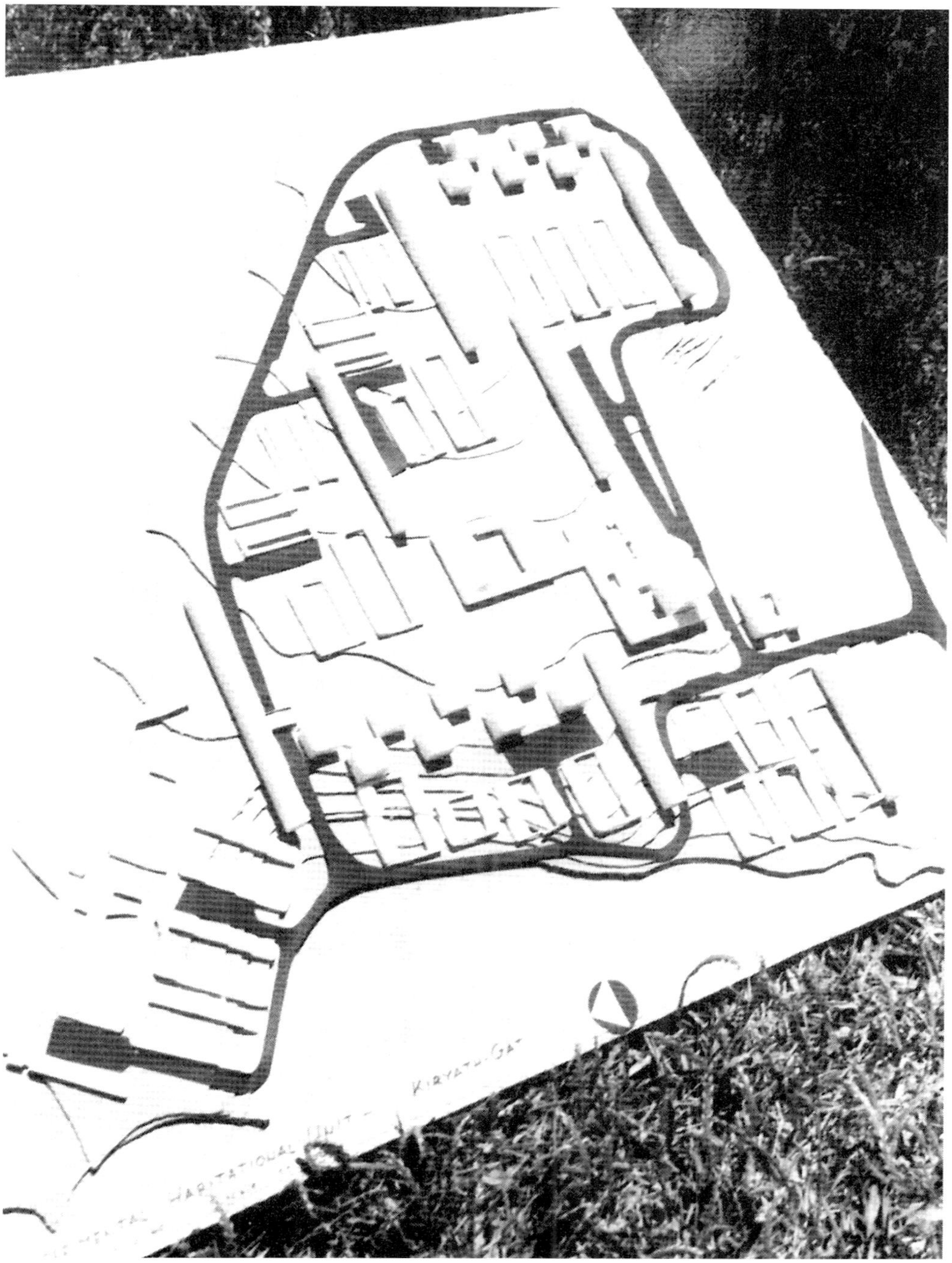

Artur Glikson, experimental residential district Kiryat Gat, later Kiryat Glikson, 1955–1965, street plan, model

Artur Glikson (Glücksohn)

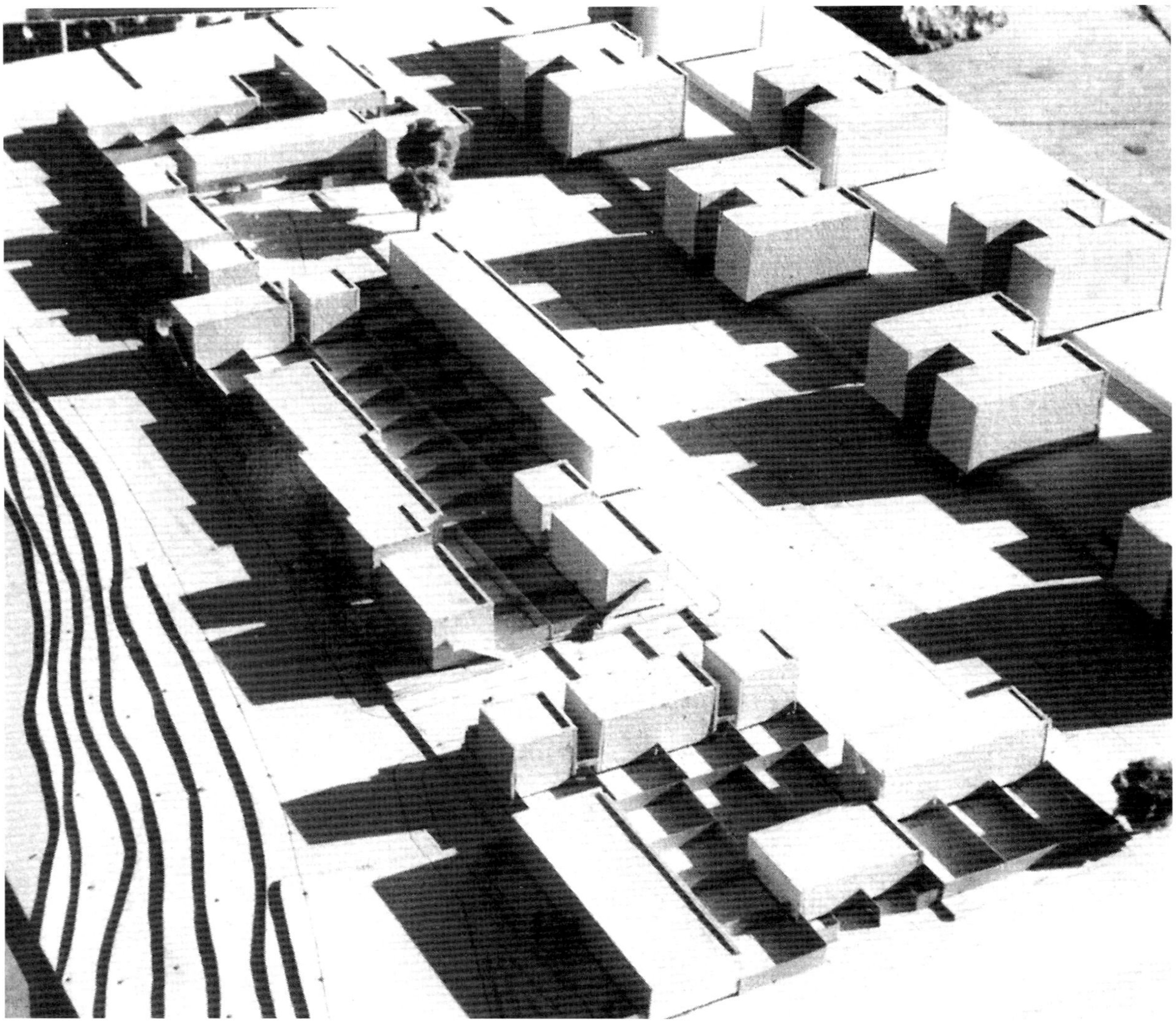

Artur Glikson, experimental residential district Kiryat Glikson, 1955–1965, model of area with apartment buildings

Artur Glikson, experimental residential district Kiryat Glikson, 1955–1965, upper-floor plan of an apartment building

Artur Glikson, experimental residential district Kiryat Glikson, 1955–1965, ground-floor plan of an apartment building

Artur Glikson, experimental residential district Kiryat Glikson, 1955–1965, view of pedestrian path between the apartment buildings

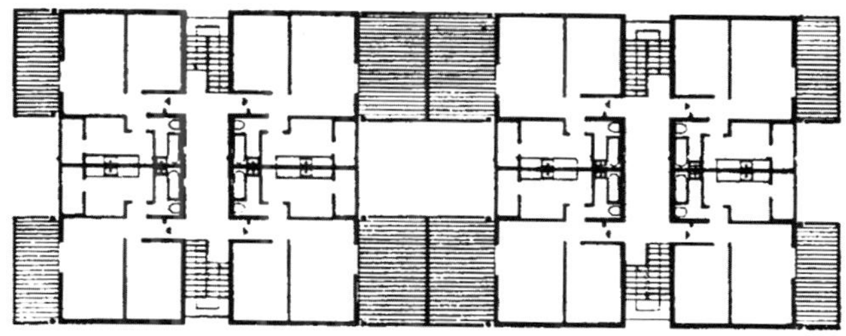

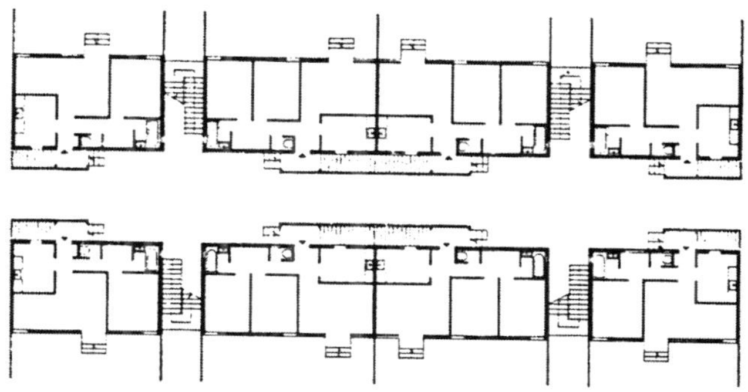

Artur Glikson, experimental residential district Kiryat Glikson, 1955–1965, site plan

Left page above:
Artur Glikson, experimental residential district Kiryat Glikson, 1955–1965, view of three-storey apartment buildings

Left page below:
Artur Glikson, experimental residential district Kiryat Glikson, 1955–1965, view of one- and two-storey apartment buildings

The Founders

Edith and Dr. Reuben Hecht

The Story of a Family and of a Silo

The life story of Reuben Hecht is inseparable from the story of the life of his father Jacob Hecht, who was born in 1879 in Gondelsheim, a small village in the Rhineland.
Jews had settled in many of the villages in this area hundreds of years before, and they played an active role in the commercial, banking, and even industrial sectors during the economic turmoil of the second half of the nineteenth century. But through all the years of their long diaspora, no Jews had ever been involved in the economic sector that the two Jewish brothers Jacob and Herman Hecht now entered: river shipping, or more precisely, Rhine shipping.

While Jacob's older brothers Nathan and Gustav pursued their university studies in Heidelberg, Jacob decided to enter the business world against his parents' wishes. At the age of seventeen he moved to Mannheim, where his uncle offered him a clerk's job in his delivery and haulage agency. At that time, Mannheim was the most modern port on the Rhine. While working in his uncle's business, Jacob Hecht expanded his knowledge, studying the technical aspects of Rhine shipping such as freight forwarding and carriage, storage and warehousing, customs brokerage, ship ownership and agenting, and the methods and management of international trade. In his free time he learned languages: English, French and Italian.
In 1898, at the age of nineteen, he applied to the naval commands at Kiel and Wilhelmshaven to serve as a volunteer sailor. He had to note that he was a Jew. The response came: no more jobs were available on board the ships.[1] When Jacob Hecht returned to civilian life after serving in the army, his brother Herman, who was working as a manager for a trade and transport company in Rotterdam, pressed him to accept a managerial position in Antwerp's shipping industry. After a two-week crash course learning the grain trade in Mannheim, Jacob started at a salary of 175 francs a month; by the end of his first year he received a bonus of 759 francs, thanks to the increased turnover and added profits his department delivered. He sent the lion's share of his bonus to his parents in Gondelsheim. He was then twenty years old.

In 1907 Jacob and his brother Herman decided to set up the Belgium River Navigation Company in Antwerp. Jacob selected the first ship, a model suitable for Rhine transport as far as Cologne and Strasbourg. After his first ship earned money, he ordered another five. Within three or four years his was the largest river shipping company in Belgium. In 1908 Jacob and Herman Hecht established the Rhenania transport company in Mannheim. The company's announced aim was to operate in all branches of shipping, transport, and haulage, but with special emphasis on grain storage and delivery on the Rhine as well as overland or via sea. The company's base capital was 300,000 marks (four years later, its equity had risen to some 5 million marks). The principal shareholders were Jacob and Herman Hecht – Herman was the chairman, but Jacob directed company policy. In 1908 Jacob married Ella Mohr, a daughter of a soap factory owner in Frankenthal, and returned with her to Antwerp. One year later, on August 15, 1909, their first

son Rudolph Charles was born. Jacob Hecht continued to run Rhenania from Antwerp while his brother Herman, at the firm in Mannheim, deferred to Jacob's authority. Within four years, the company had built a complete network of affiliates for different branches of transportation, shipping, and trade. Along with Mannheim and Antwerp, Rotterdam became a third base for Rhine transport.
Rhenania of Mannheim began to expand, opening branch offices in the immediate vicinity. The first was in Ludwigshafen on the west bank of the Rhine; Karlsruhe then was connected to the Rhine by a 5-km-long canal, and two more branches in Kiel and Mainz were opened. Heilbronn and Heidelberg were Rhenania's first bases on the Neckar, and Frankfurt and Aschaffenburg the first on the Main. All these "tentacles" were affiliates in which other investors participated, but Rhenania and the Hecht brothers retained complete control. Every branch acquired warehouses, some began building silos, and the ports were equipped with the most advanced systems of mechanical cranes.
In 1910 the Hechts founded the Duisburg General Transport Company under the Rhenania banner, followed by a long list of affiliates established first in Wesel, then in Cleve, Cologne, Ham, Gelsenkirchen, and the northern port city of Emden. The Duisburg Company and its affiliates built or bought warehouses for all kinds of goods, new silos for every type of grain handling, office buildings, and even housing for the employees.
Rhenania's success was recognised as being due primarily to one person — Jacob Hecht.
He lived and worked in Antwerp, but travelled frequently to Germany, establishing new companies and branches and ordering the most technologically advanced vessels of all kinds (ships, tugs, barges) so that Rhenania could most efficiently respond to the technical challenges facing shipping and transportation companies. After Germany's defeat in World War I, Hecht decided to settle with his family in Basle. In 1920 he founded Le Rhin, the company that represented Rhenania's interests in France, especially in Strasbourg. Rhenania represented Le Rhin all along the Rhine and throughout the Rhine district. Half a year later, he established the Neptune Shipping and Transport Co. Ltd., Basle.

Hecht's son Rudolph, who was approaching the age of Bar Mitzvah, showed interest in Judaism and Zionism, unlike his father. He changed his name to Reuben, insisted on reading the Torah in Hebrew at the synagogue, read *The Jewish State* by Theodor Herzl, and joined the Zionist youth movement Blau-Weiss.
While Jacob Hecht considered himself to be "a German Patriot of Mosaic faith", Reuben always emphasized that he was not a German citizen of Mosaic faith, but a Jew who believed in the necessity of a Jewish state. Initially, instead of studying business and economics at the University of Munich as his father wished, Reuben plunged into Zionist activity as a member of the K.J.V. (Kartell Jüdischer Verbindung), a hothouse for breeding Zionist leaders.
Within a short time, Reuben found himself in the front ranks of the association, leading seminars and evening discussions on Jewish history, Zionism, and the Land of Israel and its political, economic and settlement problems. Since he received a very generous monthly allowance from his father, Reuben invested some of the money in Zionist literature and helped finance association activities. When his father found

out about this use of his money, the monthly stipend was reduced. In 1929, as a first year student, Reuben Hecht published his first article on coins in the Land of Israel from the days of Simon the Maccabee to Simon Bar Giora and Bar Kochba.[2] From that time on, he collected ancient Hebrew coins. All the while, he was confronted with the Nazism that was becoming more and more popular among students during the 1920s. He read Hitler's book *Mein Kampf* and learned what Hitler thought about the Jews and how he planned to treat them. This confirmed Reuben's belief that Jews had no place in Germany, and he submitted a resolution to the K.J.V. that every association member must emigrate to Palestine.
In the summer of 1931, Reuben went for the first time to Eretz Israel. He then returned to the university as his father wished, and in 1933 he finished his studies and presented his doctoral dissertation on "The Structure of Rhine Shipping Transport". He graduated magna cum laude and the dissertation was printed as a book. By that time Hitler was the legally chosen chancellor of Germany. Reuben witnessed one of the many book burnings that took place across Germany between May 10 and June 21, 1933. Instead of staying in Basle and working for Neptune, Reuben joined Ze'ev Jabotinsky, who had established the Revisionist Zionist Party in Paris in 1925, and later became an active member of his party in Israel.[3]

When the Nazis came to power on January 30, 1933, the two big Hecht firms, Rhenania and Neptune, were at their peak. Together they owned 280 vessels of various sizes, twenty smaller motor vessels suitable for sailing the Rhine-Rhone Canal, and another twenty-six paddle steamers, with a total weight of 280,000 tons.
On April 1, 1933, a government decree announced that the boycott of Jewish businesses was extended to include Jewish doctors and lawyers. On April 7, a law was passed that removed Jewish government officials from their offices; in September, Jewish writers and artists were expelled from their associations by law. On September 15, the Nuremberg laws to protect German blood and honour were passed; in all there were more than 2000 pieces of anti-Jewish legislation.
During the first years of the Nazi regime, Jacob Hecht still fought for his rights. But he was forced to resign from Rhenania's management and the various conglomerate boards in Germany in autumn 1937, and then forced to sell his shares. He acquired Swiss citizenship and turned his efforts toward developing Neptune in Basle. He also agreed to Reuben's emigration to Palestine, gave him a huge amount of money to invest at the appropriate time, and arranged a job for him there with the banker Ernst Japhet, a friend from the Rhine area who had emigrated in 1933.
But Reuben's objective in Eretz Israel was to put up a silo at the port of Haifa, which the British had constructed and opened in 1933 as an outlet for the oil that was being found in the Near East. Reuben's request to the mandate government for a license to build a silo in the port of Haifa was rejected. He invested the large sum of money he got from his father between 1936 and 1938 in ancient coins and archaeological artefacts; these were to become one of the most important collections in Israel. In March 1938 Hitler annexed Austria; the Sudetenland in Czechoslovakia followed in September. During the night of November 9 to 10, 1938, the so-called Reichskristallnacht, synagogues in Germany were torched and some 30,000 Jews arrested and taken to the concentration camps of Dachau, Buchenwald and Sachsenhausen. This incident was a final warning signal to the Jews in Europe that they must flee their countries. Reuben, who was a member of the "Irgun Tzevai Leumi" (Etzel), the clandestine nationalist army, was asked by the Irgun commander David Raziel to go to Europe and rescue persecuted Jews from Nazi Germany by sending them "illegally" to Palestine – for the British authorities did not permit Jewish immigration.

No doubt Reuben was the right person to fulfil this mission; he was a citizen of Switzerland, a state that guarded his neutrality during the Nazi regime. He returned to Switzerland in January 1939, but to his father's sorrow, he did not join the Neptune company in Basle. Instead he went to Zurich, rented a three-room flat, and opened an emigration office that organized groups of European Jewish refugees and sent them by ship to Palestine. Reuben could move freely in Europe while dealing with these not always successful "illegal" activities. On September 1, 1939, when World War II broke out, smuggling Jews across the borders into Switzerland was abruptly curtailed. Two years later, Reuben went to Yugoslavia and married Edith Zilzer, a Jewish girl born in Vincovci on July 9, 1909, whom he had met when a student in Heidelberg. By the time that Reuben arrived in Switzerland with his wife, but without any money, his parents had gone to the USA and had forbidden his younger brother, who remained in Basle, from giving Reuben any financial assistance. Reuben's accidental encounter with the American consul general Sam Woods, who also worked for the American intelligence service, became a great source of help to the young couple. Woods engaged Reuben to work for American intelligence, and Edith Hecht was able to deliver information from the Yugoslav exiles in Arosa and Davos, since she spoke the language.

The State of Israel was proclaimed on May 14, 1948, and that summer a special meeting of the World Jewish Congress that was intended to clarify the ties and relations of world Jewry with the new Israeli state took place in Montreux, Switzerland. David Remez, Israel's minister of transport, was one of the participants. Reuben Hecht showed Remez his visionary plan for a "Maritime Israel" that included the building of a modern silo in Haifa. Four months later, Neptune decided to empower Dr. Reuben Hecht to open negotiations with the Israeli government about this silo, and perhaps others elsewhere as well.
First of all, Dr. Hecht had to explain the silo's function and advantages (which above all were economic) to the Israeli authorities. Hecht also declared that he and his family were ready to get involved in such a project, but the silo idea was not favourably received by the bureaucrats in various government ministries. The path to a final agreement still was a long way off, and full of serpentine curves. It was on August 9, 1950, after two years of negotiations, that a contract was signed between the government of Israel and Dr. Reuben Hecht to build a silo enterprise at the port of Haifa. Hecht named the enterprise "Dagon" after the ancient Canaanite god of earth, plant life, grain and bread, and fertility. Dagon frequently is mentioned in the book of Samuel as the great god of the Philistines, who built temples and palaces to him in Gaza. Moreover, the name resembled the old Hebrew word "dagan" meaning wheat.

Jacob Hecht placed all of Neptune's engineers and technicians at Dagon's disposal; without them it is doubtful whether the silo could have been so satisfactorily built. In the early 1950s, Dr. Hecht commissioned the architect Joseph Klarwein, who later won the first prize of the Knesset in Jerusalem, to design an artistic exterior for the silo.[4] The structure had a capacity of 20,000 tons, the tower was 67 m high. By the end of September 1955, the Dagon silo made its first deliveries.
The quantity of grain passing through the silo increased from year to year, and Hecht decided late in the 1950s to build a second silo, which went into operation on August 15, 1960. The capacity of the two silos was 45,000 tons, but this too soon was not enough. The Israeli labour sector's giant construction, industry, and service company Solel Boneh, which had built the second silo, completed a third one with a capacity of 27,000 tons in August 1962, bringing Dagon's total storage capacity to ca. 72,000 tons of grain. By

the end of 1968, Solel Boneh began construction on a fourth silo in Haifa, which was completed by the end of 1970. Dagon reached a total capacity of 100,000 tons.
The construction of a silo in the port of Ashdod, 40 km south of Tel Aviv, began at the end of 1981, after years of discussions between the Israeli government and Dr. Hecht of Dagon. The silo, whose capacity was 60,000 tons, started to operate at the beginning of 1984, fully four months before the date stipulated in the contract.
Two main points concerning Dagon's silo enterprise are worth mentioning:
1. The silos were always built using the latest systems.
2. The relationship between Hecht and the workers always was very cordial.
Throughout Dagon's existence, the company has not experienced one strike. This is a unique achievement, particularly when one considers that the enterprise operates on port lands. There have been fairly constant and bitter work disputes at Israeli ports, many of which have ended in strikes. But from the day he established Dagon, which has employed ca. 140 to 220 workers over the years, Dr. Hecht's basic outlook was that an enterprise had to look after its employees.
Today the Dagon building, with the Eastern crowns that cap its roof all around, is a well-known Haifa landmark. The building is lit up on Friday evenings and holidays.

Dagon's astounding achievements in work productivity and economy aroused unusual attention the world over. There began a regular pilgrimage to Haifa on the part of ministers from various countries, experts in agriculture, transport, ports and, naturally, grain handling, as well as by silo owners and managers. They came from Asia and Africa, and also from the leading grain-producing countries of the west, such as Norway, which adopted Dagon's working and organizational methods. Politicians, statesmen, bankers, archaeologists, public personalities, economists, educators, students, and the general public — all of them also came to visit Dagon. But it was not just the plant itself – its dimensions and aesthetic form, organization and cleanliness – that attracted all these persons whose occupations had nothing to do with grain, transportation, or ports. They also were drawn by the realization of Dr. Reuben Hecht's treasured dream since youth: an archaeological museum whose subject was grain and bread in Israel. First shown in 1956 in a small museum in the original silo, the collection was later exhibited in the new administration building built with the third silo in 1962.
Reuben Hecht was nominated as a director of the "Dagon Archaeological Museum of Grain Handling in Israel"; in 1966 the I.C.O.M. (International Council of Museums) recognized it as a museum. In 1984 Dr. Hecht founded "The Reuben and Edith Hecht Museum", which includes his own collections, and donated it to the University of Haifa. It exhibits the archaeology and history of the Land of Israel in chronological sequence, beginning with the Chalcolithic period and ending in the Byzantine era. It includes coins, weights, Semitic seals, jewellery, and artefacts from the Temple Mount excavations, Phoenician metalwork, woodwork, stone vessels, glass, and mosaics.
The art collection includes French painting of the Barbizon School, Impressionism, Post-impressionism, and the School of Paris, and Jewish art from the mid-nineteenth to early twentieth centuries. Works by Jean-Baptiste Camille Corot, Edouard Manet, Claude Monet, Camille Jacob Pissarro, Vincent van Gogh, Amedeo Modigliani and Max Liebermann and others are on display.

Dr. Hecht was an active member of various organizations and culture institutes. The list of his board memberships, not only in Israel, is endless. To mention only a few:
From 1961 until his death, he was a member of the board of governors of the Bezalel Academy of Art and Design, Jerusalem.
From 1963 until his death, he was a member of the board of governors of the Technion – The Israel Institute of Technology, Haifa.
In 1965 he founded the Shikmona Publishing Company Ltd., Haifa (since 1973 in Jerusalem), which specializes in the publication of Zionist, art and archaeology books. He remained the owner and chairman of the board until his death.
In 1970 he was the co-founder of Haifa University, and was a member of the board of governors from its inception in 1971 until his death.[5]
In 1973 he founded the Hecht Foundation at Haifa University for Zionism, Art and Archaeology, and was a member of the board until his death. During his lifetime he supported archaeological digs throughout the country.
From 1981 until his death, he was member of the international board of Beth Hatefoutzot, the Museum of the Jewish Diaspora, Tel Aviv.
Among his numerous academic degrees:
In 1984 he was awarded the first honorary Ph.D. h.c from Haifa University.
In 1988 he was awarded lifetime honorary membership in Heruth, the militant organization led by Menachem Begin, whose friend he was;[6] Yakir (Worthy) of Beautiful Israel; and a "Special Medal for Contribution to the Economy of Haifa" awarded by the Haifa Chamber of Commerce and Industry.
In the same year, the fortieth anniversary of the founding of the state of Israel, Hecht was awarded the "Israel Prize for exemplary lifelong service to the society and state".[7]

Reuben Hecht died on April 14, 1993. His wife Edith Zilzer-Hecht died on June 1, 1997.
The Israel Ports Authority became the owner of Dagon in 2003.
Reuben and Edith Hecht's private home on Mount Carmel, designed by Werner Wittkower in Modern style in the 1950s, was supposed to become a music centre according to Hecht's will.[8] But unfortunately the villa was not suited for this purpose. So the Reuben and Edith Hecht Foundation sold it to a private person and, together with Dagon and the municipality of Haifa, financed the renovation of a two-storey house built in 1893 at the centre of Mount Carmel. That building had been a community arts centre named "House Rothschild" since 1957. In October 2002 it was inaugurated as "House Hecht".

My thanks to Nichael Sharan, director general of Dagon, for the information.

Literature:

Rivka Gonen, *Grain. Dagon Collection*, Haifa 1979
Zvi Herman, *The River and the Grain*, Tel Aviv 1989
Zvi Herman, text, Oswald Adler, conception and design, *40 Anniversary of Dagon*, Israel 1991
Moshe Shamir, *Reuben Hecht*, Haifa 1995

Edith and Dr. Reuben Hecht

1 In 1898 Bruno Ahrends also was refused admittance to the Kaiserliche Werft Schiffbau of Kiel because he was Jewish. See: Warhaftig 2005, Ahrends, Bruno.
2 "On the History of Jewish Coins in Various Periods" in the monthly magazine *Der Morgen*.
3 Jabotinsky was born in 1880 in Odessa and died in 1940 in the USA. He and his wife were reinterred at Mount Herzl cemetery, Jerusalem in 1964.
4 See biography of Joseph Ossip Klarwein.
5 Brazilian architect Oscar Niemeyer designed the building.
6 Hecht served as a personal adviser to Begin from 1977 to 1983.
7 Stef Wertheimer was awarded the Israel Prize in 1991. See "Stef Wertheimer".
8 See biography of Werner Wittkower.

HILDA AND DR. RICHARD STRAUSS

The Story of a Family and of a Dairy Industry

Hilda and Dr. Richard Strauss came from an old-established German Jewish family in Ulm, whose population of approximately 60,000 in 1933 was about 2% Jewish. Hilda's parents, Berta and Fritz Bach, owned a flourishing textile company. Richard's parents, Marta and Julius Strauss, owned a metal company and were pillars of the Ulm Jewish community. Richard, the oldest son, was born September 14, 1909, studied at the universities of Frankfurt am Main, Tübingen and Berlin and earned a Ph.D. in economics and law. After an internship in Stuttgart's Ministry of Commerce, he took a position as junior manager in the family's company, destined to follow in their footsteps. Hilda Bach, born May 28, 1911, was sent after graduating high school to a prestigious finishing school in Switzerland. She envisioned a future as a successful career woman, and registered in a commercial course at the Institute of Higher Education in Berlin with the aim of eventually finding her niche in the family business. In April 1933, shortly after the Nazis came to power and one day before Hilda and Richard's wedding, laws boycotting the Jews were announced, the first in a long series of denigrating, humiliating and cruel laws. To forget this humiliation – at least for the duration of their honeymoon – Hilda and Richard decided to spend their honeymoon outside Germany. Unfortunately, reality followed them: it was in Majorca that they encountered a group of German refugees escaping the Nazis and making their way to Palestine.

On their return, Hilda and Richard did their best to settle into as normal a way of life as possible. But sitting at streetside cafes, the skiing holidays in the Alps, parties, and the good life they had previously known had all come to an end. Like many other young people and unlike the older generation, Hilda found it difficult to see any light at the end of the tunnel and began seriously considering the option of leaving Germany. Richard also came to the conclusion that their time in Germany was up and that the only way to survive was to immigrate to Palestine. His father Julius did his best to persuade him to remain, for he saw Richard as the heir who eventually would take over the family business. While he was also fearful of the future, Julius believed that the new political situation in Germany was temporary.

Hilda and Richard's first son, Michael-Peter, was born in the spring of 1934. It was Hilda who made up her mind that her son would have a more secure future, and Richard agreed. The decisive factor that led to their departure from Germany occurred when Goebbels, in one of his speeches, announced in a thundering voice that it was only a matter of time before Jews would not be allowed to leave the country. The young Strauss family loaded their suitcases onto the family car in spring, 1936 and left their home in Ulm, setting off for the Italian port of Genoa, where they were to board a ship that would take them to Palestine.

Richard's youngest brother Rudi, who had been in Palestine since 1933, met the family at the port in Jaffa and brought them to Ramot Hashavim in Sharon, a small village founded by German immigrants, where

an integration centre had been built for the new arrivals' friends from the old country. The integration of German Jews indeed proved very difficult, due to the hot and humid weather, the mosquitoes, the food, and above all the Hebrew language.[1] And besides all that, the immigrants had to find suitable occupations.

Since Hilda and Richard Strauss had received agricultural training in the Blau-Weiss youth movement in Germany, they saw their future in agriculture. With funds they brought with them and money from selling their car, they decided to purchase a farm in Nahariya, on land between the sea and the main road leading to Acre and Haifa.[2] The young family left Be'er-Tuvia and settled in a small hut on their land in 1938. Near the hut they started to build their house – which they would never leave – planting a small grove of fruit trees and a field of vegetables. And they bought a milk cow. Richard Strauss made it clear that he was not going to cultivate vegetables, like all his neighbours in Nahariya, and asked for permission to build a cowshed on his land. All the settlers were against this, telling him that Jewish Germans never drink milk straight from the cows' udders. "I will teach the Jekkes to drink fresh milk", Richard promised Hilda.[3] The Strausses did not give up, and bought a second cow and later another. Each morning Richard would go out and milk the cows into large copper jugs, load the jugs on his bicycle, and pedal from house to house trying to sell fresh milk to his neighbours. But the Jekkes continued to drink their milk out of imported cans. The couple did not know what to do with their surplus milk until Hilda began to produce cheese in her small kitchen (using a friend's recipe), but still the surplus milk problem was not completely solved. After one year in Nahariya, the Strausses entered an agricultural show; to their surprise they were awarded first prize for their milk products and honoured by the British High Commissioner.
The field of ripe strawberries near their house inspired Hilda to make a cream dessert that no doubt reminded her of one that was (and still is) very popular in Germany. She made the cream with a hand separator and served it with strawberries to the residents of Nahariya who came to her balcony, where she had set out a few tables and chairs. British soldiers stationed nearby also came to the Strauss balcony and enjoyed the dairy dessert.
Although they spent most of their time working, the Strausses never relinquished their social life. They were part of a large group of educated Jekkes (many of whom had Ph.D. degrees), who made it a point to meet and spend together the little spare time they had. This group was considered Nahariya's aristocracy. They enjoyed listening to classical music, writing poetry, reading books out loud and celebrating holidays and birthdays together with their children.

In 1939 the Strauss family was required to make a critical decision: they had to decide between agriculture and industry – and they decided to sell the cowshed with its twenty cows and set up a dairy. This marked the founding of the "Strauss Dairy, Nahariya". There were problems involved in setting up the new enter-

prise. Other inhabitants of Nahariya were not interested in having industry introduced into their agricultural community. The Strausses again faced a struggle, but did not give up, and their dairy became a given fact. They now began to purchase their milk supply from the milk farmers' kibbutzim in the Acre region. In those early days, the Strauss Dairy used between 500 and 1000 litres of milk per day.
Since Hilda's small home kitchen no longer was sufficient, Richard decided to transfer production to Ein Sara, a private farm to the south of Nahariya, where he could store his products in the local refrigeration shed. But the rabbinate threatened to boycott Strauss products because there was a pig farm at Ein Sara. In harsh and primitive conditions, Richard and Hilda continued to work at their home in Nahariya. Ten workers joined them and they produced processed cheese, some salty and white cheeses, sour cream, leben and lebenia, and butter. Most of the work was done by hand and the processed cheese was made in a primitive apparatus. The products were sold in Nahariya's cafes, groceries and restaurants and at the neighbouring kibbutzim. And Hilda began making her first attempts to produce ice cream in 1940.

In the meantime, stories of the horrors and atrocities that were taking place in Europe began to arrive. In 1938, after Richard's father Julius Strauss died of an illness in Ulm, his mother Marta came to Palestine. Hilda's father Fritz Bach also died of an illness that year. Her mother and sister were able to board the last plane to leave Germany before the gates were finally closed to Jewish emigrants. The two went to London, joining their family in Palestine after World War II ended. Richard's sister also came to live in Eretz Israel; his other sister had gone to the United States. The Strauss and Bach families escaped the Holocaust, but they arrived in Eretz Israel penniless.
Hilda and Richard's second child, Raya, was born in 1940. The 1940s were years of struggle in the history of the Jewish nation – struggle that involved bringing Jews into Palestine in the face of the British ban on free Jewish immigration, which resulted in an illegal immigration operation. Notwithstanding their daily fight for survival and their hard work in the dairy, Hilda and Richard joined the national struggle against the British. Indeed, the entire dairy was mobilized to help the Hagana: The dairy's refrigerators served as a 'slick' where weapons were hidden in milk jars. And when illegal Jewish immigrants were brought ashore in the middle of the night, they were smuggled into the Strauss Dairy dressed in work clothes, and they masqueraded as dairy labourers until such time as they could be removed to the neighbouring kibbutzim. At the same time, still prior to the War of Independence, Hilda and Richard Strauss opened the first branch of the Strauss Dairy in Haifa, in an attempt to break into the market beyond Nahariya. Hilda was responsible for producing and marketing their goods. Richard's job involved publicity and administration; he maintained contact with the authorities and met with lawyers and bankers. In the meantime, the family again received a warning from the rabbinate, for the symbol of their products was an ostrich ("Strauss" in German), which is a non-kosher animal. So they changed their logo to a picture of the Nahariya water tower.

After the state of Israel was founded, the competition among private dairies in the region became enormous, and the Tnuva dairy was the most serious competitor.[4] Tnuva distributed products from kibbutzim and was considered a socialist organization. It therefore viewed all other agriculture producers as capitalists and did not allow any of their kibbutzim to supply Hilda and Richard with milk. But the two did not capitulate and obtained milk from the kibbutzim 'black-market'.
In 1951 Richard went to Germany and brought back a machine for producing processed cheese to replace

the primitive mechanism the Strauss Dairy had been using. He was one of the first German Jews to go back to Germany and buy equipment using his own private funds. Two years later Richard brought back a new pasteurizer to modernize that system as well. When the era of milk in bottles started, he bought a bottle-filling machine in Germany.

New buildings and refrigeration rooms were added as the dairy grew, and the number of employees rose from 50 in 1950 to 150 in 1959. A production floor was built onto the main building and ice cream production was expanded. But the Strauss family still could not extricate itself from its financial difficulties.

With reparation payments he received from the German government, Richard made a desperate effort and invested his money in the purchase of second-hand dairy equipment. This created a new problem: no one knew how to operate the new equipment and they could find no expert to help. Pinhas Sapir, who was appointed Minister of Trade and Industry in 1955, was the first to recognize the important of industry in general and especially private industry. Richard's son Michael, newly discharged from the military, went to see Sapir in his Jerusalem office. Sapir approved a generous loan that saved the dairy from having to close. His business acumen confirmed, Michael decided to join his parents' firm and went to Switzerland to study milk technology in 1956. Eighteen months later he graduated with honours and then returned to Ulm, the city of his birth, for an internship at Milkana, a dairy owned by Unilever. Back in Nahariya, Michael's first objective was to institute professional production methods. It was clear to him that the dairy required a good shake-up: he would have to replace unsuccessful management personnel and outdated experts to compete in the prospective dairy market, to change the dairy's structure, create a new long-term strategy and enter new markets. Within six months, Michael replaced all the plant's management staff and professional experts and hired an expert in cheese production. At the same time, while continuing to compete with Tnuva products, he started to produce Gervais, an expensive, highly processed white cheese product.

By the end of the 1950s, the Strauss Dairies employed three hundred persons. The Strauss family owned dairies in Nahariya, an ice cream factory in Acre, and marketing companies in Tel Aviv, Be'er-Sheva and Jerusalem.

By this time, Michael Strauss realized that the company's problems had nothing to do with quality, but fell within the scope of its sales and marketing strategy. He started to seek out agents in central locations throughout the country, especially in Tel Aviv, notwithstanding competition from Tnuva and from Artic, another well-known Israeli ice cream producer.

The breakthrough in the distribution of Strauss Dairy products came when the first supermarket opened in Tel Aviv. These new kind of grocery stores started ordering not only from Tnuva, but also from Strauss, and the demand grew from day to day.

In 1968, with the move to new warehouses, the Strauss family decided to do its own marketing for the first time. They engaged marketing managers and introduced their products through "Strauss Marketing Tel Aviv Ltd" in Tel Aviv, "Strauss Be'er-Sheva Marketing" in the Negev, and "Strauss Jerusalem Marketing" in Romema in 1969. The company established branches in Eilat in the south (1978) and in Kiryat Shemona in the north (1984 – today considered one of the strongest in the Strauss organization). By 1986 the Strauss company had invested $2.5 million in a plot of land in the Petach Tikva industrial area, about 15 km east of Tel Aviv, where within eight months they built an office block and refrigeration warehouses.

In 1993 Strauss founded branches in Tiberius, Safed and Nazareth. In 1995 negotiations began between the Strauss Group and the Danone conglomerate.[5] Two years later, Danone purchased 20% of Strauss Dairies. This significant event was celebrated in the presence of both Raya and Michael and their six children, the third generation.
But neither Richard nor Hilda lived to see the partnership with this European giant. On November 10, 1975, Richard died of a heart attack at the age of sixty-four. Ten years later, on July 11, 1985, Hilda passed away. During his lifetime, Dr. Richard Strauss had distributed his property equally to his son and daughter.

Michael and Raya decided to turn the modest little house in the Strauss Dairies' yard, which had been their childhood home, into a monument to their parents. The Founders' House was inaugurated in 1986, on the first anniversary of Hilda's death, in the presence of Shimon Peres, at that time Israel's deputy prime minister. To this day, the house has been preserved exactly as it was during the lifetime of Richard and Hilda Strauss and welcomes many visitors, both school children and tourists from Israel and abroad. Official Strauss dinners are held at the Founders' House, as are all the company's board meetings. Family functions – the traditional Chanukah meals, Passover and birthdays – are held at the house, just as they were when Richard and Hilda were alive. The modest furnishings Hilda and Richard brought from Germany when they immigrated to Palestine in the early thirties still stand in the places they occupied during their owners' lifetime. The bookcase in the parlour still contains books by Max Brod, Chaim Herzog, Alexander Solzhenitsyn, Alex Hailey, and Vladimir Nabokov's *Lolita*. The silverware and Rosenthal dinner service that Hilda brought from Germany still is kept safe in the cupboards, and a picture of Ulm is on the wall.

Postscript:
An important milestone in the history of the Strauss Dairies occurred in 2004, when Strauss merged with Elite, one of the foremost confectionery manufacturers and marketers in Israel.[6] Together, they formed the largest business in the country. The process of integrating and assimilating the merger continued through 2006.
The Strauss-Elite Group operates sixteen production sites in twelve countries, including Israel, and has 6500 employees worldwide (4700 in Israel and 1800 overseas).
Ofra Strauss-Lahat, Michael Strauss's daughter, chairs the management board.

Literature:
Sarit Yishai Levi, *The Strauss Saga. The Story of a Family and of an Industry*, Jerusalem 1997 (Hebrew); English translation by Ora Cummings, Jerusalem 1998

1 Many immigrants, including Hilda and Richard Strauss, spoke only German until the day they died. They lived on an island of German culture, surrounded by the Levantine ocean.
2 In 1935, Nahariya was founded as an agricultural settlement, using funds raised from newly arrived immigrants – most came from Germany – to establish small holdings.
3 The term "Jekke", denoting German immigrants, came gradually into the language as a folklore materialized around their special and unique character: punctuality, honesty and diligence. The veterans of the Yishuv – the

name given to the Jewish community in Palestine before the state of Israel was founded – did not conceal their amusement at the habits the Jekkes brought with them from Germany. Their customary Schlafstunde – the afternoon nap – was puzzling and ridiculous as far as the veterans were concerned. But the Jekkes tended not to change their ways and ignored the ridicule and jokes made at their expense.

4 Tnuva, or Tenuvah ("fruit" or "produce" in Hebrew) is an Israeli co-operative specializing in milk and dairy products. It was created in 1926, after kibbutz movement leaders had decided to form cooperatives to distribute and export several types of food products. At first it delivered only milk. It expanded to cover other dairy products in the 1930s. Today Tnuva is Israel's largest agricultural producer and distributor.

5 The Danone conglomerate includes Gervais, one of the largest European producers of dairy products, especially cheese, and Danone, the largest European producer of dairy desserts and yoghurts. The Strausses had previously entered into partnership with the German branch of Gervais Danone in January 1969. Unfortunately, the French parent company was unable to cope with pressures from an Arab boycott that tightened around it as a result of the German branch's partnership with an Israeli company, and that affiliation lasted only ten years.

6 Not included in the merger with Elite was the Strauss company that produced ice cream, which Hilda had first attempted to make in 1940. Strauss Ice Cream signed a strategic partnership agreement with Unilever, the world's largest ice cream corporation, in 1995, granting Unilever 51% ownership. The company has four hundred employees and a plant in Acre.

Yekutiel and Shmuel Federmann

The Story of a Family and of the Dan Hotels

The "Kaete Dan" was once one of the first and best-known hotels in Tel Aviv. Designed by Lotte Cohn, the pioneer architect from Berlin, when it was built a few steps from the city beach in 1929–30 it was called a "pension" and named after Kaete Danowitz, who had commissioned the building.[1] Its style was clearly indebted to the Modernist architecture of the 1920s – a functional cubic form with a flat roof, clad in white stucco – and the building had just fourteen rooms to offer. In 1940–41, to meet an increasing demand for accommodations, the hotel was renovated and enlarged to provide twenty-two rooms. This task, and the design of the interior furnishings, was assigned to the architect Werner Wittkower, who also had been born in Berlin.[2] Since its establishment, the hotel has been a prime rendezvous not only for the German Jews known as Jekkes but also for Zionist leaders such as Aba Hillel Silver, Nachum Goldmann, and Artur Ruppin as well as artists including Bronislav Hubermann and Arturo Toscanini.[3]

In 1947 Yekutiel Federmann, also a Jekke, found himself on a balcony of the meanwhile dilapidated hotel. He was there seeking a new occupation that would be congruent with his life experiences, political views, skills and courage. Acquiring the hotel presented such an opportunity. Federmann quickly realized that a hotel industry would be a necessary part of an effective economy in a new country, assuming that the political situation was stable. Consequently he made it his aim to develop this economic sector – without ever being trained in the field – with the support of his brother Shmuel, who was two years younger. Yekutiel and Shmuel Federmann thus seized upon a nascent economic opportunity in a country that did not yet exist.

Today, sixty years later, there are twelve luxury hotels in Israel that the Federmanns have built or renovated in different Israeli cities such as Haifa, Tel Aviv, Jerusalem, Eilat, Ashkelon, and Caesarea, and all of which they still own. And except for the King David Hotel in Jerusalem, all are named "Dan" in honour of the "Pension Kaete Dan".

Who were these Federmanns, where did they come from, and what was the source of their staying power?

Their parents Zippora and David Federmann were born in Chemnitz, Germany. They ran a bakery and four pastry shops in various city locations and had five children – two girls and three boys – to support.

Yekutiel (Ksil), the oldest son, was born on November 11, 1914, and his brother Shmuel (Semo) on December 23, 1916, in Chemnitz. Both parents and children had Zionist views. When the National Socialists came to power on January 30, 1933, and Chemnitzers took to the streets to celebrate the event, the four pastry shops owned by the Federmanns were among the first Jewish businesses in the city to be looted. In addition, young Yekutiel had to watch while members of the Sturmabteilung (SA) forced his father to remove Communist Party slogans from the walls. These events strengthened his Zionist awareness and motivated him to work actively against the National Socialists. Yekutiel Federmann became an active member of the international Zionist youth movement Hechalutz, which was founded in Odessa in 1905 and later merged with the first European Jewish student organization Kadima; his name was on the regional leadership list in Berlin. Although he was one of the youngest in the group, Yekutiel began to coordinate activities between the organization's branches in Austria and Czechoslovakia.

With the introduction of the Nuremberg Laws on September 15, 1935, Jewish students were banned from so-called "Aryan" schools. It became an urgent necessity to organize an educational framework for these young people while they awaited certificates enabling them to immigrate to Palestine. At the request of Giora Yoseftal, secretary of the Youth Aliya in Germany, and his wife Senetta, Yekutiel, along with Recha Freier and Professor Franz Ollendorf, established a Jewish school in Berlin.[4]

In addition to this legally sanctioned task, Yekutiel Federmann also was involved in illegal activities. In the Berlin headquarters of the Hechalutz youth movement, located at Prenzlauer Strasse 16 (today Karl-Liebknecht-Strasse), he secretly met with other young comrades. They decided to establish contacts with other non-Jewish opponents of the Nazis, whose help they used to seek out locations where Jews could be hidden and supplies stored. They also planned escape routes to Austria and Czechoslovakia. The day after the Pogrom night of November 9–10, 1938, the boys were denounced and arrested by the Gestapo. Only Yekutiel and a second comrade were able to escape.

With forged papers, Yekutiel was able to pass through thirty control points and finally, after three days and three nights, he reached London. There he was appointed head of the Youth Immigration Office, replacing Teddy Kollek, who later was for many years the mayor of Jerusalem. Yekutiel's mission was to bring as many Jewish children as possible out of Nazi Germany to London and to arrange lodgings for them in different hachshara campsites in England, where the young people would be prepared for life in Palestine prior to being sent there. To fulfil his mission, Yekutiel travelled between Berlin and London with false papers, an action that put his life, and those of his helpers, constantly in danger. He meanwhile observed that, as the German Wehrmacht became increasingly powerful, his rescue project was meeting with less and less success. Inventive as he was, Yekutiel was able to make contact with high British officers who – in their weaker moments, as he described it – issued certificates for Palestine to his young people from Germany. Secretly, Yekutiel had also obtained blank immigration forms with which he enabled those over the age of eighteen to immigrate to Palestine as well.[5] In view of these experiences, Federmann became increasingly aware of the necessity of founding a Jewish state.

Yekutiel Federmann travelled for the first time to Palestine in March 1938, on a small French boat with a group of Jewish young people. He had previously married his long-time girl friend Bela Reiner, also born in Chemnitz, who had joined him in London. The young couple took the opportunity to visit Eretz Israel before they returned to their mission in London.

When the German Wehrmacht invaded Poland on September 1, 1939, and England and France declared war on Germany, Yekutiel could no longer operate his rescue mission. In March 1940, he and his wife immigrated to Eretz Israel.

Yekutiel could not abandon the idea of continuing to fight the Nazis, but even his pilot's license did not help him to get into the British Royal Air Force. So he accepted an offer from the intelligence branch of the Hagana underground movement, called "Shai", to work as a waiter in a Haifa café that was frequented by officers and sergeants of the British Royal Army. There he could overhear their talks and pass on the contents to the intelligence service. This advance information enabled the Hagana to circumvent hindrances, such as searches for illegal immigrants or weapons, which would have had the worst imaginable consequences for many of their actions. In the summer of 1942, when the German marines reached Tobruq Bay, the British army moved its base to the port district of Haifa. The British soldiers needed to be supplied with underwear and uniforms, which prompted Yekutiel to commission the two textile factories then operating in the country to produce these items. The factories were "Ata" in Kiryat Ata, recently established by the Jewish textile engineer Hans Moller from Brno, and "Lodzia" in Tel Aviv, which had been founded by a Polish family from Lodz.[6]
Soon Yekutiel was also providing the military with food and supplies for their billets. Beyond this, he used military trucks to import leather and cotton from Egypt, textiles from India, cork from Malta, shoes, shirts and underwear from Turkey. And courageous, energetic and resourceful as he was, he also smuggled in weapons and munitions for the Hagana, primarily from Egypt.

Other members of the Federmann family in Chemnitz had left the city in 1938 after the November pogrom and settled in Brussels, where they opened a pastry shop on a main street. When the German Wehrmacht invaded in 1940, the family scattered in different directions. Younger brother Shmuel was caught while fleeing to Spain and was brought with four thousand other persons to Camp Miranda, in the northern part of the country, where he was held prisoner for three years. Before the end of the war, Shmuel was able to board a ship with 751 Jewish refugees that reached Haifa in January 1944. And it was his brother Yekutiel who, with his connections to the English occupation forces, was able to gain his release from the camp in Atlit where illegal refugees were confined. From then on, Shmuel stood loyally at his brother's side in all his endeavours. Shmuel soon met his future wife Ruth Stekelmacher, who had come to the country in 1939 with the Children's Aliya after the Germans invaded Czechoslovakia. Yekutiel and Shmuel helped their parents Zippora and David Federmann, who had fled Germany via Spain and Portugal, stayed in a refugee camp in Jamaica, and wound up in Cuba, to immigrate to Eretz Israel. The other Federmann children Susi and Paul put down roots in Mexico, while Marta and her husband Fritz had already come to Palestine in 1933.

In 1947 Yekutiel Federmann faced his decision in the matter of the hotel "Kaete Dan". The brothers interested foreign investors and, five years after the founding of the state of Israel, next to the site of the "Kaete Dan" (which had been torn down), they built the 120-room "Dan Tel Aviv", Israel's first luxury hotel.
And since it was still difficult to find qualified personnel, the Federmann brothers took the initiative and established "Dvir", the country's first hotel school, in Haifa in 1959. They designed the training programme for all personnel – from waiter to director, from chambermaid to cook – that was authoritative for decades

in every hotel in the country. By the end of the 1960s, the Federmanns were able to acquire four more hotels: the "Dan Accadia Herzlia-on-sea", the "King David Jerusalem", the "Dan Carmel" in Haifa and the "Dan Caesarea".
Early in the 1980s, sons Michael (Mickey) and Ami joined their respective fathers Yekutiel and Shmuel Federmann as directors of the hotel chain. With great elan they established a group of new hotels including the "Dan Panorama Tel Aviv", "Dan Panorama Haifa", "Dan Panorama Jerusalem", the "Dan Panorama Eilat", and the "Dan Eilat".

The brothers Yekutiel and Shmuel Federmann became known in Israel and abroad as businessmen who had the power to make visions into reality and who refused to give up their optimism in difficult times. They developed the tourism industry, whose success is highly dependent upon the political situation. The 1965–66 recession, the wars of 1967 and 1973, the unstable situation since 1987 in the entire region, riots and acts of terror have repeatedly paralysed tourism in Israel. As a result, hotels must often close their doors. But the Federmann brothers always have been able to get through these times of crisis without closings. They have either reduced personnel or decided to renovate one or another hotel during such difficult periods. They have never given up their hope for better times.

Yekutiel Federmann died in Tel Aviv on January 18, 2002, at the age of eighty-seven. His brother Shmuel died on January 15, 2006, at the age of eighty-nine.
A plateau on Mount Carmel with a view of the Mediterranean was recently dedicated as "Yekutiel Federmann Square".
A boulevard on Mount Carmel will soon be named after Yekutiel und Shmuel Federmann.
In November 2004, the Weizmann Institute of Science in Rehovot held a celebration marking the tenth anniversary of its chair in hotel management. The chair, which is integrated into the Faculty of Agriculture, Food and Environment Quality Sciences, had been endowed by the Federmann families and now was renamed after Yekutiel Federmann z"l (in blessed memory).

For twenty-five years, the Dan Hotels Corporation Ltd. has been registered on the Tel Aviv stock exchange, with 87% of its shares owned by the Federmann family. The company founders are the brothers Yekutiel and Shmuel Federmann. Yekutiel's son Michael Federmann is the chairman of the board of directors, and the company's deputy chairman is Shmuel's son Ami Federmann. The company today owns and operates twelve hotels throughout the country having a total of 3150 rooms, and the chain employs some 2500 persons. Overseas tourists represented about 45% of the total bed nights in 2004; the rest were local. The Ministry of Tourism classifies most of the hotels owned by the chain as first class hotels.

Most of the information here is derived from the book *Hamelonaim* by Menachem Portugali, Shaul Maizlish, Aharon Shacham, Israel 2000.
My special thanks for her assistance to Shoshana Danziger, who has been the secretary to the Federmanns dynasty for decades.

1 See biography of Lotte Cohn.
2 See biography of Werner Wittkower.
3 The term "Jekke" apparently was coined due the German immigrant's habit of keeping on his jacket, or "Jacke", in the scorching heat of summer. See also "Hilda and Dr. Richard Strauss", note 3.
4 Recha Freier founded the Children's and Youth Aliya, which rescued thousands of Jewish children and teenagers. Franz Ollendorf taught there. Later he was a professor of electronic engineering at the Technion, Haifa.
5 The British mandate government only allowed children under the age of eighteen into the country.
6 "Ata" stands for the initials of "Arigai Totzereth Artzeinu", or "fabrics made in our land"; see biography of Eugen Szekey.

Stef Wertheimer

The Story of a Man and a Metal Industry

Stef Wertheimer was barely eleven years old when he was forced to leave Nazi Germany with his family and find refuge in Palestine. Fifteen years later in Nahariya, the northern coastal town established by German Jews, he founded his metal cutting tools company ISCAR with little more than a sander and two soldering irons. In 2006 the American investor Warren Buffett acquired 80% of the firm for $4 billion. Stef Wertheimer's son Eitan, today chairman of the board of ISCAR, discussed the deal: with the proceeds, Stef Wertheimer could fulfil his long-desired aim of expanding industry in the Galilee, where Jews, Arabs and Druse live and work alongside each other. He would be able to establish additional industrial parks and move forward with realizing his vision of a "Marshall Plan" for the Middle East.

Stef Wertheimer came from a Jewish family that had lived for over three centuries in Kippenheim, in the Black Forest near Freiburg, where he was born on July 16, 1926. His father Eugen Wertheimer, whose leg had been amputated after war injuries suffered at Verdun in World War I, was a grain dealer. Stef Wertheimer attended grammar school in his hometown, and went to a secondary school in Ettenheim for a few months, before he and his parents and siblings fled Germany via Basel in February 1937 and settled in Tel Aviv. His separation from Germany was painless, Wertheimer has often related to journalists — his high school teacher was eager to see him go. But from then on, he never completed any academic programme. To his father's displeasure, he dropped out of school in Tel Aviv at the age of fourteen. After apprenticing to an optician and becoming trained in photomechanics and precision engineering, Wertheimer was called to serve in the British mandate's military force. He repaired optical instruments for the Royal Air Force as far afield as Bahrain. Developments during World War II led him into the Jewish underground organization Palmach, the forerunner of the Israeli army, in 1945. He participated in actions against the British mandate government and, in connection with the action "Black Sabbath", was arrested for illegal possession of weapons on June 29, 1946, and interned for four months. Afterward he worked as a precision mechanic in a munitions factory run by Palmach until the start of the War of Independence. When the state of Israel was founded in 1948, he was appointed to a position of responsibility in the new Israeli army.

In 1950 Wertheimer ended his seven years of military activities and moved to Nahariya, where the Strauss family also had lived since 1938.[1] In a corrugated-iron garage, Stef Wertheimer began to build his company, formally establishing it as ISCAR in 1952. It should be mentioned that during this period, Stef Wertheimer and his young family lived for fifteen years in a one-family house built in 1937 in the Modern style by the architect Josef Neufeld.[2] ISCAR's rapid development after the 1967 Six-Day War was aided by De Gaulle's call for a weapons embargo. It became necessary to launch production of aircraft replacement parts, which led

to important recognition for the company's production capabilities. As a result, in 1977, Stef Wertheimer – now a representative of the newly formed Shinui reform party in the Israeli Knesset – sought to back export-oriented economic development. He gave up his political career after three and a half years, much to his regret; the Knesset was so focused on questions of military security at the time that economic matters could not be addressed.
Therefore, Stef Wertheimer decided to go his own way politically as an advocate for economic development and peace in Israel, in addition to pursuing his business activities. He made it his life's task to communicate the experiences that had enabled him to become a successful industrialist to those who were interested, and to advise and promote budding entrepreneurs, wherever they might come from. The belief that Israel's productive activities with its neighbours will lead to peace in the entire region has continued to be his credo until today.
Wertheimer is an excellent craftsman and also formulates his observations with a craftsman's precision in concise propositions that he tirelessly repeats in public. He maintains: "My objective is not to make money, I am engaged in producing products." He goes on to state: "Education and progressive industry. There is no other way. Whoever wants to work and is able to work will not make war," adding, "If the Israelis and Arabs were busy meeting deadlines ... they would have neither the time nor the desire to fight each other."

In 1981, having just completed his term in the Knesset, Stef Werthemer decided to develop a beautiful but barren area in the western Galilee. His idea was not simply to expand his own ISCAR, Ltd. metalworking business, but above all to find a way to enhance the economic stability, industrial productivity, and employment opportunities of the entire region. He also wished to further Israel's economic independence by encouraging young entrepreneurs in their new initiatives, mainly in export-oriented industries. His multi-pronged mission took the form of an economic development centre. He believed in furthering creativity in a variety of forms: industrial production in a new robotically-run metal-cutting tools factory, entrepreneurship in incubator spaces, art and culture in several on-site museums and sculpture gardens, and education in the form of a school for kindergarten through twelfth grade and technical training centres.
In 1985 Wertheimer established his first model economic development centre on the premises of ISCAR, the Tefen Industrial Park. He envisioned the Tefen model as a business incubator where research and development focused on exports could take place, and created a business environment designed to support small and mid-sized companies.
After more than twenty years, the Tefen Industrial Park today accommodates some thirty companies in various fields of industry, hi-tech and services. The Open Museum also is situated there, realizing Wertheimer's underlying idea of eliminating the division between the spheres of art and industry, developing mutuality between creativity and productivity.
The Art Gallery shows changing exhibitions of painting, sculpture and other media, emphasizing Israeli art by the best Israeli artists. "The Museum for German-Speaking Jewry — The Centre of the Jekkes Legacy" was inaugurated in the summer of 2005. The museum, whose curator is Ruthi Ofek, features a permanent display of items and documents describing and commemorating these Jews and their significant contribution to the settlement, culture and industry of Eretz Israel and the state of Israel. An exhibition about the contributions of German Jewish architects in Palestine 1918–1948, based on the biographies in this book, is on display on the ground floor of the museum.[3]

Stef Wertheimer

On display upstairs is an exhibit of which Wertheimer is very proud: a series of photographs documenting the history of the synagogue in Kippenheim, where he was born. In one photo from the 1930s, National Socialists can be seen plundering the synagogue's interior. Then come four additional photos that show the step-by-step reconstruction of the synagogue. Stef Wertheimer financed this restoration.
The Tefen Sculpture Garden consists of some one hundred permanently installed pieces. The purely Israeli collection reflects various approaches in conception, material and style. The sculpture garden is integral to the Industrial Park – a human environment incorporating industry and art. Tefen Industrial Park also features his son Eitan Wertheimer's automobile collection, which illustrates the development of motor vehicles during the twentieth century. The collection includes some thirty classic models dating from 1930 to the present.
Tefen's Education Department offers guided tours and activities in the Museum and Park on themes encompassing industry, art and the environment. The tours and activities are available in three languages: Hebrew, Arabic and English. They are adapted to various age groups, with an emphasis on experiential activities and creativity for children and youth.
A few minutes away from the Tefen Industrial Park is Kfar Vradim (Roses Village), a residential community that Wertheimer established to further the overall development of the region. It is now home to about 1500 families.

As a result of Tefen's great success, Wertheimer subsequently established five more industrial parks in Israel, which he nicknamed "kindergartens for young entrepreneurs". In 1992 Tel Hai, located near the town of Kiryat Shemona in Galilee, was opened. This economic development centre includes Israel's only museum of photography. The park has achieved a successful synergy with nearby Tel Hai College.
The Omer economic development centre, established in 1993, is located in the southern Negev region, 6 km from Be'er-Sheva, near the attractive residential suburb of Omer. It is home mostly to high-tech companies, drawing on the expertise of nearby Ben Gurion University.
Wertheimer opened his next park in 1998 in Lavon, which lies just south of Tefen. It houses industry as well as the Zur educational centre, where technical and entrepreneurial courses for Arabs, Druse, and Jews are offered. A residential area offering residents low-density, high-quality housing is five minutes by foot from the centre.
And Dalton, a fourth industrial park on the Dalton plateau of the Galilee, is being established in 2006.
The four industrial parks in Galilee employ hundreds of local Jews, Arabs and Druse. Employees are promoted on the basis of neither national extraction nor religious allegiance, but according to one concept alone: "Industrialization should become our common religion." This is another Wertheimer credo.
The industrial parks represent his vision, which advocates creativity in industry as well as in culture, art and education. Wertheimer calls this vision "Zionism's Third Stage": namely that Zionism's goal now – after the two previous stages of settlement and security have been achieved – is to create economic independence based on industry and export. The parks serve plants and companies both in their early stages of development and as well-established enterprises, and provide an uplifting, pleasant work environment.

Wertheimer believes that a plan similar to the American Marshall Plan, which was used to help rebuild Western Europe after World War II, can be implemented in the non-oil-rich countries of the Middle East.

Instead of aid in the form of money, he proposes developing infrastructure, industry and technical education as a means for bringing economic prosperity to this region. "Jobs, and only jobs, are an alternative to war," Wertheimer repeats to every person who visits him at his ISCAR headquarters in Tefen. Sustainable peace, development, and democratization in this part of the world will be achieved only through the creation of jobs, investment in entrepreneurial education, industrial and technical training, the expansion of trade, and economic growth focused on export industries. Terrorism is best combated when people have productive jobs and work together.

On June 24, 2002, Wertheimer made a statement to the United States House Committee on International Relations in Washington D.C. under Chairman Henry Hyde in which he presented his Marshall Plan for the Middle East, an area he defined more precisely as the Eastern Mediterranean region. Thought it was delivered over four years ago, his statement has not lost any of its pertinence.
Here are some excerpts from that speech:
"Congressman Hyde has been voicing the need for a new bold approach to certain parts of this area. He has used the term 'a new Marshall Plan' to describe his vision. ... I am here to make a few observations and, perhaps, to expand the concept that Congressman Hyde has envisioned. He and I – and I know many others – share an interest in calming my region. I believe there is only one solution: a vigorous plan for industrial development that will be enhanced sometime in the future by a political solution to the Arab-Israeli conflict.
What is needed is not continuing aid, but rather the willingness of the U.S. and other OECD countries to make a limited-term investment in the future of the Eastern Mediterranean.[4] Unlike social welfare, the proposed plan will make people self-sufficient rather than continually dependent. It is a programme that will offer hooks rather than fish.
My testimony is based on fifty years of successful entrepreneurship in a developing region. I started my own metal tool cutting company, ISCAR, Ltd., in 1952, not long after the end of the Israeli War of Independence. It is now one of the two leading companies in its field in the world, with annual revenues of $1 billion. I have also built four industrial parks in Israel that generate an additional $1 billion, much of which derives from the 150 emerging industries that have been launched in the parks' incubator spaces.
My own experience allows me to make two points with conviction. First, since my own corporation grew during times of war on Israeli soil, I can vouch that we need not wait for a peace agreement before embarking on this plan. *We should begin as soon as possible*. Second, having launched my company from a remote area in the Galilee, I can testify that it is possible for the Eastern Mediterranean to be competitive in the global market ...
The main way that I can contribute to Congressman Hyde's vision for a Marshall Plan is through Tefen, my model of an industrial park that has been extremely successful in Israel. Its formula could be exported. Today there are four parks in Israel based on this model, and a fifth will soon be constructed in the north.[5] In addition, it will also soon be tested for the first time on foreign soil: in Gebze, Turkey.[6]
Only two years ago, the model was to be built in Gaza. I was engaged in a partnership with the Palestinians to build twin parks, one near Rafah, the other just across the border in Israel. Leaders of both Israel and the Palestinian Authority approved the plan. The Harvard University School of Design completed a planning study of the area. Unfortunately, however, the second Intifada has postponed that project.

The Tefen model stresses creativity through an unusual combination of aims: to provide high quality products to a global market, to advance entrepreneurial education and industrial training, to foster new indigenous industries, and to showcase art and culture. To these ends, the four parks all have incubator spaces, educational and training facilities, museums, and sculpture gardens.
As in any business enterprise, Tefen's success can be quantified in numbers. The model park and its two replications in the Galilee and one in the Negev have launched 150 new firms that currently generate $1 billion in sales and have given rise to 5000 new jobs. They prove that this part of the world can compete successfully in the global market ..."
Stef Wertheimer concluded his speech with an appeal:
"While economic disparities are not the only issue plaguing this region, an ambitious programme of industrial development in the Eastern Mediterranean will bring positive political, economic, and social results. This will prove to be the best investment for the future.
In summary, I would welcome the support of this Committee, which would greatly enhance the prospects of peace. A long-term solution to the problems besetting us now rests on narrowing the gap of wealth distribution. Industrialization is the key to achieve this."

Soon after his appearance in Washington, Stef Wertheimer offered his economic development model for an industrial park to the neighbouring state of Turkey. Together with Turkish partners and in collaboration with Sabanci University, in 2005 he created what in Turkish parlance is called "Technopark". The Tefen model in Gebze is located about 40 km southeast of Istanbul.

A great deal of information is available to visitors interested in the activities of ISCAR and the various industrial parks, including dozens of *yezur ve-yezira* (creature and creation) bulletins as well as copies of articles and interviews with Stef Wertheimer in local and foreign publications such as *The Philadelphia Inquirer, Financial Times, The Economist, Die Zeit, Handelsblatt*, and *Die Welt*. And the book *The Tefen Model* and videos on various topics in several languages also are available in the Museum shops.
Stef Wertheimer has established technical and entrepreneurial programmes and served in volunteer leadership positions at some of the world's most distinguished educational institutions, including Harvard University and the Technion in Haifa. In addition, he has been awarded honorary doctorates from the Technion, Tel Aviv University, Ben Gurion University of the Negev, and the Schechter Institute of the Jewish Theological Seminary of New York. But none of the awards he received throughout the world has been more significant to him than his country's highest honour, the Israel Prize, which he received in 1991.[7]
As Stef Wertheimer looks from his office window at the rocky landscape of northern Israel, toward the Mediterranean to the west, the Lebanese border to the north, and the Sea of Galilee and Jordan to the east, he is convinced that the Tefen concept is ready to be exported to the Arab world.
In every interview he gives, he emphasizes: "We need to give opportunities to the Arabs; their success is the guarantee of our peace."

Literature:

Erez Navon (ed.), *The Tefen Model*, Tefen 2003
yezur ve-yezira 3/2002; 5/2003; 6/2003; 7/2004; 8/2004
Handelsblatt, 15/16 November 2002
Die Welt, 19 February 2003
Ettenheimer Stadtanzeiger, 15 May 2003
Die Zeit, 22 May 2003
tachles 33, 15 August 2003
The Economist, 20 September 2003
Financial Times, 22 September 2003
The Philadelphia Inquirer, 16 November 2003
tachles 4, 23 January 2004
The Wall Street Journal, 19 February 2004
haaretz, 6 May 2006
The Wall Street Journal, 8 May 2006

1 See chapter on Hilda and Dr. Richard Strauss.
2 See biography of Josef Neufeld, where the house is pictured (Josef Neufeld, one-family residence K., Nahariya, 1937).
3 Exhibitions of this material have also been mounted in Tel Aviv, Haifa, Jerusalem, Berlin, Dessau, Braunschweig and New York.
4 OECD – Organization for Economic Cooperation and Development
5 Now constructed.
6 Now constructed.
7 Dr. Reuben Hecht was honoured three years earlier. See chapter on Reuben Hecht.

List of Architects

Adler, Leo (biography. p. 256); see: Warhaftig 2005

Ahlfeld, Ludwig Eliezer-Arieh
Born 1902 Nordhausen/Saxony, died 1984 Omer/Israel
Studied at the Technische Hochschule of Hanover and Karlsruhe
Immigrated 1939 to Palestine. See: Warhaftig 2005

Ascher, Gad
Born 1908 Berlin, died 1965 Tel Aviv
Studied at the Technische Hochschule of Berlin and Stuttgart
Immigrated 1933 to Palestine. Director of the public works department, Tel Aviv. See: Warhaftig 2005

Ascher, Siegfried
Born 1877 Berlin
Independent architect in Berlin, many buildings
Immigrated 1934 to Palestine. See: Warhaftig 2005

Baerwald, Alex (biography p. 28)

Ben-Uri (Wasbutzki), Meir
Born 1908 Riga, died 1983 Haifa
Studied at the Technische Hochschule Berlin
Immigrated 1933 to Palestine. Architect in the municipality of Haifa. See: Warhaftig 2005

Berger, Josef
Born 1898 Vienna, died 1989 London
Studied at the Technische Hochschule Vienna and Adolf Loos's private school; private practice with Arthur Berger (brother) and Martin Ziegler, residential buildings
Immigrated 1934 to Palestine. Private practice in Haifa
Moved 1937 to England, private practice in London

Berlowitz, Yona (Alfred)
Born 1881 Tilsit, died 1958 Tel Aviv
Studied at the Technische Hochschule Berlin; practice in Berlin
Immigrated 1934 to Palestine. See: Warhaftig 2005

Bernstein, Shlomo (Salomon) (biography p. 140); see: Warhaftig 2005

Bienheim, Yehuda (Karl Ludwig) (biography p. 308); see: Warhaftig 2005

Blumann, Shlomo (Salomon)
Born 1894 Berlin, died 1969 Tel Aviv
Studied at the Technische Hochschule Berlin; private practice in Berlin
Immigrated 1935 to Palestine. See: Warhaftig 2005

Blumenfeld, Alex
Born 1905 Berlin, died ?
Studied at the Technische Hochschule Berlin; private practice in Berlin
Immigrated 1934 to Palestine. See: Warhaftig 2005

Bruck, Ze'ev (Wilhelm) (biography p. 332); see: Warhaftig 2005

Brutzkus, David Anatol
Born 1910 St. Petersburg, died 1999 Jerusalem
Studied at the Technische Hochschule Berlin under Hans Poelzig
Immigrated 1935 to Palestine. Private practice in Jerusalem

Brutzkus, Eliezer Leonid
Born 1907 St. Petersburg, died 1987 Jerusalem
Studied at the Technische Hochschule of Munich and Berlin
Immigrated 1933 to Palestine. City planner in Jerusalem

Burstein, Ruth
Born 1913 ? Germany
Studied at the Technische Hochschule in Danzig
Immigrated 1945 to Palestine

Crzellitzer, Fritz
Born 1876 Berlin, died 1942 Tel Aviv
Studied at the Technische Hochschule Berlin. Private practice in Berlin
Immigrated 1934 to Palestine. See: Warhaftig 2005

Cohn, Lotte (biography p. 76); see: Warhaftig 2005

Engelmann, Paul (biography p. 246); see: Warhaftig 2005

Epstein, Fritz
Born 1877 Dresden, died 1960 Bad Ems
Private practice in Kassel and Frankfurt/M.
Immigrated 1933 to Palestine. Practice in Tel Aviv
Returned 1956 to Frankfurt/M. See: Warhaftig 2005

List of Architects

Fenchel, Heinz-Chaim
Born 1906 Berlin, died 1988 Tel Aviv
Studied at the Kunstakademie Berlin. Worked for UFA in interior design
Immigrated 1937 to Palestine. Interior designer in Tel Aviv. See: Warhaftig 2005

Frenkel, Chanan (biography p. 138); see: Warhaftig 2005

Friedjung, Eliyahou (Bruno)
Born 1908 Austria, died 1984 Haifa
Studied at the Technische Hochschule Vienna
Immigrated 1934 to Palestine. Architect in the municipality of Haifa

Friedmann, Robert (biography p. 222); see: Warhaftig 2005

Gad (Goldberg), Dora
Born 1912 Romania, died 2003 Caesarea
Studied at the Technische Hochschule Vienna
Immigrated 1938 to Palestine. Private practice in Tel Aviv; interior designer
Retrospective exhibition in Tel Aviv 1994

Galil (Hoffmann), Gad
Born 1905 Budapest, died 1973 Tel Aviv
Studied at the Technische Hochschule Braunschweig
Immigrated 1933 to Palestine

Gerstel, Moshe (biography p. 204); see: Warhaftig 2005

Gerstenfeld, Abraham
Born 1892 Poland, died 1959 Haifa
Studied at the Technische Hochschule Vienna
Immigrated 1935 to Palestine. Private practice in Haifa

Gidoni-Mandelstamm, Elsa (biography p. 320); see: Warhaftig 2005

Gitai (Weinraub), Munio (biography p. 150); see: Warhaftig 2005

Glikson, Artur (biography p. 362); see: Warhaftig 2005

Goldberger, Alfred
Born 1908 Vienna, died 1979 England
Studied at the Technische Hochschule Vienna

Immigrated 1933 to Palestine. Private practice in Haifa
From 1954 buildings in Far East; from 1965 in England, many buildings

Goldmann-Bustin, Jochanan (Hans)
Born 1897 Vienna, died 1972 Haifa
Studied at the Technische Hochschule and the Kunstakademie in Vienna
Immigrated 1934 to Palestine

Goldner, Leo
Born 1911 Baja, Hungary, died ?
Studied at the Technische Hochschule Berlin
1941 deported, until 1945 in various camps including Dachau
1948 moved to Israel. Private practice with Abraham Axelrod,
Tel Aviv; many buildings. See: Warhaftig 2005

Goldschmidt, Trude (Gertrud)
Born 1901 ? Germany
Studied at the Technische Hochschule Munich
Immigrated ? to Palestine

Haller, Ze'ev (Wilhelm) (biography p. 196); see: Warhaftig 2005

Hed (Hecht), Edgar (biography p. 134); see: Warhaftig 2005

Heimann, Nathan
Born 1884 Vienna, died 1974 Tel Aviv
Studied at the Technische Hochschule of Munich and Berlin; private practice in Breslau
Immigrated 1938 to Palestine. See: Warhaftig 2005

Herz, Gidon
Born 1904 Germany, died 1974 Tel Aviv
Studied at the Technische Hochschule Stuttgart
Immigrated 1933 to Palestine. Private practice in Tel Aviv

Hoffmann, Otto
Born 1898 Vienna, died 1974 Jerusalem
Studied at the Technische Hochschule Vienna; private practice in Vienna
Immigrated 1935 to Palestine

Imberg, Paul
Born 1877 Berlin, died 1962 New York

Private practice in Berlin and Danzig
Immigrated 1935 to Palestine; 1956 to the USA. See: Warhaftig 2005

Jacobowitz, Georg
Berlin architect and garden architect. As of 1934 in Tel Aviv. See: Warhaftig 2005

Kalitzki, Bruno (biography p. 240); see: Warhaftig 2005

Kaminka, Gideon (biography p. 342); see: Warhaftig 2005

Kauffmann, Richard (biography p. 36); see: Warhaftig 2005

Kaufmann, Oskar (biography p. 158); see: Warhaftig 2005

Kaufmann, Richard
Born 1886 Freiburg, died ?
Studied at the Technische Hochschule, Munich and Berlin; private practice in Frankfurt/M.
Immigrated 1933 to Palestine. See: Warhaftig 2005

Kissin, David
Born 1901 Moscow, died 1978 Tel Aviv
Studied at the Technische Hochschule Berlin
Immigrated 1933 to Palestine. Private practice in Tel Aviv. See: Warhaftig 2005

Klarwein, Ossip Joseph (biography p. 288); see: Warhaftig 2005

Klein, Alexander (biography p. 184); see: Warhaftig 2005

Kornberg, Fritz (biography p. 44); see: Warhaftig 2005

Krakauer, Leopold (biography p. 54); see: Warhaftig 2005

Kuczynski, Dov (Bernhard) (biography p. 70); see: Warhaftig 2005

Lavie (Loevisohn), Yehuda (Ernst)
Born 1910 Berlin, died 1998 Tel Aviv
Studied at the Technische Hochschule Berlin
Immigrated 1934 to Palestine. Private practice in Tel Aviv. See: Warhaftig 2005

Lazarus, Otto
Born 1887 Berlin, died ?

Studied at the Baugewerbeschule and the Technische Hochschule Berlin; worked in Berlin
Immigrated 1933 to Palestine. See: Warhaftig 2005

Leschnitzer, Georg
Born 1885 Tarnowitz/Upper Silesia, died 1950 Tel Aviv
Architect and sculptor in Berlin
Immigrated 1934 to Palestine. Private practice in Tel Aviv. See: Warhaftig 2005

Lesser, Willy
Born 1887 Berlin, died ?
Immigrated 1934 to Palestine. See: Warhaftig 2005

Levy, Alexander
Born 1883 Berlin, died Auschwitz
Studied at the Technische Hochschule Berlin; private practice in Berlin
Immigrated 1920 to Palestine: the "Pagoda" in Jugendstil, Tel Aviv
Returned 1930 to Berlin; 1933 to Paris; deported to Auschwitz. See: Warhaftig 2005

Lewinski, Philipp
Born 1889 Germany, died ?
Studied at the Technische Hochschule Braunschweig; private practice in Berlin
Immigrated 1934 to Palestine. See: Warhaftig 2005

Lewinsky, Kurt
Born 1909 Hildesheim, died 1952 Tel Aviv
Studied at the Technische Hochschule Berlin
Immigrated 1933 to Palestine

Loeb, Max (biography p. 110); see: Warhaftig 2005

Lustig, Leopold
Born 1889 Kattowitz, died ?
Studied at the Technische Hochschule Dresden
Private practice in Dresden and Berlin
Immigrated 1934 to Palestine. Private practice in Tel Aviv. See: Warhaftig 2005

Mansfeld, Alfred (biography p. 151); see: Warhaftig 2005

Mendelsohn, Erich (biography p. 210); see: Warhaftig 2005

Menkes, Theodor (biography p. 348); see: Warhaftig 2005

Mertens, Chanan (Heinrich)
Born 1912 Austria, died 1982 Tel Aviv
Studied at the Technische Hochschule Vienna
Immigrated 1934 to Palestine. Head of housing department in Tel Aviv

Meschulam, Chaim
Born 1904 Filipopol/Bulgaria, died 1985 Tel Aviv
Studied at the Technische Hochschule Darmstadt
Immigrated 1929 to Palestine, Chalutz. Private practice in Tel Aviv

Mestechkin, Shmuel (biography p. 144); see: Warhaftig 2005

Metrikin, Yakob
Born 1902 Litau, died 1981 Jerusalem
Studied in Oldenburg
Immigrated 1925 to Palestine. Private practice in Jerusalem, many buildings for "Tnuva"

Neufeld, Joseph (biography p. 88); see: Warhaftig 2005

Neumann, Alfred
Born 1900 Vienna, died 1969 Quebec
Studied at the Kunstakademie Vienna under Peter Behrens
Deported to Theresienstadt; 1949 to Israel. Private practice in Haifa. Professor at the Technion Haifa

Ofenberger, Alexander
Born 1907 Stanislavov/Poland, died 1957 Haifa
Studied at the Baugewerbeschule Vienna
Immigrated 1933 to Palestine. Private practice in Haifa.

Pavell (Pawel), Chanan (Heinz)
Born 1909 Stettin, died 1976 Tel Aviv
Studied at the Technische Hochschule Stuttgart
Immigrated 1934 to Palestine. Private practice in Tel Aviv. See: Warhaftig 2005

Pick, Kurt
Born 1890 Liss/Prussia, died 1959 Tel Aviv
Studied at the Technische Hochschule Berlin; private practice in Frankfurt/M.
Immigrated 1933 to Palestine. See: Warhaftig 2005

Pienaker, David (biography p. 316); see: Warhaftig 2005

Pinkerfeld, Jacob (biography p. 82); see: Warhaftig 2005

Pinthus, Alexander
Born 1983 Germany, died 1981 Haifa
Studied at the Technische Hochschule Karlsruhe
Immigrated 1933 to Palestine. Professor at the Technion Haifa

Polatshek, Otto
Born 1908 Poland, died ?
Studied at the German Technische Hochschule Brno
Immigrated 1932 to Palestine
Worked in offices of Richard Kauffmann, Arieh Sharon;
architect in the municipality of Herzlia; after 1947 private practice

Posener, Julius
Born 1904 Berlin, died 1996 Berlin
Studied at the Technische Hochschule Berlin under Hans Poelzig
Immigrated 1935 to Palestine. Returned 1961 to Berlin. Architectural historian, author.
See: Warhaftig 2005

Rading, Adolf (biography p. 230); see: Warhaftig 2005

Ratner, Jochanan (Eugen) (biography p. 62); see: Warhaftig 2005

Rau, Heinz (biography p. 300); see: Warhaftig 2005

Reich, Arthur
Born 1889 Germany, died ?
Studied at the Technische Hochschule Dresden;
private practice in Glewitz, Upper Silesia
Immigrated 1938 to Palestine.

Reich, Itzchak
Born 1890 Russia, died 1970 Tel Aviv
Studied at the Technische Hochschule Vienna
Immigrated 1926 to Palestine. Archtitect in the municipality of Tel Aviv.

Reifenberg, Heinrich Julius
Born 1894 Berlin, died 1968 London
Studied at the Technische Hochschule Berlin. Private practice in Berlin
Immigrated 1933 to Palestine; 1938 to London. Private practice in London. See: Warhaftig 2005

Reinsch, Kurt (biography p. 264); see: Warhaftig 2005

Reiss, Arthur
Born 1904 Heilbronn am Neckar, died ?
Studied at the Staatliche Bauschule Munich
Immigrated 1933 to Palestine
Private practice in Hod Hasharon
See: Warhaftig 2005

Rings, Josef (biography p. 178); see: Warhaftig 2005

Roibitschek, Max
Born 1894 Podebrad/Czechoslovakia, died 1991 Haifa
Studied at the Technische Hochschule Vienna
Immigrated 1933 to Palestine. Architect in the municipality of Haifa

Rosenthal, Harry (biography p. 270); see: Warhaftig 2005

Roth, Helene
Born 1904 Göding/Moravia, died 1995 Tel Aviv
Studied at the Technische Hochschule Vienna; private practice in Vienna
Immigrated 1933 to Palestine. Private practice in Tel Aviv; renowned interior designer

Rubin, Carl (biography p. 102); see: Warhaftig 2005

Salinger, Hellmut-Chaim
Born 1896 Berlin, died 1991 Jerusalem
Studied at the Technische Hochschule of Darmstadt and Stuttgart; private practice in Berlin
Immigrated 1933 to Palestine. Architect in the municipality of Jerusalem
Author of three books in German. See: Warhaftig 2005

Salkind, Nachum
Born 1895 St. Petersburg, died 1976 Tel Aviv
Studied in St. Petersburg; active in Berlin after 1920
Immigrated 1933 to Palestine. Private practice in Tel Aviv, many public buildings

Salomon, Arieh-Franz
Born 1892 Berlin, died 1960 Jerusalem
Studied at the Technische Hochschule Berlin; private practice in Berlin
Immigrated 1933 to Palestine. See: Warhaftig 2005

Schallinger, Gideon
Born 1909 Czechoslovakia, died 1978 Haifa
Studied at the German Technische Hochschule Brno
Immigrated 1930 to Palestine. Private practice in Haifa

Schapiro, Heinrich
Born 1900 Vilna, Poland, died 1984 New York
Studied at the Kunstakademie and the Technische Hochschule Berlin;
close colleague of Hans Poelzig, Berlin
Immigrated 1934 to Palestine; 1946 to USA. See: Warhaftig 2005

Scheller, David (Dagobert)
Born 1911 Berlin, died 1981 Tel Aviv
Studied at the Technische Hochschule Berlin
Immigrated 1936 to Palestine. Private practice in Tel Aviv, many interiors. See: Warhaftig 2005

Schiller, Uriel (Otto) (biography p. 354); see: Warhaftig 2005

Schönberger, Joseph
Born 1912 Frankfurt/M., died 1982 Jerusalem
Studied at the Technische Hochschule Darmstadt
Immigrated 1935 to Palestine. Private practice in Jerusalem, many religious buildings
See: Warhaftig 2005

Schragenheim, Arthur Abraham (biography p. 282); see: Warhaftig 2005

Shani (Steinbock), Jehoshua
Born 1901 Lodz, died 1956 Tel Aviv
Studied at the Technische Hochschule Danzig
Immigrated 1926 to Palestine, Chalutz. Private practice in Tel Aviv, many buildings

Sharon, Arieh (biography p. 122); see: Warhaftig 2005

Siegel, Hans
Born 1890 Berlin, died 1984 Haifa
Studied at the Technische Hochschule Berlin; private practice in Berlin
Immigrated 1933 to Palestine. See: Warhaftig 2005

Sobelsohn, Hans
Born 1890 Vienna, died 1961 Haifa
Studied at the Technische Hochschule Vienna; private practice in Vienna

Chief architect 14th Zionist Congress
Immigrated 1926 to Palestine. Private practice in Haifa, many buildings

Stolzer, Eugen (biography p. 174); see: Warhaftig 2005

Stolzer-Segal, Judith (biography p. 336); see: Warhaftig 2005

Strauss, Walter
Born 1892 Germany, died ?
Studied at the Technische Hochschule Stuttgart; private practice in Stuttgart-Cannstatt
Immigrated 1934 to Palestine. Architect in the municipality of Haifa

Strick, Nassim
Born 1902 Pinsk/Russia, died 1967 Tel Aviv
Studied at the Technische Hochschule Vienna; private practice in Vienna
Immigrated 1934 to Palestine. Architect in the municipality of Haifa. See: Warhaftig 2005

Szekey, Eugen (biography p. 294); see: Warhaftig 2005

Trostler, Ruben
Born 1908 Austria, died ?
Studied at the Technische Hochschule Vienna; private practice in Vienna
Immigrated 1938 to Palestine. Private practice in Jerusalem, many buildings

Tversky-Genosar, Aharon
Born 1911 Russia, died 1967 Tel Aviv
Studied at the Technische Hochschule Darmstadt
Immigrated 1935 to Palestine. Private practice in Tel Aviv

Unger, Yehuda Kurt (biography p. 356); see: Warhaftig 2005

Weitzmann, Siegfried
Born 1886 Berlin, died 1960 Tel Aviv
Studied at the Technische Hochschule Berlin; private practice with Arthur Korn in Berlin
Immigrated 1936 to Palestine. See: Warhaftig 2005

Weltsch, Ze'ev Willy
Born 1887 Prague, died 1978 Haifa
Studied architecture and construction at the Technische
Hochschule Prague; private practice in Hamburg
Immigrated 1933 to Palestine. Private practice in Haifa. See: Warhaftig 2005

Wiener, Alfred
Born 1885 Potsdam, died ca. 1977 Tel Aviv
Studied at the Technische Hochschule of Dresden and Berlin
Private practice with Dipl Ing. Jaretzky, Berlin; many apartment and office buildings
Immigrated 1938 to Palestine. See: Warhaftig 2005

Witt, Arieh (Hans)
Born 1908 Berlin, died 1985 Jerusalem
Studied at the Technische Hochschule Berlin
Immigrated 1934 to Palestine. Practiced in Jerusalem. See: Warhaftig 2005

Wittkower, Werner (Joseph) (biography p. 326); see: Warhaftig 2005

Yelin, Eliezer
Born 1888 Jerusalem, died 1945 Jerusalem
Studied at the Technische Hochschule Darmstadt
1913 returned to Jerusalem. Partnership with civil engineer Wilhelm Hecker, many buildings
See: Kroyanker 2006

Zeisler, Eliezer
Born 1892 Poland, died 1976 Tel Aviv
Studied at the Technische Hochschule Vienna
Immigrated 1933 to Palestine. Private practice in Tel Aviv, sometimes with Else Gidoni-Mandelstamm

Zohar, Yeheskiel
Born 1901 Yugoslavia, died 1960 Haifa
Studied at the Technische Hochschule Stuttgart
Immigrated 1925 to Palestine, Chalutz. Private practice in Haifa, many buildings in the Modern style

Bibliography

Achleitner, Friedrich: *Österreichische Architektur im 20. Jahrhundert*, Vol 2, Salzburg 1982
Adiv, Uriel M.: *Richard Kauffmann (1887–1958). Das Architektonische Gesamtwerk.* Dissertation Technische Universität Berlin, Berlin 1985
Adler, Leo: *Vom Wesen der Baukunst*, Leipzig 1926. Reprint Berlin 2000
Adler, Leo: introduction in: *Bruno Kalitzki*, Berlin – Leipzig – Wien 1929
Adler, Leo (ed.): *Wasmuths Lexikon der Baukunst*, Berlin I/1929, II/1930, III–IV/1931
Adler, Leo (ed.): *Neuzeitliche Miethäuser und Siedlungen*, Berlin 1931. Reprint 1998, epilogue: Myra Warhaftig
Agassi, Uzi: *W. J. Wittkower: habriza baa mimarav. "The Cool Breeze Comes From the West"*, Israel 1993
Amitai, Mordechai (ed.): *Nahalal / chazon behitgashmuto*, Tel Aviv 1971
Avissar, Oded: *Sefer tveria*, Jerusalem 1973

Bab, Julius (ed.): *Wesen und Weg der Berliner Volksbühnenbewegung*, Berlin 1919
Baffa Rivolta, Matilde and Augusto Rossari: *Alexander Klein*, Milano 1975
Bakacsy, Judith (ed.): *Paul Engelmann und das mitteleuropäische Erbe*, Wien 1999
Baudenkmale in Berlin. Bezirk Wilmersdorf. Ortsteil Grunewald. Ed.: Senatsverwaltung für Stadtentwicklung und Umweltschutz, Berlin 1993
Bauhaus-Archiv (ed.): *Der vorbildliche Architekt. Mies van der Rohes Architekturunterricht 1930–1958 am Bauhaus und in Chicago*, Berlin 1986
Bauhaus-Archiv (ed.): *hannes meyer*, Berlin 1989
Bein, Alex: *Toldot haityashvut hazionit*, Jerusalem 1942
Bein, Alex: *Theodor Herzl. Biographie*, Frankfurt/M. – Berlin – Wien 1983
Bentwich, Norman: *Ben-Shemen. A Children's Village in Israel*, Israel 1960
Berents Catharina: *Art Déco in Deutschland*, Frankfurt/M. 1998
Bie, Oscar: introduction in: *Der Architekt Oskar Kaufmann*, Berlin 1928
Blumenfeld, Kurt: *Im Kampf um den Zionismus*, Stuttgart 1976
Botstein, Leon: *Judentum und Modernität*, Wien – Köln 1991
Bruno Taut 1880–1938. Exhibition catalogue. Ed.: Akademie der Künste Berlin, Berlin 1980

Campbell, Joan: Der Deutsche Werkbund, Stuttgart 1981 [*The German Werkbund. The Politics of Reform in the Applied Arts*, Princeton University Press 1978]
Claus, Sylvia: *Plastische Architektur. Das Werk des Architekten Harry Rosenthal (1892–1966)*, Zürich 2006

Deutsche Bauausstellung Berlin 1931. Amtlicher Katalog und Führer, Berlin 1931
Dresslers, Willy Oskar (ed.): *Dresslers Kunsthandbuch*, Berlin 1930

Ehlgötz, Hermann: *Essen*, Berlin 1925
Elkin, Rivka: *Mordechai Kampinski – Adrichal*, Omer 1991
Engelmann, Paul: *Dem Andenken an Karl Kraus*, Wien 1967
Engelmann, Paul: *Ludwig Wittgenstein. Architekt.* Wien – München 1970
Erlik, Abraam: *Leopold Krakauer*, Tel Aviv 1987

Essen. Architekturführer, Essen 1983
Eulenberg, Herbert: introduction in: *Neue Werkkunst. Robert Friedmann*. Berlin – Leipzig – Wien 1930. Reprint Berlin 2000, epilogue: Wolfgang Voigt

Feilchenfeld, Werner, Dolf Michaelis and Ludwig Pinner: *Haavara-Transfer nach Palästina*, Tübingen 1972
Festschrift zum 60. Geburtstag: Adolf Loos, Wien 1930

Gebauer, Gunter, Alexander Grünenwald, Rüdiger Ohme et al.: *Wien. Kundmanngasse 19*, München 1982
Glikson, Artur: *Regional Planning and Development*, Leiden 1955
Glikson, Artur: "L'unité d'Habitation Intégral" in: *Le Carré Bleu* 1, Paris 1962
Glikson, Artur: *Two Case Studies of Rural Planning and Development in Israel*, Israel 1964
Glikson, Artur: *The Ecological Basis of Planning*, Den Haag 1971
Glikson, Artur: "Man, Region, World. On Regional Planning", in: *Ministry of Housing Quarterly*, Tel Aviv 1978
Göckede, Regina: *Adolf Rading (1888–1957)*, Berlin 2005
Gonen, Rivka: *Grain. Dagon Collection*, Haifa 1979
Gravagnuolo, Benedetto: *Adolf Loos. Theory and Works*, New York 1982
Gruber, Gerhard: *Eugen Szekely – Freibad Pernegg. Denkmalpflege-Seminar*, Graz 1989
Günther, Sonja and Dietrich Worbs (eds.): *Architektur-Experimente in Berlin und anderswo. Für Julius Posener*, Berlin 1989

Hänsel, Sylvaine, Beate Kruger, Sabine Noack et al.: *Die Jarrestadt*, Hamburg 1981
Hansen, Antje: *Oskar Kaufmann*, Berlin 2001
Heinze-Mühleib, Ita: *Erich Mendelsohn. Bauten und Projekte in Palästina 1934–1941*, München 1986
Heinze-Greenberg, Ita and Regina Stephan: *Luise und Erich Mendelsohn. Eine Partnerschaft für die Kunst*, Stuttgart 2004
Herbert, Gilbert: *Gropius. Hirsch & The Saga of Copper Houses*, Technion, Israel 1980
Herbert, Gilbert and Silvina Sosnovsky: *Urban Developments in Down-Town Haifa during the British Mandate*, Technion, Israel 1984
Herbert, Gilbert and Silvina Sosnovsky: *Bauhaus on the Carmel and the Crossroads of Empire*, Jerusalem 1993
Herman, Zvi: *The River and the Grain*, Tel Aviv 1989
Herman, Zvi (text), Oswald Adler (conception and design): *40 Anniversary of Dagon*, Israel 1991
Herzl, Theodor: *Altneuland*, Haifa 1962
Herzl, Theodor: *Der Judenstaat*, Reprint Augsburg 1986 [*The Jewish State*, Filiquarian Publishing, LLC, USA 2006]
Hilker-Siebenhaar, Carolin (ed.): *Wegweiser durch das jüdische Berlin. Geschichte und Gegenwart*, Berlin 1987
Hirdina, Heinz (ed.): *Neues Bauen. Neues Gestalten*, Dresden 1991
Hitchcock, Henry-Russell and Philip Johnson: *Der Internationale Stil*, Braunschweig – Wiesbaden 1985
Hocquél, Wolfgang: *Leipzig. Baumeister und Bauten*, Berlin – Leipzig 1990

Bibliography

Huse, Norbert (ed.): *Mendelsohn. Der Einsteinturm*, Stuttgart – Zürich 2000

Illera, Christa: *Der Architekt Leopold Krakauer. 1890–1954*. Dissertation Technische Universität Wien, Wien 1992

Illing, W.: introduction in: *Naumann & Kalitzki Architekten Chemnitz*, Berlin 1925

Ingersoll, Richard: *Munio Gitai Weiraub. Bauhaus Architect in Erez Israel*. Exhibition catalogue, Milano 1994

Kaminka, Gideon: "*... ins Land, das ich dir zeigen werde*", Zürich 1977

Kaminka, Gideon: *Schwieriges Israel*, Zürich 1980

Katz, Shaul and Michael Heyd (eds.): *Toldot Hauniversita Haivrit Beyerushalym*, Jerusalem 1997

Kirsch, Karin: *Die Weissenhofsiedlung*, Stuttgart 1993

Klein, Alexander: *Das Einfamilienhaus – Südtyp*, Stuttgart 1934

Kroyanker, David: *adrichaluth hamedina shebaderech*, Jerusalem 2006

Landauer, Gustav and Heinz-Joachim Heydorn: *Aufruf zum Sozialismus*, Frankfurt/M. 1967

Lasker-Schüler, Else: *Das Hebräerland*, München 1986

Lehmann, Siegfried: *Raayon vehagshama*, Israel 1978

Luft, Gerda: *Heimkehr ins Unbekannte*, Wuppertal 1977

Mezger-Szmuk, Niza: *Batim min hachol*, Tel Aviv 1994

Mendelsohn, Erich and Regina Stephan: *Gebaute Welten*, Stuttgart 1998

Mendelsohn, Erich and Bruno Zevi: *Erich Mendelsohn. The Complete Works*, Basel 1999

Mendelsohn, Erich, Ita Heinze-Greenberg et al.: *Gedankenwelten*, Stuttgart 2002

Miller Lane, Barbara: *Architektur und Politik in Deutschland 1918–1945*, Braunschweig 1986 [*Architecture and Politics in Germany, 1918–1945*, Harvard University Press 1968]

Mosse, George L.: *Jüdische Intellektuelle in Deutschland*, Frankfurt/M. – New York 1991 [*German Jews Beyond Judaism*, Bloomington and Cincinnati 1985]

Müller-Wulckow, Walter: *Architektur der Zwanziger Jahre in Deutschland*, Königstein im Taunus 1925–1932. Reprint 1975

Naor, Mordechai and Dan Giladi: *Eretz-israel bamea haesrim*, Israel 1990

Naor, Mordechai and Dan Giladi: *Ben Shemen Youth Village. 70 years 1927–1997*, Tel Aviv 1997

Neufert, Ernst: *Bau-Entwurfslehre*, Braunschweig 1984

Offenberg, Mario (ed.): *Adass Jisroel. Die jüdische Gemeinde in Berlin (1869–1942). Vernichtet und Vergessen*, Berlin 1986

Oppenheimer, Franz: *Genossenschaftliche Kolonisation in Palästina*, Köln 1910

Osborn, Max: introduction in: *Oskar Kaufmann*, Berlin – Leipzig – Wien 1928. Reprint Berlin 1996, epilogue: Myra Warhaftig

Oswalt, Philipp and Susanne Rexroth (eds.): *Wohltemperierte Architektur*, Heidelberg 1994

Patishi, Dov: *Kirya betzel alonim*, Tel Aviv 1983
Pegels, Otto: *Adolf Rading 1888–1957*. Dissertation Technische Universität Aachen, Aachen 1992
Perry-Lehman, Meira and Michael Levin (eds.): Leopold Krakauer. Painter and Architect, 1890–1954, Jerusalem 1996
Pfankuch, Peter (ed.): *Adolf Rading*, Berlin 1970
Pinkerfeld, Jakob: *The Synagogues of Israel from the 'Geonim' till the 'Chassidim'*, Jerusalem 1946
Pinkerfeld, Jakob: *The Synagogues in Italy. Their Architectural Development since the Renaissance,* Jerusalem 1954
Pinkerfeld, Jakob: *Bishvilei omanut yehudith*, Israel 1957
Pinkerfeld, Jakob: *The Synagogues of North Africa*, Jerusalem 1974
Pollak, Adolf: *Zionismus*, Berlin 1934
Portugali, Menachem et. al.: *Hamelonaim*, Israel 2000
Posener, Julius: *Fast so alt wie das Jahrhundert*, Berlin 1990
Posener, Julius: *Heimliche Erinnerungen*, München 2004

Ratner, Jochanan: *Ani vechaye*, Tel Aviv 1983
Recknagel, Steffi: *Das Renaissance Theater*, Berlin 2002
Reimann, Max: introduction in: *Wilhelm Haller*, Berlin – Leipzig – Wien 1930
Reinharz, Jehuda: *Hashomer hatzair begermania*, Israel 1989
Richter, Tilo: *Erich Mendelsohns Kaufhaus Schocken*, Leipzig 1998
Rings, Josef: *Siedlungsform. Gesetze. Baugedanken. Ziele*, Essen 1923
Rinswer, Eleonore: *Öffentliche industrielle und gewerbliche Bauten der Ersten Republik in Graz*. Dissertation, Innsbruck 1990
Ruppin, Artur: *Dreißig Jahre Aufbau in Palästina*, Berlin 1937

Scheer, Regina: *Ahawa. Das Vergessene Haus*, Berlin – Weimar 1992
Schoenberger, Joseph: *Miqvaot*, Jerusalem 1974
Shamir, Moshe: *Reuben Hecht*, Haifa 1995
Sharon, Arieh: *Kibbutz + Bauhaus. an architect's way in a new land*, Stuttgart – Israel 1976
Shoshani, Eliezer: *hakvutza vehakibbutz beisrael*, Tel Aviv 1973
Sosnovsky, Silvina (ed.): *Jochanan Ratner. The Man. The Architect and his Work*, Haifa 1992 (English and Hebrew)
Spiegel, Erika: *Neue Städte in Israel*, Stuttgart 1966
Spur, Günter and Wolfram Fischer: *Georg Schlesinger und die Wissenschaft vom Fabrikbetrieb*, München – Wien 2000
Steirische Jubiläums-Kunstschau, Graz 1928
Stöhner, Ulrich-Klaus: *Untersuchung über den Beitrag Alexander Kleins zur Entwicklung und Bewertung von Grundrissen im Geschosswohnbau.* Dissertation Technische Universität Berlin, Berlin 1976
Szymanski, Beate: *Der Architekt Adolf Rading* (1888–1957), München 1992

Talmi, Ephraim and Menachem: *Lexikon zioni*, Israel 1977

Bibliography

Tel Aviv Neues Bauen 1930–1939. Ed.: Institut für Auslandsbeziehungen, Stuttgart and Architekturmuseum der Technischen Universität München, Tübingen 1993
Tel-Aviv's Modern Movement. The White City of Tel-Aviv. A World Heritage Site. Ed.: Municipality of Tel Aviv–Yafo, 2004
Tuvia, Miriam and Michael Bone (eds.): *binyan haaretz*, Israel 1999
Twenty Years of Building. Ed.: Engineers', Architects' and Surveyors' Union, Israel 1940 (Hebrew)

Warhaftig, Myra: *Deutsche jüdische Architekten vor und nach 1933. Das Lexikon*, Berlin 2005
Whittick, Arnold: *Eric Mendelsohn*, London 1964
Wijdeveld, Paul: *Ludwig Wittgenstein. Architekt*, Basel 1994
Wingler, Hans M.: *Kleine Bauhaus-Fibel*, Berlin 1974
Yishai Levi, Sarit: *The Strauss Saga*, Jerusalem 1998
Zevi, Bruno: *Erich Mendelsohn*, Zürich 1983
Zweig, Max: *Lebenserinnerungen*, Gerlingen 1987

Periodicals

Architektur des XX. Jahrhundert, Berlin
Architectural Design, London
Architectural Record, New York
Architectural Review, London

Baugilde, Berlin
Bauwelt, Berlin
Basler Magazin, Basel
Berliner Architekturwelt, Berlin

Das Werk, Zürich
Der Architekt, Köln
Der Monat, Brünn
Der Neubau, Berlin
Der Städtebau, Berlin
Deutsche Bauzeitung, Berlin
Deutsches Bauwesen, Berlin
Die Neue Stadt, Frankfurt/M.

Energy and Buildings, The Netherlands

Habinyan, Tel Aviv

Habinyan bamisrah hakarov, Tel Aviv
Haus Hof Garten, Berlin
Het Landhuis, Den Haag

Innendekoration. Darmstadt

Journal of Israel Association of Engineers & Architects, Tel Aviv
Journal of Israel Association of Town Planning, Tel Aviv
Jüdische Rundschau, Berlin

Kunstblatt, Potsdam
Kunst und Kirche, Darmstadt

L'Architecture d'Aujourd'hui, Paris

Moderne Bauformen, Stuttgart

Österreichische Kunst, Wien

Viviendas, Madrid

Wasmuths Monatshefte für Baukunst, Berlin
Wochenschrift des Architekten-Vereins zu Berlin, Berlin
Zeitschrift für Ästhetik und allgemeine Kulturwissenschaft, Stuttgart
Zentralblatt der Bauverwaltung, Berlin